W9-BPJ-988

Also by George Howe Colt

November of the Soul

The Big House

Brothers

THE
GAME

Harvard, Yale, and America in 1968

George Howe Colt

SCRIBNER

New York   London   Toronto   Sydney   New Delhi

Scribner
An Imprint of Simon & Schuster, Inc.
1230 Avenue of the Americas
New York, NY 10020

First Scribner hardcover edition October 2018

For information about special discounts for bulk purchases,
please contact Simon & Schuster Special Sales at 1-866-506-1949
or business@simonandschuster.com.

The Simon & Schuster Speakers Bureau can bring authors to
your live event. For more information or to book an event,
contact the Simon & Schuster Speakers Bureau at 1-866-248-3049
or visit our website at www.simonspeakers.com.

Interior design by Kyle Kabel

Manufactured in the United States of America

1   3   5   7   9   10   8   6   4   2

Library of Congress Cataloging-in-Publication Data is available.

ISBN 978-1-5011-0478-7
ISBN 978-1-5011-0480-0 (ebook)

For my father, who taught us to stay until the end of the game.

And for my brother Ned, who saved the ticket.

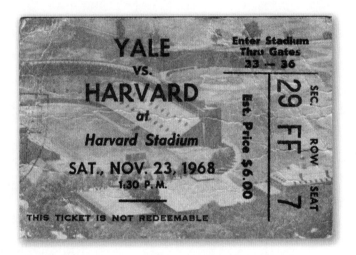

Contents

Contents

THE
GAME

Prologue

I grew up going to Harvard football games in the 1960s. My father, a Harvard alumnus, worked in the college's fund-raising office, and I lived a Harvard-saturated childhood. I swaddled my schoolbooks in glossy Harvard book covers; I thumbtacked my father's old Harvard pennants along the molding of my bedroom wall; I listened to *Veritas*, his album of Harvard fight songs. Each evening when he came home from his office in Harvard Yard, I'd fish a copy of the *Crimson* from his briefcase and read the sports page. On fall Saturdays, my brothers and I followed our parents up the concrete steps of Harvard Stadium—the ancient, horseshoe-shaped hulk that looked like the Colosseum, but with a wedge missing—and took our seats among the tweed-jacketed professors and bow-tied administrators near midfield. A few rows behind us, Harvard's president, Nathan Pusey (Dad called him "Nate"), a thin-lipped man with a face as smooth and immobile as alabaster, sat with his wife, who knitted an endless series of crimson scarves as she watched the game.

When I was twelve, everything about Harvard football seemed outsized and heroic, from the monumental stadium to the musclebound players to the band's trampoline-size bass drum, reputed to be the largest in the world and guarded, according to my father, by the six strongest men at Harvard. (Not to mention the forty-foot-plus urinals—surely also the world's largest—that lined the east and west walls of the men's room underneath the stands.) It mattered deeply to me whether Harvard won or lost, especially when it came to the Yale game, a clash of civilizations that seemed no less significant than that of Athens and Sparta. (Harvard, of course, was Athens.) I followed the action on the field as closely as the most avid alumnus, and far more closely than the Harvard students, who were so blasé that when the cheerleaders shouted "Gimme an H!" I half expected them to shout back, "Why should I?" The moment the final whistle blew, my brothers and I raced onto the field to ask the players for their autographs and, if we were feeling brave, their sweat-stained chin straps.

In 1968, I was fourteen. I was no longer going to every Harvard home game—and I was certainly no longer running around on the field afterward asking players for their chin straps. I was letting my hair grow a little longer. I had bought my first pair of bell-bottoms (striped). On my turntable, *Veritas* had been replaced by *Sgt. Pepper.* I still devoured my father's copy of the *Crimson* each night, though I read it as much for news of antiwar protests as for news of the football team. I still enjoyed Harvard football games, even if I now looked forward to the halftime show, in which the band made fun of LBJ, the Pentagon, and everyone over thirty, almost as much as to the game itself. And in mid-November when my father asked me whether I wanted to go to the Yale game, I said of course.

Two-a-Days

When Pat Conway decided to play football again, the one thing he didn't want to do was embarrass himself on the field. Now he'd embarrassed himself before he'd even gotten to the field. It was the first day of practice. In the locker room, listening to the other players joking and laughing as they put on their uniforms, he had pulled on his football pants and drawn the laces tight. But something didn't feel quite right. He snuck a glance at the players nearby and realized what it was. He had forgotten to put on his girdle, the thick cloth wrap that contained pads for his backbone and hips. The girdle went on *before* the pants. He looked around sheepishly, worried that someone had noticed, but everyone was busy lacing up shoulder pads or putting on cleats. Conway took off his football pants, cinched the girdle around his waist, and pulled the pants back on. He reached for a crimson stirrup sock and tugged it up his leg—until he realized that the socks, too, went on *before* the pants. He felt like a fool. He'd forgotten how to put on a football uniform. He unlaced his pants one more time.

Of the 117 candidates for the 1968 Harvard football team who returned to Cambridge on September 1 for three weeks of preseason practice, Pat Conway was, perhaps, the most unlikely. He was twenty-four years old, six years older than some of his teammates. He hadn't played football in more than three years. He knew almost no one on the team. He'd be trying out for safety, a position he had never played. Six months ago, he had been dodging mortar fire in Vietnam.

Conway had played football for Harvard before. A *Sporting News* high school All-American from Haverhill, Massachusetts, he had arrived in the fall of 1963 and quickly established himself as a star halfback on the freshman team. (On November 22, after his 48-yard touchdown run gave Harvard a 7–6 lead over Yale, he had been standing on the goal line, ready to receive the second-half kickoff, when the referee walked over and told him that President Kennedy had been shot. Although shaken, the hyper-competitive Conway pleaded with the official not to tell anyone else so they could finish the game.) Sophomore year, Conway started at fullback for the varsity, but he was floundering academically and Harvard put him on probation. The following autumn, falling still further behind, he left school, enlisted in the Marines, and was sent to Vietnam. While his Harvard teammates were playing Yale in November 1967, he had been digging foxholes at Khe Sanh Combat Base. His tour almost up, he had reapplied to Harvard for the spring semester. By the time his paperwork came through, more than 30,000 North Vietnamese troops had surrounded the base. It would be months before Conway was able to fly home.

Conway hadn't expected to play football when he returned to Harvard for his senior year. But that summer he'd gotten a letter from Coach John Yovicsin saying he had a year of eligibility left; did he want to rejoin the team? Yovicsin told Conway they already had someone—the captain, Vic Gatto—at right halfback, his favorite position. But they needed a safety. Conway said he'd give it a try.

The last time he had touched a football was at Khe Sanh, before all hell broke loose. Someone had come across a battered old ball, and Conway and a few other marines had tossed it around for half an hour one afternoon. Conway never saw the ball again; he assumed it had blown up in a mortar attack.

He had no real expectation of making the team. But ever since

4

he'd started playing Pop Warner in the seventh grade, fall had meant football. Returning to college after almost three years away wouldn't be easy. Playing football might help him get back to his old life.

Besides, Conway was lonely. He had spent July and August in Cambridge, going to summer school and living alone in a dorm in Harvard Yard, where he had spent his freshman year five years before. He was almost as old as some of his teachers. Everyone he'd been with at Harvard the first time around was off at graduate school or out in the real world. Playing football, he would meet some people. And not just any people, *his* kind of people: blue-collar guys, regular guys, guys who knew how to work hard. If he didn't make the team, at least maybe he'd make a few friends.

That summer, Conway took long runs on the Charles River footpath. He "did stadiums"—bounding up and down the steep Harvard Stadium steps. Once in a while he was able to persuade an old high school teammate to throw a football with him. Most of the time, he was on his own. By the start of preseason, he was in pretty good shape, but football shape was something different, and he had no idea what to expect once the hitting began.

* * *

For most of the 116 other players who showed up that first day, there was a comfortable, back-to-school feel. They joshed and kidded, giving each other grief about a particularly colorful T-shirt or the length of someone's sideburns. At the same time, they were surreptitiously sizing one another up: whose biceps looked especially prominent, which of the incoming sophomores looked as if they might be players. Over dinner they talked about their summers.

It had been a strange, unsettling few months. The summer had seemed to begin on June 6, when Robert Kennedy was assassinated, only nine weeks after the assassination of Martin Luther King Jr. Quarterback George Lalich and linebacker John Emery had been up late watching a movie in a Connecticut motel room, preparing to play for Harvard in the NCAA baseball tournament, when the show was interrupted with news of the shooting. They spent the rest of the night watching the coverage and wondering what the country was coming to.

The summer had ended, a week before preseason began, with the Democratic National Convention in Chicago. Offensive tackle Joe McGrath had been there, working as a congressional aide and staying in a hotel across from Grant Park, where the antiwar demonstrators gathered. One night McGrath had been in the hotel basement, mimeographing the latest draft of the party platform, when a few dozen Chicago policemen, bloodied and furious after an encounter with rock-throwing protestors, came in to regroup. Another night, he'd walked out of the hotel and seen a mass of policemen lined up across from thousands of demonstrators, who were shouting "Oink oink" and "Fascist pigs." Every so often, billy clubs flailing, the police charged into the crowd, which scattered into the park before coming forward to renew its taunts—at which point the police charged again. For several nights, as delegates at the convention argued over whether to adopt an antiwar plank into the party platform, downtown Chicago itself resembled something of a war zone, as thousands of police and National Guardsmen, employing what one senator called "Gestapo tactics," teargassed and clubbed protestors, bystanders, and journalists alike.

Between those disturbing events, the Harvard players had settled into their summer jobs. Many of them had worked in construction, which not only paid well but helped them stay in shape. Lalich had been a rod buster at a Chicago steel mill. Cornerback Mike Ananis had unloaded two-by-fours at Boston lumberyards. Not every player did heavy lifting: tackle Bob Dowd had been a counselor at a boys' camp in New Hampshire; guard Tommy Lee Jones had acted in a summer repertory theater at Harvard, playing the title role in a blues adaptation of the fifteenth-century morality play *Everyman*; halfback Ray Hornblower had run with the bulls

at Pamplona before bumming around Spain. Defensive tackle Rick
Berne had driven across the country with a friend. It had been a
mind-expanding trip: from the Deep South, where their shaggy
hair and New York license plates had earned them hard stares that
Berne would recall the following summer when he saw a movie
called *Easy Rider*, to San Francisco, where they'd wandered among
the flower children in Haight-Ashbury before ending up in Golden
Gate Park in a vast swirl of barefoot, half-naked hippies smoking
pot in broad daylight.

*   *   *

The first few days of preseason were always a time of unbridled
optimism. The grass on the fields had just been cut, the lines were
newly chalked, the uniforms were freshly washed. Everything
seemed possible. Before practice even began, there was Picture
Day, in which the players, dressed in their crimson game uniforms, posed for Boston photographers on the emerald greensward
of Harvard Stadium, where they were encouraged to assume a
variety of "action" poses rarely, if ever, seen in games: helmetless
halfbacks in stiff-arming, Heisman-esque positions; quarterbacks,
arms cocked, leaping like ballet dancers in mid-jeté; linebackers
pouncing like cartoon cats on footballs that lay, conspicuously
unattended, on the grass.

The players' spirits were high, their coach's somewhat less so.
John Yovicsin was cautious by nature, and he had even more reason to be this year, his twelfth at Harvard. Despite having ended
the previous season with a near-upset of heavily favored Yale,
Harvard had tied for fourth place in the eight-team Ivy League.
Of twenty-two starters, fourteen had graduated, including five
who had been named All-Ivy. There were only fourteen returning
lettermen, the fewest in the league. By the time preseason started,
due to injuries over the summer, they were down to eleven. The
biggest blow was the loss of senior defensive back John Tyson,

whom the press book described as "Harvard's top candidate for All-East and All-American honors." Yovicsin told reporters that Tyson couldn't play because the knee he'd injured last season hadn't healed, but most of the players knew the real reason: Tyson had quit the team to devote himself to black activism. It was Tyson's shoes that Yovicsin hoped Pat Conway could fill.

Harvard did have one bona fide star: its captain, Vic Gatto, the squat, muscular halfback who entered the season as the fourth-leading rusher in Harvard history. Gatto was joined by junior Ray Hornblower, a whippet-fast halfback who had come out of nowhere the previous year to finish fifth in the league in rushing, to give Harvard what might be the top running tandem in the league. Whether the offensive line—it had only one returning letterman, the aspiring actor Tommy Lee Jones—would be able to open holes for their talented running backs was another matter. "At offensive tackle the picture is desperate," the *Crimson* observed. On defense, there were a few veteran linebackers and several promising sophomores, but, as Yovicsin told the press, "I've never gone into a season with as many question marks." In almost every preseason poll, Harvard was picked to finish in the bottom half of the Ivy League. "Harvard Outlook Not Too Bright" was the gleeful headline in the *Yale Daily News*. Even Harvard's director of sports information, whose job required him to be optimistic, conceded that the football team, after overachieving for two seasons, might have its first losing campaign in ten years. "The well," he said, "has finally run dry."

* * *

Two-a-days, as the twice-daily preseason practice sessions were known, were all about finding out who wanted to hit. This year, the players had a temporary reprieve before the hitting began. Alarmed by the number of cases of heat exhaustion in the early days of practice—including twenty-four deaths among high school and college players in the previous eight years—the NCAA had decreed that the first three days of the 1968 preseason be conducted without pads. Coaches grumbled. You couldn't tell who the real football players were until you saw them hit. But for a brief honeymoon period, practice had a summer-camp feel, as the players, in T-shirts, shorts, and helmets, improved their conditioning, rehearsed their footwork, and learned plays. On the morning of the fourth day, the walk to the fields was quieter than usual.

It wasn't that the players hated hitting—you didn't play football unless you liked to hit. It was that there was so much of it. Even the quarterbacks, running backs, and ends—the so-called skill positions—did a lot of hitting, when they weren't throwing and catching and handing off. The linemen who, by implication, toiled at unskilled positions, did nothing *but* hit, spending four hours a day smashing into each other. There were a variety of ways to accomplish the smashing. There was the Hamburger Drill, in which a defensive lineman squared off against an offensive lineman and a running back. There was Bull in the Ring, in which the players formed a circle with one man in the center, and, as a coach called out their names, the players on the perimeter, in quick succession, tried to knock him down. There was the Board Drill, in which two linemen, straddling a two-by-four on the ground, rammed into each other like sumo wrestlers, each trying to toss the other aside. When the linemen weren't smashing into each other, they were smashing into inanimate objects like the seven-man sled, which they shoved back and forth across the field, with a coach going along for the ride on the steel frame, goading them like a galley master. When practice was almost over and the hitting finally, mercifully, stopped, there were wind sprints—fifty yards at top speed, over and over, until the players were so exhausted they could hardly stand up.

All this took place in the heat and humidity of the city at the end of summer, when even the faintest breeze off the Charles felt like a blessing. In high school, most of the players had coaches who made it clear that only sissies drank water during practice. Mindful of the NCAA's concerns about dehydration, the Harvard coaches weren't quite so draconian, but they were loath to spare even a minute for a water break. The players lived for the rare occasions when the managers appeared on the field, scurrying from group to group with metal trays stocked with water-filled Dixie cups, half of whose contents had sloshed out along the way. Some of the players had heard about a new Day-Glo lemon-lime "sports drink" called Gatorade, developed by scientists at the University of Florida, and they pleaded with the trainers to get them some, but were told to make do with water. If they were feeling faint, they could gobble down some salt pills. When his teammates complained about the 90-degree heat, Tommy Lee Jones, who, before taking up acting had spent his summers working on oil rigs, would growl, "You pussies, it's a *hundred* degrees in Texas."

Unlike other Division I colleges, Ivy League schools prohibited spring practice, so there had been no organized football since the final snap of the Yale game nine months earlier. Although the coaches issued a manual of suggested exercises, there was no required off-season conditioning program. The players were expected to arrive at camp in shape; how they accomplished this was up to them. For those, like Gatto, who, the moment his Park League summer baseball season was over, launched into a systematic regimen of push-ups, pull-ups, sprints, and distance runs (Gatto was never really *out* of shape), preseason was exhausting enough. For those who had put off exercising till the waning days of August and then jogged around the block a few times, it was agony. Even if you came to camp in shape, *hitting* shape was something else. For the first three or four days of full-pad workouts, your body was so sore it took several minutes to get out of bed in the morning. Just when you thought you might not be able to get out of bed at all, your body, miraculously, began to adjust. The wear and tear, however, continued to accrue. A lineman's hands got bruised and cut from the constant jousting, clawing, and fending off. His forehead developed new creases where his helmet jammed into it with each collision.

Ten days in, starting center Ted Skowronski had a purple stripe across his brow so dark and persistent that the team doctors, concerned he might have some sort of blood disorder, sent him to Massachusetts General Hospital for tests. Skowronski was devastated. Three years ago, he had arrived at Harvard for his first day of freshman football practice to find himself on tenth string. He had worked his way up over the years, but no matter how well he performed in practice, he remained on the bench; playing in JV games, dressing for the varsity, and cheering his lungs out but getting in only long after the outcome had been decided. In low moments, Skowronski worried that maybe he just wasn't good enough and wondered whether it might be time to give up. He had seen dozens of players, tired of sitting on the bench, quit the team. But he knew he couldn't. Not with the name Skowronski. One of his brothers had been a two-year starter at guard for Harvard; another was the starting left tackle and co-captain of the NFL champion Green Bay Packers. Ted Skowronski had to live up to the family name. Now, in his last season at Harvard, he was one of only nineteen players remaining from the 132 who had come out for the freshman team three years earlier. Just as he had finally made first string, however, it seemed his football career might be over.

The tests came back negative. The purple stripe was merely a particularly colorful bruise, part of the normal wear and tear of playing on the line.

*　*　*

The fortunes of the 1968 Harvard football team would depend largely on players like Skowronski, seniors who had spent two years on JV and were only now getting the chance to start. Being an underclassman on a John Yovicsin team could be maddening. All the players knew that the coach favored seniors who had worked their way up through the program. Only in rare cases, when a first-stringer was injured, or when an underclassman like Gatto, who was so clearly superior, came along, would sophomores or juniors start. It was hard to argue with the results—Yovicsin hadn't had a losing season since 1958—but it didn't seem fair that underclassmen could outplay seniors in practice but sit on the bench when game day arrived. Indeed, some of them had become so disgruntled that after the 1967 season, unbeknownst to their coach, they had talked about not coming out for the team senior year.

In high school, most of them had played for coaches straight out of central casting: chain-smoking Rocknes whose locker room–pacing, vein-popping, expletive-spewing pregame pep talks worked the players into such a frenzy they were practically frothing at the mouth as they took the field. After that, John Yovicsin took some getting used to. Formal and reserved, almost courtly, Yovicsin, who seemed older than his forty-nine years, was often mistaken for a Harvard professor. A regular worshiper in the Congregational church, "Yovvy," as the *Crimson* referred to him (a nickname that seemed more impertinent than affectionate), didn't smoke or drink, and spoke firmly but softly; his saltiest language ran to "Dag-gone it," "cheese and crackers," or, in extremis, "Christopher Columbus!" After a Harvard player got into a fight with an opponent during last year's Penn game, Yovicsin came into the locker room and said, "Boys, I've told you many times: no fisticuffs on the field." His pregame speeches focused on technical details; he left the emotional preparation to his players. "I don't believe in psychological pressure such as pep talks," he told the *Crimson*. "That is a thing of the past. . . . Anyway, our boys are too intelligent to fall for that." Dressed in a herringbone tweed jacket, a crimson V-neck sweater, a carefully knotted tie, and a Tyrolean fedora atop his neatly combed, going-gray hair, Yovicsin spent much of the game pacing the sideline, arms folded, a troubled expression on his handsome face.

Earlier in his career, Yovicsin might have been considered an admirable exemplar of taciturn, square-jawed rectitude, but in the sixties he seemed to exemplify the out-of-touch authority figures against which young Americans were rebelling. Players grumbled about his formal approach and remote air. A few wondered whether he even knew their names. (He did.) Some rolled their eyes at his antiseptic pregame speeches, imitated his generic instructions (*Boys, you've got to be better!*), or joked about his fastidious practices, which Yovicsin, checking his clipboard and stopwatch, programmed to the minute; if the players were in mid-drill and it was time for the next item on his agenda, he'd blow his whistle and move the team along. Each afternoon when Yovicsin walked out of his office in Dillon Field House for practice, the first thing he did was turn around and check the clock on the wall. One day, halfback Jimmy Reynolds moved the clock's hands a few minutes forward. When Yovicsin came out, he turned around, looked up at the clock, and, to the team's amusement, was visibly flustered at the thought that he might be a minute or two late.

It was ironic that so many members of the team felt distant from their coach. Despite his impeccable garb and patrician manner, Yovicsin came from a background more like that of his players, most of whom were from working-class families, than like that of his employers. He had grown up during the Depression in Steelton, a company town in central Pennsylvania where immigrants from Eastern Europe worked in the foundries for Bethlehem Steel. Yovicsin's father, a welder who left Serbia when he was seventeen, had steered his son toward sports as a way out of the mills. (A trace of a Slavic accent could still be heard in the coach's speech.) The lanky Yovicsin had starred in football, basketball, and track (he was a high jumper and pole-vaulter) at Steelton High, and then, on scholarship, at Gettysburg College.

He had been coaching in relative obscurity at Gettysburg when Harvard hired him, in 1957, to resurrect its moribund football program. His first year began with a seven-touchdown loss in a scrimmage with tiny Williams College and ended with a 54–0 shellacking by Yale, the most lopsided defeat in the rivalry's eighty-two-year history. But he updated Harvard's antediluvian offense from single wing to T-formation, started a junior varsity program, expanded the use of game films, and beefed up the alumni recruiting network. In 1961, Harvard tied for the Ivy League title.

Even when he won, Yovicsin was criticized. A skilled tactician, an "x's and o's guy" who was attentive to every detail, Yovicsin often said that he considered defense to be the most important part of the game, followed by kicking. Offense, by implication, was almost an afterthought. Indeed, his Harvard teams were known for two things: the impregnability of their defense and the predictability of their offense, which seemed an endless loop of off-tackle runs and end sweeps. Yovicsin, alumni said, was unaware that the forward pass had been legalized in 1906. Yovicsin's methods worked—in 1966 his team tied for the Ivy title again—but no matter how well the coach did, the alumni grumbled that with the talent Harvard had he should be doing even better.

Yovicsin was accused of being an old-fashioned coach, but in one area he was far ahead of his time. In 1964, Harvard had been the first team in the Ivy League—and among the very few in college football other than at historically black institutions—to start a black quarterback, a milestone that had provoked little comment in liberal Cambridge, but had earned the coach hate mail from around the country. And though he was said to be distant from his players, he was protective of athletes who made mistakes, and at postgame press conferences went out of his way to single out less-celebrated players—someone who'd made a good block or performed well on punt coverage. After cornerback John Ignacio separated his shoulder in preseason, he'd been surprised and touched when Yovicsin visited him that night in the infirmary. When linebacker Gerry Marino was in danger of flunking out sophomore year, he went to Yovicsin, who listened sympathetically and helped him get tutoring. Two years later, when his grades were down, his graduation was in doubt, and he had no idea what he wanted to do with his life, Marino would go to Yovicsin again;

and though it was spring and the senior could no longer be of use to him on the football field, the coach was equally concerned, and arranged a session with a psychologist for career counseling.

Yovicsin's restraint wasn't just a matter of temperament. Few of his players knew that in the spring of 1965, their coach had undergone open-heart surgery at the Mayo Clinic to replace a defective valve. The doctors put him on a heavy dose of cardiac medication and told him he could continue coaching but had to be careful not to overdo it. Given his job, it wasn't an easy prescription to follow. Yovicsin worked fourteen-hour days during the season, rarely getting home to his wife and four children in Framingham before ten o'clock. Nor did the players know that from time to time, when his heart began to fibrillate, Yovicsin quietly checked into the hospital, where cardiologists, using electrical stimulation, were able to coax his heartbeat back to normal.

* * *

Midway through two-a-days, everyone began to get a little stir-crazy. In the Ivy League, there were no athletic scholarships, though most of the football team was on need-based financial aid; no one *had* to play, and no one got cut. But every few days, someone dropped off the team: a sophomore who realized he wasn't going to get much playing time, a junior who just couldn't take one more Hamburger Drill and decided to spend the last days of summer at the beach. The next day, his locker was empty. Of the 117 players who showed up on the first day of preseason, 29 would be gone by the end of the three-week session. Those who stayed couldn't take a second off. They had to go all out in every drill, scrimmage, and wind sprint, knowing that each night while they slept, the coaches were discussing that day's sessions, evaluating every man, and then revising the depth chart—the mimeographed list of players ranked by position that was the first thing the players saw each morning when they walked into Dillon Field House.

The Game

The players were staying in Kirkland House, a dormitory just across the river from the fields. Their quarters were monastic: two single beds, two bureaus, two desks, no TVs, no radios, no posters, no fans. After lunch, when the players returned to their rooms to rest, they pulled down the shades and turned off the lights to create the illusion of coolness, but it was so hot that they worked up a fresh sweat just lying there. The beds weren't big enough for the larger players, but they were too tired to worry about that, too tired to talk, too tired to do anything but lie there as still as possible, trying not to think about the afternoon practice. They didn't really want to fall asleep, because if they dozed off, it seemed only seconds later they'd hear the manager's knock on the door that meant it was time to get up; it was better to lie there, the minutes passing, dreading the knock. And when the knock came, they couldn't pretend they hadn't heard it, because the manager was instructed to stay there, knocking, until they came to the door. So they'd haul themselves out of bed and walk slowly, gingerly, back to the field house, pull on a uniform still clammy with sweat—and no matter how often the uniforms were laundered they never lost their sour smell—and head out for a second session more exhausting than the first.

Dinner was the high point of the day. Training table meals almost always began with New York strip steaks, as many as they wanted, and ended with buckets of ice cream and hot fudge sauce. After dinner, the players met with their position coaches to watch film and go over the playbook. Any distraction from the routine was welcome, even the lecture on venereal disease by the official from the Massachusetts Department of Public Health who came by one evening to remind them that in the age of free love, love wasn't always free. But by then they were too tired even to *think* of anything other than sleep. Seconds after their heads hit the pillow, it seemed, the manager was knocking on their door, and it was time to get up and do it all over again.

Sometimes the need to escape was so great, however, that after the last meeting of the night, Ted Skowronski and reserve end Tony

Smith, who had roomed together in Cambridge that summer, would walk two blocks up to Harvard Square just to get a whiff of what they were missing. They had to remind themselves that there was a real world out there. They'd stand near Out of Town News, taking it all in: the hippies in front of Holyoke Center swaying and singing along as a guitarist strummed "Hey Jude"; the high school students bumming cigarettes and hoping to scrounge up some pot before heading home to the suburbs; the antiwar protestors handing out pamphlets; the unpublished poet hawking dittoed copies off his work in the incense-patchouli-and-marijuana-scented summer night. If they were feeling adventurous and the line wasn't too long, they might get a strawberry cone with jimmies at Brigham's. Or they'd slide into an empty booth at Hazen's, put a dime in the jukebox, and sip coffee while listening to Cream's "Sunshine of Your Love" or "Born to Be Wild" by Steppenwolf, songs that had defined their summer. And then, taking a final glimpse of the Square and fixing it in their minds, the way a pothead held the smoke in his lungs as long as possible before exhaling, they'd walk back to Kirkland House.

Mornings were the worst. As the players straggled down Boylston Street and the sun began to hint at the heat that lay ahead, George Lalich vowed to all within earshot that once he was finished with football, he'd never again do so much as a jumping jack before noon. Crossing Anderson Bridge, Skowronski had fantasies of jumping in the Charles and floating downriver to Boston—anything to save him from the misery that awaited. Seeing the stadium loom in the distance, some of the players might break into a plaintive chorus of "Please Mr. Custer, I Don't Wanna Go," or, thinking of what they'd rather be doing on the field than smashing into one another, they'd sing Van Morrison's "Brown Eyed Girl": *Making love in the green grass / Behind the stadium / With you, my brown-eyed girl.* As they got closer, the smell of the dew on the freshly mowed grass, a smell that on the first day of practice had made Lalich tingle with anticipation, now made him feel slightly nauseated.

The Game

* * *

After Parris Island, Harvard two-a-days didn't seem so bad. For Pat Conway, the challenges of preseason were more mental than physical. Learning to play defense was like learning another language. On offense you knew where you were going before the play began; on defense your responsibility depended on how the offense set up, and might change as the play developed. In the middle of a play, Conway's fellow defensive backs would suddenly shout "Go east! Go east!" or (like so many Horace Greeleys) "Go west!"—thus alerting each other which way they should rotate. That was confusing enough, but Conway was dyslexic and had always had trouble with left and right. When his teammates called out "Go west," Conway would visualize a globe with the North Pole on top, then locate California on the left and head that way. If he heard "Go east," he'd think Atlantic Ocean and head right. Conway had never told anyone he was dyslexic, and though he felt a little foolish on the field when it took a second or two to get his bearings, he certainly wasn't going to tell anyone now.

Conway may have been laboring in some of the drills, but it was clear to his coaches and teammates that he was going to be good. He was big (six feet two, 185 pounds), he was fast (he had run a 9.9 hundred-yard dash for his high school track team), and he was so conscientious and eager to learn that the other defensive backs went out of their way to help him, though they knew they might end up playing less because of it. Conway tended to hang out with the sophomores, despite the age difference, because they, too, were new to the team, feeling their way along, trying to fit in both on and off the field. Each night after dinner, defensive backfield coach Loyal Park quizzed his men, firing questions at them about their assignments. *Third and long, your side of the field, right hash mark, fourth quarter. What are you looking for?* A wrong answer earned a withering comment from the coach. Afterward, Conway went straight to his room and pored over the playbook; he and his roommate tested each other on formations and rotations. Conway had never studied so hard. He knew he had to learn the stuff until it was second nature; by the time the season started, he certainly couldn't be pausing in the middle of a play to figure out where the North Pole was.

*   *   *

Like Conway, each player in camp was fighting his own private battle. Bruce Freeman, a rangy, redheaded sophomore end from southern California who had played little as a freshman, was hoping to get a chance to show what he could do. But the night before he was scheduled to fly back to Boston, his father had died of a heart attack. Freeman, who was on scholarship, assumed he could no longer afford Harvard and resigned himself to attending the local community college. But the admissions office quickly came up with a new financial package that enabled him to return. He arrived in camp a week late, after the funeral, and was struggling to catch up, trying not to think about his father until he was back in his room. At night, his dreams about him seemed so real that he'd wake up thinking his father was alive—and then remember.

Fritz Reed had ten days to learn an entirely new position. Last year he had started at end. This year, Yovicsin, desperate for help on the offensive line, moved him to tackle in the second week of preseason. Reed, who had played end since he was a high school sophomore and had co-captained the Ohio All-Star South team at the position, was deeply disappointed and a little insulted. "I thought tackles did nothing but grunt and groan and just plod straight ahead," he admitted to a reporter. But the sleepy-looking junior was a fast learner—he had, in fact, an IQ of 169—who adapted to his new role with characteristic humor. "Well, I guess I'm down here with the farm animals again," he'd announce as he walked into the locker room.

And then there was Alex MacLean. The coaches were counting

on him to start at middle guard, but the former JV player, worried that he might not be up to the responsibility, had spent the month of August trying to eat his way out of the job, half-hoping he'd arrive in such bad shape that the coaches would give up on him. On the first day of preseason, the five-foot-nine senior had weighed in at 230 pounds, 30 over his playing weight. The coaches made him wear a long-sleeved rubber shirt under his pads, the kind wrestlers use to make weight for an upcoming bout. But now that he was in camp, MacLean, reminded of how much he loved football, was working hard and hoping that in his anxiety he hadn't blown his big chance. Between drills, he'd untuck the front of his rubber shirt and a small river of sweat would pour out.

* * *

Most players were so involved in their own struggles that they were only dimly aware of what was going on in other corners of the practice field. But everyone knew Yovicsin's most pressing task was to find a quarterback. Last year's starter, Ric Zimmerman, arguably the greatest passer in Harvard history, had graduated. So had his backup. Of the four quarterbacks in camp, only George Lalich had any varsity experience—and that for a grand total of twelve minutes.

If based on passing ability alone, the job would be Frank Champi's. A junior who had played JV the previous year, Champi had what coaches called "an arm." (Last spring he had broken the Harvard javelin record.) Players paused during practice just to watch him hurl perfect spirals fifty or sixty yards down the field. But Champi, a balding, bespectacled young man from the working-class Boston suburb of Everett, was self-conscious and unobtrusive to the point of invisibility. You didn't notice him—until he threw a pass. Yovicsin and his assistant coaches wondered whether he had the personality to lead a team. A team had to believe in its quarterback. Champi, it appeared, had trouble believing in himself.

If Champi was the most introverted member of the team, Lalich, last year's third-string quarterback, he of the twelve minutes of varsity playing time, was among the most extroverted: an irreverent, street-smart jokester from the South Side of Chicago who seemed always to be at the center of a knot of players, cracking people up. When, early in camp, Yovicsin told the *Boston Globe* that the team had "a big hole" at quarterback, Lalich had quipped, "*I'm* the quarterback. Who's this guy *Big Hole?*" The line became a running joke. Lalich, a relief pitcher on the baseball team, wasn't in Champi's league as a passer, but he was a decent thrower and a resourceful scrambler, and the coaches could see how the players, particularly the seniors, responded to him. During breaks in practice, just when the players were about to buckle in the heat, the tousle-haired, pie-faced Lalich would grab a tackling dummy and waltz around the field crooning Sérgio Mendes's bossa nova version of the Beatles' "Fool on the Hill," and the mood lightened. The coaches suspected that Lalich's self-deprecating humor masked some underlying insecurity, and they took every opportunity to boost his confidence. Going into two-a-days, they had assured him that the quarterback job was his, and backfield coach Pat Stark helped him choose the style and brand of ball he wanted to use during the season (Wilson's "The Duke"). But each time they saw Champi launch another 50-yard dart, they couldn't help wondering whether they were making the right choice.

* * *

Two weeks in, just when the players thought they might explode if they didn't get to hit someone besides each other, Harvard scrimmaged the University of New Hampshire. It was a sobering experience. The defense had trouble stopping a weak New Hampshire offense. The offense struggled to make a first down. Lalich was erratic, though it was hard to fault him because he spent most of his time dodging tacklers who had eluded his patchwork offensive line. The entire team looked sluggish in the 16–7 loss. Afterward, an assistant coach told a reporter he'd be happy if Harvard managed to win five games.

Things were no more encouraging the following week during the annual intrasquad scrimmage: the players' last chance to impress the coaches before the season started. It was their first time back in Harvard Stadium since Picture Day, but the grand setting only made their performance look more feeble. On one of the day's final plays, starting cornerback Mike Ananis separated his shoulder making a tackle. Harvard was down to ten returning lettermen. The opening game was a week away and it wasn't clear who would be healthy enough to play.

And then, suddenly, two-a-days were over. The players moved into their regular dorms, the rest of the students came flooding back, and classes began.

Asked by the *Crimson* to evaluate his team's prospects, Coach Yovicsin didn't sound optimistic.

"If everything works out, we'll have a football team," he said.

"A good football team?" asked the reporter.

"A football team," Yovicsin replied.

*   *   *

On September 28, 1968, the Harvard football team opened its ninety-fifth season against Holy Cross in front of 23,000 spectators at the stadium. In a players-only huddle before the game, Vic Gatto told his teammates that although few people believed they'd amount to much this year, they were going to win the Ivy League championship; in fact, they had a very good chance of going undefeated. Tommy Lee Jones was not the only one who thought their captain might be a little delusional.

Indeed, for much of the first half, Harvard continued its mistake-filled play of preseason. They had gone into the game intending to keep the ball on the ground, but Holy Cross stacked its defense against the run, and Gatto and Hornblower were stymied. Harvard tried passing, but Lalich was tentative and ineffective, in part because his offensive line was unable to stave off the Holy Cross defenders. (The *Harvard Alumni Bulletin* would describe the line's first-half performance as "jelly-like.") Midway through the second quarter, the offense had run seventeen plays and gained fourteen yards; Harvard was behind 13–0. "It looked as if the Crimson was in for a long day, perhaps for a long season," observed one sportswriter.

The coaches made some adjustments to Harvard's blocking assignments, and the offense began to click. With more time, Lalich found his targets, especially his biggest one, Pete Varney, the six-foot-two, 245-pound sophomore who had taken over Fritz Reed's spot at end. At the half, Harvard trailed 13–12. Going into the fourth quarter, Holy Cross was ahead by one touchdown and was driving for another when Ananis's replacement intercepted a pass deep in Harvard territory. Lalich led Harvard to a touchdown and followed it with a two-point conversion pass to Varney that tied the score at 20. A few minutes later, Holy Cross went for it on fourth and one from midfield, but their fullback was met by what seemed to be the entire Harvard defense—whereupon Lalich drove his team down the field and scored the winning touchdown himself on a one-yard plunge.

The players were relieved. They knew they had been fortunate to win. Harvard fans left the stadium feeling mildly encouraged, especially by their new quarterback, who, after a shaky start, had shown poise in leading the team on two fourth-quarter scoring drives. Lalich finished with eleven completions in nineteen attempts for 139 yards and was awarded the game ball. ("Harvard Let George Do It and He Did" was the headline in the *Boston Herald*.) Seven of those passes went to Varney, a two-time first-round choice in the Major League Baseball draft who, it was said, had turned down an $80,000 signing bonus to attend Harvard. Conway, who'd had cortisone injections in each ankle two days before the game, started at safety and made five tackles. Afterward, a reporter asked him whether, playing football for the first time in several years, he had been nervous or scared. "Scared?" Conway replied. "You don't get nervous or scared playing a football game. You get nervous or scared being under incoming and live artillery. . . . You get excited and enthused about playing football."

II

Hell No, We Won't Go!

.

When the 1968 Harvard football team moved back into their dorms for the start of the school year, they returned to a Harvard that bore little resemblance to the college at which the seniors had arrived three years earlier.

In the fall of 1965, nearly half the freshman class of 1,211 had been drawn from Northeastern prep schools. There were 61 students from Exeter alone. Coats and ties were required at dinner, and many students wore them to class as well. Informal dress meant button-down Oxford shirts, chinos, and Bass Weejuns. (Sartorial renegades opted for madras pants or tassels on their loafers.) Hair was short and neatly parted, if not crew-cut. The burning issue on campus was "parietals": the hours during which girls—in 1965, they were invariably referred to as girls—were permitted in men's dorms, their comings and goings recorded in notebooks placed in each entryway. Students caught with a member of the opposite sex in their room outside the hours of four to seven on weekdays or eleven to eleven on weekends (midnight after home football games) could be, and often were, suspended. Radcliffe students, who attended Harvard classes but were quartered in dorms a half-mile north of Harvard Yard, were warned by their proctors that females under the age of twenty-one who spent the night in a man's room could be prosecuted under the Massachusetts fornication law of 1692.

In the fall of 1965, Harvard Square was a backwater of coffee shops, antiquarian bookstores, and mildly seedy all-night cafeterias. Harvard social life centered around its eleven "final clubs," well-appointed sanctuaries where prep school grads played backgammon, sipped postprandial brandies, and chatted up returning alumni for jobs on Wall Street. Although an obscure lecturer in psychology named Timothy Leary had made national news two years earlier when he was dismissed after conducting experiments with a chemical compound called lysergic acid, alcohol was the drug of choice. Students caught smoking marijuana were sent to University Health Services (UHS) for a stern talking-to and some psychotherapy. When a reporter for a national magazine arrived on campus to do a picture story on "pot parties at Harvard," she had a hard time finding volunteers and ended up having to supply the raw materials herself. In the previous spring's Freshman Riot, an annual ritual that was generally more wholesome than riotous, hundreds of students had crawled across Memorial Drive on their hands and knees, blocking traffic as they pretended to search for a "lost" contact lens. Although the first American combat troops had landed in Vietnam in March, many Harvard students would have been hard-pressed to locate the country on a map.

Three years later, in the fall of 1968, the incoming freshman class was the most diverse in Harvard history. (The admissions office nevertheless managed to find room for 49 students from Exeter.) Coats and ties were technically still required at dinner, but some students wore "ties" made of string or toilet paper, others wore their coats and ties over T-shirts, and one student wore his coat and tie without any shirt at all. Blue jeans, boots, and sandals were in; not even the most unrepentant preppie would have ventured forth in tasseled loafers. (Sartorial renegades opted for pin-striped bell-bottoms and paisley shirts.) Cambridge barbers reported that business was down 20 to 60 percent. Although the faculty had agreed to expand parietals, the new hours were ignored by students and administrators alike. The story went that the master of Adams House, seeing a couple emerge from an entryway early one morning, stared fixedly at a point above their heads and said, "Good morning, gentlemen." More and more undergraduates were moving off campus to escape the university's oversight altogether.

In the fall of 1968, Harvard Square was the closest thing New England had to Greenwich Village or Haight-Ashbury. Students ogled flowered shirts and outrageous buttons ("Fornicate for Freedom!") at Truc; checked out psychedelic posters and underground newspapers at Serendipity; or people-watched at Forbes Plaza, the open area in front of Holyoke Center that the *Crimson* called "a pot Rialto." Coach John Yovicsin wasn't the only over-thirty observer to refer to Harvard Square as "the zoo." Harvard's preppie culture was increasingly marginalized: "College's Final Clubs Enjoy Secluded Life in a World That Pays Little Attention to Them," a *Crimson* headline read. Surveys suggested that 40 percent of undergraduates had smoked marijuana, and every so often a student on a bad acid trip was carted off to UHS. By now, the *Crimson* had a reporter assigned to "the pot beat." There were 500,000 American troops in Vietnam. Each week more than 500 of them were killed. Even Harvard's Young Republican Club was against what was now called, simply, "the war."

The previous academic year had ended in turmoil, uncertainty, and despair. At the 1968 Class Day Exercises, six days after Robert Kennedy's death, a graduating senior delivered a Class Ode that, while based, as per tradition, on the university's alma mater (*Fair Harvard, thy sons to thy jubilee throng . . .*), was far from the customary nostalgic farewell:

> Fair Harvard, your sons are unsure of themselves
> As they step through your dignified gate.
> Wise prophets to whom they appeal for a word
> Are silenced by bullets and hate. . . .

It was with no little apprehension that Harvard College opened for its 333rd academic year in September 1968.

The Game

* * *

One night in early October, after meeting with their defensive line coach at the Varsity Club, the oak-paneled retreat where the football team took its training-table meals, Rick Berne and Alex MacLean walked down Quincy Street to Burr Hall for a meeting of the Harvard-Radcliffe Students for a Democratic Society.

Berne and MacLean, who played next to each other on the defensive line, were a Mutt-and-Jeffish pair. At six feet two, 230 pounds, Berne, a junior tackle, was one of the largest players on the team, with a long El Greco face that ended in a lantern jaw. He was brash and boisterous, a smart aleck with an assertive bass voice who loved nothing better than a Saturday night at the Pi Eta, a frat-like club frequented by athletes and known for its rowdy parties. At five feet nine and 200 pounds, MacLean, a senior, was round-faced and a bit doughy; if you saw him in the shower you'd never guess he was the starting middle guard for the Harvard football team. A semi-observant Quaker, he was charming and thoughtful, a good listener with a droll sense of humor who could often be found in the Quincy House darkroom developing his black-and-white landscape photographs. MacLean and Berne shared a love of football, an irreverent view of authority, and a deep conviction that the Vietnam War was politically and morally wrong.

MacLean and Berne weren't hard-core members of SDS, the student radical group with chapters on more than three hundred college campuses. Indeed, they weren't sure they really *were* members; there were no dues, there was nothing to sign, and anyone was welcome at meetings. Neither of them was as radical as MacLean's girlfriend, Delia O'Connor, a Radcliffe junior who could rattle on so ardently and interminably about the Albanian liberation movement of 1942 or the workers' struggle to "seize the means of production" that some of her non-SDS friends cringed when they saw her approach in the dining hall. MacLean and Berne didn't join any of the SDS working groups on civil rights, labor, or South

Africa, or act in the political skits SDS staged in the dining halls, although MacLean, who was taking some courses in the Visual Studies department, designed a few posters to help publicize SDS demonstrations. They weren't among the core group who did most of the talking at meetings; in fact, they didn't talk at all. But unless it conflicted with football, they tried to attend as many meetings and marches as they could.

When MacLean and Berne arrived at Burr B, the 207-seat lecture hall was nearly full, but Delia had saved them places. (Unlike John Yovicsin's football practices, SDS meetings rarely started on time.) Three years earlier, when MacLean was a freshman, SDS had had trouble attracting students to its table at the Orientation Week activities fair in Memorial Hall. By the fall of 1968, the Harvard-Radcliffe chapter of SDS was the largest in the country and its meetings were often standing-room only. With each new horror that year—the Tet Offensive, the assassinations, the carnage at the Democratic convention in Chicago—an increasing number of students had become "politicized." Many of those already politicized had become radicalized. Students had returned to campus in September with a sense that push was coming to shove. And if the majority of Harvard students dismissed SDS as an annoying group of scruffy, self-righteous, attention-seeking pests who joined because it was the only way they could get a girlfriend, no other campus organization seemed to oppose the war in a sufficiently emphatic manner. The Harvard-Radcliffe Young Democrats, by far the largest political group on campus two years earlier, now had so few members it was in danger of folding.

In the fall of 1968, Harvard SDS was feeling pressure to do something even more emphatic. The previous spring, Columbia's chapter had gained worldwide attention when its members took over several university buildings and occupied the president's office. After seven days, the administration had called in the police, who removed the students in a bloody operation that left more than a hundred protestors needing medical attention. Harvard students returned to school in September to find the words "TWO, THREE, MANY COLUMBIAS!," the latest SDS rallying cry, spray-painted on the walls and sidewalks of Cambridge.

On September 27, Mark Rudd, the former president of Columbia's SDS chapter, had come to Harvard to talk about the occupation. (Columbia had expelled him, so he had plenty of time for proselytizing.) MacLean and Berne hadn't been able to attend because it was the night before the Holy Cross game, but they had heard about it. The occupation's "main lesson," Rudd told an overflow crowd of eight hundred in Lowell Lecture Hall, was "pretty much embodied in our slogan, which was 'Up Against the Wall, Motherfucker.'" Near the end of his presentation, Rudd dismissed his audience, many of them devout SDSers, as a "nonradical group." The crowd hissed, but the implication—that Harvard activists were too much talk and not enough up-against-the-wall-motherfuckerism—hit a nerve. That fall, there was a growing feeling that a confrontation at Harvard might be looming.

* * *

That Rick Berne had become a student radical shocked those who had known him as a freshman. If you had wanted to cast a television sitcom about a stereotypical jock, you could have done worse than choose Berne. All-Upstate in one of the top high school football leagues in New York, he had been heavily recruited and didn't hesitate to remind his new teammates of it. At Harvard, where false modesty was an art form, this was considered a little uncool. He carried himself with a macho swagger that a few of his teammates found off-putting. Before the first drill on the first day of freshman football practice, he had gotten into a fistfight with a teammate over his place in line. He played with gung-ho ferocity and considered it a coup to knock an opponent out of the game. Coming from a big-time high school program, Berne found freshman football at Harvard disorganized and rinky-dink and didn't mind saying so.

During the first game, losing to lowly Tufts on a field that didn't even have stands, Berne, furious after Harvard fumbled in the fourth quarter and wondering how an All-Upstater from Syracuse had ended up on a third-rate field losing to a third-rate team, came off the field cursing loudly. An elderly alumnus on the sideline said, "Son, that kind of talk isn't the Harvard way."

"Oh, really?" snarled Berne, moving toward the startled gentleman. An assistant coach rushed over and steered Berne to the bench.

Berne lived up to the jock stereotype off the field as well, playing the wild man at parties and cold-calling the prettiest girls in the *Radcliffe Register*, a booklet containing tiny black-and-white photographs of entering Cliffies, as Radcliffe women were known. (After a cute freshman—the future actress Lindsay Crouse—hung up on him before he'd even begun his date-seeking spiel, he vowed to look beyond Radcliffe for feminine companionship.) He had been a good student in high school but had come to college to play football, and whenever a player dropped off the team to devote more time to his studies, Berne dismissed him as a wuss. Assigned an essay, "The Person I Most Admire," for his freshman expository writing class, Berne wrote about Ernie Davis, the Heisman Trophy–winning Syracuse star who had spoken at Berne's seventh-grade football team banquet, and who, several years later, had died of leukemia. Berne worked hard on the piece, larding it with three-syllable adjectives in what he assumed was the Harvard style, and telling a couple of his teammates, "Well boys, here's my first A." When the instructor read it aloud in class (*Ernie Davis was a great football player...*), several Cliffies tittered. Afterward, when the instructor asked for comments, they savaged it as mercilessly as Berne had ever savaged an opposing quarterback, using words like *clichéd* and *puerile*. When Berne got back to his room, he called his father. "Dad, I've had it with this place. Tell the Syracuse coach I'll be there on Monday." His father told him to hang in there, that things would work out. (His paper received a D.)

The Game

Berne was a two-way starter as a freshman, playing more minutes than anyone else on the team. The following year, listed in preseason forecasts as a "sophomore to watch," Berne, at defensive tackle, worked his way up to second string. He was thrilled when, in early November, he was one of three sophomores named to the forty-five-man traveling squad that would fly to Philadelphia for the Penn game. His parents and a dozen other family members would be there. Because of the smaller number of players on the trip, the coaches put together a makeshift kickoff team. Berne was on it. Most players on kickoff teams are fairly fast, and though Berne was quick for a big man, he worried that he might lag five or ten yards behind his smaller, speedier teammates as they beelined down the field. He didn't want to look like an idiot. On Harvard's first kickoff, Berne was so intent on trying to keep up that he never saw the Penn player who came from the side and smashed into his right knee.

Berne had ruptured his meniscus and torn both his medial collateral ligament and his anterior cruciate ligament. The surgeon who operated on Berne told him that it was one of the worst knee injuries he'd ever seen. There was some question whether he'd ever play football again, or even whether he'd walk without a limp.

* * *

Berne was crushed, but it never occurred to him that he wouldn't play again. Football was who he was. At the same time, his injury had an unintended consequence: he was forced to pay attention to the world beyond sports. Before it, he had spent almost all his free time with his teammates; now he decided to branch out and meet people with other interests, to try some things he might not have tried before, to stick his toe into the countercultural waters of the mid-sixties.

Berne lived in Adams House, one of eight large dormitories to which students applied at the end of freshman year. Over time, each house had developed a reputation: Eliot was the "preppie ghetto"; Winthrop the jock house; Dunster a haven for radicals; Adams the preferred haunt of artists, hipsters, and would-be men of letters. In the ecumenical spirit of the era, Harvard had recently engaged in some social engineering, diverting a few token literati to jockish Winthrop and diluting artsy-fartsy Adams with a dozen or so football players, of which Berne was one. It was rumored that Harvard put more athletes in Adams not just to offset the aesthetes but to have a chastening effect on the house's growing number of antiwar activists.

Berne might have preferred a more athletically inclined house, but he had come to appreciate Adams. It was the closest house to Harvard Yard, so he could sleep late and still get to class on time. It had its own indoor swimming pool, the site of notorious late-night co-ed skinny dips. And it was full of the kind of people Berne might never have gotten to know before his injury. The suite just downstairs in his entryway included a painter, a political activist, and a keyboard player whose rock band had already released a demo. Berne liked to hang out in their living room, listening to the Who, smoking a little pot, and talking about music, politics, and the war. He went to a poetry reading by Allen Ginsberg; he saw *The Battle of Algiers* at the Brattle (the kind of movie theater he would previously have scorned as an "art house"); he read not only *The Sporting News* but *Avatar*, a hippie weekly whose use of four-letter words had led a Boston judge to ban it as obscene. His circle of friends widened to include several Cliffies, though for dating purposes he continued to forage at Lesley and Pine Manor, nearby women's colleges. Berne hardly abandoned the jock life for that of an Adams House bohemian, and still spent more time partying at Pi Eta with his football buddies than studying at Lamont Library. But his consciousness was expanding. And when his teammate Alex MacLean invited him to an SDS meeting, he went.

*   *   *

That Alex MacLean was at Harvard in the first place still seemed astonishing. He was even more severely dyslexic than Pat Conway. The son of a Quaker activist and a National Institutes of Health neurophysiologist, MacLean was in second grade when he was diagnosed. Though his dyslexia was detected early and he had extensive tutoring, he couldn't really read on his own until eighth grade, and throughout high school he dictated most of his papers to his mother. Sports had boosted MacLean's confidence. At Sidwell Friends, a Quaker private school in Washington, D.C., he had been captain of the football team, a standout fullback and middle linebacker. But his SAT verbal score was so low that when he visited Wesleyan, the interviewer all but told him not to bother applying. Harvard seemed an even longer shot, especially after he walked into his interview and, reminding himself to make eye contact with the interviewer, tripped over an open briefcase and sent a slew of admissions folders flying. The interview itself had gone well—the man seemed interested in his senior project on why tumbling pigeons tumbled (MacLean tended a dovecote on the family farm)—until he'd been asked how, given his test scores, he planned to keep from flunking out. "I know I'm going to have to take some guts," he blurted out. Although he scrambled to explain himself—given his dyslexia it might be wise to take a few less demanding courses—he assumed he'd blown whatever small chance he'd had. But Harvard had a reputation for taking an occasional gamble on unconventional candidates, and apparently it saw something in MacLean.

MacLean was a good athlete and a hardworking player, but in the regimented world of football he was a little offbeat and spacey. At practice, he'd appear on the field without his helmet; someone would remind him and he'd run back to the locker room to fetch it. On game days, when the defense had its final meeting an hour before kickoff, he'd straggle in late, pulling on his football pants, looking for one of his cleats. Traveling to away games, when most players wore a sport jacket and khakis, MacLean would show up in a vintage woolen suit his father had outgrown, whose wide lapels and thick stripes made him look like a Roaring Twenties gangster. MacLean had his own quixotic style. People at the *Crimson* still talked about the time he tried out for the photography staff. Asked to submit a photo essay about sex, the other applicants shot something metaphorical (kittens cuddling, teenagers holding hands), but MacLean shot the real thing—nothing too graphic, but no question what the couple in the photos was up to. Even in an era of growing sexual openness, this created something of a scandal, and an offended staffer ripped the pictures out of the Assignment Book in which *Crimson* "compers" pasted their work for inspection. MacLean didn't make the cut.

MacLean and Berne had crossed paths at a varsity football game in 1966, during MacLean's sophomore year. MacLean, a third-stringer who hadn't suited up for the game, wound up sitting behind an obnoxious freshman who, in a voice that could be heard several rows away, was criticizing the players on the field and intimating how much better the team (which would share the league title that year) would be if *he* were out there: "Fucking Ivy League football; I can't believe I came here to play." MacLean was appalled. When the game was over, he left the stadium shaking his head, thinking what an asshole the guy was.

The following year, MacLean found himself playing next to that asshole on the second unit. During lulls in practice, sitting on the bench while the first team was on the field, they got to know each other. MacLean realized that beneath Berne's macho bluster lay a smart, inquisitive, and howlingly funny person whose values were not all that different from his own. They became friends. When Berne blew out his knee, MacLean visited him in the hospital. As Berne recovered, MacLean introduced him to his social circle, many of whose members were involved in the antiwar movement.

MacLean's own involvement was fairly recent. Both his parents were against the war—as a Quaker, his mother was a committed pacifist—and Vietnam was a frequent topic of family dinner-table conversation. By the time he arrived at Harvard, MacLean was against the war, too, but what with football and trying to keep up with his studies—his dyslexia made writing even the shortest essay torture—he didn't join in any antiwar activities. In the fall of MacLean's sophomore year, Robert McNamara had given a speech at Quincy House after which hundreds of demonstrators had surrounded the defense secretary's car and shouted "Murderer!" MacLean had felt a little sorry for the man. McNamara's son had been a few classes behind him at Sidwell; he, too, had difficulty reading, and MacLean had tried to be something of a mentor to him.

But as the war continued to escalate, MacLean wanted to do something more than just complain about it at the dinner table. In April 1967, when heavyweight boxing champion Muhammad Ali claimed conscientious objector status as a Muslim and refused induction, saying, "I ain't got no quarrel with them Vietcong," it made a deep impression. Six months later, on October 21, MacLean was in upstate New York, playing football against Cornell, when hundreds of Harvard students joined 100,000 other antiwar pro-testors in the March on the Pentagon. When he got back to Cambridge, everyone was talking about the march, which had ended with hundreds of protestors teargassed, beaten with billy clubs and rifle butts, and arrested. Delia's sister had been among the gassed. MacLean was outraged and sickened by the violence. The march marked a turning point in the antiwar movement—"From Dissent to Resistance," a *Crimson* headline read—as well as for MacLean. A few days later, when friends told him that SDS was going to picket a recruiter from the Dow Chemical Company, which supplied the military with napalm, he decided to go.

By the time he arrived at Mallinckrodt Hall, the chemistry building at the north end of campus, SDS's picket line had become a sit-in; the protestors had taken up residence in the hallway, effec-tively trapping the recruiter in a conference room and refusing to let him leave until he signed a pledge that Dow would never again hold job interviews at Harvard. MacLean found space among the students to sit. As the hours passed, various Harvard deans and masters picked their way through the several hundred tightly packed protestors, reasoning, remonstrating, cajoling, and pleading, as well as warning them that they were at risk of suspension. There were rumors that the police would be called in to remove the students by force. (Unbeknownst to the protestors, among the onlookers emerging from their offices to see what was happening was the Harvard chemistry professor who had invented napalm.)

MacLean was conflicted. He wanted to support the cause, but he also felt that he owed a great debt to Harvard, which had taken a chance on him. He didn't want to embarrass the people who had admitted him by getting suspended. He was secretly relieved when, in mid-afternoon, he realized it was time for football practice. Feeling guilty, he excuse-me'd his way through his fellow demonstrators and hurried down to Dillon Field House. At six o'clock, when the Dow recruiter, having been detained for seven hours, was finally allowed to leave, MacLean was preparing for the Dartmouth game. He would not be one of the seventy-four students placed on probation for their role in what the dean of students called "the blackest day in Harvard history" and the leader of the sit-in called "one of the most exciting days I ever spent at Harvard." But after Dow, as it would be known, MacLean began attending meetings of SDS. He was one of the first varsity athletes to join the radical antiwar movement at Harvard.

*   *   *

McNamara and Dow became legend, their names invoked by the SDS faithful as the names of famous battles are invoked by the veterans who fought them. They also marked the rapid evolution of student attitudes toward the war. After McNamara, 2,700 Harvard undergraduates had signed a letter to the defense secretary apologizing for the protestors' bad manners. After Dow, there was no apology.

The draft had changed everything. For the first few years of the war, college students with the intellectual and financial wherewithal had been able to avoid serving by going to graduate school, extending their 2-S student deferment until they turned twenty-six and aged out of the draft. This not only boosted applications to graduate schools but ensured that the war was fought largely by those without the means to go to college, much less grad school. Then, in July 1967, with the number of call-ups exceeding 20,000 a month, the government declared an end to grad school deferments, making exceptions only for medicine and a few other disciplines considered "vital to the national interest." Knowing that the moment they received their diplomas they'd become "draft bait," Harvard seniors had to make a decision. Would they serve? Go to prison? Flee to Canada? Apply for conscientious objector status? Find a sympathetic doctor to exaggerate an old knee injury or a case of flat feet and try for a medical deferment? Develop an interest in teaching—an exempted occupation in certain circumstances—at least until the war was over? Students shared strategies for flunking the physical: taking amphetamines or gulping down ten cups of coffee to spike their blood pressure above the acceptable limit; feigning homosexuality or insanity to get deferred on psychological grounds. Discussions about the war that had once been theoretical now had life-and-death implications. All fall, in the dining halls and dorm rooms, the question echoed: "What are you going to do?"

You could no longer postpone the decision by taking time off, as one in four Harvard students had done before the war. Those who left school now, however briefly, lost their student deferments. "The once traditional leave of absence now means military service," observed the *Crimson*. "Many who would have taken a year off to work or to 'find themselves' have been forced to remain in school." The chief psychiatrist at UHS suggested that the record number of Harvard students being sent to mental hospitals might reflect the inability of troubled students to take a break from college without being drafted. At the same time, it became more difficult to get kicked out. Reluctant to send students to Vietnam, the Administrative Board grew increasingly unwilling to suspend or expel misbehaving undergrads, and professors—most of whom opposed the war—began bumping Ds up to Cs so that students wouldn't flunk out. (Many years later, sociologists would identify this moment as the birth of Ivy League grade inflation.)

MacLean wasn't worried about the draft. He was applying for conscientious objector status, but even if he didn't get it, he wasn't going to serve. He hadn't decided whether he'd go to Canada or to prison—he just knew that one way or another he wouldn't fight. From his mother's pacifism and his years at Sidwell Friends, he had been brought up to believe that conflicts should be resolved without violence. His uncle had been a CO during World War II. MacLean believed that all wars were wrong, but that the Vietnam War was even more wrong than most. He didn't plan to make a public statement of his beliefs, like his SDS friend who had turned in his draft card at the Arlington Street Church rally in Boston last October, or like the Harvard junior he'd read about in the *Crimson* who had burned his. He admired those men, but he wasn't a very public person and he didn't want to go on record unless he had to. He planned to work on his CO application after football season was over.

Now that there was a very real chance they'd have to fight the war themselves, many more students felt the urgent need to stop it. The ranks of SDS swelled. At the same time, the group's focus changed. Frustrated by its inability to sway the United States government from its course in Vietnam, SDS turned its attention to a target closer to home: Harvard, and, more specifically, its Reserve Officers' Training Corps. Established in 1916 to prepare for the looming world war, ROTC groomed college students across the country to serve as military officers. (Almost half of all Army officers on active duty in Vietnam were ROTC grads.) In 1968, there were 208 undergraduates enrolled in the Harvard chapter, including two members of the football team, defensive end Joe McKinney and offensive tackle Joe McGrath, the senior who had worked as an aide at the Democratic National Convention. Some, like McKinney, had signed up because they were considering a career in the military; others, like McGrath, because they expected to be drafted and would rather go to Vietnam as officers than as infantrymen. For both, ROTC, which awarded scholarships and a monthly fifty-dollar stipend, was also a way to help pay for college. In return, they promised to serve for two years after graduation. They took courses in battle tactics and leadership from military personnel who had been given faculty appointments. Each Monday afternoon, they donned uniforms, shouldered World War II–era M-1 rifles, and drilled on a practice field near the stadium before hurrying over to Dillon Field House to change into their football gear.

Until the fall of 1968, few students had been aware of ROTC's existence—though some may have noticed an occasional uniformed cadet crossing the Yard and wondered what soldiers were doing on campus. But after SDS launched its campaign to abolish ROTC at Harvard, starting with a petition drive in the dining halls and a rally outside Memorial Hall, it was impossible to be a Harvard student and not know what the initials stood for. Almost overnight, ROTC became a symbol of what SDS called Harvard's "complicity" in the war. As SDS stepped up its anti-ROTC rhetoric, the administration, as a precautionary measure, moved Monday drill from the stadium practice field to a parking lot near ROTC headquarters on a quiet street near the Divinity School. But there were occasional reports of uniformed cadets being spat at or called "baby killers"; cadets on their way to drill learned to avoid the Yard, where they were more likely to bump into demonstrators chanting, "ROTC MUST GO." Whether because of their size or their affability, neither McKinney nor McGrath ever suffered anything more than a scornful look. McGrath, however, would learn that his bid for membership in the Fox, a final club, had failed because he'd been blackballed by an ROTC-hating member.

Before Dow, the relationship between SDS and the Harvard

administration had been wary but amiable and, at times, even playful. In the spring of 1967, SDS had challenged the college deans to a softball game, and when the administration team found itself a man shy, the head of SDS had filled in at shortstop, where he combined with the second baseman, the dean of freshmen, for a few adroit putouts. After Dow, there would be no more softball. In January 1968, in his annual report to the Overseers, Harvard's president, Nathan Pusey, dismissed the radicals as "Walter Mittys of the left" who "play at being revolutionaries"—a comment, wrote a *Crimson* editorialist, that exemplified "Pusey's blindness to the magnitude of disaffection at Harvard."

Pusey was a ripe target for radical ire. A classics scholar from Council Bluffs, Iowa (and the first Harvard president born west of New York), he was a modest, unpretentious, principled man who attended Harvard football games on Saturday afternoon as faithfully as he attended Memorial Church services on Sunday morning—both rituals for which not a few students and faculty members viewed him with distrust. In 1953, his first year as Harvard president, Pusey had won praise for defending several faculty members from attacks by the red-baiting senator Joseph McCarthy. But by 1968, most students viewed him as hopelessly out of touch. Freshmen started rolling their eyes when, in his welcoming remarks each fall, he pointed out that the university, like the papacy, was one of the last surviving medieval institutions. It didn't help that Pusey's Midwestern stolidity was underscored by an unlined face of almost infuriating blandness; he looked, it was said, like the back of a spoon. While the SDS platform called for Harvard to be "an instrument of social change, with decentralized decision-making stressing love and morality," Pusey viewed it as an academic ivory tower that should remain above the political fray and take no public position on the war. SDS insisted that Harvard, with its ROTC program, its Dow recruiters, its defense department contracts, and its professors shuttling back and forth to Washington to advise the government, was already doing so.

In private, Pusey referred to radical student activism as "the McCarthyism of the left." Other observers characterized the activists as spoiled upper-middle-class children whose anti-establishment activities were an attempt to assuage their guilt over their privileged lives and to act out against their overly permissive parents. Harvard's chief psychiatrist asserted that many of them were "emotionally ill"; indeed, the administration's response to more than a few had been to suggest they see a University Health Services therapist. In the Autumn 1968 issue of *Harvard Today*, Dean of the Faculty Franklin Ford described the radicals as "wreckers" who, unable to succeed as students in more traditional ways, tried to prove they were "the victims of a worthless system" by destroying it. His concerns were not exaggerated. If Harvard did not comply with their demands, vowed an SDS leader, "We are going to bring this university to an end, as you know it."

Yet even as colleges across the country were paralyzed by sit-ins and occupations, the administration and much of the faculty assumed that Harvard was immune to a Columbia-style take-over. People cited the coziness of the house system and the close faculty-student relationships as deterrents, but at bottom there was the feeling that it could never happen here. After all, this was Harvard.

* * *

That fall, MacLean had moved off campus, in large measure to avoid parietals, and was more or less living with Delia in an apartment near Central Square. It wasn't a hippie pad by any means, but MacLean used his interest in design to build his own bed and a funky lamp wrapped in silver wire. Delia sewed him a purple-and-maroon velvet quilt. MacLean painted the radiator blue. They hung out with Berne and their other activist friends at the cafeteria in Lehman Hall, a building set aside for commuters that had become a meeting spot for student radicals—the place to talk about the latest news from Vietnam, discuss the anti-ROTC campaign, and find out when the next rally was taking place.

MacLean sometimes wondered whether the rallies had any effect. People had been rallying, marching, debating, sitting-in, leafleting, sponsoring debates, signing petitions, and holding teach-ins for years, and the war had only gotten bigger. Sometimes he thought it was all just so much pissing in the wind. But he had to do *something*. Berne, after his trip across the country that summer, had returned to school determined to dedicate himself fully to the cause. He wasn't going to be one of those moderates who sat around the dining hall and talked about the immorality of the war but weren't out demonstrating because they didn't want to jeopardize their business school applications. "That's a cop-out," Berne would say. "It's time to take a stand." Berne, one of the football players assigned to Adams House to help counterbalance the radicals, had *become* one of the radicals.

Their commitment was reinforced by a controversial new course. Soc Rel 148, "Social Change in America," had been conceived the previous spring, when, amid the growing call for classes with more "relevance," a cadre of grad students, many of them SDS members, created a course on radical politics. It was sponsored by Social Relations, a relatively young department known as a place where alienated students could find a sympathetic ear without going to UHS psychiatrists and having the visit noted in their permanent records. (In the department's signature course, Soc Rel 120, "Analysis of Interpersonal Behavior," students sat around an oval table and talked about whatever was bugging them—sex, drugs, religion, parents, Vietnam, Harvard—while other students observed them through a one-way mirror.) Soc Rel 148, according to its prospectus, would examine "three of America's central social problems: imperialism, race, and labor." The course was not only *about* radical politics, it was *taught* by radicals, a mix of graduate and undergraduate students, most of them members of SDS: the first class in Harvard history with undergrad instructors.

Grades, it was rumored, would be pulled out of a hat. When Pusey saw a flyer announcing the course, he thought it was a prank. Three-hundred-fifty students enrolled.

Faculty members denounced Soc Rel 148 as a disgrace to Harvard's academic standards. There was no doubt that the course was a roaring gut, even more roaring, perhaps, than such legendary guts as Nat Sci 10, "Introduction to Geology" (commonly known as "Rocks for Jocks") and History 1375, "Man and the Sea" ("Boats"). The reading load was minimal: MacLean's section read excerpts from *The Wretched of the Earth*, by the Marxist philosopher Frantz Fanon, which encouraged colonized peoples to take up arms against their oppressors, and *Fanshen*, a book by the Harvard dropout William Hinton that praised the Communist land-reform movement in rural China. Students were assigned only one or two short papers, took no exams, and though there was general agreement that grades were meaningless (a manifestation of Harvard's repressive system that got in the way of real learning), didn't complain when they realized they had to be practically comatose not to get an A. But for MacLean, Berne, and their fellow students, it was a revelation to learn that in 1953 the CIA had helped engineer the coup that deposed the democratically elected prime minister of Iran, consolidating power in the hands of a corrupt and brutal Shah—the very Shah to whom Harvard had awarded an honorary degree last June. Or that in 1956, the United States, desperate to avoid a Ho Chi Minh presidency, had conspired to block free elections in Vietnam, the country in which it was now waging a war to defend "democracy." At a time when it was hard to discern the relevance of parsing Chaucer or memorizing the photosynthesis formula, it seemed appropriate—even imperative—to discuss the validity of the Geneva Accords or the morality of training military officers on college campuses. Soc Rel 148, which students referred to as "the SDS course," had the not-unintentional effect of serving as a training ground for the radical left. "Propaganda for credit," one critic called it.

But that fall, even as its ranks swelled, there was dissension within SDS. The majority of its members were associated with the New Left, a national movement that used nonviolent civil disobedience to push for a wide range of reforms but focused most on ending the war. They were being challenged by a small but strident faction from the Progressive Labor Party, a militant Marxist-Leninist organization dedicated to forming a worker-student alliance that would rise up and overthrow the capitalist oppressors. Progressive Labor dismissed the New Left as insufficiently radical, contemptuously referring to it as the "New Right"; the New Left considered PL too radical, as well as inflexible, humorless, and shrill. The groups' ideological differences were evident in their chants: the New Left stuck with "HELL NO, WE WON'T GO!" while the PL had escalated to "HO, HO, HO CHI MINH, DARE TO STRUGGLE, DARE TO WIN!" The New Left flashed the peace sign. PL brandished the clenched fist.

Ideologically, MacLean and Berne sided with Progressive Labor. Temperamentally, they were more in tune with the New Left. PLers, many of whom wore work shirts and cut their hair short to demonstrate solidarity with the proletariat, frowned on drugs and rock and roll as frivolous and antirevolutionary. The New Left, on the other hand, didn't believe that puffing on a joint while listening to "White Rabbit" was incompatible with the struggle to dismantle the military-industrial complex. No self-respecting PLer would have dared show his clean-shaven face at the be-in MacLean and Berne had attended on the banks of the Charles one sunny spring Sunday afternoon, at which hippies, peaceniks, and other assorted free spirits had gathered to smoke dope, watch mimes and jugglers, sway to a guitar-and-bongos jam session, and contemplate the occasional fugitive helium balloon. To MacLean and Berne, however, politics and the counterculture were of a piece.

Some SDS members found it surprising that anyone who played a violent, establishment sport like football could truly be interested in dismantling the war machine. But MacLean and

Berne, the only football players in SDS, were, in a way, prize recruits, evidence of the group's broadening appeal and the next best thing to getting an ROTC cadet to join. Their presence was also useful on a practical level. As factions grew increasingly confrontational, arguments occasionally turned physical. Whenever their friend Jamie Kilbreth, a PL leader (and MacLean's Soc Rel 148 section man), got wind that a meeting might be particularly acrimonious, he invited MacLean and Berne along. The two players joked about being "Kilbreth's bodyguards," but MacLean felt a little uncomfortable in the role because it played into the jock stereotype—not to mention that even if he hadn't been a pacifist, he would have had no desire to fight.

*　*　*

After trying to eat his way off the football team that summer, MacLean had reclaimed both his confidence and his physique (he lost more than twenty pounds to the rubber suit) to become a dependable starter. Although Berne wasn't starting, he was one of four defensive tackles in the regular rotation. After seven months of grueling rehab, he retained the faint trace of a limp, but his rebuilt knee was holding up. Each day he had to get to the trainer's room a couple of hours early for physical therapy; when he took the field, his entire leg was mummified in bandages and tape. Before every game, the team doctors injected his knee with cortisone; the following morning, no matter how much time Berne spent in the ice bath, they had to drain a syringeful of fluid from the cantaloupe-size joint. Berne still played with an edge, but he no longer believed that injuring an opponent was something to celebrate or that someone who dropped off the team to devote more time to his classes was a wuss.

At most colleges, athletes were assumed to be conservative, and football players were assumed to be the most conservative. The previous spring, when radicals occupied the Columbia library, a squadron of jocks (or "students of considerable athletic attainment," as the *New York Times* referred to them) had formed a human barricade in an attempt to starve out the protestors. When supporters of the occupation began tossing grapefruits and hunks of cheese to demonstrators on the second floor, the athletes used their considerable athletic attainment to leap in the air to intercept them. After a group of students finally broke through the blockade, a reporter was heard to observe, "That's Columbia for you—never could hold on fourth and one."

At Harvard, too, athletes were commonly assumed to be hawks. *Crimson* accounts of early antiwar demonstrations invariably described the muscular, short-haired men in crewnecks, khakis, and loafers who showed up to heckle the demonstrators as "jocks" or "jock types." In fact, by the fall of 1968, most of the players on the football team were against the war, even if they weren't out there demonstrating. Junior linebacker Dale Neal wrote so many antiwar letters to his hometown Illinois newspaper that the editor gently let him know he couldn't use any more. Before the team's first game, backup middle guard Mike Georges had pasted a Eugene McCarthy "flower power" decal on his helmet—although his teammates weren't entirely sure whether it was an antiwar statement or whether the irascible Georges simply wished to thumb his nose at the coaching staff. In any case, after a sharp-eyed alumnus complained, Yovicsin made Georges take it off.

Many of the players had grown up in the kinds of communities from which the majority of those serving in Vietnam had been taken. Many had high school classmates who had enlisted or been drafted. End John Kiernan's best friend, with whom he had played football at Milton High, had joined the Marines. In August 1968, he had been shot in the arm during a firefight just south of Da Nang in an area nicknamed Dodge City because of the frequency of Vietcong ambushes. The following spring, he would be carrying a letter from Kiernan in his flak jacket when he was hit in the chest by a grenade. He was hospitalized for thirteen months. When Kiernan visited him at Chelsea Naval Hospital, his friend showed him the letter; it was riddled with shrapnel holes and stained with blood.

Kiernan and his Harvard teammates felt both fortunate and guilty to be on an Ivy League campus playing football when people they knew were risking their lives overseas. But they didn't speak of the war on the field or in the locker room. Whether they were members of SDS or ROTC, no one proselytized, criticized, or ostracized. In fact, no one talked about it at all. Guys whose views might have made them mortal enemies in the Yard were close friends on the football field. In Dillon Field House, lion and lamb were likely to greet each other with affectionate obscenities. There was tacit agreement that football was a politics-free zone, the one place where they could get away from the war—and from the election, the riots, and the other issues that preoccupied students back on campus. The players marveled at how, once they crossed Anderson Bridge, all that stuff seemed to fade away, and the only thing that mattered was the next game.

*　*　*

Bucknell was one of those games in which everything went right. Before the first quarter ended, Harvard led 31–0. In the second quarter, Yovicsin started sending in the backups. By the fourth quarter, he was sending in the backups to the backups to the backups. In all, sixty-six Harvard players, many of them not even listed in the program, got into the game. Seven different players scored. Four weeks after several hundred feminists picketed the Miss America Pageant in Atlantic City, carrying signs that read "Welcome to the Cattle Auction," and tossing bras, girdles, hair curlers, and false eyelashes into a trash can labeled "Freedom," the *Crimson* write-up of the game proved that sexism was alive and well in at least one corner of the Harvard campus: "The Bucknell backfield boasted a Vassar at halfback and a Radcliffe at wingback, but Harvard treated them more like Lesley girls as the Crimson rolled to an easy 59–0 triumph over Bucknell Saturday."

Most Harvard fans expected the score to be only slightly less lopsided the following week, in the team's Ivy League opener against Columbia. Since the League began play, in 1956, Columbia had lost more than twice as many games as it had won, often by staggering margins. Last year, Harvard had beaten Columbia by five touchdowns. During the takeover that spring, when student radicals taunted authorities with an old school football cheer—WHO OWNS NEW YORK? WHY, WE OWN NEW YORK! WHY, WE OWN NEW YORK! WHO? C-O-L-U-M-B-I-A!—cynics noted that it was the first time in many years that the cheer contained a grain of truth.

The events of April were still being felt on October 12, when 17,182 spectators gathered at Baker Field, the rickety wooden stadium overlooking the Harlem River on the northern tip of Manhattan. Among those in attendance was Grayson Kirk, the Columbia president who had been forced into early retirement after last spring's disaster. Kirk was so bitter that he sat on the Harvard side and cheered lustily for the visiting team. Wrote his Harvard seatmate, "He told me that he plans to attend every Columbia home game this year and, as he did for the Harvard game with me, sit on the visitors' side and root against the Lions."

The Lions might have won had their coach not elected to keep the ball on the ground almost the entire first half, an unusual choice given that their quarterback had set three Ivy League passing records the previous week, albeit in a four-touchdown loss to Princeton. In the second half, the Columbia coach turned his quarterback loose, and he proceeded to pick apart the Crimson defense. Harvard barely held on to win, 21–14. The Bucknell game, sportswriters concluded, had been a fluke, and Harvard was sinking back to its natural level.

III

God Plays Quarterback for Yale

One hundred and twenty miles southwest of Harvard Yard, in New Haven, Connecticut, hopes could hardly have been higher for the 1968 Yale football team. The previous year, following a string of disappointing seasons, the Bulldogs had put together one of the most glorious campaigns in recent memory. After losing their opener, they won eight straight games, outscoring their opponents by an average of twenty-three points and capturing the Ivy League title for the first time since 1960. Their closest game had been the last: a come-from-behind 24–20 win over Harvard so thrilling that, as 68,135 fans poured out of the Yale Bowl, everyone agreed that there would never be another Harvard-Yale game as exciting as the one they'd just seen.

This year, with twenty-eight returning lettermen, the most in the league, the team was expected to pick up where it had left off. The *New York Times*, *Sports Illustrated*, *Street & Smith's*, *Playboy*, and almost every preseason poll picked Yale to repeat as Ivy League champion; many people assumed they would go undefeated. Indeed, the outlook was so bright that one of head coach Carmen Cozza's main concerns was to make sure the team didn't get complacent. At an organizational meeting in January, he had quoted his old college coach, Woody Hayes, who said that in football there was no such thing as standing still—if you weren't getting better, you were getting worse. "Boys," said Cozza, "We're going to get *better.*"

It's not that there weren't concerns. Ten starters had been lost to graduation, including the entire defensive line. But on offense, eight of eleven starters were back from an attack that had been one of the most explosive in Yale history. They had two All-Ivy interior linemen. They had the finest pair of ends in the league. And they had what the *New York Times*, in its preseason college football roundup, called "two of the best offensive backs in the nation." One was Calvin Hill, a halfback who could run, catch, and throw with equally devastating effect. The other was quarterback Brian Dowling.

Dowling was the most sensational Yale football player since Albie Booth, the pint-sized halfback known as "Little Boy Blue," who had given Bulldog fans something to cheer about during the Depression. *Sports Illustrated* called Dowling the most exciting Ivy League back since Dick Kazmaier, the Princeton halfback who won the 1951 Heisman Trophy as the country's top player—an award for which Dowling himself was being touted this year. He had been written up in *Time* and *Newsweek*. His picture had appeared in the *New York Times* on three occasions. He had been the subject of a five-minute special report on the *CBS Evening News* with Heywood Hale Broun. Howard Cosell, at Yale to speak at a Master's Tea, had stopped by Dowling's room to meet the young phenom. At a time when most colleges were too cool to have a Big Man on Campus (or, if they had one, he was likely to be the head of SDS), Dowling was the Biggest of BMOCs. Yale students hung bedsheet banners painted with his uniform number from their windows. Grown men asked for his autograph. Women from colleges across the Northeast wrote to ask him for a date. The *Yale Daily News* called him God.

If Dowling was a deity, he was a modest and unassuming one. In an era that prized self-expression, in which outsized personalities like Muhammad Ali and New York Jets quarterback "Broadway

Joe" Namath were redefining what it meant to be a sports star, the Yale captain was a throwback: a soft-spoken straight arrow who never sought the limelight, though it often sought him. With a football in his hand, however, he was as daring and unpredictable as any athlete in the country. "With Dowling on your side," said a teammate, "you never know what's going to happen—but you know you're not going to lose." Indeed, except for two games in which he had been injured, he hadn't lost a football game since the seventh grade.

*   *   *

Dowling grew up in Cleveland Heights, the second of six children, five of them boys. When they weren't in school, in church, or at the piano (their mother made all her children take lessons), he and his brothers were outside playing sports: baseball in the front yard, using trees as foul poles and the brick steps as a backstop; basketball in the driveway, shooting at the hoop their father had bracketed to the garage; football in the vacant lot across the street. Inside, there were Browns and Indians games to watch on TV; box scores to study in the *Plain Dealer*; baseball cards to sort, trade, and flip; and endless living-room-floor games of dice baseball (double ones was a strikeout, double sixes a grand slam). When he was old enough, Dowling signed up for every football, basketball, and baseball league he could. The skinny, well-mannered boy excelled in all of them.

On his first play from scrimmage at Saint Ignatius High School, Dowling intercepted a pass and returned it for a score. In his first start as quarterback, he threw five touchdown passes. In his three years on the varsity, two as starting quarterback, his team won twenty-nine of thirty games. Its only loss was the final game of his junior year. Competing for the city championship in Municipal Stadium in front of 37,673 people on Thanksgiving Day, Dowling played through a sprained ankle, a bruised kidney, and chipped bones in his back, before a broken collarbone on the final play of the first half sent him to the hospital. (Because Dowling was the team's quarterback, safety, punter, and kick returner, it took four players to fill in for him in the second half.) In his high school career, he threw for 2,350 yards and thirty-four touchdowns, averaged over 35 yards a punt, intercepted a state-record thirty-three passes, and was named to several All-America teams. He also led the basketball team to a city championship, batted over .400 for the baseball team, and reached the regional tennis singles final. By the time the twelve-letter man graduated, he had become one of the most celebrated high school athletes in Cleveland history.

Dowling was recruited by more than eighty colleges, including such powerhouse football programs as USC, Michigan, and Notre Dame. Ohio State was especially keen in its pursuit of the home-state hero: its coach, Woody Hayes, spent four hours in the Dowling living room one evening; OSU alumnus Jack Nicklaus called long-distance from Florida to ask whether Brian would play a round of golf with him next time the Masters champ was back in Ohio; Governor James Rhodes stopped by the house and put in a pitch for matriculating in-state. Dowling listened politely, but he didn't want to go to OSU. Its quarterbacks spent most of their time handing off. He was leaning toward USC, another perennial contender for the national championship.

Dowling wouldn't have considered Yale had it not been for his father, a successful businessman who came to all his son's games and was supportive without being pushy. Emmett Dowling knew Brian had his heart set on a big-time football school, but he asked him to consider the Ivy League. Touring east coast colleges with his father in the spring of his junior year, Brian liked Princeton's campus best, but the Tigers still used the single wing, an old-fashioned offensive formation in which the quarterback rarely passed. At Harvard, he met with John Yovicsin, but the meeting seemed perfunctory and the coach didn't even offer to show Dowling and his father the stadium. At Yale, Dowling immediately hit it off with Carmen Cozza, who was also from the Cleveland area. Cozza drove them out to the Bowl, where they stood on the field and gazed up at the 70,000 empty seats. "Wouldn't it be great to play here in front of a full house?" Cozza asked.

Yale deployed every resource at its disposal to woo Dowling. Clint Frank, Yale's 1937 Heisman winner, called him to talk Yale football. Mike Pyle, captain of Yale's undefeated 1960 team and starting center for the Chicago Bears, wrote him a three-page letter, assuring him that playing at Yale wouldn't keep him from playing in the NFL. Cozza sent him *Why Yale?*, a pamphlet enumerating the presidents, senators, Supreme Court justices, and CEOs who had attended the school, as well as *The Yale Football Story*, a book recounting the exploits of Walter Camp, Pudge Heffelfinger, and other legends from the turn-of-the-century glory days when the Bulldogs were always at or near the top of the national rankings and tickets for their games were among the most sought-after in sports. Cozza told Dowling that he wouldn't be the only blue-chip recruit in his class; two other high school All-Americans were likely to attend. Dowling narrowed it down to USC, Michigan, Northwestern, and Yale. His father encouraged him to choose Yale—"Why go cabin when you can go first-class?"—and said that if Brian didn't like it, he'd pay his way to another school. When Dowling called Cozza to tell him he was coming, the coach was stunned. An editorial in the *Plain Dealer* praised the decision as the rare triumph of education over big-time sports.

*   *   *

In his first weeks on the freshman team, Dowling couldn't help having second thoughts: Yale didn't seem so first-class after all. The players had to take a fifteen-minute ride on a cramped yellow school bus just to get to practice. The locker room consisted of a hook or two for each player in a World War I–era armory that also housed the polo stables. The practice field smelled of manure. The equipment, varsity hand-me-downs, looked as if it might have been worn by Albie Booth. (One player wrote to his high school coach and begged him to mail him his old shoulder pads.) On Thursdays, there were no tackles at practice—all four of them took Biology 11, which held labs that day—and the team had to make do with tackling dummies. The coach of the Bullpups, as the freshman team was known, was an avuncular ex–Green Bay Packer named Harry Jacunski, who introduced a vocabulary "word for the day" at the beginning of each practice, served milk and cookies at optional Tuesday-night film sessions, played scratchy records of the Whiffenpoofs singing fight songs to fire up the team during drills (the players blocked and tackled to the strains of "Daddy Is a Yale Man" and "Goodnight, Poor Harvard"), and used note cards to help him through his pregame pep talks. Reaching for an inspirational finish before his team took the field one day, Jacunski, peering through thick horn-rimmed glasses, concluded, "And so, boys, I want you to go out there and . . ."—there was a pause as he switched to the next card—"win!"

If the freshman football program seemed amateurish, Dowling had to admit that the team itself was loaded with talent. The other high school All-Americans—Calvin Hill and end Bruce Weinstein—could have played for any college in the country, and Cozza had persuaded an unprecedented number of All-State players to join them at Yale. Theirs would one day be regarded as the greatest recruiting class in the school's history. As the season progressed, the coaches occasionally sent over members of the freshman team to drill with the varsity. One afternoon, Weinstein and tackle Kyle Gee practiced double-team blocking against the varsity's best player, a six-foot-four, 240-pound defensive tackle who would captain the team the following year. To the shock of the coaches, the two freshmen pushed the junior down the field again and again. It would be the last time they were invited to practice with the varsity.

Even in this august group, Dowling stood out. His style was, admittedly, unorthodox. He threw from a three-quarters delivery, like a shortstop slinging a baseball. His passes wobbled, yet when the receiver looked up, the ball always seemed to be right there. He ran with a long, loose-limbed stride that looked almost leisurely— until you tried to catch him. But he had unerring instincts and a genius for ad-libbing. Back to punt on fourth and one in a close game against Cornell, he saw an opening and decided to run. He made the first down with a yard to spare. A 15-yard penalty, however, erased the gain, making it fourth and sixteen from deep in Yale territory. Jacunski told him, in no uncertain terms, to punt this time. Dowling, however, seeing the Cornell defenders come up the middle, took off around end for 20 yards and another first down. Cozza, getting a look at the freshmen from atop the viewing tower, was so furious he almost fell as he scrambled down the scaffolding, yelling, "Make that kid kick the ball!" But that kid had a way of making things come out right that seemed almost charmed. His teammate Pat Madden would long remember a play in the Columbia game when Dowling took off downfield, holding the ball, as he often did, to his coach's consternation, away from his body, in one capacious hand. Any other player carrying the ball like that, Madden knew, would surely have fumbled—or gotten his arm ripped off. Indeed, after a long gain, Dowling ended up buried under four Columbia defenders. But from deep within the pile of pale-blue jerseys, there extended a lone, dark-blue-shirted arm, at the end of which a hand held out the football.

Dowling led the freshman team in rushing; completed 57 percent of his passes for eleven touchdowns and almost 1,000 yards; did most of the punting and some of the placekicking; and, when the defense couldn't stop a potent Princeton offense, convinced Coach Jacunski to put him in at safety, where he helped preserve a narrow victory. The freshmen won all six of their games, finishing with a 45–20 thrashing of Harvard in front of 5,000 spectators, an unheard-of crowd for a Bullpups game. Every Old Blue, as Yale's ultra-loyal graduates were known, in attendance was salivating at the thought of Dowling and company playing varsity for the next three years.

* * *

Dowling came along at an opportune time for Yale football—and for Carmen Cozza. The youngest of five children born to Italian immigrants in Depression-era Ohio, Cozza had never set foot in New England before 1963, when he was hired as an assistant coach at Yale at the age of thirty-two. As he would write years later, "It was a culture shock for the son of an Italian laborer from the Midwest to be transported suddenly into the elite, old-money atmosphere that marked Yale and the Ivy League at that time." It didn't seem likely that he would be there long. In 1965, in Cozza's opening game as head coach, Yale lost to the University of Connecticut, an upstate school intended to serve as an early-season warm-up—a "patsy" or "cream puff," as such opponents were known—before Yale began Ivy League play. Letters from irate alumni poured into the athletic department, urging that Cozza be fired. "There's a train for New London at 5:40 p.m.," read a telegram addressed to the coach. "Be under it." As Dowling's Bullpups racked up victories, the varsity won only three games that season, finishing with a dreary shutout loss to Harvard.

Win or lose, Cozza had the players on his side. Many of them had come to Yale because there was something about Carm Cozza that felt right. With a closely cropped fringe of prematurely silver hair surrounding his bald pate, Cozza had a wrestler's build, a strong jaw, and a straightforward manner that contained not an iota of pretension. He worked his players hard but never berated or made fun of them. He never used profanity. If someone made a mistake, he didn't criticize him in front of others; if someone did something good, he pointed it out in front of the team. He tried to find a role for everyone on the squad. He wasn't one for stem-winding pregame speeches; he spoke briefly and frankly. His players knew he meant what he said and they didn't want to disappoint him. During games, he patrolled the sideline in slacks, sneakers, windbreaker, and a Yale baseball cap, which he windmilled above his head in delight after a particularly fine play.

Each day the players walked past a sign in the locker room that read, "Football is not only a game. It is a way of life." It was Cozza's favorite quote. If some of the players thought it a little hokey, they took to heart its implication that football's lessons of hard work, loyalty, and sacrifice were equally applicable off the field. A football team, said Cozza, was a family. A devout Catholic, he led the team in the Lord's Prayer before each game. He often invited players home for dinner, and on Sunday mornings he visited injured players in the infirmary, bringing brownies baked by his wife. He kept a close eye on his players' grades, not just to make sure they stayed eligible but to make sure they stayed on track to graduate. If they had to miss practice for a lab, so be it. He was proud that the team had a higher GPA than the student body as a whole; in fact, because of the structure imposed by the football season, the players' grades were usually better in the fall than in the spring.

But Cozza was no softy. A fiercely competitive man who had pitched in the minor leagues before turning to coaching, he hated losing as much as anybody. In his mid-thirties, he was in better shape than many of his players; running wind sprints with the team, he easily kept pace with all but the fastest. He encouraged them to play handball in the off-season to improve their agility; sometimes he took on two at a time and destroyed them both. After his dismal first season as head coach, he was all the more determined to win. And with Dowling and company moving up to varsity, he had the tools to do it.

*　　*　　*

Charley Loftus had high hopes, too. As Yale's sports information director since 1943, Loftus had been responsible for numerous innovations in the fledgling profession of sports publicity: joint telephone press conferences with opposing coaches, typed play-by-play accounts of games supplied to press box writers at the end of each quarter. It had been Loftus who insisted that the Harvard-Yale game be called "The Game." It had been Loftus who came up with the idea to photograph the Harvard and Yale captains together for the program cover. In twenty-three years at Yale, Loftus, who could make a press release about a JV hockey game sound like a Fitzgerald novel, had covered almost three thousand athletic events. He knew a great story when he saw it.

Although Loftus, a hard-drinking, chain-smoking serial raconteur, spent his career proclaiming the glories of Yale, he was, like Cozza, something of an outsider, having grown up a townie in New Haven and gotten his B.S. in journalism from Ohio University. He brought to his work an outsider's blend of reverence and skepticism. If, occasionally, he seemed eager to prove that he was as clever as any Yalie (when an alumnus demanded he write "something big" about the football team, he responded with a 182-letter word from Aristophanes), he was not above tweaking Old Blues. He once proposed that Yale drop its bulldog, Handsome Dan, as mascot and replace him with his own prizewinning Old English sheepdog, Fezziwig Clyde—a notion that had gullible alums harrumphing into their dry martinis. Ironically, the outsider-turned-insider—the "y" in Charley, he insisted, stood for Yale—was incapable of straying far from campus. Loftus intimated that an inner-ear infection made travel difficult, but those closest to him knew that a phobia kept him from venturing beyond the New Haven city limits. Even trips to the Yale Bowl made him so anxious he required a police escort.

Loftus saw Dowling as next in the roll call of Yale gridiron giants. It didn't hurt that Dowling was a three-sport star who had gone on to lead the freshman basketball team in scoring and rebounding, play center field for the baseball team, and win a few doubles matches for the tennis team. Or that with his tousled hair and blue-green eyes, he was as handsome as a Hollywood leading man, yet had the quiet, unaffected manner of the altar boy he had once been. Before Dowling played a varsity down, Loftus was extolling him as the contemporary incarnation of Frank Merriwell, whose last-second heroics and manly but modest personality had won the day for Yale on and off the field in a series of popular turn-of-the-century dime novels. Loftus's efforts soon bore fruit: "Another Merriwell in Making at Yale" was the headline in the *Providence Evening Bulletin*; "Yale QB Tabbed 2d Merriwell" was the title of a syndicated column by Red Smith. When reporters asked Dowling about his fictional alter ego, Loftus couldn't have scripted a more Merriwellian response. "I've never read any of the books," Dowling said. "But from what I understand, Frank Merriwell was quite a guy."

*   *   *

On September 24, 1966, in his first varsity game, Dowling threw for two touchdowns in a win over Connecticut.

The following week, playing Rutgers in a torrential rain, Dowling was running the option early in the second quarter when, as Charley Loftus wrote, his right knee was "ripped asunder by a jarring tackle," and he was carried off the field.

That night, Dowling's father died.

He had known his father was seriously ill but had no idea that the illness would be fatal. In May, they had played a round at the Yale Golf Course. Emmett Dowling had gotten a blister on his foot—which was nothing unusual, except the blister never healed. Six weeks later, when the family gathered in the backyard for their annual Fourth of July cookout, he fainted. He spent most of the summer in the hospital, his red and white blood cell count alarmingly skewed. When Dowling returned to school in September, his father knew he was dying of leukemia but was hoping for a remission long enough to see Brian play at least once for the Yale varsity. Too ill to travel, however, he had listened to the Connecticut game on a special radio hookup from his hospital bed. "Maybe I can get to the Rutgers game," he whispered to his wife. But by then, he couldn't even listen to the radio. He slipped into a coma and died that night at the age of forty-nine. On Sunday morning, Dowling was at breakfast when the assistant to the president of the university walked across the dining hall toward him, and Dowling knew.

In the weeks following the funeral, Dowling felt as if he were in a twilight zone. He had lost his father; he had also lost football. His knee required surgery that would force him to miss the entire season. He considered leaving school. But after talking it over with Cozza, he decided it wouldn't make things any better. Dowling spent weeks on crutches, then endless afternoons doing leg lifts with sandbags draped over his shin. Without him, the team struggled to a 4-5 record. Dowling sat in the stands at Harvard Stadium on a bitterly cold November afternoon and watched Yale conclude its season with a 17–0 loss.

*　　*　　*

In the 1967 preseason, though everyone pretended otherwise, all eyes were on Dowling and his surgically repaired knee. Dowling himself wasn't worried, but he couldn't wait to get the initial hit over with. He got his chance on the first play of the first intrasquad scrimmage, when he fumbled the snap. As he picked up the ball and began to run, one could almost hear the collective intake of breath among onlookers—and the exhalation when, after being tackled, Dowling hopped to his feet, intact. The news traveled all the way to Boston: "Yale QB Dowling Passes Big Test" was the *Globe* headline. Then, eleven days before the opening game, while doing the Monkey Roll, a routine warm-up in which players leapfrogged over one another, Dowling landed awkwardly and fractured his right wrist.

By the following day it seemed the entire Yale campus had gone into mourning. "Another season down the drain," one student told the *Yale Daily News*. In "An Open Letter to Yale Football Fans," the *News* sports editors acknowledged that Dowling's fluke injury was "a crushing blow" but implored students not to succumb to despair. "Giving up is no way out," they wrote. "It's our football team, and they need our support. Win or lose, they'll try harder if we will." The players themselves were shaken. Dowling, the doctors said, would be in a cast for six weeks. The 1967 season seemed to be over before it began. Indeed, the team fumbled five times and lost its first game, to Holy Cross: only the fifth time in ninety-seven seasons that Yale had lost its opener. Cozza, going into the final year of his contract with a 7-11 record—and, even worse, without a win over Princeton or Harvard—knew he had little margin for error. In the locker room after the game, the coach who almost never raised his voice raised it. "This may be my last year of coaching here, but I'm not going down without a fight," he roared. "If any of you guys aren't with me, don't bother showing up at practice on Monday." The following week, Yale barely squeezed by Connecticut.

For the second straight year, Dowling faced missing most of the season. How could it happen again? Would he ever get to play varsity football at Yale? But after an evening spent pacing his dorm room floor, he reminded himself he'd be back in time to play at least a few games that season. The next day he was out at practice, fielding punts and passing left-handed, listening in on huddles, handing out towels, trying to make himself useful.

In fact, Dowling's wrist healed far more quickly than anticipated, though Cozza, not wanting to get everyone's hopes up, including his own, kept the news a secret. In the third game of the season, against Brown, a murmur rippled through the stands when Dowling trotted onto the field in the fourth quarter. He was in for only one play—at flanker, where he was safely removed from the fray—but, like the vision of Zapata on his white horse that was said to inspire his Mexican revolutionaries in mid-battle,

Dowling's brief appearance gave hope to fans and teammates alike. Help was on the way.

The following week, Dowling started against Columbia. Playing with his knee heavily taped and his wrist cushioned in foam rubber, he spent most of the 21–7 win handing off. "I'm just glad to see him come through the game alive," said Cozza. Facing heavily favored Cornell, Dowling ran for 51 yards on the second play of the game. Yale fans shuddered when he got up from the tackle with a bloody face, but after a trip to the locker room to have his broken nose wrenched back into place, he returned to lead Yale to a 41–7 victory. A year after a provocative *Time* cover had asked, "Is God Dead?" a chant arose from the Yale student section: "GOD IS ALIVE! GOD IS ALIVE!"

All the promise of that undefeated freshman year blossomed against Dartmouth. Dartmouth had won five Ivy titles in ten years. They came into the game without a loss. They had the league's top-rated defense. They were favored by two points. They lost by forty-one. Yale scored four touchdowns in the first seventeen minutes. It was 35–2 at the half. Cozza put in the second team, and they kept scoring. He put in the third team, and they kept scoring. "It's like Carm has created a Frankenstein and he doesn't know what to do with it," Bruce Weinstein told Kyle Gee. At the height of the slaughter, reserve defensive back John Waldman looked across the field at the Dartmouth players lined up on the sideline; they were all watching the Yale offense with slack-jawed expressions. He looked up and down the Yale sideline: his teammates wore the same awed look. The final score was 56–15, the worst beating Yale had administered to Dartmouth since 1896. In the locker room after the game, Cozza was at a loss for words.

As Yale continued to run roughshod over its opponents, the school embraced its team with the kind of fervor normally associated with state universities in the Midwest. Much of the adulation centered on Dowling, whom sportswriters called "Superman," "Wunderkind," "the Magic Man," "Lochinvar," and, to Charley

Loftus's gratification, "Merriwell." But all the players basked in the attention. There were pep rallies and bonfires. Restaurants and barbershops filled their windows with photos of the team. Students packed three-hundred-seat Harkness Hall for Football 10a, an informal weekly session in which Cozza narrated the most recent game film; they gave the coach a standing ovation when he stepped to the podium. Alumni who a year earlier had demanded Cozza's ouster now agreed they'd always thought him a fine coach. On game day, the New Haven Railroad added extra trains to accommodate the tide of alums coming up from New York City. "It should be recorded for all time and not on the sports page, what Yale's charismatic football team has done to this normally sedate university community," declared a *Yale Daily News* editorial. "Quite simply, it has turned Yale into a frenzied, screaming, rock-'em-sock-'em football school, where the marching band trudges home through a cheering New Haven from the Yale Bowl, where myriads of posters festoon the college walls with naughty slogans, where even the cynics sport 'Blue Power' buttons, and where renditions of 'Bulldog Bulldog' or 'Boola Boola' or 'Bingo Bingo' are sung by sober-minded fans as they cross the campus for classes."

The euphoria reached fever pitch for the Princeton game. A saying at Yale had it that the coaches wanted to beat Dartmouth and the alumni wanted to beat Harvard, but the players wanted to beat Princeton. They wanted to beat Harvard, too, of course, but with Harvard there was an underlying, if grudging, mutual respect. Their dislike of Princeton was visceral. Asked why he found Princetonians objectionable, one Yale undergraduate said simply, "They're pompous, snotty rah-rahs." In 1967, Yale's animus was whetted by the fact that they hadn't beaten Princeton in seven years. Players and fans were still smarting from the 1964 game, a rout in which Princeton tailback Cosmo Iacavazzi scored on two long runs and, after each, had hurled the ball into the Yale Bowl stands—the kind of insult-to-injury flourish that, years later, would become routine but at the time was a breach of gridiron etiquette akin to letting out a Bronx cheer in church. In 1966, when Dowling was out with his knee injury, Yale had the game all but won when, on fourth down from the Princeton 30-yard line, Cozza elected to punt. The snap was low, the punt was blocked, and a second-string Princeton end ran it back for the winning touchdown. Afterward, in the locker room, several players wept.

In the week leading up to the 1967 game, film of the blocked punt was played on a continuous loop outside the locker room, intercut with footage of Iacavazzi hurling the football into the Yale Bowl stands. But with Dowling healthy, there was a sense that this time, things would be different. The campus was seized with a collective frenzy. HATE PRINCETON banners appeared in dorm room windows. TWEAK THE TIGER'S TAIL buttons appeared on students' shirts. The *Yale Daily News* described the Yale-Princeton rivalry as a Holy War and the upcoming game as Armageddon. Each night, bands of students held roving rallies, involving so much symbolic crushing of Princeton-colored oranges that by mid-week, Yale dining halls stopped serving the fruit. On Wednesday night, hundreds of undergraduates made a pilgrimage to the courtyard of Dowling's dorm, where they settled beneath his second-floor room and chanted "WE WANT GOD! WE WANT GOD!" until, like the Pope appearing on his balcony at St. Peter's to bless the faithful, the quarterback came to the window and spoke to the crowd below. Someone tossed up an orange and Dowling crushed it against the wall, triggering a roar. On Friday morning, eight hundred students gathered in front of Ray Tompkins House, the neo-Gothic home of Yale's athletic department, to send the team off to New Jersey, working themselves into such a pitch of excitement that they began to rock the team buses before an alarmed Cozza told the drivers to take off.

Early in the game, Dowling pitched to Hill, who ran a sweep to the right before pulling up and throwing back to Dowling, who had drifted, unnoticed, down the field. Catching the pass on the Princeton twenty, Dowling strode into the end zone and fired the ball into the upper reaches of Palmer Stadium. Playing in biting cold, with intermittent rain and a smattering of hail, against a team that had beaten Harvard by five touchdowns the previous week, Dowling passed for two touchdowns and scored twice himself in the team's 29–7 win, clinching Yale's first Ivy title since 1960. Players carried Cozza off the field on their shoulders. Fans tore down one of the goalposts and carried a fifteen-foot chunk into the Yale locker room, where they presented it to the coach. An inebriated senior named George Bush was one of several Yale students detained by Princeton campus police for refusing to come down from their perches on a goalpost.

It was a day in which Dowling could do no wrong. Late in the second quarter, when the rain started up again, a chant arose from the Yale student section: "MAKE IT STOP, BRIAN, MAKE IT STOP!" Dowling raised his arms for quiet, and though a causal relationship could never be definitively established, it was indisputable that the sun emerged at some point during the fourth quarter. The headline in the *Yale Daily News*: "God Plays Quarterback For Yale."

A week later, in front of the largest crowd at the Yale Bowl since the 1954 Army game, Yale trailed Harvard by three points with two minutes left when Dowling, his back foot slipping on the soggy turf, threw a 66-yard touchdown bomb to end Del Marting to win the game, 24–20. "His timing was poor," Charley Loftus crowed to reporters in the press box. "Merriwell would have waited until there were only seven seconds left."

*   *   *

It wasn't just what Dowling did but the way he did it that dazzled fans and demoralized defenses. Although the six-foot-two, 195-pounder was an extraordinary athlete, he would never have been chosen to appear in an instructional film for young quarterbacks. Over the years, writers would describe his passes, variously, as loopers, bloopers, floaters, lobs, knuckleballs, beanbags, balloons, loaves of bread, marshmallows, custard pies, rainbows, cotton candy, blimps with engine trouble, and "great lumbering auks." Dowling himself good-naturedly called them his "flutterballs." (Weinstein thought the fluttering made them easier to catch; it was if the football had handles.) Defensive backs, convinced Dowling's throws would fall short and they'd have an easy interception, dropped off their coverage—only to watch the football sail over their head and into the receiver's waiting arms. "He doesn't look very good passing," said the Penn coach after Dowling flutterballed Yale to a lopsided victory over his team. "All he does is kill you."

Dowling's running was no less exasperating. He could look as if he were out for a Sunday stroll—describing one touchdown run, Red Smith wrote that the quarterback "loitered" across the goal line—but his long-legged gait ate up ground. (In wind sprints at the end of practice, just as teammates were convinced they'd catch him, he'd take a few strides and be out of reach.) He was maddeningly elusive, capable of scrambling for a seeming eternity before throwing for a big gain or loping for a first down. "He was like a ghost," said an opposing lineman. "You were so sure you had him. And then you didn't." In one intrasquad scrimmage, two beefy Yale defenders broke into the backfield, each determined to get a big hit on Dowling. At the last second, like a matador working with two bulls, Dowling stepped away, and they knocked each other to the ground.

Many quarterbacks who threw perfect spirals or ran like gazelles couldn't read the field. Dowling was blessed with what freshman coach Jacunski called "panoramic peripheral vision" and an uncanny awareness of where every player was, even, it seemed, when his back was turned. As defenders closed in on him, he continued to hold out for the big play long after most quarterbacks would have thrown the ball away to avoid being tackled behind the line. (In 1967, he averaged 15.5 yards per completion; of every eleven Dowling passes, one was a touchdown.) Four decades later, on a charity golf outing, a current Yale coach asked the legendary quarterback how, back to pass, he chose his receiver. How did he read his progressions? Did he watch the safety? Did he key on the linebackers? Dowling shrugged and said, "I just threw it to the guy who was open."

* * *

As the 1968 season got under way, the pressure on Dowling was enormous. Yale fans were counting on him to lead the team to an undefeated season and a second straight Ivy League crown. Dowling himself expected nothing less. He possessed a preternatural confidence—not the in-your-face cockiness of some star players but the laid-back calm that in great athletes can be mistaken for carelessness. Junior year, on the morning of the Dartmouth game, Cozza thought his quarterback might be nervous about taking on the undefeated Indians in his fifth varsity start and sought him out in the lounge at Ray Tompkins House for a game of pool. Waiting for the right moment as they moved around the table, he began to talk soothingly to Dowling, telling him not to worry, that everything would be all right. Dowling politely cut him off. "Coach, don't worry, we're going to kill 'em," he said, lining up a shot. That afternoon, Yale scored the first four times they had the ball.

Dowling played without doubt or fear; the possibility of losing never crossed his mind. No matter how dire the circumstance, he was unflappable; third and ten didn't faze him any more than second and one. Sportswriters described his affect on the field as "nonchalant"; Thomas Bergin, a Yale professor of romance languages and devoted Bulldog fan, wrote of his "serenity." In four years of Yale football, his teammates saw him flustered only once: when, as Dowling crossed the goal line at the end of a long run, the Yale cheerleaders fired off a miniature cannon, primed with wads of paper, as they did after every Yale touchdown. In this case, the blast happened to hit Dowling on his calf, startling him so that he dropped the ball and turned his head in surprise.

Dowling's confidence was reflected in his play-calling. On first down, when most teams ran the ball, he often chose to pass—sometimes even on the game's first play. On third and short, when most coaches called for the fullback up the middle, he was just as likely to throw the bomb. If Dowling's calls seemed whimsical, they were based on logic—albeit the logic of a high-stakes gambler, not an accountant. And woe to those who expected Dowling to play it safe just because Yale had a big lead. "Heck no," he told a reporter. "That's when you have the other team retreating." Dowling's decisions often made Cozza, a disciple of conservative, run-it-up-the-gut Woody Hayes, squirm. But ever since he'd seen Dowling run from punt formation on fourth and sixteen freshman year, Cozza had learned not to intervene too much; it would be like telling Jackson Pollock to paint by numbers.

The self-assured Dowling, in fact, had a soothing effect on his tightly wound coach, who entered the 1968 season more relaxed—relatively speaking—than his players had ever seen him. In practice, Cozza took an occasional turn throwing against the defensive backs. He allowed a bespectacled, 125-pound reporter from the *New Haven Register* to don pads and spend an afternoon drilling with the team. (*Paper Lion*, George Plimpton's account of playing training-camp quarterback for the Detroit Lions, had just been published.) And one afternoon near the end of two-a-days, when the team was dragging in the heat and Cozza stalked off the field in apparent disgust, the players were flabbergasted when, five minutes later, the neighborhood ice-cream truck drove up with Cozza at the wheel. "You guys stink," he said, as he hopped out and began tossing them Eskimo Pies.

There was an obvious bond between the quarterback who had lost his father and the coach who had three daughters and no sons. (When Emmett Dowling died, Cozza had missed two days of practice to fly to Cleveland for the funeral.) They could often be seen talking quietly on the sideline, Cozza, one hand on his cheek, listening thoughtfully. They looked more like two friends, one team member thought, than like coach and player. Dowling called the coach Carm. During two-a-days, Cozza promised his oft-injured quarterback that if he stayed healthy all year and the team went into its final game undefeated, he'd let him return a kickoff against Harvard.

Quarterbacks are rarely elected captain—Dowling was the first to hold the office at Yale since 1926—but it would have seemed wrong to choose anyone else. In some ways the role didn't suit him. He wasn't a backslapper. He never gave a single speech before a game. Other than to call the plays, he didn't talk all that much. But there was no doubt who the leader of the team was. His teammates kidded him about being God, but when asked about Dowling by reporters, they sounded almost as if they meant it, using words like *faith, belief, aura,* and *mystique.* Said one: "All the reassurance I need before a game is to know that Brian Dowling is alive and healthy."

*　　*　　*

Had Dowling been a different person, his teammates might have resented the attention he got. But he never boasted, was quick to redirect praise toward his offensive line and receivers, and treated everybody with the same quiet respect. It wouldn't have occurred to him to complain to the officials after a bad call or show up an opponent. Except for his moment of payback in Palmer Stadium, he'd hand the ball to the referee after scoring as matter-of-factly as if he were returning a book to the library. When all of Yale went into depression after he fractured his wrist, no one heard the injured man himself complain or even express disappointment. Indeed, Dowling seemed slightly embarrassed by the fuss people made over him. He would just as soon be one of the guys. Each year, the Yale trainers jokingly maintained an All-Ugly Squad, composed primarily of linemen who had lost teeth or gotten stitches. The handsome Dowling, of course, had little chance of being chosen. But as he came to the sideline after breaking his nose in the Cornell game, Dowling, pointing to his bloody face, crowed "U.S.! U.S.!"—thrilled that he might earn a place on the Ugly Squad.

Off the field, Dowling was amiable, if somewhat reserved. Like most Yale football captains, he was tapped for Skull and Bones, the most exclusive of Yale's nine "secret societies," whose alumni included William Howard Taft, McGeorge Bundy, and George H. W. Bush. But no one pegged Dowling as socially or politically ambitious, much less a devoted clubman. And though he switched majors from sociology to economics in his junior year and had to give up varsity basketball to bring up his grades, he would never have been mistaken for a grind. (Yale legend had it that if Dowling walked into a lecture hall at the beginning of the semester, when students were choosing classes, the other students applauded, certain they had found a gut.) He hung out with his roommates in front of *Batman* and *Hogan's Heroes*, and joined an occasional road trip to Briarcliff or Vassar. On Saturday nights at DKE, while his frat brothers celebrated another Yale victory by knocking down whiskey sours, Dowling sipped a 7-Up and responded politely to the people who sought to warm themselves in his glow. Sunday morning he was always up in time for ten o'clock Mass at St. Mary's. Like many great athletes, he wasn't given to introspection or reflection. He seemed incapable of the world-weary irony and facetiousness that constituted the lingua franca of many Yale students. "Nothing ever bothered Brian, at least not outwardly," Cozza would write many years later. "I don't know what made him tick inside."

He felt most himself on the playing field. He wanted to go pro, hoped to be drafted by his hometown Browns, the team he'd grown up watching with his father. And as he checked the college football scores in the *New York Times* on Sunday mornings that fall, if he occasionally wondered what it would have been like had he gone to USC, where a tailback named O. J. Simpson was setting records, he was glad that he had chosen Yale. When he heard "Boola Boola" or "Down the Field" played in the varsity locker room, the songs that had seemed so corny three years earlier now triggered a palpable feeling of pride.

* * *

On September 28, 1968, Yale opened its ninety-sixth football season against Connecticut in front of 33,373 fans at the Yale Bowl. The largest stadium in the world when it opened in 1914 ("We suppose the Yale Bowl . . . can be seen through a telescope from Mars," observed the *New York Times*), the Bowl was beginning to show signs of wear, but its 70,869 seats—eighteen miles' worth—had been given a fresh coat of Yale blue for what was expected to be a banner year. Yale was favored by three touchdowns.

In the first half, the defense recovered three fumbles and intercepted a pass, and the offense converted all four turnovers into touchdowns. The final score was 31–14. Afterward, in the locker room, tackle Kyle Gee said to his teammates, "One down, eight to go."

The win came at a cost. In the fourth quarter, Calvin Hill, hit by a defensive back as he leaped high for a Dowling pass, flipped upside down and landed on his head. He was carried from the field on a stretcher and taken by ambulance to the Yale infirmary.

At most colleges, players who "got dinged" or had their "bell rung"—they didn't like to use the word *concussion*, which made it sound serious—were asked by their trainers how many fingers they were holding up and who was the president of the United States. If they answered correctly, they were sent right back into the game. At Yale, things were different. The head trainer, Bill Dayton, had come to Yale from Texas A&M after being fired for objecting to Coach Bear Bryant's practice of rushing players back on the field before their injuries had healed. At Yale, concussed players were kept out of action for a minimum of ten days.

Fortunately, the concussion Hill sustained was a mild one,

and he seemed fine when Cozza visited him in the infirmary on Sunday morning with a plate of brownies.

* * *

On Monday morning, two days after Yale's victory over Connecticut, students came down to breakfast to find a comic strip on the op-ed page of the *Yale Daily News*. It depicted a quarterback addressing a huddle. *O.K. team, this play is the same as the last one . . . "The Cleveland Clutch." The front line just blocks like hell. The ends run straight down the field, and you backs tear off around the ends. I'll either pass downfield, or roll out to one of the backs, or I'll run the ball myself, or maybe I'll just punt it.* In the last panel, the quarterback, whose huge helmeted head rested on a pencil-thin neck, turned to the reader with a sheepish grin. *Actually, "The Cleveland Clutch" is a very flexible play.*

Bull tales, as the comic strip was titled, was the work of a junior named Garretson "Garry" Trudeau. A third-generation Yalie, Trudeau had played football in junior high but given it up when he went off to boarding school and got interested in art. At Yale, he wrote for the campus humor magazine and became one of the thousands of undergraduates who flocked to the Bowl during the 1967 season, besotted with the team and its charismatic quarterback. In Trudeau's case, his hero-worship was tempered with wry bemusement. He expressed his thoughts in a few cartoon strips, and showed them to an editor at the *Yale Daily News*. "They're all right," said the editor. "We publish pretty much anything."

Over the course of the fall, Trudeau would introduce other characters to *bull tales*, including a self-conscious freshman named Mike Doonesbury, but he always returned to the football team. Though other players made cameo appearances, the strip revolved around "B.D.," the endearingly single-minded quarterback who never took off his helmet, even on road trips to Briarcliff. Although a few players grumbled that the strip reduced them to stereotypical dumb jocks, like everyone else on campus they checked the *News* each morning to see if there was a fresh installment and, if so, whether they might be in it. Players passed it around on the bus to practice, ribbing Dowling for whatever his alter ego had done that day. With Loftus as the quarterback's Boswell and Trudeau as his Daumier, Dowling's legend grew.

* * *

In its second game of the season, Yale rolled to a 49–14 victory over Colgate. Even without Calvin Hill, the offense amassed 520 yards on a Yale-record 103 plays. The defense held Colgate to 9 yards rushing and 99 passing. Yale, which hadn't lost since the first game the previous year, won its tenth consecutive victory.

Yale's offense was even more impressive in its Ivy League opener against Brown. Before many people in the crowd of 29,511 found their seats, Yale led 14–0. It was 28–0 at the half, 35–13 at game's end. Yale established a school-record 614 yards of offense: 307 on the ground, 307 through the air—the *beau ideal* of a balanced attack. Dowling produced 303 of those yards, rushing for 111 and completing seven of nine passes for 192 more, in what the *New York Times*'s Dave Anderson called "the most spectacular individual offensive performance in Yale's distinguished football history." Dowling, said the Brown coach, was "the most exciting football player in the country."

Late in the third period, Dowling was on the bench when Charley Loftus, watching from the press box, realized his Merriwell was only three yards shy of the Yale single-game record for total offense. He got word to Cozza, who sent Dowling back in. After gaining a yard on a keeper around end, Dowling was hit out of bounds by a Brown player, triggering an outraged roar from Yale fans. Dowling hopped to his feet, seemingly unhurt—then suddenly buckled to his knees. It turned out to be nothing serious, but the incident put a scare into Yale coaches and fans, and reminded them just how much the 1968 season depended on their quarterback.

IV

The Melting Pot

When Ray Hornblower showed up for the first day of Harvard freshman football practice, some of his teammates wondered whether he'd wandered into the wrong place by mistake. The slender halfback with blue eyes, blond hair, dimpled cheeks, and upper-crust accent—and a funny last name masking-taped to the front of his helmet—looked more like a choirboy than like a football player. (He had, in fact, been singing in choirs since he was seven.) "Who's this Hornblower guy?" Gus Crim, the 210-pound fullback who had turned down Ohio State to come to Harvard, muttered to Rick Berne. "I'm playing on a team with *this*?" And then they saw the choirboy run. There was another surpassingly fleet player on the freshman squad that year, a black halfback from Brooklyn. One afternoon after practice, the players arranged a match race. Hornblower won going away. He started out eighth on the depth chart; by the time the season opened, he was first.

*   *   *

Ralph Hornblower III was not, as was often assumed by Harvard fans, a Proper Bostonian. He grew up in Greenwich, Connecticut, and summered at Squibnocket Farm, a 1500-acre family compound on Martha's Vineyard. His father worked on Wall Street as a partner in Hornblower & Weeks, the brokerage founded by Ray's great-grandfather in 1888. But on both sides of the family, college had, for generations, meant Harvard. His parents had taken him to every Harvard-Yale game since he was six, and he had thrilled to the exploits of Charlie Ravenel, the undersized quarterback from Charleston, South Carolina, whose improvisational daring had earned him the nickname "the Riverboat Gambler." Despite his slight frame, it was assumed that young Hornblower would one day play football for Harvard. His father's father had captained the hockey team in 1911; his mother's father had been the intercollegiate 440 champion in 1909. But the best athlete in the family may have been his mother. Legend had it that her Beaver Country Day softball team had gotten together at a reunion and beaten a group of Harvard freshmen. Ray would always remember the autumn afternoon when he and his mother were tossing a football on the back lawn. Ray was nine. His mother, wearing a fur coat, had waved the ball and called out, "Okay, Ray, run at me!" And Ray had run at her, as fast as he could, driving his head into her stomach and knocking her back a yard or two. "My God, you really *hit!*" she exclaimed, beaming. From that moment on, Ray was determined to run the football with total abandon.

Two years later, while eleven-year-old Ray was starring on his sixth-grade football team, his mother lay in bed, dying of leukemia. One afternoon, he overheard her on the phone, telling a friend how her son was tearing up the Fairfield County private school league. "I know he's going to make it," he heard her say. "He's going to be the next Charlie Ravenel." A few months later, she was dead.

As a middle-aged man, Hornblower would look back and see that much of what drove him on the football field was a desire to vindicate his mother's faith in him. To that end, he might have been wise to prep somewhere other than St. Paul's, a small boarding school in the woods of southern New Hampshire known more for its prowess at squash than for its mastery of football. Since its founding in 1856, St. Paul's had played mostly intramural sports, in which three stuffily named clubs—Isthmian, Delphian, and Old Hundred—competed against one another. A St. Paul's football team wouldn't begin playing other schools until 1962, a year before Hornblower arrived. Hornblower became a star at St. Paul's, running with quicksilver elusiveness and throwing the option pass with an accuracy his father attributed to years of family duck-hunting on the Vineyard. But his star didn't shine far beyond Concord. When his high school coach phoned John Yovicsin to tell him about his talented senior, the Harvard coach seemed to be under the impression that St. Paul's was a big Catholic school up near Manchester.

At Harvard, Hornblower led the freshman team in scoring. The following summer, he came down with mononucleosis, having indulged in some French kissing at a debutante party on Long Island. He spent most of August, when he should have been running wind sprints on the beach, lying on a couch at Squibnocket Farm and gazing at the Atlantic. Hornblower began his first varsity season on the bench, but in the third game, when the reserves were sent in during a rout of Columbia, he took a pitchout and sped forty yards for a touchdown. Two games later, he played so well in the third quarter of a tight contest against Dartmouth that although the outcome was still in doubt, the coaches left him in. "Little Ray Hornblower," as the *Harvard Alumni Bulletin* referred to him in its account of the game, had been a starter ever since.

For Harvard alums, many of whom came from similarly privileged backgrounds, Hornblower's emergence was a boon; he was one of their own. Whenever he ripped off a long run, a frisson of self-satisfaction rippled through the choice seats between the forties, like a gust of wind rippling the surface of the Charles. (The similar frisson that followed a good run by reserve halfback Jim Reynolds might have been less robust had those alumni known he wasn't one of the Massachusetts Reynoldses, whose ancestry could be traced back to Paul Revere, but one of the New Jersey

Reynoldses—in fact, a parochial school kid from an Irish-Catholic family of nine children whose father worked at a Staten Island shipyard.) Hornblower wasn't the only dyed-in-the-wool New England preppie on the 1968 team—Tony Smith, the ridiculously handsome second-team end, had arrived at Harvard by way of New Canaan and Choate—but Hornblower was the only starter. Jack Fadden, the Harvard trainer, himself the son of Irish immigrants, called him the Last of the Mohicans.

To his teammates, Hornblower was the kind of self-assured rich kid who seemed to have been born and raised in Harvard Yard. Although the WASP world of final clubs and debutante balls was losing its hold in the anti-establishment sixties, there remained redoubts to which private schoolers could retreat. Hornblower lived in Eliot House, the "preppie ghetto" whose master, the famously patrician classics professor John Finley, handpicked its three-hundred-fifty students and was said to favor applicants from Groton, St. Paul's, and his own alma mater, Exeter. (In the spring, croquet wickets sprouted as unfailingly as the daffodils on the Eliot courtyard lawn.) Saturday night after the football game, while many of his teammates were guzzling keg beer at the Pi Eta, Hornblower could be found nursing a bottle of Budweiser at the Owl, a final club whose alumni included Harry Elkins Widener '07, the millionaire bibliophile who went down on the *Titanic* and in whose memory Harvard's main library was named. Yet the princely Hornblower wasn't a "snot," as stuck-up preppies were called. He had a disarmingly bluff manner and something of an egalitarian streak, sponsoring Crim, Berne, and several other public school teammates for Owl Club membership. The teasing to which his fellow players subjected him was good-natured. When Fritz Reed caught sight of Hornblower in the locker room, fastening garters to his black dress socks on his way to an Owl Club formal dinner, the offensive tackle razzed the halfback unmercifully. Knowing that Hornblower's girlfriend was the great-granddaughter of Teddy Roosevelt, the players asked, "Hey, aren't you dating Margot Rockefeller?" Hornblower would shake his head in exasperation and respond, "Her name is *Roosevelt*, for God's sake!" Hornblower's play made him immune to any real barbs. That was one of the reasons he liked football. It was the same reason why generations of players from less privileged backgrounds had liked it: on the field your background didn't matter. The only thing that mattered was whether you could turn the corner on a defensive end.

Hornblower's breezy self-assurance wasn't quite as breezy as it seemed. If some of his public school teammates felt out of their element in classrooms dominated by jaded preppies from St. Paul's and Groton, Hornblower felt out of his element on the football field among the gritty players from local powerhouses like Everett and Malden Catholic. He was aware that prep school athletes, who tended to play the glamour positions like halfback and quarterback, were assumed to be soft and had a reputation for quitting when they realized they weren't going to be first or second string. Hornblower was determined to subvert the stereotype. On warm-up laps around the field, when most players ran just fast enough not to get yelled at by the coaches, Hornblower would race out in front, straining to be first. He knew that his teammates were probably cursing him under their breath, muttering, "What an asshole," but he *had* to be first, every practice, every day.

Hornblower was abetted by some technical help. Most running backs used half-inch spikes on their cleats, switching to three-quarter- or even one-inch spikes if the field was soggy. Hornblower used one-inch spikes no matter what the conditions. They gave him better traction. He credited them with his uncanny ability to cut. On sweeps, he'd run toward the sideline, plant his foot, and—as two or three would-be tacklers, unable to stop as suddenly, zoomed past—head off across the field in nearly the opposite direction, like a sailboat executing a perfect tack. (In a publicity photo, a helmetless Hornblower, football cradled against his chest, was shown cutting sharply to the left while his abundant, surfer-blond hair cut sharply to the right.) The problem with the seemingly magical spikes was that the longer they were, the greater the risk of twisting an ankle or wrenching a knee, which is why other running backs didn't wear them—and why inch-long spikes would be banned in 1972. Hornblower, eager to hold his own among the public schoolers, believed the risk worth taking.

Hornblower had another secret weapon. Sophomore year, Margot Roosevelt introduced him to a psychiatrist she'd met at the Harvard Christian Fellowship. Dr. Armand Nicholi, a Harvard Medical School faculty member, was a specialist in Freud. He was also a former varsity football player at Cornell who, at a time when sports psychology consisted largely of coaches calling their players pussies in an attempt to goad them to greater heights of aggression, was interested in how psychology could be used to maximize athletic performance. He started working with Hornblower on what, years later, would be called visualization techniques. To perform at his best on Saturday afternoon, Nicholi told Hornblower, he should spend Friday night and Saturday morning in a quiet spot, rereading his clippings and replaying his longest runs in his mind. He encouraged Hornblower to set specific goals. Hornblower decided that his goal in 1968 was to run for 100 yards each game.

Whatever the reasons, something was working. Against Columbia, Hornblower had run for 93 yards, his new career high.

*   *   *

Even Harvard's most devoted fans assumed that the team's three-game unbeaten streak would come to a halt against Cornell on October 19. Cornell had twenty-seven lettermen coming back from a team that had finished third in the league. Their defense boasted nine returning starters, including the league's largest player, a six-foot-five, 250-pound tackle who had been an honorable-mention All-American the previous year. Furthermore, Harvard was hurting. Gatto checked into Stillman Infirmary on Tuesday with an infected foot and wasn't released until Friday afternoon. Lalich, his back sore from the Columbia game, couldn't throw the ball all week, and was listed as the team's third-string quarterback, available only in an emergency. It looked as if Frank Champi would start, but on Saturday morning Lalich told the coaches he felt well enough to play.

Under a steady rain in front of 16,990 hardy fans, Harvard's defense held Cornell to eight first downs and didn't allow them inside the twenty. Although the footing was sloppy, Lalich threw for 102 yards, while Gatto ran for 76, in the process breaking Harvard's career rushing mark, set in 1953. It would be Hornblower, however, who propelled the offense in the team's 10–0 victory, running twenty-six times for 138 yards, earning honors as Ivy League Back of the Week, and generating a sheaf of new press clippings to pump himself up for the next game.

*   *   *

For much of the first half of the twentieth century, Harvard was composed largely of students like Hornblower: New England prep schoolers who had grown up assuming that admission to the college was their birthright. Abbott Lawrence Lowell, scion of one of Boston's oldest, wealthiest, and most socially prominent families, and Harvard's president from 1909 to 1933, had done his best to keep it that way. To the consternation of Lowell and many alumni, Harvard's demographic complexion began to change under his successor, James Bryant Conant. A brilliant chemist who had grown up in middle-class Dorchester, Conant was troubled by Harvard's social and economic exclusivity and encouraged a more meritocratic admissions policy that would make it a truly national institution. "We should be able to say that any man with remarkable talents may obtain his education at Harvard whether he be rich or penniless, whether he come from Boston or San Francisco," he wrote in his first annual report. Slowly, Harvard's student body became, relatively speaking, more socially, ethnically, and geographically diverse. In 1953, for the first time, there were more public schoolers than private in the entering freshman class—a milestone not quite so egalitarian as it seemed, given that only 2 percent of American high school graduates attended private schools.

The demographics of the College, were, in fact, coming closer to those of its football team. An oft-told joke had it that to play for Harvard you had to have been born on Beacon Hill or belong to the Porcellian, the oldest and most prestigious of Harvard's final clubs—unless you were one of the South Boston Irishmen recruited to block for them. In fact, the football team had long been a pocket of ethnic and socioeconomic variety. As far back as the turn of the century, when 80 percent of Harvard students were private school graduates, a story in the *Crimson* complained that immigrant sons from public schools were pushing prep schoolers off the squad.

On the 1968 roster, twenty-eight of eighty-eight players had attended private school, but the number was misleading; of those, twelve were PGs: players who, after graduating from Boston-area public schools, were encouraged to undergo a year of postgraduate polishing, on scholarship, to prepare them for the academic and social demands of Harvard. Indeed, six players on the team, including Pat Conway, had PG'd at Exeter, which over the years had come to serve as a kind of de facto farm team for Harvard football—and, at the same time, a way station at which future Harvard players could boost their test scores to an acceptable level.

More than a third of the players on the 1968 team had been culled from Boston-area public and parochial schools—"local boys," as the sportswriters called them, many of them the sons or grandsons of immigrants who had arrived in the great tide that had transformed the city at the turn of the century. A critical mass of seniors, including the captain, Gatto, were Italian-American, and calls of *cinque* or *otto* could occasionally be heard in the locker room as they played morra, an ancient Italian game, not unlike rock-paper-scissors, in which contestants threw out a hand, showing zero to five fingers, and guessed what the sum of all the fingers would be. More than a few players, like Conway, were Irish-American, including cornerback Neil Hurley, whose parents had emigrated from Galway and County Cork as teenagers and bequeathed their son the faint brogue that overlay his Boston accent. Skowronski's grandparents were from Poland, Lalich's from Serbia; Ignacio's father, a geographic outlier, had been a farmer on Guam. (Harvard's 1968 press book contained a "Pronunciation Guide"—unnecessary in the days of Hamilton Fish and Endicott "Chub" Peabody—that provided broadcasters with phonetic spellings: "ska-RON-ski," "ig-NAH-she-o," and so on.) While the locker room chatter was still dominated by Boston-ese, Yovicsin's alumni recruiters were bringing in an increasing number of "horses"—as football players were referred to in admissions parlance—from farther afield: safety Tom Wynne was from Arkansas; defensive tackle Ed Sadler was from Tennessee; defensive end John Cramer was a fifth-generation Oregonian whose great-great-great-grandmother had crossed the Great Plains by covered wagon in 1864. The team's annual end-of-preseason New England clambake was the first time Cramer had seen a lobster. He had to ask his Boston teammates for operating instructions.

The team varied by age (twenty-four-year-old Conway was the oldest, eighteen-year-old safety Fred Martucci the youngest); marital status (Lalich, McKinney, and defensive back Ken Thomas were married and lived off campus); temperament (there were free spirits like MacLean, teetotaling Midwesterners like Crim, and hard-partiers like defensive tackle Steve Zebal); and interests (MacLean and Berne had their SDS meetings, punter Gary Singleterry his Christian Science services). You never knew what hidden talents a teammate might possess. That fall, Joe McGrath was struggling with a midterm music paper in which he had to analyze a Bach fugue. He asked his fellow lineman Fritz Reed, who was also taking the class, for help. Reed took McGrath and the score down to the Adams House music room, where he sat at the piano and sight-read the piece flawlessly before explaining to the astonished McGrath how the fugue was structured.

The most unusual résumé on the team may have belonged to Tommy Lee Jones. The son of a cowboy turned oil rigger, Jones was an eighth-generation Texan whose life had revolved around hunting, fishing, and football until the afternoon during his junior year in high school when he wandered into a room where a group of students was rehearsing for a production of *Mr. Roberts*. Jones was spellbound. He auditioned for the school's next show, Dylan Thomas's *Under Milk Wood*, and was cast in a small part. Since arriving at Harvard, the "talented thespian," as the press book called him, had performed in plays by Pinter, Euripides, and Brecht; the previous spring he had won raves in the title role of a multimedia adaptation of *Coriolanus*, for which he had dragooned several linebacker teammates into appearing onstage as appropriately muscular centurions. Being both a jock and a "Loebie" (Harvard actors spent much of their time at the college's Loeb Drama Center) took some juggling. After practice, while his teammates dawdled in the locker room, Jones sometimes had to rush off to rehearsal, occasionally in costume. "Are you bolting so you can go do that to-be-or-not-to-be shit?" Reed would shout.

Offstage, Jones was a man of few words, which he measured out in a gravelly Texas twang and punctuated with long, enigmatic pauses. His face, with its deep-set eyes, high cheekbones, pockmarked cheeks, and square jaw, usually wore an expression as impassive as granite. The first week of freshman year, Joe McGrath was unpacking in his room in Mower Hall when he heard a strange, rhythmic thumping. He went outside and found a sturdy-looking freshman in cowboy boots, squatting on his haunches, throwing a hunting knife into the trunk of a tree. McGrath introduced himself. "I'm Tommy Lee Jones," the young man replied, and went right back to his throwing. Jones, who kept his radio tuned to the only country station in Boston, could occasionally be heard croaking scraps of Hank Williams in a tuneless bass in the locker room, and every so often, when his teammates got him going, his face relaxed into a disarming grin. He was generally so terse, however, that when he did clown around, it was all the more unexpected. Defensive end John Cramer was talking with Jones in the shower one day after practice when he felt something warm on his calf. He looked down and realized that Jones, grinning innocently, had pulled the well-worn gag of peeing on his leg.

Jones belonged not to jock-dominated Pi Eta but to the Signet Society, the invitation-only literary club that counted T. S. Eliot and James Agee among its former members. An English concentrator (what other colleges called "majors" Harvard called "fields of concentration"), he was writing his honors thesis on the influence of Catholicism on the work of Flannery O'Connor. One evening, John Ignacio found himself sitting next to Jones at dinner at the Varsity Club, discussing *Look Back in Anger*, the play by John Osborne. Ignacio soon realized that while he was talking in a basic way about its plot, Jones was dissecting its structure, its characterizations, its place in contemporary drama. As he listened, Ignacio realized that *this* was what people meant when they said that you'll learn more at Harvard from the people you have dinner with than from your professors.

At six feet, 195 pounds, Jones was an unusually sturdy leading man ("hulking," said the *Crimson*, in its review of *The Caretaker*), but the smallest player on the offensive line. Although he wasn't one to overpower an opponent, like Skowronski, he was the fastest of the linemen, had excellent technique, and played with an almost unsettling intensity. Guard Bob Jannino considered him the most focused person he'd ever met. The team could be ahead by four touchdowns in the final minute and Jones would still be going at it as if the game were tied. In practice, when the coaches instructed the players to perform a drill at half speed, most were grateful for the respite, but Jones continued at full throttle. Once, when Jim Reynolds and Neil Hurley were freshmen, the coach brought the team over to practice with the varsity. In one drill,

Reynolds and Hurley held blocking dummies while the varsity offense ran simulated plays. It was a noncontact exercise; when the offensive linemen reached the defensive backs, they were supposed to pull up into blocking position and run in place for a few seconds. Instead of pulling up, one offensive lineman kept running and blocking. The annoyed freshmen decided to teach him a lesson. The next time he came at them, Hurley dropped to his knees in front of Reynolds, who cudgeled the guy to the ground with the blocking dummy. The guy sprang to his feet and peered intently at Reynolds, who clenched his fists, ready, if necessary, to fight. "Good work," the guy said, in a low, raspy voice. "Keep it up." He turned and ran back to the huddle. It was Jones.

*   *   *

At many big-time football schools, players lived in the same dorm, hung out together, and became a distinct cult, set apart from their classmates. At Harvard, athletes were scattered throughout the campus—though Winthrop House had such a profusion that visiting Cliffies joked about making sure to bring along a piece of raw meat. Even so, the team spent more time together than many families. Practice ran from five to seven—it started late so premeds could finish their labs—but most players came early to get their ankles taped, and after the long walk to the Varsity Club for dinner, there were meetings, films, and scouting reports. Some nights, they were lucky if they got back to their rooms by ten to begin studying.

Although most of the players went their separate ways off the field, many of them belonged to the Pi Eta, which was quartered in a three-story brick building on Boylston Street. On Saturday nights after the game, they gathered with their guests at "The Pi" to drink beer and dance. (At the height of the party, one of Tommy Lee Jones's suitemates, a senator's son from Tennessee named Al Gore, might be seen flopping around on the floor doing the Gator with his girlfriend, Tipper, a blonde BU student whom the players thought was very cute.) On Sunday afternoon, players convened in the basement to watch the NFL doubleheader on the club's color TV, while linebacker Gerry Marino and cornerback Mike Ananis prepared the ritual Pi Eta Sunday-night spaghetti supper in the kitchen. They had assembled the ingredients on Saturday morning before the game, getting up early to take the subway to Haymarket, where Marino, all four of whose grandparents had emigrated from Sicily, went from stall to stall, haggling in pidgin Italian as he selected tomatoes and peppers and onions and garlic, before heading to Capone's butcher shop for pork chops, short ribs, and ropes of hot sausage. On Sunday, Marino prepared the bolognese sauce; Ananis, the grandson of Lithuanian immigrants, was relegated to making the salad.

Ananis, another local boy—his father, a former All-American running back at Boston College, owned a Cambridge bar—was the kind of selfless player it took to make a team. The five-foot-nine senior had started at cornerback the previous year. In the Yale game, he had intercepted two Brian Dowling passes and was on the verge of intercepting a third when he slipped in the mud and gave up the winning touchdown bomb. This year, when he separated his shoulder in the final preseason scrimmage, he was devastated. But Ananis, for whom sports had been a refuge after his mother died of cancer when he was nine, decided that if he couldn't play, he'd do everything he could to prepare his replacement, sophomore Rick Frisbie: instructing him in practice, encouraging him from the sideline during games, going over his assignments with him during time-outs. He continued to custom-make T-shirts for new members of the Headhunters, as Harvard's kickoff team was known, staying up late at his Lowell House desk and painstakingly Magic Markering a skull skewered by a bloody knife over the word HEADHUNTERS in Hells Angels–style lettering, with the player's name inscribed on the skull's forehead. And he continued to take a hand in the scout team's "Instant Replays."

No one knew who came up with the idea, but Instant Replays were inspired by long Monday nights at the Varsity Club spent watching movies of next Saturday's opponent. Video replay technology had recently come to television, but the Monday night sessions still used reel-to-reel films, so if a coach wanted to show a certain play again, he had to rewind the film, and the Harvard players got a kick out of seeing their opponents scurry backward to their presnap positions.

One afternoon at practice before the Holy Cross game, the scout team, joking around, tried to run one of the opponent's plays backward in real life, just the way it had looked on the rewinding film: the halfback, retreating, returned the ball to the quarterback, who spun back to the line and inserted the football between the center's legs. During breaks, the scout team—which, composed of second and third stringers, tended to have more time on its hands—painstakingly rehearsed their new play-in-reverse. On Friday at the end of practice, they unveiled it for the rest of the defense, running the Holy Cross handoff forward, then backward, then forward, then backward, to their teammates' guffaws.

Instant Replays became a Friday tradition. As the season went along, the plays became increasingly ambitious, the execution more polished. Ananis assumed the role of choreographer, rehearsing the sophomores and juniors until their little ballet looked just like the film. The rest of the defense began to look forward to the scout team's latest production.

*   *   *

Halfway through the season, the Harvard football team was coming together. The offensive line was jelling. The seniors who had considered quitting were glad they hadn't. Most important, quarterback George Lalich was turning out to be the leader Yovicsin had hoped for. Up till now, Lalich's Harvard football career had been beset by bad luck. Freshman year, he'd been slowed by mononucleosis.

Sophomore year, he'd lost thirty pounds to colitis. Junior year, he'd been buried on the bench behind the greatest passer in Harvard history and contemplated giving up football. Finally healthy, and at the helm of an undefeated team, he was having the time of his life.

On the field, he was all business, though every so often he'd break the huddle with a "Lalich for All-American on three," or some other tension-dissolving quip. Off the field, his wisecracking kept the team loose, and though he was closest to the seniors, he included all the players in his repartee. He was the chief dispenser of nicknames: blond third-string quarterback Dave Smith was "Surfer Boy"; swarthily handsome Bob Jannino was "Animal," which soon devolved into "Aminal." When it was his turn to lead calisthenics before practice he'd guide his teammates through an air-guitar riff from Hendrix's "Purple Haze" or a spirited chorus of "I'm a Little Teapot, Short and Stout," leaving the team in stitches, if less than fully stretched.

Everyone liked Lalich. They liked his father, too. An ebullient car dealer who flew in from Chicago for every game, Steve Lalich was a locker room fixture who regaled the players with tales of dropping out of school during the Depression to become a professional boxer, fighting under the name Denny O'Keefe. (Irish pugilists were bigger draws than Serbian.) He became such a part of the team that the players awarded him a game ball. Most of them viewed the son as a younger and equally lighthearted version of the father. Few knew, however, that the quarterback's wisecracking persona masked the fact that he was, as he put it, "essentially scared out of my mind most of the time." Before each game, he got so nervous that his body shook with the dry heaves. Once on the field, though, he played with resourcefulness and grit. And with each win, his confidence grew.

On defense, the unquestioned leader was linebacker John Emery. All football players like to think of themselves as tough. "Emma," his teammates agreed, really *was* tough. The tobacco-chewing son of a Boston-area carpenter who had died the week before the

1966 Yale game, Emery was an imposing sight: a five-foot-eleven, 210-pound block of muscle with a neck almost as wide as his head and a Fu Manchu he'd started growing in preseason and decided he'd keep as long as Harvard kept winning. Though frequently double-teamed, he almost always led the team in tackles; his helmet was festooned with miniature football decals—actually, silver duct tape scissored into lopsided ovals by the managers—that were awarded by the defensive coaches to players who had made key contributions in the previous game. Emery, the defensive signal caller, wasn't a big talker, but there was never any doubt who ran the huddle. One evening in practice, when Pat Conway seemed to be daydreaming, Emery grabbed him by the face mask and head-butted him so forcefully that Conway nearly lost consciousness. "Pay attention," Emery growled. Off the field, he was thoughtful, empathetic, and determinedly private. On Friday nights before big home games, when Yovicsin had the team stay in a hotel to remove them from the distractions of campus, Emery had permission to stay behind. After dinner with the team, he'd attend Mass at a church in downtown Boston, then sit awhile on a bench on the Common, alone with his thoughts, before taking the subway back to his Adams House room.

*　*　*

Captains of football teams tend to be linebackers and linemen, rugged-looking behemoths whose very appearance can unsettle opponents. Vic Gatto was a halfback, and at five feet six he was the shortest player on the team and, invariably, on the entire field. Before each game, when the captains of the opposing teams met at midfield for the coin toss and Gatto shook hands with some six-foot-three, 240-pound tackle, fans couldn't help thinking of David and Goliath. Gatto was the first backfield player to captain the Harvard varsity since 1953. He was elected in one of the swiftest votes in memory.

Gatto's diminutive stature often led opponents to underestimate him. In the fall of 1965, when the freshman team took the field for its first practice, Alex MacLean—at five feet nine, no Goliath himself—noticed Gatto and thought, "What is he doing here? What could he be *thinking?*" Not long afterward, trying to tackle Gatto, MacLean reflected on how easy it was to misjudge someone. Not only was Gatto fast (he ran a hundred yards in under ten seconds, the gold standard for football players), he was also exceptionally strong, with a low center of gravity that made him hard to bring down. With 185 well-muscled pounds on his five-foot-six frame, Gatto was "built along the lines of a hydrant," noted the *Harvard Alumni Bulletin*. Though his legs were so short that he had a hard time managing the tall concrete steps when doing stadiums, they were extraordinarily powerful. Teammates couldn't help gaping at his calves, which seemed as cartoonishly oversized as Popeye's forearms. Disappearing among the giants on the line of scrimmage, Gatto, legs churning, would somehow emerge, unscathed, on the other side, then use his speed to escape his pursuers. He had a knack for the big play; his seven touchdown runs for the freshmen had covered 16, 45, 55, 65, 65, 73, and 90 yards. He not only broke the freshman record for points scored in a season but also for interceptions, though he was usually covering receivers at least a half foot taller. For the varsity, he ran the ball, threw the option pass, returned kickoffs and punts, and blocked as crisply as an offensive lineman. Yovicsin called him "Mr. Everything."

By then, Gatto had acquired not only a handful of Harvard records but an impressive collection of sobriquets inspired by his unusual physique. The *New York Times* called him the "truncated torpedo," the *Boston Globe* "Little ol' Git Gat," the *Yale Daily News* the "stumpy speedster," and the *Princeton Alumni Weekly* "Harvard's Mighty Mouse"—though if Gatto was to be compared to a mouse, it could be said that with his big ears, wide grin, and unfailingly upbeat attitude, he had more in common with Mickey. The *Crimson* referred to him, over the years, as the "squat scatter," the "mighty mite," the "sawed-off sensation," and the "Galloping Gnome."

Gatto had been outplaying bigger kids since he was a ten-year-old among twelve-year-olds on his Pop Warner team in Needham, a suburb of Boston. In elementary school, he wasn't particularly short for his age, but by the time he got to high school he had all but stopped growing. Gatto knew he was small, but even as a sophomore starter on the Needham High basketball team he never *felt* small. When opposing players and fans called him "shorty" or "midget," he didn't let it bother him. He didn't consider his size something to overcome; he took for granted that he could do whatever he needed to do on the field.

Resilience may have been a family trait. Gatto's grandparents had emigrated from Sicily, settling in Cambridge, where his grandfather opened a corner variety store. After his wife returned to Italy, suffering from what, years later, would be known as postpartum depression, Gatto's grandfather raised their five children on his own. All of them had to take after-school jobs to help the family make ends meet. Gatto's father had been a fine athlete, but while he worked his way through high school and college he'd had little time for sports. A successful insurance and real estate broker, he was determined to see his children excel at the games he'd never had a chance to play himself. From the time Vic was two, he had him out in the backyard playing catch. But it wasn't the companionable back-and-forth tossing the phrase implies; as Vic grew, it became almost as much work as play. It wasn't enough to catch the ball. It had to be caught the right way: how you positioned your hands, how you reached for the ball, what shoulder you were looking over. Held to such exacting standards, some sons might have turned their backs on their fathers, or on sports, but Gatto developed an ability to let the criticism wash off him while staying focused on his goals.

It isn't necessary that the captain be one of the best players on the team, but it helps. "Gatti" was not only the best player on the Harvard team, he was one of the hardest working and one of the smartest. He seemed always to be in the right place at the right time. One afternoon in practice, backfield coach Pat Stark corrected a player's positioning: "You're supposed to line up *here*," he said. "No," Gatto piped up politely, "I think he's supposed to be over here." Gatto was right. Fullback Gus Crim, who witnessed the moment, realized that Gatto knew what *everyone* on the offense was supposed to do on *each play*. Having him on the team was like having a coach on the field. The team's hulks marveled at how someone so small could hit so hard. When his teammates saw him take devastating shots from opponents fifty pounds heavier and bounce to his feet as if nothing had happened, they were determined to work even harder themselves. When they saw him play through injuries that might have kept lesser players off the field—during the 1967 season, according to trainer Jack Fadden, Gatto had been hampered by "two bad knees, two hamstrings, bum feet, and one bum shoulder," yet didn't miss a game—they were inspired to play through their own aches and pains.

Unlike his coach, Gatto was a congenital optimist. On the night he was introduced as captain at the team banquet, he predicted that the 1968 squad had a good chance to go undefeated, provoking an indulgent chuckle from the alumni in the room. But Gatto believed it. He never doubted himself; he never doubted his teammates. His belief in them helped them to believe in themselves. When Ted Skowronski, finally starting after two years on JV, worried he might not be up to the task, Gatto said, "Skow, you should have been playing all these years. You're a great player, you can do it." Gatto was at the center of a tight group of seniors, but he tried to make sure that every member of the squad felt valued. During passing drills, Gatto had an ongoing wager with backup halfbacks Jimmy Reynolds and John Ballantyne, betting nickels and dimes on who'd make the most receptions. It was just a game, but the juniors, who weren't getting much playing time, felt important because the great Gatto was including them.

Gatto would have been a fine captain in any era, but he was

the ideal captain for the 1968 squad. On a team of diverse personalities playing in a contentious time, he cut across all lines. With
his round face, ready laugh, and glass-half-full attitude, he had
a knack for bringing people together. Though he was passionate
about football, Gatto, a history concentrator, had a wide range
of interests. He went to all of Tommy Lee Jones's plays at the
Loeb, and not just because Jones blocked for him. He could be
seen around campus cheering at a wrestling match, taking in a
Quincy House concert, pausing on his way to class to listen to
an anti-ROTC speech in the Yard. He was against the war but
listened respectfully to differing views. In a judgmental time, he
was remarkably nonjudgmental.

Gatto wasn't what the players called a "rah-rah type"; in 1968,
rah-rah wouldn't have worked at Harvard. But he knew how to
unite a team. Before he was captain, the offense and defense had
met separately before the game. At the start of the 1968 season,
Gatto told the coaches that he wanted the team to be together
just before they took the field. So after the offense and defense
received final instructions from their respective coaches, the entire
team crowded together in the squad room under the stands. After
Yovicsin spoke, the coaches left, and Gatto, giving what the players
thought of as "the real speech," in his surprisingly deep voice, quietly told the team what they needed to do to win the game—and
that now they were going to go out and do it.

*   *   *

In 1903, William James, speaking at the Commencement Dinner on "The True Harvard," suggested that people were drawn
to the college, among other reasons, "because she cherishes so
many vital ideals, yet makes a scale of value among them; so that
even her apparently incurable second-rateness (or only occasional
first-rateness) in intercollegiate athletics comes from her seeing so
well that sport is but sport, that victory over Yale is not the whole

of the law and the prophets." James wrote those words at a time when the football team's fans were so numerous that Harvard had just begun building what was then the country's largest stadium to accommodate them. Nonetheless, Harvard, where it was considered a virtue never to be caught caring too much about anything (especially Harvard), had long prided itself on its ability to keep athletics in perspective. When Yale scored its first touchdown in the 1934 Harvard-Yale game, Harvard students held up a placard that read "Who Gives a Damn?" By mid-century, Harvard students had given up writing fight songs in favor of writing satires of fight songs, like that composed in 1945 by sophomore Tom Lehrer (and rendered in hoity-toity Brahmin-ese):

Fight fiercely Harvard, fight, fight, fight,
Demonstrate to them our skill.
Albeit they possess the might, nonetheless we have the will!
How shall we celebrate our victory?
We shall invite the whole team up for tea.

In the forties and fifties, prior to Yovicsin's arrival, Harvard students may have had little choice but to feign being above it all because the team was so inept. In the sixties, the alumni still lived and died with the team, albeit quietly—"at Harvard it isn't considered proper to show any emotion at a football game," a player lamented—but the students who attended games viewed the proceedings with ironic condescension, as if they were observing a quaint, mildly amusing ritual from an earlier era. "I don't mind if we lose, so long as we lose interestingly," said one.

For the players, Harvard's apathy took some getting used to. Most of them came from public high schools where football players were treated not merely with respect but with adoration. At Harvard, few people other than their roommates knew they played, and, if they did know, they weren't likely to pay much attention. Harvard was full of people who were good at what they did, and the fact that what you were good at was playing football was considered no more worthy of veneration than singing for the Glee Club or writing for the *Advocate*, the college literary magazine. The players, while larger, on average, than their fellow students, didn't dress much differently, and in most cases their hair was appropriately shaggy. They could walk the campus in virtual anonymity. On the Friday afternoon before the Dartmouth game, Vic Gatto was sitting in the hallway of Dillon Field House being interviewed by a writer for the *Globe*. Several passing students asked him for directions to the weight room. Not one of them recognized the captain of the undefeated Harvard football team.

If anything, being a football player at Harvard carried something of a stigma. Most of the players wouldn't have been caught dead wearing their "DeeHa" (DHA: Department of Harvard Athletics) sweatshirts to class, lest they risk being dismissed as a jock (the adjective *dumb* was implied) who might not have been admitted had he been unable to catch a buttonhook or manhandle a quarterback. "I hate snobbery toward jocks," observed Harvard sociologist David Riesman, who hardly did athletes a favor when he added, "The jocks at Harvard are no threat to anybody. They don't even get the prettiest girls."

* * *

In the mid-sixties, Harvard students were especially disinclined to get excited about football. Ever since the first football game had been played in 1869, the sport, with its elaborate strategy, precise formations, and unbridled violence, had been likened to war. Coaches spoke of their teams as "armies" who "fought for every inch"; players were assigned to offensive and defensive "platoons"; linemen "battled in the trenches"; linebackers "blitzed"; quarterbacks were "field generals" who threw "the long bomb." As football was likened to war, war was likened to football. Thirty-three years after starting at halfback for the 1912 Army team, Dwight Eisenhower compared the invasion of Normandy to a football game. Like many military commanders, he believed that football players made the best soldiers: they were aggressive, decisive, determined, and accustomed to following orders and sacrificing for the team. Football fields—many of which, like Harvard's (also known as Soldiers Field), were named to honor the war dead—were seen as ideal spawning grounds for the military. "Football! Navy! War!" proclaimed naval Commander Thomas Hamilton in 1942. "At no time in history have these words been more entwined and inter-meshed than they now are." Several years later, during the Cold War, the presidential briefcase that contained the nuclear launch codes became known as "the football."

For almost a century, football's association with war had been embraced. During the sixties, however, that association was viewed with disdain, at least in Cambridge. The qualities football prized—discipline, conformity, aggression, and teamwork—were the antithesis of peace, love, and doing your own thing. Many students considered it frivolous or even immoral to cheer young men running up and down the field in mock battle when, on the other side of the world, young men were fighting and dying in earnest. Far better—and far cooler—to chant "HELL NO, WE WON'T GO!" in Harvard Yard than "HOLD THAT LINE!" at Harvard Stadium. More than a few students who attended the games were there less for the football than for the halftime show, in which the Harvard band—irreverent, hip in a nerdy way, and decidedly antiwar—could be counted on to comment acidly on the issues of the day. The band's antics infuriated many alumni, who believed that the stadium on a Saturday afternoon was one of the few places left where the world still seemed right side up.

* * *

But in the fall of 1968, something extraordinary was happening on the Harvard campus. As the football team continued, improbably, to win, the students began to pay attention. More experienced fans told each other there was nothing to get excited about yet. The Cornell victory was all well and good, but the team hadn't played Dartmouth.

"It is hard to convey exactly how much beating Dartmouth means to people around Cambridge," a writer for the *Harvard Alumni Bulletin* observed. "The Game, steeped in tradition, is sort of a gentlemen's contest; it compares with the Dartmouth conflict the way two men playing backgammon in the Harvard Club compare with a street fight on the West Side. The Dartmouth game is a bitter class struggle, a defense of civilization against the onslaught of barbarians." Each year, Harvard sportswriters sounded this note: caricaturing the Dartmouth team, whose mascot was the Indian, as uncouth savages swarming down from the New Hampshire wilderness, trailed by a horde of boorishly enthusiastic and hard-drinking fans, to invade cultured Cambridge. (Dartmouth always came south to play Harvard; its own 21,416-seat stadium was deemed too small for a clash of such import.)

The reason behind Harvard's exaggerated condescension was, of course, that those barbarians from the north tended to beat the gentlemen from the south. In thirteen seasons under Coach Bob Blackman, a cherubic man considered something of a tactical genius, Dartmouth had trampled over Harvard seven times on their way to five Ivy championships.

This year, as was frequently the case, Harvard came into the game undefeated; Dartmouth, surprisingly, did not. In preseason polls, Dartmouth had been picked to finish second or third in the league. Plagued by injuries, however, it had already lost two games—more than it usually lost in an entire season. But the previous week, the team had looked more like its old self, demolishing Brown 48–0. With Dartmouth getting back several of its injured players, the Harvard game was rated a toss-up.

Over the years, Dartmouth had taken up residence in the Harvard psyche. Nonetheless, on the eve of the 1968 game, longtime Boston sportswriters noted how relaxed the Harvard team was. At the Friday walk-through, when local photographers traditionally took photos of the offensive and defensive starters in their sweatsuits, the defense struck a turn-of-the-century football players' pose: John Emery and Lonnie Kaplan reclining on the grass; Alex MacLean resting an arm on Tom Wynne's shoulder; Rick Berne gazing contemplatively off into the sky; Pat Conway mock-heroically admiring his biceps; and, *mirabile dictu*, John Yovicsin looking on with a grin. At the end of practice, the scout team performed its latest Instant Replay, reversing one of Blackman's razzle-dazzle extravaganzas, to hoots of delight.

The next day, Gatto gathered the team around him. "We think we can be champions," he told them. "But the role of a champion is different from that of a contender. When you're the favorite, the other team is looking to you. We have to go out and prove that we can be champs from the start of the game. We've got to stomp them from the beginning."

In front of a sell-out crowd of 39,909, Harvard did just that. The first time Dartmouth had the ball, it was on its own forty-one. Three plays later, the Harvard defense had pushed them back to the thirty. A week after Dartmouth amassed more than 600 yards against Brown, Harvard held them to fewer than 200. Harvard's offense was no less impressive. Lalich ran for 60 yards, passed for 119, and engaged in the kind of swashbuckling play for which Dartmouth was famous; hit after a 25-yard scramble, he shoveled the ball to Gatto, who ran for another 16. Gatto rushed seventeen times for 71 yards, caught five passes for 67 more, and completed one pass for 22.

Hornblower exceeded his hundred-yard goal for the second straight game, amassing 121 yards on twenty-one carries. He had entered the game fourth in the Ivy League in rushing; after it, he was first.

The final score was 22–7: Harvard's largest margin of victory over Dartmouth in forty years. The win, Harvard's fifth straight, even had a few revved-up fans daydreaming about going through the entire season without a loss. "It would be nice to go undefeated," a freshman dean admitted. "But I wonder if a Harvard team can do it. I think the players think there's something immoral about it."

V

Opening Up the Club

By mid-October, Bob Levin had settled into something of a routine. After a training-table dinner with his teammates in the basement of Ray Tompkins, he headed back to his room in Calhoun, one of twelve residential "colleges"—Yale's Oxbridgean name for its dorms—to study for an hour or two. Then, most nights, he strolled east on Elm Street to a white clapboard house overlooking the New Haven Green. Downstairs, he usually found several of his friends in conversation in front of the fireplace. There was Paul Moore, a *Yale Daily News* columnist active in the draft resistance movement. There was Ray Nunn, chairman of the Student Advisory Board and a leader in the effort to persuade Yale to offer a major in Afro-American Studies. There was Ray Dellinger, who'd been in the thick of things at the Democratic National Convention in Chicago that summer with his father, David, a Yale alumnus and pacifist who'd helped organize the antiwar demonstrations.

At first glance, Levin might have seemed out of place. He was a football player, and not just any football player. There was general agreement that the six-foot-one, 220-pound fullback, second on the team in rushing last year behind Calvin Hill, was the fiercest competitor on the Yale squad. "On the field, he looked like he wanted to kill you," recalled a teammate. In drills, players who realized they'd be going up against Levin one-on-one tended to get a hollow feeling in their stomachs and experience a sudden urge to step out of line and retie their shoelaces. In games, Levin shrugged off devastating hits as casually as a banker might flick a piece of lint off his suit. His teammates still talked about a play in the 1967 Dartmouth game, when, after a thunderous head-on collision, Levin spat out pieces of three teeth and jogged back to the huddle. The Dartmouth player, out cold, was carted off on a stretcher.

Off the field, though, Levin was what teammates called "a teddy bear." He was a patient after-school tutor to underprivileged elementary schoolers in New Haven. He was a mild, thoughtful man who was increasingly troubled by the war and was moving slowly leftward. He looked forward to coming to this basement room and talking into the night with his friends about the upcoming presidential election between Hubert Humphrey and Richard Nixon, about the tension between the civil rights and Black Power movements, and about Vietnam.

That Levin and his friends were discussing these issues not at a meeting of SDS but at one of the college's most prominent senior societies was an indication that the sixties, at long last, had arrived at Yale. The eight "societies"—fifteen-man clubs whose members often went on to wield great influence in Washington or on Wall Street—were the essence of old-line Yale. In contrast to Harvard's final clubs, refuges in which young men from "the right families" and "the right schools" could relax and drink to excess among their own kind, Yale's societies were intended to promote not only bonding but intellectual and moral growth among a cross section of young men distinguished less by their lineage than by their campus accomplishments. Drinking and revelry were secondary to interpersonal exploration; in fact, several of the societies were dry. (For drinking and revelry, Yale had its frats.) Each spring, in a highly anticipated ritual, the societies "tapped" new "delegations" of soon-to-be seniors. Levin had been tapped for Skull and Bones, the oldest and most prestigious of the secret societies, whose initiation ceremony was rumored to involve naked wrestling and a coffin, though not, presumably, at the same time. But when outgoing Bonesman George Bush clapped him on the shoulder and uttered the words that most Yalies would have given their Bass Weejuns to hear—"Skull and Bones, accept or reject?"—Levin had done the unthinkable and turned down Bones in favor of Elihu.

Elihu was something of an outlier. Founded in 1903 and named for Elihu Yale, the college's eponymous benefactor, it was the first *non*secret senior society. Unlike Skull and Bones and the other societies, which met in blocky, windowless buildings known as tombs, Elihu was quartered in the kind of pleasant-looking colonial house that could be found on almost any village green in New England. It was the only society with windows—though its wooden blinds were usually kept shut. The first society to tap a minority member—a Native American in 1910—Elihu had long been reputed to be more open to Jews than its peers. Its members gravitated toward the arts, politics, the law, and, in recent years, social activism. According to the 1968 *Yale Banner*, the college's yearbook, it was also "conspicuously lacking in dogma and mumbo-jumbo." But in at least one important aspect, it adhered to senior society tradition: each Thursday night, after a formal dinner at a long refectory table, an Elihu delegate delivered an oral autobiography, an intimate sharing of the self that could take as many as three hours. Levin, a modest man unaccustomed to talking about himself, had some trepidation about presenting his "auto." But when the appointed night arrived, he found himself speaking openly about his childhood in Skokie, his relationship with his girlfriend, and his polio.

*   *   *

Levin was one of hundreds of children in Chicago to be infected in the epidemic of 1952. He had been five the summer the doctor came to the house to break the news to his parents. He spent five days in the contagious ward—the nurses rolled his bed over to the window so he could see his parents waving at him when they visited—before the fever broke and he was moved to the recovery ward, where doctors could assess the damage. As he looked around him and saw children on crutches, children who couldn't walk at all, and children sealed inside metal-and-glass capsules called iron lungs to help them breathe, Levin understood that he'd been relatively lucky. He had some paralysis in his left leg, which made it difficult but not impossible to walk, and in his neck, which left his head lolling to one side. He would stay in the hospital less than two weeks. He would need no braces. He would, however, have to postpone kindergarten and devote an entire year to physical therapy. Three times a week his mother drove him ninety minutes across town to a South Side hospital where he walked slowly back and forth while holding on to parallel bars, strengthening his ravaged muscles. At home he lay on the kitchen table and watched cartoons as his mother massaged his legs. By the time he entered school, a year late, his limp was no longer noticeable and his head stood straight.

Levin, who didn't tell anyone he'd had polio, became a determined, physically fearless boy who loved sports and, as it turned out, was good at them. From the moment he started playing football in the fourth grade, he realized that the essence of the game lay in hitting the other guy harder than he hit you. Levin almost always hit the other guy harder. At the same time, he was an unusually bighearted young man. In elementary school softball games, Levin, who was invariably chosen to captain one of the teams, always put himself at the bottom of the batting order so the less-athletic kids would get a turn at the plate before recess was over. He spent the summer after his junior year in high school working at a camp for severely disabled children, and found, to his surprise, that he liked the job. That fall, he made All-State, and was recruited by Notre Dame, Stanford, and forty other schools. His father, a former Army lieutenant, wanted him to go to West Point, and Levin won an appointment to the Academy. But his mother fretted about this new conflict in Vietnam. What if it hadn't ended by the time he graduated? Levin wasn't worried—if he had to fight, he'd fight, just as his father had in World War II. Then Levin visited Yale. It was raining and New Haven looked dreary, but forty minutes into a two-hour meeting with Coach Cozza, he knew he wanted to play football for this manifestly decent man.

*　　*　　*

The Yale at which Bob Levin arrived in the fall of 1965 was in something of a time warp. Founded in 1701 by ten Connecticut ministers who deemed Harvard spiritually lax, Yale had long been regarded as the more conservative of the two institutions. Its conservatism was encouraged by its geography. Harvard's campus was inseparable from Cambridge; few undergraduates could get to class in the Yard—ground zero for student protests—without navigating the hubbub of Harvard Square. Yale, behind its cast-iron gates, waterless moats, and turreted Gothic walls, had the feel of a medieval cloister. Its back was turned, architecturally, on the city that surrounded it. Students rarely ventured beyond its walls, except to escort a date back to her room at the Hotel Taft or to cheer on the football team at the Bowl. Yale's admissions catalogue focused less on the glories of New Haven, a struggling industrial city, than on the convenience of being ninety minutes from Manhattan.

Indeed, the Yale of 1965 hadn't changed all that much since 1951, when, on the occasion of its 250th anniversary, *Time* magazine had described it as "perhaps the most inbred of all Ivy League colleges." Twenty percent of Levin's freshman class came from five prep schools, forty-three men from Andover alone. Twenty percent had fathers who had attended Yale. Nearly half the faculty had graduated from Yale. Students were required to attend meals in coats and ties, many of which had been purchased at J. Press, the York Street haberdashery whose ad in the *Yale Daily News* stated, "For more than 63 years this organization and its productions have formed a quasi-official part of the moulding process at Yale." After being weighed and measured, freshmen had to pass a physical education test—sit-ups, pull-ups, a hundred-yard swim—and pose for nude "posture" photos. Those whose posture was deemed insufficiently erect were required to attend remedial classes in which they warded off lordosis by lifting weights: Yale men stood up straight.

In the classroom, students took a prescribed number of courses in the natural sciences, social sciences, and humanities. Although the concept of the gentleman's C was fading, it was still considered good form to maintain a laissez-faire attitude toward one's studies. "No man ever went to Yale to learn anything," observed one wag. "God gave us Columbia and Harvard for that." A Yale man was measured by his extracurriculars, not by his intellect; the pathways to status ran through varsity athletics and the a cappella groups, and election to a senior society was considered the pinnacle of achievement. The Saturday-night social scene revolved around Yale's six fraternities, the most popular of which was DKE, known for having the most jocks, the best bands, the booziest parties, and the longest bar in New Haven. On Monday evenings, students flocked to Mory's, the 104-year-old alehouse where generations of Yalies had carved their initials into battered oak tables, drank from silver trophy cups, and listened to the Whiffenpoofs sing "Aura Lee" and "Bright College Years" (the Yale alma mater, sung by moist-eyed alums at the end of every football game, whose last lines saluted—presumably in ascending order of importance—"For God, for country, and for Yale"). Like Mory's, Yale remained proudly, steadfastly, all-male; as at Harvard, women were allowed in students' rooms only during parietal hours. Prep schoolers still set the tone. Conformity was still considered a virtue. Only one student in Levin's freshman class had long hair; one evening in Commons, the freshman dining hall, two St. Paul's boys conspired to walk by and "accidentally" spill milk on his head.

If "Mother Yale" was in something of a time warp, its devoted alumni—and a surprising number of its students—wanted to keep her that way. That they failed was in large measure due to three Yale men who didn't do what was expected of Yale men.

A *Mayflower* descendant who had grown up summering on Martha's Vineyard, Kingman Brewster Jr. '41 had never been afraid to go his own way. As an undergraduate who objected on principle to secret societies, he had shocked the Yale community by turning down a tap from Skull and Bones. "The world we shall live and work in is being refashioned," he wrote, at twenty, in his first editorial as chairman of the *Yale Daily News*. "Parts of the Yale machinery that are rusty with complacency and stiff with tradition will have to be hauled out and re-examined." In 1963, when the forty-four-year-old Brewster was named Yale's seventeenth president, he would be in position to do something about that rusty machinery. Seeing the country changing rapidly, he was convinced that if Yale continued to serve a student body composed largely of wealthy white Protestants like himself, it would atrophy into irrelevance. "I do not intend to preside over a finishing school on Long Island Sound," he confided to a friend shortly after his inauguration.

To that end, in 1965, Brewster appointed a new dean of admissions, twenty-nine-year-old R. Inslee Clark Jr. '57, a handsome, gregarious, crew-cut alumnus universally known as "Inky." Clark also seemed an unlikely agent of change, and not just because his name constituted a veritable parody of WASP nomenclature; as a Yale undergraduate, he had been editor of the *Banner*, president of the Inter-Fraternity Council, a varsity golfer, and a member of Skull and Bones. But he had come to New Haven not from Andover but from a public school on Long Island, and his father not only hadn't gone to Yale, he hadn't gone to college at all. As an undergraduate, Clark chafed at what he described as "a certain inbreeding, parochialism, and clubbiness." As dean of admissions, he opened up the club. During his first year, in what amounted to a purge, he fired most of his aging staff and replaced them with a younger and more diverse group, including the college's first black admissions officer. He increased the number of schools the staff visited from six hundred to a thousand, many of them in the inner city or in remote rural areas that Yale had previously ignored. For the first time, Yale began to admit students based more on how well they had done in school than on the names of those schools or on where their fathers had gone to college. For the first time, Yale began to admit applicants regardless of whether their fathers could afford to send them, becoming the first college in the country to adopt a need-blind admissions policy.

For much of the twentieth century, the proportion of private to public schoolers at Yale had been about 60 to 40. That had begun to change under Clark's predecessor; indeed, in 1963, for the first time, there were—just barely—more public schoolers than private schoolers in Yale's entering freshman class, the benchmark Harvard had reached ten years earlier. Under Inky Clark, however, the demographics of Yale's student body were radically transformed— virtually overnight. In 1966, when the first class chosen by Clark arrived on campus, the percentage of public to private schoolers was 58 to 42. The number of students from Andover was nearly halved. The percentage of alumni sons dropped from 20 percent to 12. The percentages of Jews and African-Americans nearly doubled. The average SAT scores were the highest in Yale history. It would not go unnoticed that Clark, in the process, had also assembled the skinniest Yale class since 1951 and the shortest since 1945.

Alumni, not a few of whose sons were rejected to make room for "Inky's Boys," as these students were dubbed (not always affectionately), were outraged. The conservative author William F. Buckley Jr. '50 called the new admissions policies "egalitarian hocus-pocus" and accused Yale of discriminating against alumni sons. "You will laugh," he wrote in *The Atlantic*, "but it is true that a Mexican-American from El Paso High with identical scores on the achievement tests, and identically ardent recommendations from their headmasters, has a better chance of being admitted to Yale than Jonathan Edwards the Sixteenth from St. Paul's School." Pledging to undo Clark's work and promote an admission policy under which any alumni son deemed capable of passing grades would automatically be admitted, Buckley campaigned for a seat on the Corporation, Yale's governing board. His quest was unsuccessful, but not because the Corporation approved of Clark, who was called before them to explain his new approach. "You're admitting an entirely different class than we're used to," a prominent banker pointed out. "You're admitting them for a different purpose than training leaders." (Yale's self-proclaimed mission was to educate the nation's future leaders.) Clark explained that as America changed, its leaders would come from a wider variety of backgrounds. The banker was unconvinced. "You're talking about Jews and public school graduates as leaders," he said. "Look around you at this table. These are America's leaders. There are no Jews here. There are no public school graduates here."

Even as they railed against Brewster and Clark, conservative Yale alumni reserved their greatest wrath for a third impeccably pedigreed Yale man who went against the grain. Chaplain William Sloane Coffin '49 (Pilgrim ancestry, Andover graduate, third-generation Bonesman) had given a hint that his theological approach might be unorthodox when, at the Freshman Assembly in 1959, in his first official Yale prayer, he beseeched the Lord to "forbid our using our education to buy our way into middle-class security." Coffin practiced what he preached, first as a civil rights activist and Freedom Rider who was arrested and jailed in Mississippi, then as an eloquent, charismatic, and highly visible antiwar leader who pledged support for draft resisters at rallies across the country. To those who scorned antiwar activists as cowardly draft dodgers, Coffin—a ruggedly handsome former World War II paratrooper and CIA agent—offered an eloquent rejoinder. He was, wrote an admiring Norman Mailer, "one full example of the masculine principle at work in the cloth." To many Yale students, Coffin was a hero and a role model. To many Yale graduates, he was an embarrassment and a disgrace. The letters department of the *Yale Alumni Magazine* swelled to accommodate the avalanche of mail from Old Blues calling for Coffin's dismissal and vowing to withhold their donations to the university as long as he was employed.

*　　*　　*

Over the next few years, alumni howled as they saw the Yale they had known dismantled. By the fall of 1968, when Levin arrived for his senior year, 65 percent of Yale's entering freshman class were public school graduates—a higher percentage than at Harvard. The coat-and-tie rule had been abolished, the freshman phys-ed requirement had been dropped, and nude posture photos had been eliminated (Inky's Boys had balked). In the classroom, distribution requirements had been waived and numerical grades had been replaced by a pass-fail system. It was unclear whether the latter change was provoked more by the policies of Margaret Mead, who graded the six hundred students in her "Introduction to Anthropology" class so generously that she was said to have singlehandedly boosted Yale's communal GPA by an entire point, or by radical sociologist Robert Cook, who, to demonstrate the superficiality of grades, allowed his students to grade themselves, whereupon, as the *Banner* put it, they "made the existential sacrifice of giving themselves all 100s."

Parietals were still on the books, but they were largely ignored and rarely, if ever, enforced. Fraternities drew fewer pledges each year, and two houses folded. (A *Banner* article on frats was titled "The Benign Irrelevancy.") Mory's was, increasingly, the bailiwick of gray-haired alums. In an anti-elitist era, even secret societies were no longer regarded with unadulterated reverence; the only thing more prestigious than a tap from Skull and Bones was turning down a tap from Skull and Bones. So few students bought tickets to the 1968 Prom that the administration had to help pay for the big band that had played at Yale's formal dances for more than half a century, though they drew the line at springing for the psychedelic light show the students had requested. Meanwhile, the Senior Dinner, at which the comedian-activist and write-in presidential candidate Dick Gregory was invited to speak, sold out. Although Yale's reputation for bibulousness was exceeded in the Ivy League only by that of Dartmouth, alcohol was no longer necessarily a Yale man's intoxicant of choice. A 1967 poll found that 35 percent of Yale undergraduates had smoked marijuana and 10.5 percent had tried LSD. "It used to be that a freshman could think he was really putting something over on the authorities if he could get a senior to buy booze for him," observed the *Yale Daily News*. "Now the freshmen and sophomores are selling grass to the seniors and juniors." The October 18, 1968, issue was headlined "Pot Prices Hit New High." By then, one could detect the sweet scent of marijuana amid the familiar odor of beer on Saturday nights at DKE. A few intrepid students were outfitting themselves not at J. Press but at the Army-Navy surplus store. The preppies who'd poured milk on their long-haired classmate during freshman year now had long hair themselves.

The changes had occurred so precipitously that it was common to hear people refer to "The Old Yale" and "The New Yale." Writing to the alumni magazine in the fall of 1968, a member of the class of 1935 concluded, "Gentlemen: Except for the buildings and the name, the Yale University that meant so much to so many of us almost ceases to exist."

* * *

In one important aspect, Yale hadn't changed: it was still all male. Aside from an occasional sighting of a female grad student in the library, the only time most Yale men encountered the opposite sex was on weekends, when busloads of females from women's colleges across New England pulled into New Haven for mixers at Yale's residential colleges. "Yale men would line up from the door of the bus all the way to the door of the dance," recalled a 1970 graduate. "The women would exit the buses and find themselves walking—parading might be a more apt description—through this tunnel of men, much like a football team entering the field of competition." In dining halls cleared of tables and supplied with watery beer and a local band playing Rolling Stones covers, Yale men followed a time-honored strategy: as one student put it, "You'd get blind drunk, pick out a girl, and hope for the best." At the end of the evening, the women climbed back on the buses and vanished as suddenly as they'd arrived. Yale men unable to wait for the weekend went on road trips, driving seventy or eighty miles to Smith, Vassar, or Briarcliff in search of feminine companionship. Carless Yalies tried their luck at George & Harry's, a bar-restaurant where, it was said, one could pick up townies (or, as some called them, without occasioning so much as a raised eyebrow, "street meat"). When a Yale senior walked into the Silliman College dining hall one evening with a good-looking blonde on his arm, the entire room rose in a standing ovation. "Treat Yale as you would a good woman," counseled the opening paragraph of Yale's *Freshman Handbook*. "Take advantage of her many gifts, nourish yourself with the fruit of her wisdom, curse her if you will, but congratulate yourself in your possession of her."

Harvard, of course, was hardly a shining exemplar of gender enlightenment. Although Radcliffe students had been attending Harvard classes since 1943 in a "coordinate" role, the prospect of full co-education was another matter entirely. "I'm not quite sure people want to have crystalline laughter falling like a waterfall down each entry of the House at all hours," observed John Finley, master of Eliot House. "I should think it would be a little disturbing if you were taking advanced organic chemistry."

But at least Harvard *had* a Radcliffe. Yale had no analogue. Its resistance to co-education seemed especially obstinate given that beyond its walls, women—many of them veterans of the antiwar movement who had been turned off by its pervasive male chauvinism—were beginning to push for gender equality. In the wake of the 1966 founding of the National Organization for Women, "women's liberation groups" were forming across the country to "raise consciousness" about the constraints women faced at home, in the workplace, and in higher education. Some of that raised consciousness was beginning to be imported by those busloads of women who descended on Yale for football weekends. "Freshman and sophomore year, your date was arm candy," a football player from the class of 1969 recalled. "Junior and senior year, she was part of the conversation."

But as college after college went co-ed, Yale remained all male, to the relief of alumni aghast at the thought of "girls" showering at Payne Whitney Gymnasium or carving their initials into the tables down at Mory's. "In the course of 267 years, the word 'Yale' has taken on a meaning of its own in which the element of masculinity is clearly dominant," a member of the class of 1926 wrote to the *Yale Alumni Magazine*, arguing against co-education. "Witness how easily we speak of a Harvard intellectual, a Princeton socialite, a Yale man. The turtleneck sweater, the curved pipe, the bulldog shoes may bring a laugh, but underneath it all lies a pride that every Yale man understands." Some undergraduates shared his position. "With coeducation there will be extra temptations and tensions that are not at Yale now," a sophomore fretted. "The students here could lose their intellectual drive." But the public schoolers Yale was recruiting in ever-larger numbers were inclined to see single-sex education less as a proud tradition than as an unnatural anachronism. Indeed, candidates of all stripes were increasingly turning down Yale in favor of colleges with women on the premises. (That the preferred college was almost always Harvard made the situation even more distressing.) This, at least, provided an argument for co-education that appealed to Old Blues: football coach Carmen Cozza was losing coveted recruits because they failed to appreciate the advantages of an all-male campus.

Concerned about the effect on admissions, Brewster had begun discussions with Vassar about selling its campus and moving to New Haven to become a "coordinate college," in an arrangement not unlike that of Harvard and Radcliffe. Spoofing the proposed merger at the 1967 Cornell game, half the Yale band formed a massive Y and marched, stem-first, into the other half's waiting V. Three weeks later, "the Vassar flirtation," as the press called it, ended when the Poughkeepsie college decided to go co-ed on its own, leaving an embarrassed Yale to its own devices. In September 1968, Yale's plight became all the more awkward when Princeton announced its intention to admit one thousand female undergraduates the following year, leaving Yale the only Ivy without plans for some form of co-education aside from Dartmouth—which, situated as it was in the wilds of New Hampshire, was deemed a special case.

That fall, fed up with the administration's foot-dragging, a group of students decided, in the words of the *Yale Daily News*, that "the easiest way to bring girls to Yale was to bring girls to Yale." They announced plans for Coeducation Week, a trial balloon of sorts in which female students from colleges across the Northeast would be invited to attend Yale classes, eat in Yale's dining halls, and sleep in vacated Yale suites. "The idea is to take the male-female relationship out of the absurdly pressured situation of a weekend date," one of the organizers explained to the *New York Times*. "A lot of the guys think of women simply as objects, or dumb broads, but they're human beings too." Not everyone was thrilled. "The value of Coeducation Week is questionable and the potential harm is obvious," a *Yale Daily News* editorial maintained, adding that a "hastily-organized, shoddily-conducted coed frolic" could do "irremediable damage" to any plans for co-education the administration might have. Some predicted the experiment would be no more edifying than an extended mixer; others accused it of being a pretext for a bacchanal. (A local clergyman delighted in referring to it as "The Great Screw-In.") Brewster worried about the possibility of sexual assault—what if a girl were raped in a Yale residential college? But when he realized that students were determined to go ahead with or without his blessing, he reluctantly went along with the plan. The event was scheduled for early November, the week before the Penn game.

* * *

In the fall of 1968, Yale students seemed exercised more about co-education than about Vietnam. Although antiwar sentiment was widespread, the issue that was convulsing campuses around the country hadn't completely breached Yale's thick stone walls. Yale activists remained remarkably genteel. "No matter how deep the agony is over the war or the cities, the Yale student is still essentially a voyeur," a *Banner* essayist noted. Two weeks before Harvard students held a Dow recruiter hostage for seven hours, fifteen hundred Yale students turned out to protest LBJ's Vietnam policy when his wife spoke at the college. Not wanting to disrupt the First Lady's speech, however, they limited their protest to a ten-minute silent vigil outside Commons while she spoke inside on "Beautification in America." A September 1968 *Yale Daily News* editorial observed, "Over the past several years Yale has developed a reputation for hosting lovely demonstrations—well organized, beautifully choreographed, devoid of violence and generally free of abusive or inflammatory rhetoric."

The group that on other campuses was providing a great deal of abusive or inflammatory rhetoric was struggling for its own survival at Yale. Founded in 1965, Yale SDS disbanded the following year for lack of interest. Revived in 1967, by the fall of 1968 it was "singularly dormant," according to the *Yale Alumni Magazine*, which observed that the "half-dozen or so radicals who had comprised it" were "finding it difficult to get anyone in the University to take the group seriously." A teach-in on the moral implications of ROTC drew fewer than a dozen students, most of them friends of the speakers. Members began driving to Boston to attend Progressive Labor Party meetings. "We're six months behind Harvard in everything," said Mark Zanger, the group's most outspoken member.

Yale's radicals may have been fewer and better-behaved than Harvard's, but the university itself had a national reputation in the antiwar movement, thanks to its chaplain—especially after the 1967 March on the Pentagon, at which Coffin and his fellow Yale alumnus Dr. Benjamin Spock '25 turned over 996 draft cards they'd collected from students across the Northeast, 43 of them from Yale. In the spring of 1968, the chaplain and the pediatrician were sentenced to two years in prison for conspiring to "counsel, aid, and abet" young men to refuse service in the armed forces. Many alumni were irate, all the more so when Coffin announced his intention to offer Yale's Battell Chapel as a sanctuary for draft resisters. Accusing Coffin of treason in a letter to the alumni magazine, a member of the class of 1948 concluded, "I think he should be lined up before a firing squad." Outrage was hardly assuaged when alumni opened their August 1968 copy of *Playboy* to find that the subject of the magazine's monthly interview was none other than Yale's outspoken chaplain, out on bail while his conviction was appealed.

*   *   *

Even as campuses across the country were brought to a halt by student unrest, Yale remained relatively quiescent, in large measure because of its president. Unlike Harvard's Pusey, Brewster was an unusually accessible college head: receiving students at the President's House on Hillhouse Avenue, pausing to chat as he strolled the campus (often with his wife and their dogs, a black Labrador and a golden retriever), and even dropping in on students in their rooms. Unlike Pusey, who regarded campus activists with obvious distaste when he couldn't avoid them, Brewster sought them out and took their concerns seriously. In the fall of 1968, when a group of black students that included sophomore cornerback Kurt Schmoke marched to Brewster's home to demand that Yale admit more minority students, Brewster rose from his sickbed to meet them. His receptiveness was disarming; it was harder to rebel against the Man when the Man was sympathizing, and often agreeing, with you. Brewster, an early supporter of civil rights, had awarded an honorary degree to Martin Luther King in 1964, a time when many Northern whites considered King a rabble-rousing criminal. Although he would not come out publicly against the war until 1969, Brewster, whose eldest son was a conscientious objector, was sympathetic to the antiwar movement and fiercely defended Coffin's right to speak his mind, while just as fiercely criticizing his tactics. At Harvard, the revolutionaries had an obdurate president and administration against which to butt heads; at Yale, the president, the chaplain, and the dean of admissions *were* the revolutionaries.

Yalies might make fun of their president's patrician affect ("Kingman Brewster wears 3-piece underwear" someone scribbled on the newly erected Saybrook College graffiti wall), but in an era in which most university presidents were reviled, or at best tolerated, by their students, "The King," as undergraduates called him, was remarkably popular. The mere fact that he had turned down Skull and Bones twenty-eight years earlier, suggested the 1968 *Banner*, "may explain why students today refer to their president very simply as 'stud.'" Brewster, who in appearance and charm could have been mistaken for a Kennedy cousin, was satirized in a *bull tales* strip: a scruffy student radical known as Megaphone Mark (inspired by SDS leader Mark Zanger) walks into the office of the college president, a debonair fellow named King, and announces through a bullhorn that he is taking over the room. "*Oh, yeah, well alrighty,*" says President King, getting up from his chair. "*Let me just get together here a few of my personal effects.*" In the last panel, Megaphone Mark, who has been eager for a confrontation, buries

119

his head on the desk in despair as King adds, *"Before I go, shall I show you where I keep my sherry and cigars?"*

*　*　*

There was another factor that helped Yale through the tumult of the mid-sixties: football. Yale had always been more gung-ho about the sport than Harvard, where manifestations of school spirit were considered, as one student put it, "plebeian." (Yale was *better* at football, too: in the rivalry's ninety-three-year history, Yale had won 46 times to Harvard's 31.) In the mid-sixties, as Yale cast aside tradition after tradition, it did not abandon this one. If anything, it clung to it more fiercely. Football continued to play a central role in undergraduate life. It lay at the heart of "Bulldogism," a word Yalies invoked to describe the essential spirit of the college. And as old-guard alumni and activist undergrads battled for the soul of Yale, there was one thing on which both sides could agree: the excellence of Dowling, Hill, and company. "They have brought the Old Blue, with their bulletproof glasses and thick tweed coats, and the skinny long-haired juniors with their glazed eyes together when they couldn't get together anywhere else," observed the *Yale Daily News.* The *Yale Alumni Magazine* put it more diplomatically: "At a time when an understanding gap has frequently separated alumni from students, football has provided a bridge of common interest." Hawks and doves nested side by side in the Bowl.

It helped that Yale's two most prominent liberal icons were among the team's most rabid fans. Not only was Brewster a fixture at the Bowl, cheering vigorously from his seat directly over the tunnel from which the Yale team emerged onto the field, his camel-hair topcoat adorned by a "Blue Power" button, but he attended pep rallies and showed up, on occasion, at the players' postgame parties. On the eve of the 1967 Princeton showdown, when a crowd of two thousand sign-waving undergraduates marched to his home, he had delighted them by ripping apart an orange and leading them in a chant of "FUCK PRINCETON!" Coffin, whose childhood hero had been the legendary Yale halfback Clint Frank, was a fine athlete; in 1961 Sargent Shriver had hired him to develop a physical fitness program in the Puerto Rican rain forest for a new Kennedy initiative called the Peace Corps. He was notoriously competitive on the tennis court and the touch football field. (In one Thanksgiving game, he told his twelve-year-old niece, "Don't let that guy past you"—that guy being Kingman Brewster. The obedient niece rammed the Yale president flat on his back, as Coffin tossed the winning touchdown pass.) Friends with several of the players, Coffin attended Yale football games, his children in tow, whenever his protest schedule permitted. In February 1968, he delivered the invocation at the mid-winter football banquet in Woolsey Hall, then sprinted over to the Law School, still in his tuxedo, to speak at a teach-in on draft resistance, where his arrival prompted a standing ovation.

It was fortuitous that Yale's years of relative turmoil coincided with its years of glory on the gridiron. "Our kids are so busy rooting for their ball club that they don't even think about burning their draft cards," said Charley Loftus proudly. As Yale's P.R. man (and a longtime member of the Selective Service board in New Haven), Loftus may have been somewhat disingenuous; certainly he knew that more than a few Yale kids *were* thinking about burning their draft cards, or at least turning them over to their chaplain. But in the fall of 1968, pregame rallies drew far more Yalies than antiwar protests, and on Saturday afternoons, as Dowling and Hill ran wild in the Bowl, Vietnam could seem very far away. The following spring, as SDSers egged on students at a sputtering antiwar demonstration on campus, it would seem perfectly natural when half the crowd burst into song:

> Bulldog! Bulldog!
> Bow, wow, wow,
> Eli Yale!

*   *   *

Bob Levin hadn't been particularly political when he arrived at Yale, but junior year, as he read about Khe Sanh, the Tet Offensive, and the protests at Columbia and Harvard, he started questioning what his country was doing in Vietnam. He began attending Sunday services at Battell Chapel to hear Coffin's impassioned antiwar sermons. He talked about the war with R. W. B. Lewis, professor of English and Master of Calhoun College, who had marched on the Pentagon with Coffin. He made a point of meeting the left-leaning luminaries Lewis invited to the college, including Joseph Heller (who signed his copy of *Catch-22*); Norman Mailer (who regaled Levin and several other students with boxing stories while almost singlehandedly working his way through a fifth of bourbon); and Reverend Malcolm Boyd, the so-called beatnik priest and author of *Are You Running with Me, Jesus?* (whose contribution to the Saybrook graffiti wall was "Jesus has a real penis"). He took a course on African-American history with Eugene Genovese, a controversial Marxist professor who had written extensively on slavery, and realized how much he didn't know about his own country. He discussed the upcoming election with his friends. Like many of them, Levin had been an ardent RFK supporter; he had tried to transfer his enthusiasm to Eugene McCarthy, but it wasn't the same.

Senior year, Levin resigned from DKE; though he liked hanging out with his teammates, he wasn't a big drinker, and he was spending more and more time at Elihu. Too, he was spending almost every weekend with his girlfriend, a smart, funny Vassar sophomore named Meryl Streep, whom he'd met on a blind date on the first football weekend of junior year. (Levin's teammates agreed Meryl was very pretty, if somewhat shy.) Meryl, who'd been a cheerleader in high school, loved football and came to his games; Bob, in turn, attended concerts of the Vassar Night Owls, the a cappella group in which she sang. They talked about trying to stay together after he graduated. But, like many of his classmates, Levin had no idea what he'd be doing next year. Everything depended on the draft. Part of him would have liked to resist, to turn over his draft card to Coffin, but he knew how profoundly that would disappoint his father. If drafted, he'd probably serve, but he would rather not fight a war he didn't believe in. Although he was applying to law school, his draft board made it clear that it wouldn't keep him from being called up. He thought about teaching, which might not only earn him a deferment but was something he'd loved ever since that eleventh-grade summer working with disabled kids. Meanwhile, influenced by his nightly discussions at Elihu, he was turning more and more against the war, though he wouldn't get actively involved until the spring, beginning on the afternoon he and Meryl tacked up posters on Cross Campus for an antiwar rally.

There were other players who were against the war, including guard Bart Whiteman, an introspective English major from Greenwich Village who wrote folk songs, hoped to become a writer, and attended antiwar protests whenever they didn't conflict with football. But most were not the type to be out demonstrating. Despite Yale's reputation as a preppie stronghold, only three starters on the team—Whiteman, Marting, and Gee—had attended prep schools, and many of the players were from conservative, patriotic, blue-collar towns in the Midwest. (Most were "bursary boys"— students on scholarship who bused dining hall dishes or reshelved library books to help pay their way through Yale.) Dowling had an older brother in the military who was likely headed to Vietnam, as did linebacker Mike Bouscaren, who not only supported the war but, with his roommates, formed the Anti-Blip Coalition (ABC), a tongue-somewhat-in-cheek group dedicated to scorning students— Blips—they deemed long-haired, pot-smoking protestors. The seniors, of course, would soon face the draft themselves. Most were trying to put off thinking about it until after the football season, but it couldn't help weighing on them. One Sunday, tackle Fran Gallagher was interviewed on *Yale Football with Dick Galiette*, a local television show on which Cozza appeared each week, accompanied by a player or two. Asked about his postgraduation plans—"What's in store for you next year, Fran?"—Gallagher blurted out, "I'm just going to do whatever it takes to stay out of Vietnam." Host and coach were momentarily speechless.

Backup defensive tackle Mick Kleber was one of the few seniors on the team who knew exactly what was in store for him. Kleber, the son of a marine colonel who had won a Bronze Star at Iwo Jima and served three tours in Vietnam, was at Yale on a Navy ROTC scholarship. He owed his first four years after graduation to the Marines, almost certainly in Vietnam. A photograph of the broad-shouldered Kleber sitting alone in Naval Science 402A, "The History of Amphibious Warfare"—in which he was the only student—had illustrated an anti-ROTC article on the front page of the *Yale Daily News.*

That summer, Kleber's father had become commanding officer of the Marine Barracks in Philadelphia. The barracks were adjacent to the Naval Hospital, where soldiers who'd been severely injured in Vietnam went for surgery, rehab, or long-term care. Each week, Colonel Kleber made his son come with him to the hospital to visit the men. It was the time of the Tet Offensive, the most deadly period of the war thus far, and the hospital was overflowing with wounded men. Some were missing limbs, some had suffered catastrophic brain injuries, some had disfiguring burns. Kleber couldn't forget the soldier who, having lost a leg, placed a flip-flop on his bed next to a sign: FOR SALE: LEFT SHOE. CHEAP. Kleber was deeply shaken by his visits, but he'd soon be heading to the place these men had come from, and he knew he had to put up a strong front. Each week, he went back to the hospital. Each week, there were more new arrivals.

Kleber returned to Yale that fall determined to live his senior year as fully as possible, knowing it might be his last. It was less a matter of eat-drink-and-be-merry—though Kleber had always done plenty of that—than of exploring the richness of life. An American Studies major, he threw himself into his thesis on

Hemingway and pondered the author's conception of a hero as someone who lives up to a code of courage, honor, and endurance in a chaotic and often hostile world. At the suggestion of Erich Segal, a Yale classics instructor and marathon runner with whom Kleber had studied, he drove seventy miles to Sarah Lawrence to sit in on lectures by Joseph Campbell, a professor of folklore and mythology whose ideas about the archetypal nature of "The Hero's Journey" were beginning to attract attention. At departmental receptions, Kleber got to know sculptor Donald Judd and painter Josef Albers, with whom he had long discussions about the nature and purpose of art. He devoured books, frequented Yale's galleries, and saw films (including *Yellow Submarine*, the Beatles' new animated movie, on which Segal, one of its screenwriters, had sent the Fab Four on a psychedelic Hero's Journey of their own). With images of Hemingway's bullfighters, Campbell's heroes, his father at Iwo Jima, and the soldiers he'd met that summer swirling in his mind, Kleber was full of questions: How would he handle himself in Vietnam? What was *his* code? What was *his* journey?

*   *   *

And all along, there was football, a collective dream in which Kleber, Levin, and everyone else at Yale could lose themselves, at least for one last autumn. Though it was a disheartening time for the country, it was a glorious time to be a football player at Yale, a throwback to the days when football was the talk of the college and those who played it were the school's leaders. When players walked across campus, students and teachers they'd never met wished them luck. At the end of Friday classes, professors went to the blackboard and wrote down predictions for the next day's score. On Saturday afternoons in the fall, Sterling Library was closed. There was no point in keeping it open; everyone was at the Bowl.

*   *   *

The Yale Bowl—"that damn pan," as a Princeton player called it in a Fitzgerald short story—was, essentially, an enormous concrete saucer nestled in the ground. Even on the sunniest of days, its playing surface, which lay twenty-seven-and-a-half feet below sea level, could be a little spongy. On October 19, when Yale met Columbia in a driving rain that kept all but 17,724 fans at home, the field was a quagmire. The *New York Times* reported, "What was to have been a confrontation between the best quarterbacks in the East, Marty Domres of Columbia and Brian Dowling of Yale, became instead a battle of amphibious forces today, and the surer-footed Elis sloshed their way to a 29–7 victory." Although Columbia scored first, it would be their only score, as Yale's jury-rigged defense held the Lions to 130 yards. In the battle of the quarterbacks ("D-day," reporters dubbed it), Domres, second in the nation in total offense going into the game, managed only 97 yards; Dowling ended up with 204, well under his season average but, as one sportswriter noted, perfectly respectable given that he was "operating in a swamp under a 15-mph wind."

That night, Bob Levin was at Woolsey Hall, where the Vassar Night Owls were appearing at the sixtieth annual Whiffenpoof Jamboree, one of the most-anticipated events on the Yale fall calendar. In the group's penultimate number, Meryl, in a simple black dress, stepped into the spotlight and sang the solo on "Moonlight Becomes You." Offstage, she was modest and unassuming. On stage, she was as self-assured as Brian Dowling on a football field. Levin invariably marveled at the transformation. Tonight, as usual, she had the audience hanging on every note. It was always a thrill for Levin to see her perform, but he had never been so proud.

The following week, playing at Cornell in near-freezing temperatures and intermittent rain, Yale took the opening kickoff and scored in five plays, finishing off with a 46-yard touchdown pass from Dowling to Marting. It looked as though, once again, the rout was on. But the team wasn't playing with its usual sense of urgency, and, after turning the ball over several times, Yale was up only 13–7 at the half. Cozza was furious. He had worried that a team with so much talent might get complacent. Just showing up, he told them, was not enough.

Yale scored the first time they had the ball in the second half, and though the expected offensive avalanche never materialized, the team pulled away to win, 25–13. After the game, Levin, who had run for 55 yards, was one of the few players to earn Cozza's praise. Yale's string of consecutive victories now stood at thirteen.

VI

Playing Football for the Man

In September 1968, during the first week of school, when a steady stream of students showed up at his office to go over their class schedules or discuss a roommate problem, Dunster House Senior Tutor Roger Rosenblatt met with an economics concentrator named John Tyson. A husky, muscular senior with a modest afro, neatly trimmed beard, and wire-rimmed glasses, Tyson wanted to talk about the courses he was considering. Rosenblatt had learned from Tyson's folder that he played varsity football and was such a talented defensive back that professional teams had been scouting him. After they wound up their discussion of Tyson's courses, Rosenblatt asked him how football was going. Tyson said he wasn't playing. Rosenblatt asked why. "I don't want to be a hired gladiator in the Colosseum," Tyson replied. Although the expression struck Rosenblatt as a trifle melodramatic, he was impressed by the matter-of-fact way in which the young man said it, with neither hostility nor boastfulness. He had clearly given the matter a great deal of thought. There were other things he would rather do with his life, Tyson said, than play football.

A few days later, Rosenblatt got a telephone call from John Yovicsin. The coach begged him to talk to Tyson and persuade him to rejoin the team. Something in the coach's tone of voice made it clear he couldn't believe that his star safety was giving up football, and that if only the senior tutor would speak to him, Tyson would come to his senses. As he listened, Rosenblatt realized that Yovicsin didn't seem particularly concerned about Tyson's life beyond the football field. He told the coach he was sorry but he wouldn't try to talk Tyson back on the team.

*　*　*

That anything could be more important to John Tyson than football would have been unthinkable only a few years earlier. His life had revolved around the game from the day he had first picked up a football at the age of ten in Montclair, New Jersey, where he'd grown up the youngest of six children. His father, a West Indian immigrant with an eighth-grade education, percolated with entrepreneurial schemes but was employed as a handyman. His mother had taught sixth grade in a segregated school in Mississippi before moving north in the thirties and finding part-time work as a housekeeper for a wealthy white family. Money had been tight even before Tyson's father died of a brain tumor when John was nine. Tyson's parents had always stressed the importance of getting an education and working hard in order to succeed in a world dominated by whites. "You've got to be better than to be equal to," their mother often told her children, reinforcing her lessons, if needed, with a switch from the lilac bush that grew near the front door.

Her youngest rarely needed reinforcing. From an early age, he was determined to be the best at whatever he did. After winning a scholarship to a Catholic grammar school, Tyson, like the handful of other black students, was automatically placed in the lowest of the three academic groups in his grade. He begged his mother to talk to the teacher because, as he put it, "I don't want to be with the dummies." He was moved up to the second group, from which he eventually worked his way to the first. Whenever his older brother George ran laps around the block to get in shape for high school football, ten-year-old John took off after him, determined to keep up. George was too proud to stop before his little brother did. Finally, after ten or twelve laps, John, exhausted, would slow to a halt, and, after a few more strides, so—gratefully—would George.

Playing on his first football team, in the Pop Warner league, Tyson met a skinny boy named Ron Burton. Two of the team's top athletes, they started out fiercely competitive, but were soon making plans to play on the same high school team and the same college team, and then go pro together—the kind of plans many boys make, but in their case, a real possibility. Burton, at quarterback, and Tyson, at halfback, were among the best players their town had ever seen. In their senior year, Montclair High went undefeated, won the state championship, and was ranked third in the country. Both players were named All-State, Tyson for the second time. Recruited by scores of colleges, Tyson and Burton settled on Colgate. Then a Harvard alumnus invited Tyson to spend a day in Manhattan. They ate at the Harvard Club and motored up the Hudson on a private yacht. When he returned to Montclair, Tyson, whose friends called him "Big Time"—because whatever his dream, he always dreamed big—told Burton that if he got in, he couldn't say no to Harvard.

*   *   *

Tyson starred on Harvard's freshman team. On offense, he and Gatto were the starting halfbacks; on defense, he and Gatto were the starting safeties. Several of his teammates thought Tyson was the best football player they had ever seen. After the season was over, Yovicsin asked Tyson to play defense for the varsity. He wanted Gatto and senior Bobby Leo as his starting halfbacks, and the team needed help in the secondary. Tyson was deeply disappointed, but he didn't complain. "I'll be the best safety this place has ever seen," he told Burton. That summer, after spending his days doing construction work in Manhattan, Tyson rushed back to Montclair to work out with Burton at their old high school field. For the first half of practice, Tyson ran pass patterns so Burton could sharpen his throwing. For the second half, Tyson lined up five yards in front of Burton and back-pedaled while the quarterback fired the ball a few feet to one side of his friend or the other, over and over, until it was too dark to see. By the end of the summer, Tyson could catch the ball just as easily running backward as he could running forward.

Sophomores almost never started for John Yovicsin. Tyson not only started but was one of the top players on the team. At five feet ten and 190 pounds, he was a rare combination of speed (he ran a 9.7 hundred-yard dash), power, and fearlessness, equally good at defending against the run or the pass. When it came to hitting, Tyson, pound for pound, had no equal. Players on the Harvard defense who had tried to tackle him in freshman scrimmages were relieved that he played on *their* side of the ball now. During games, he worked himself into a remarkable state of intensity, muttering "Bust up . . . Bust up" in the huddle, exhorting himself to explode the upcoming play. In Tyson's sophomore year, Harvard's defense gave up only one touchdown through the air—for all of twelve yards. That it was Tyson who had given up that touchdown was an irony lost on none of his backfield mates, who were well aware that on a defensive secondary acknowledged to be the best in the Ivy League and among the best in the east, Tyson was, hands down, the outstanding player. Tyson was the only sophomore named first-team All-Ivy. By the end of the season, pro scouts were coming to see him play.

Tyson never talked to his teammates about going pro. He wasn't one to brag. He carried himself with quiet dignity and always stood up for what he believed was right. Defensive backfield coach Loyal Park, whose motivational techniques tended toward confrontation and humiliation, had, at some point, reduced every member of the 1966 starting defensive backfield to tears—with the exception of Tyson. "He'd try that stuff on John, but John was not going to be shaken," Tyson's fellow safety Tom Williamson recalled. "John was a rock of a man. Loyal learned not to mess with him."

Junior year, Tyson was named one of the top defensive backs in the East by *Street & Smith's* in their annual college football preview. After the BU game, in which he made nine tackles and an interception, Yovicsin told the press, "We've never had anybody who played safety better than Tyson." On one play, going for an interception, Tyson sprinted toward the sideline, hurdled the Harvard bench, and somersaulted into the first row of the stands. "Before the crowd could react," observed a *Crimson* sportswriter, "he was back on the field."

In the fourth quarter of the fourth game of the year, playing on a rain-soaked, chewed-up Cornell field, Tyson was cutting toward the ball when his knee buckled and he dropped to the ground. He had torn both his anterior cruciate ligament and his medial collateral ligament. He would miss the rest of the season. The hardest hitter on the team had blown out his knee on a play in which he hadn't been touched.

* * *

When John Tyson arrived as a freshman in the fall of 1965, no Ivy League college enjoyed a better reputation among African-Americans than Harvard. Exactly one hundred years earlier, it had been the first of the Ivies to enroll a black student, a transfer from Oberlin named Richard Greener, who won the Boylston Prize for Oratory when he graduated in 1870—four years before a black student would graduate from Yale, seventy-seven years before a black student would graduate from Princeton. Indeed, in the late nineteenth century Harvard was sufficiently welcoming that, as the historian Samuel Eliot Morison noted in *Three Centuries of Harvard*, "Southerners avoided Harvard after the Civil War because it admitted negroes on the same terms as whites, allowing them to eat at Memorial Hall, room in college dormitories, and participate in debating and athletic contests." In 1890, two black students graduated from Harvard; one was chosen by his classmates to be their class orator, the other, W. E. B. Du Bois, to be a Commencement speaker.

But there were limits to the college's hospitality. In 1907, Harvard president Charles Eliot assured members of the Southern Club, a social organization for students from the South, that should the number of black undergraduates grow to such a point "as to impede the progress of the College," limitations would be imposed. In the early twenties, his successor, Abbott Lawrence Lowell, instituted a policy excluding black students from the freshman dorms in Harvard Yard, saying he felt sure they were "anxious to avoid unnecessary antagonisms" and could find accommodations in private homes. When both black and white alumni protested, Lowell, who at the same time was working energetically to limit the number of Jews at Harvard, explained that the number of Southerners in the college was increasing, and he didn't wish to offend them. (Freshman housing would be off-limits to black students, formally at first, and then informally, into the 1950s.) In 1931, Lowell assured Du Bois, who by then had helped found the NAACP, "The negro presents no problem peculiar to Harvard. The numbers coming here are not large, and as their object is to get an education they do not seek to be publicly conspicuous." In 1947, Corporation secretary David W. Bailey struck a similar note, observing that Harvard "has no 'Negro policy'"; indeed, he pointed out, it didn't even keep count of its black students. The count would have been easy to keep: between 1865 and 1941, an average of slightly more than two black undergraduates per year were enrolled at Harvard. After the war, those numbers modestly increased—though not to universal approbation. In 1952, two white students burned a five-foot cross in front of Stoughton, Holworthy, and Hollis, the freshman dorms in which nine African-American members of the Class of 1955 were housed.

In the early 1960s, prodded by the civil rights movement, the Harvard admissions office quietly worked to recruit more black students. Tyson was one of forty-two in his entering freshman class, by far the largest number in the school's history. That same year Yale would enroll twenty-three black freshmen, Princeton sixteen.

For nearly a century, the small number of black students Harvard admitted had come from the upper middle class—the sons of doctors, lawyers, and professors. These students, many of whom had attended predominantly white secondary schools, were raised with the belief that success was achieved by excelling in what some of them referred to as "the white man's world." Having gained admission to what many considered the academic and social pinnacle of that world, they worked hard to prove to Harvard—and to themselves—that they belonged, by trying to be, as one student put it years later, "whiter than white." For some, this meant keeping their distance from their black classmates. An article in the *Crimson* noted that "standard procedure" in the early sixties "was for Negroes, passing one another in the Yard, to cast down their eyes or become immediately engrossed with tying their shoelaces." (Approaching such students, Martin Kilson, Harvard's only black faculty member, would mischievously call out "Hey, spook! Hey, Negro!" until the mortified young man acknowledged him.) In 1963, when students formed the Association of African and Afro-American Students (commonly known as Afro), the country's first black student group at a predominantly white college, some black alumni objected, asking Harvard not to sanction what one called "self-jimcrowism and self-segregation." Presumably, those critics were pleased when, in December 1965, it was announced that an African-American had been accepted into the Spee Club. "He is believed to be the first Negro to accept membership in a final club at Harvard," wrote the *Crimson*, in its account of what, in the long march of civil rights, was a peculiarly Harvardian footnote.

By the time Tyson arrived, Harvard was no longer just cherry-picking black seniors from Exeter and Andover but seeking out students from inner-city public schools in Detroit and Los Angeles. Unlike the sons of the so-called black elite, who'd grown up speaking the language of integration and nonviolence, these younger students were more likely to speak the language of black nationalism and Black Power, more likely to quote Stokely Carmichael than Martin Luther King. Often the first in their family to attend college, they were less likely to have been steeped in the culture of genteel academic discourse on which Harvard was based, less likely to consider the election of a "Negro" to a final club as cause for celebration, less likely to accept being called "Negro" rather than "black," less likely to worry about being, in Lowell's phrase, "publicly conspicuous." It is generally agreed that the fall of 1965 marked the appearance in the Freshman Union dining hall of the "Soul Table," a table at which black students congregated. (In its early years, the decision of whether to sit there would be, for some, psychologically and politically fraught.) Many of the men at the Soul Table believed that instead of bending themselves to fit Harvard, Harvard should do a little bending to fit them.

Harvard had opened its doors a bit wider, but did little to make black students feel at home. In 1965, of nearly four hundred tenured professors on the faculty, none were black; of nearly two thousand offerings listed in the *Courses of Instruction*, only fifteen contained the word *Negro* or *black* or *Africa*. Although the administration had one black dean, not a single admissions officer was black, nor was a single psychiatrist or psychologist at University Health Services. Most of Harvard's black employees served food in the dining halls. "I was in Harvard but not of it," W. E. B. Du Bois wrote in 1890. Seventy-five years later, Harvard's black students, though more numerous, could have said the same.

For Tyson, the decision of whether to sit at the Soul Table wasn't as fraught as it was for many of his friends. Sometimes he sat there, sometimes he didn't, unconcerned that, either way, he might be making a statement. (Indeed, his discomfort was less racial than socioeconomic. Tyson was shocked by how wealthy his classmates were, and by how oblivious they seemed to the fact that not everyone had grown up the way they had.) Harvard was far less integrated than the community he had left. At Montclair High, he had been one of 197 black students in his graduating class of 536; on his football team, seven of eleven starters were black. His high school friends were a tight multiracial pack who sat with one another at lunch and hung out in one another's homes. Montclair was hardly a racial Eden; Tyson's eldest sister could recall the days when black shoppers had been barred from certain downtown department stores. But when Tyson had watched the civil rights struggle play out on his family's television set, the fire hoses and German shepherds of Birmingham seemed a long way from Montclair.

* * *

On July 12, 1967, not long after Tyson and Burton had begun their summer workouts at Woodman Field, in preparation for their junior seasons, Newark erupted in riots. Newark was seven miles down the road from Montclair. Tyson, Burton, and their friends did their back-to-school shopping there, at Gimbels, S. Klein, and Bamberger's. They went ice skating at Branch Brook Park. They took school trips to the Newark Museum. They had grown up thinking of Newark as their New York City. Now, on TV, they watched the downtown streets they knew so well burn into the night. On the third day of the uprising, Tyson and Burton were stunned to hear that someone they knew had been killed. Billy Furr, a twenty-four-year-old unemployed baker from Montclair, was Burton's mother's godson, a good-natured but hapless young man who, caught up in the looting, had grabbed a six-pack of beer moments before a police car roared up. A *Life* magazine photographer who happened to be on the scene documented what happened next: Furr running away, a helmeted policeman shooting him in the back, Furr collapsing on the sidewalk. (Furr was one of twenty-one African-American civilians killed in Newark that week.) The photos shocked black and white readers across the nation. Tyson and Burton read and reread Burton's mother's copy of the magazine.

The Game

*   *   *

The events in Newark, one of more than a hundred cities to be paralyzed by riots in the summer of 1967, resonated with Tyson that fall as he began to recover from his knee injury. His own athletic career on hold, he paid close attention to the proposed boycott by black athletes of the 1968 Olympic games, to be held in Mexico City the following autumn. The idea had been raised at the first National Conference on Black Power in Newark, which started three days after the riots ended. "For years we have participated in the Olympic Games, carrying the U.S. on our backs with our victories, and race relations are worse now than ever," said Harry Edwards, a San Jose State sociology instructor and former discus thrower who stood six feet eight and wore dark glasses and a black beret. "But it's time for the black people to stand up as men and women and refuse to be utilized as performing animals for a little extra dog food."

In late November, Tyson read a column by Arthur Daley, a white sportswriter for the *New York Times*, in which he asserted that a boycott "would not put the slightest dent in the Olympics" and "would deprive a dozen or so fine Negro athletes . . . the opportunity of instilling pride in members of their race." Daley held up Jesse Owens's four-gold-medal performance at the 1936 Olympics in Berlin as a more promising path toward racial justice. Angered by Daley's patronizing tone and by his implication that black athletes should keep their mouths shut off the playing field, Tyson asked Tom Williamson, his fellow safety on the football team, whether he would draft a letter to the *Times*. Williamson, a straight-A social studies concentrator, said he would be glad to help.

Published on December 10—and signed by Tyson, Williamson, and middle guard Stan Greenidge, the only other black starter on the 1967 team—the letter expressed admiration for the would-be boycotters. "These young men are willing to sacrifice long-nurtured ambitions and almost certain glory for the affirmation of an ideal," they wrote. "They are saying to their people and the world that gold medals and momentary plaudits are meager consolation for being denied the fundamental right of human dignity." Later that month, Tyson had reconstructive surgery on his knee.

* * *

As he began the long and painful process of rehabilitation, Tyson pondered his own role as a black athlete. He wondered whether he might have something in common with those Olympic boycotters. Even at Harvard, black students were often assumed to be athletes—"What sport do you play?" was a question that came up early in conversation with whites—and if they *were* athletes, they faced the assumption that if they hadn't been, they wouldn't have been admitted. (As far back as 1907, President Eliot observed that black students at Harvard won recognition "on account of their remarkable athletic merit.") Tyson liked his teammates. He had never experienced overt racism on the field, though like other African-American team members he suspected that black players had to drastically outperform their white counterparts to earn a starting spot: "You've got to be better than to be equal to," as his mother had told him. But the more he thought about it, the odder it seemed that he spent his Saturday afternoons playing in front of an audience composed almost entirely of wealthy white alumni, who, if they were to see him coming down the sidewalk at night, might well cross to the other side of the street. That winter, as he flexed his injured knee in the trainer's room, Tyson found himself wondering, "Why am I playing this game? Why am I working so hard—and for what?"

In the spring, Tyson took a course on African history and culture, the only such course offered at Harvard. He began to let his hair grow out. He got increasingly involved in Afro, which, like black student groups across the country, was turning its attention from injustices in the Deep South to injustices in its own institution. Why didn't Harvard have more black students? Why didn't Harvard have more than one black faculty member? Why were black students stopped and asked to show their bursar's cards by campus police as they crossed the Yard after dark? Tyson started spending less time around athletes, more around nonathletes. He started spending less time in the trainer's room rehabbing his knee and more time sitting around with Al Gore and his other roommates, talking about race, politics, and the war.

Tyson had met Gore their first week at Harvard when Gore knocked on his door in Lionel Hall, seeking his vote for president of the Freshman Council. Many years later, when his friend was running for president of the United States, Tyson would admit that, having watched the civil rights struggles on TV, he had grown up assuming that people with Southern accents must be stupid or evil or both. Gore, the son of a Democratic senator from Tennessee, was neither; he was smart, outgoing, funny, and, unlike many privileged students at Harvard, interested in hanging out with people different from himself. On his freshman rooming form, Gore had asked to be placed with a black student. Though that black student wasn't Tyson, but rather a West Coast hipster with a predilection for sunglasses, bell-bottoms, and marijuana, it was with Tyson that Gore became close. Like Tyson, Gore dreamed big; he told him about his White House ambitions. Like Tyson, Gore loved sports (he had captained his high school football team), and their friendship grew against a background of fierce but friendly competition: handball games, impromptu push-up challenges, and even, one memorable spring evening in the Yard, a beer-chugging contest, the outcome of which would be debated over further beers for years to come. At the end of freshman year, Gore invited Tyson to be part of a nine-man rooming group that included Tyson's teammate Tommy Lee Jones. They requested Adams House but were assigned to Dunster, known for flower-power scruffiness and left-wing activism.

Their sophomore year had been relatively laid back: shooting pool in Dunster's basement grill; watching *Star Trek* and *The Tonight Show* on TV; tossing frisbees in the courtyard; holding late-night bull sessions, sometimes over a joint. On Saturday afternoons, Gore, who played end for the Dunster House football team, would stroll down to the stadium and cheer on Tyson and Jones. Junior year, as the country seemed to be fracturing before their eyes, their circle spent less time watching Johnny Carson and more time watching Walter Cronkite. That year, Tyson and Gore shared a bunk bed (Tyson, coming straight from two-a-days, had gotten there first and taken the bottom bunk), and they often stayed up late discussing race, war, and politically charged literature—including *Soul on Ice* and *The Autobiography of Malcolm X*—until they'd talked themselves to sleep. Just as Tyson was exploring his identity as a black man in America, Gore, a government major whose father had been one of the first senators to speak out against the Vietnam War, was pondering his responsibility to his country and to himself. He was against the war, but he couldn't stop thinking about the boys he cut tobacco with every summer on the family farm, who didn't have the ways to avoid the draft he and his Harvard friends had. Gore knew that if he didn't serve, one of those boys would likely have to go in his place. Through months of bunk-to-bunk give-and-take, each roommate encouraged the other to act on his ideals.

*　　*　　*

On April 4, 1968, Martin Luther King was assassinated. Riots broke out in more than a hundred American cities. The following evening, George Lalich and several other Harvard football players were flying back to Boston on a plane bearing the baseball team home from its annual spring training trip to Florida. Their flight was scheduled for a brief layover at Dulles, the D.C. area's new airport. As the plane came in low over Washington on its approach, Lalich and his teammates were shocked by what they saw below: entire city blocks of the nation's capital in flames. Lalich couldn't help thinking of the scenes of Atlanta burning in *Gone With the Wind*. At Dulles, as he and his teammates wandered into the terminal to stretch their legs, he was taken aback by the glares of the airport personnel, most of whom were black, as they served the all-white team.

It was a time when even the most well-intentioned whites were resented. On the night of King's death, nearly a hundred Harvard students walked to a black section of Cambridge to express their sympathy. They were turned away by a few dozen men, one of whom told them, "Get out of our neighborhood—leave us alone."

When Tyson and Gore got back to Dunster House from spring break, they stayed up until four in the morning, talking and crying. "We were sick from watching our nation burn up," Tyson would recall. "You didn't want to believe what you were seeing and what had happened. How were we going to stay together as a people?"

On the afternoon of April 9, five days after King's death, twelve hundred members of the Harvard community—students, faculty members, administrators, alumni, and a smattering of local politicians—gathered in Memorial Church to recite the Lord's Prayer, sing "We Shall Overcome," and hear President Pusey eulogize King as "a great man and a great citizen." An air of unease hung over the proceedings, however, as the mourners, all but a handful of whom were white, were keenly aware of what was taking place outside the church, where the vast majority of Harvard's black students had gathered on the steps for a service of their own. They spoke not only of their anguish at King's death but of their anger at Harvard. "Martin Luther King would have called those people in there hypocrites," said Jeff Howard, president of Afro, pointing to the church behind him. "If they come out of there with tears in their eyes, we want it to be plain that we don't want their tears. We want black people to have a place here at Harvard."

The following morning, the *Crimson* front-page headline read: "Blacks Hold Own Service for King as Pusey Eulogizes Him in Church. Speakers Call Harvard Racists." Next to a lengthy article, there was a photograph of the students leaving the Memorial Church steps. In the foreground, at the head of the line, was John Tyson, wearing his Harvard Athletics warm-up jacket. Inside the paper, there was a half-page notice.

TO FAIR HARVARD

Do you mourn Martin Luther King?

Harvard can do this:

1. Establish an endowed chair for a Black Professor
2. Establish courses relevant to Blacks at Harvard
3. Establish more lower level Black Faculty members
4. Admit a number of Black students proportionate to our percentage of the population as a whole

In an essay in the 1969 yearbook, Tyson's classmate Herbert Nickens would call King's assassination "the watershed of race relations at Harvard." For white Harvard, the segregated service and the *Crimson* ad were a profound shock. Over the past few years, the administration had responded to Afro's concerns by counseling patience. "A lot of Harvard people acted as if they were doing you a big favor by letting you into their famous university and letting you take their fancy classes—you shouldn't be complaining, you should be grateful," Tom Williamson, Tyson's backfield mate and co-author of the letter to the *New York Times*, would recall. Pusey continued to equivocate, saying he had no comment on black student dissatisfaction "except that I regret it and feel sad about it." But it was clear that the patience of Harvard's black students was at an end.

For black Harvard, the tragedy had a galvanizing effect, wrote Nickens, bringing together the children of the black bourgeoisie and the children of the inner city into "a cohesive, self conscious community." In the days that followed, the majority of the college's African-American students ate their meals together and spent their evenings together, grieving and brainstorming. Afro quickly formed an "ad hoc negotiating committee" of ten students to press their concerns with the administration. Tyson was one. Tom Williamson was named chair.

Only a year apart, Tyson and Williamson were, in some ways, representative of the two different generations of black students at Harvard. Though Montclair was no ghetto, Tyson had grown up in a single-parent household with few advantages. Though Williamson, the son of a retired Army officer, was no prep schooler, he had grown up in an affluent Northern California suburb that, aside from his family, was entirely white. Williamson had come to Harvard believing that if he worked hard enough and achieved as much as—or more than—any white student, he might be able to change people's attitudes about race. Williamson had succeeded on Harvard's terms so well that he had recently won the ultimate symbol of collegiate success, a Rhodes Scholarship—the third black student in the country to win one in the sixty-six-year history of the award. But when King was murdered, he realized that the model of assimilation he'd been following all his life wasn't working. He had been invited to speak at the service inside Memorial Church, a signal honor, but when Afro leaders asked him to speak at the outside service, he knew he had to make a choice. And the choice was clear. "I didn't want to collaborate with the people inside," he told the gathering on the church steps.

Tyson, Williamson, and their fellow committee members debated how to persuade the administration to take their concerns seriously. The more militant among them, saying there was little point in trying to negotiate with racists, called for occupying buildings; some talked of carrying guns. Although Tyson voiced skepticism about Harvard's willingness to change, he and several other committee members favored sit-ins and protest marches. Williamson and his fellow moderates argued that taking over a building or leading a sit-in might give them momentary satisfaction but could hurt their chances of achieving their long-term goals. Better to work with the largely sympathetic faculty to bring about change. In the end, the committee agreed to try the moderate approach.

Over the following weeks, Ad Hoc Committee members led meetings in every Harvard house to discuss King's death and talk about what it meant to be a black student on an overwhelmingly white campus. They met with the dean of admissions, who promised to bring along black undergraduates on recruiting trips, to hire black admissions staffers, and to enroll a substantially higher number of black students. They met with the faculty, which agreed to look into establishing a concentration in Afro-American Studies. In mid-May, the dean of the faculty announced that a full-year course on African-American history and culture would be introduced in the fall. Social Sciences 5, The Afro-American Experience, would be Harvard's first course devoted to the history of black Americans. It would be taught by Frank Freidel, a popular white history professor and biographer of Franklin D. Roosevelt. Over the final weeks of the spring term, Tyson and other Ad Hoc Committee members offered their suggestions as Freidel put together a syllabus.

Tyson told his friend Burton about helping to shape Soc Sci 5. It was only one course, he said, but it showed there *was* a chance to change things at Harvard. It felt good, he said, to be doing meaningful work.

But there was a long way to go. That spring, the Ad Hoc Committee arranged a meeting with Pusey to discuss its grievances. When members arrived at his office in Massachusetts Hall, Tyson and Williamson were dismayed to find that the first thing the Harvard president wanted to talk about was not Harvard's racial issues but the prospects for next year's football team.

* * *

If football had loomed less large to Tyson before Martin Luther King's death, it seemed almost irrelevant now. He had more important things to do than bust up opposing halfbacks. Even if he had wanted to play again, he worried that he wouldn't be the player he had once been, that he had lost his 9.7 speed. In any case, he was no longer showing up for physical therapy. Some of the players heard that he was thinking of quitting the team. They wondered whether Tyson, one of the most visible black students on campus, was being pressured not to play by more militant members of Afro. They were surprised when, in a *Crimson* article about black athletes at Harvard, Tyson said the university was "definitely racist."

Vic Gatto held out hope that Tyson would play that fall. In May, before school was out, the newly elected captain asked Tyson to meet with him. Gatto and Tyson had liked and respected each other ever since freshman year, when they'd played side by side on both offense and defense. Gatto told Tyson how much he wanted him to come back to the team. Tyson was polite but firm. He had decided not to play. He felt that he was being used by Harvard, he told Gatto, and that by playing football, he was supporting an institution that discriminated against black people. Gatto was disappointed but told Tyson he respected his decision.

It had been hard for Tyson to tell Gatto. It was far harder to tell Ron Burton. They had been playing football together since they were children. That June, when Burton called Tyson to tell him it was time to start their summer training, Tyson told him he had given up the game. "I've got other things going on now," he said. "I want to find a way to help my people." Burton, one of seven blacks in his 450-member class at Colgate and the only black starting quarterback in the Northeast, was sympathetic; after King's assassination, he had taken part in a campus sit-in. But he was more interested in leading a team than in leading a movement. Tyson told Burton he had been thinking a lot about his role as a black athlete. "I don't have to play any more football for the Man," he said. Then he added, "My knee's not right, anyway."

Playing Football for the Man

* * *

In the fall of 1968, one of Tyson's freshman roommates saw him from across the Yard. They hadn't crossed paths much in the last two years, and the roommate was surprised to see him with an afro and a beard, and wearing a dashiki. He was walking with a slight limp.

It was the first fall since he was ten years old that Tyson wasn't playing football. But he was hardly idle. He was continuing his work with the Ad Hoc Committee, which was pressing for an Afro-American Studies department at Harvard. He was tutoring black schoolchildren in Roxbury. He was teaching Afro-American history to black inmates at Norfolk State Prison. He had gotten involved in the antiwar movement; in May, he'd been one of 442 Harvard undergraduates to sign a "We Won't Go" pledge, vowing that as long as the United States was involved in this "unjust and immoral" war, they would not serve in the armed forces. Every other week, he was meeting with Roger Rosenblatt and a handful of students to discuss the work of James Baldwin, Richard Wright, Ralph Ellison, and other African-American novelists and poets. Unable to find a course in Harvard's celebrated English department that examined the work of a single black writer, Tyson had been one of several Dunster students to approach Rosenblatt, the senior tutor who had refused Yovicsin's request to talk Tyson back onto the team—and, conveniently, a young English instructor who had a reputation for being relatively hip—to ask whether he'd help. Word of the informal seminar spread, and though they got no academic credit, by the end of the semester there were two dozen students squeezed around the long wooden table in the Junior Common Room. (The following fall, when Rosenblatt was asked by the English department to teach Black Fiction in America for credit, more than four hundred students would enroll.)

Tyson and the Ad Hoc Committee were also trying to figure

out what had gone wrong with Soc Sci 5, The Afro-American Experience. In September, 250 students, including Tyson and 50 or 60 other black undergraduates, had enrolled. Almost from the beginning, there had been trouble. A number of black students, many of them freshmen, said that the lectures were simplistic and homogenized, that the reading list had too many white authors, and that, most crucially, a course on the Afro-American experience should be taught by an Afro-American. "As the course now stands it is hardly relevant to black students because we're still seeing history through the white man's eyes," said one. Another scoffed, "The lecture series might better be called 'Negro Heroes I Have Known'—it consists of black equivalents of the George Washington cherry tree tale." In the middle of one lecture, in the kind of confrontation that was becoming increasingly common at Harvard, a black freshman had taken over the podium to denounce the course and Professor Freidel. Assistant Professor of Government Martin Kilson, still the only African-American member of the college's faculty, attacked Soc Sci 5's critics, calling their arguments "racially bigoted and disgustingly anti-intellectual," and accusing them of trying to reduce the course to "a platform for black nationalist propaganda." This set off a vitriolic exchange that occupied the pages of the *Crimson* for weeks. The critics were hardly mollified when Freidel, who had given up his pet course on the New Deal to teach Soc Sci 5, suggested that the freshmen might not understand the way Harvard courses worked, and that his lectures had "gone over the heads of some of them."

For Tyson and the Ad Hoc Committee, the dispute was deeply distressing. The course they had helped create with such hope had become a lightning rod for black students' anger toward Harvard. In early November, the committee arranged to interview disgruntled students and prepare a critique of the course. It became apparent that their efforts to mediate the conflict might already be too late. On November 14, a *Crimson* summary of the controversy noted that "less than two months after its first class meeting, there is some question whether the infant course will, or even should, survive."

That Soc Sci 5's most vocal critics were freshmen was no surprise. Over the last several years, each new class of African-Americans at Harvard had been more militant than the last, and those entering in the fall of 1968, in the wake of King's assassination, were particularly outspoken. Less than a decade after black students at Harvard had been reluctant to acknowledge each other while walking across the Yard, a black student seen in the company of a white student was at risk of being labeled an Uncle Tom.

Tyson was spending more time with his black friends and was increasingly adopting the vocabulary of black nationalism. But he had grown up in Montclair; he could not, like some of his friends, call *all* whites racist. He remained close to Al Gore and his Dunster House suitemates. They still stayed up late talking about the country's problems.

*   *   *

On October 16, four days after the Harvard football team beat Columbia, the American sprinters Tommie Smith and John Carlos stood on the victory podium at the Mexico City Olympics, bowed their heads, and raised black-gloved fists during "The Star-Spangled Banner." The image shocked the nation. If Tyson had been at Harvard Stadium three days later, when Harvard played Cornell, he might have seen an image less dramatic but no less indelible: when the crowd rose to sing the national anthem, three black spectators remained seated, staring straight ahead, fists in the air, ignoring the pointed looks and pursed lips of the nearby Harvard alumni and their wives, who were too polite—or too scared—to say anything.

But Tyson wasn't there. Although he was still listed in the press book as "a top pro prospect because of his sprinters' speed," he didn't go to Harvard football games that fall. He rarely talked about football anymore, though Burton could tell that he missed it. The two friends remained close, but for the first time they were on different paths. Burton had his sights set on the NFL. Tyson was thinking of divinity school.

One evening, Tyson was talking with a friend about plans for the future. Tyson showed him a letter. It was from the Dallas Cowboys. The team wanted to draft him despite his knee injury and planned to offer him a substantial signing bonus. Tyson told his friend he'd been putting on a uniform every fall since sixth grade. Football, he said quietly, had become a major part of his identity—at least in the eyes of others. But he had come to realize that he could no longer accept any definition of self that did not come from within. Henceforth, he planned to follow what he called "a spiritual path."

When Tyson's former teammates saw him around campus, they said hi, but encounters could be a little awkward without the common ground of football to fall back on. Some of the players couldn't understand how someone as talented as Tyson could give up the game. The emergence of Pat Conway had eased the loss, but Gatto couldn't help wondering what it would have been like to have Conway *and* Tyson in the defensive backfield at the same time.

*   *   *

If people were surprised that Harvard came into the Penn game, on November 2, undefeated, they were even more surprised that Penn did, too. Penn hadn't had a winning record since 1959; for the last five years they had taken turns in the Ivy League cellar with Columbia and Brown. But Penn had twenty-seven returning lettermen, and even in their leanest years, they were one of the hardest-hitting teams Harvard faced. The previous week, Penn had stunned perennial powerhouse Princeton, 19–14. The oddsmakers rated Harvard a slight favorite.

Some of the 25,000 fans were still finding their seats in Harvard Stadium when Pat Conway leaped high to intercept a pass on Penn's first offensive series. On Penn's second possession, Conway dove in front of the receiver on a sideline route and picked off another pass. By the end of the first quarter, Harvard was up 21–0. Their third touchdown, a 70-yard punt return by Vic Gatto, made the captain the second leading scorer in Harvard history. Harvard won, 28–6, for their sixth straight victory.

VII

The Most Dangerous Back in the History of the Ivy League

On the first day of Yale freshman football practice in 1965, as the team went through a battery of conditioning tests, halfback John Waldman found himself in line for the standing broad jump behind one of the most physically impressive players he'd ever seen. Waldman was five feet nine and 145 pounds. This man—he looked more like a grown man than a teenager—must have been at least six feet three and 210 pounds. Waldman watched him step up to the mat, which had been marked out to twelve feet. Waldman had been impressed when some of the players ahead of them had jumped nine, even ten feet. Now he looked on in amazement as the man bent his knees, swung his arms, and leaped clear off the end of the mat.

Many years later, a former sports editor for the *Yale Daily News* recalled Calvin Hill as "a player so gifted his presence in the Ivy League seemed preposterous." Hill was bigger and stronger than most linemen, yet faster than all but a few defensive backs. He could pass like a quarterback and catch like a wide receiver. He could also kick; once, in a scrimmage, he booted a 52-yard field goal, which, had he done it in a game, would have been Yale's longest in more than forty years. Carmen Cozza said that Hill was the only player he'd ever coached who could have started—and starred—at all twenty-two positions. NFL scouts had been watching him since sophomore year. Hill, however, was an atypical prospect. His heroes were not athletes but spiritual leaders and civil rights activists: Martin Luther King, William Sloane Coffin. He hoped to be drafted by a team from a city that had a divinity school, so he could attend classes at night.

* * *

Hill's great-grandfather was born into slavery in 1847, a hundred years before Calvin's birth. Hill's father had been a sharecropper in South Carolina during the Depression. One day in the early 1930s, Henry Hill had taken a drink of water without the permission of the owner's son. There had been a fight. Fearing for his life, Hill and his wife fled north, to Baltimore, where he found work in construction. They settled in Turner Station, a segregated neighborhood populated largely by black Southerners who had come to work at Bethlehem Steel, the world's largest steel mill. Its smokestacks lined the horizon across Bear Creek and turned the sky gray.

Calvin Hill might have ended up at Bethlehem Steel, too, had it not been for his father. Henry Hill had left school after second grade; his wife, Elizabeth, a seamstress who had finished tenth grade, taught him to read and write after they were married. (He had put an X instead of a signature on their marriage certificate.) He was determined that their only child get the education he hadn't gotten himself. When Hill was three months old, his father purchased a set of encyclopedias from a door-to-door salesman. One of Hill's earliest memories was of his father pointing to the volumes and saying, "When you learn to read, everything you need to know will be in those books." After Hill began school, his father came home each evening wanting to hear about his son's day, set aside time for homework as well as time to play catch in the backyard, took an active role in the PTA, and reminded him that being a Hill was something to be proud of. When Hill was in second grade, the teacher at his segregated school asked the students what they wanted to be when they grew up. Hill, who had read somewhere that the president of the United States made $100,000 a year and lived in a big house, said he wanted to be president. The teacher told him he couldn't, because he was black. Hill, upset, told his father, who did his best to explain the way the world worked, but also told him that if he wanted to be president, he could be president. In Turner Station, that possibility seemed especially far-fetched. "My vision was one where you went to high school, you graduated, and you went to work with Bethlehem Steel," Hill would say many years later. "That's what most of the men in my community did. He felt there was more for me. He wanted his only child to use his mind to make a living instead of his back. He'd take me over to the Bethlehem Steel plant to see guys getting out of work, guys who were dog-tired or dirty and gritty—and just asking me to think about that as a goal." Years later, when Hill graduated from Yale, he framed his degree and gave it to his father. Henry Hill kept it in his bedroom so it would be the first and last thing he saw each day.

As Calvin was about to enter ninth grade, their family physician told the Hills about the private school in New York his son had attended. Looking for a more diverse student body in the midst of the civil rights movement, the school had a scholarship available for a qualified minority student. Hill, who made straight As, didn't want to leave Turner Station, but his father insisted he apply. He won the scholarship, and, in September 1961, his parents drove him to Riverdale Country School, in a well-to-do part of the Bronx. Other than visits to his grandmother in South Carolina, it was the first time the fourteen-year-old had been away from home. Somewhere along the New Jersey Turnpike, the radio happened to play Ray Charles's latest single, "Hit the Road Jack," which did nothing to allay his apprehension. When they arrived, the student who gave Hill a tour of the manicured twelve-acre campus asked him where he wanted to go to college. Hill had no answer. The student said he wanted to go to Brown. The name meant nothing to Hill. "Don't worry," his father told him before he said good-bye. "You're as good as anyone there. But don't forget you're no better than anyone there either."

Hill had been raised in a city still under the sway of Jim Crow. The only whites he'd ever spoken to were the drugstore owner, the ice-cream man, and his teammates on the Red Shield Boys Club, an integrated baseball team sponsored by the Salvation Army. At Riverdale, he was one of half a dozen African-Americans in a student body of more than four hundred. "I had never heard of atheists or agnostics," he recalled. "I didn't realize there were different nationalities among white folks, like Italians and Germans. I didn't realize there were other religions, like Judaism." Homesick and miserable the first few months, he ended up thriving. Among his closest friends were a Jew from Long Island, an Italian-American from the Bronx, and an Episcopalian from Greenwich, Connecticut.

In Turner Station, Hill had been a standout in baseball and basketball, but his parents, worried that the sport was too rough, hadn't let him play tackle football. When Riverdale's football coach noticed the tall, sturdy teenager in the locker room one afternoon, he invited him to come out for the team. Because Hill was new to the sport, the coach put him on the freshman squad. In his first game, he scored four touchdowns.

Hill led the varsity to three straight undefeated seasons. Senior year, at quarterback, he averaged ten yards a carry, ran for seven touchdowns, threw for twelve more, and was named a *Parade* high school All-American. (At a postseason all-star banquet, he met a halfback from New Jersey named John Tyson, with whom he would stay in touch.) A Yale alumnus who happened to see him play alerted the Eli coach. "I saw him throw a pass 60 yards accurately, punt, run the ends like a deer and back up the line on defense," he wrote. "I made inquiry and was told that he is a fairly good student. . . . Needless to say, Hill would make a wonderful addition to the freshman squad in New Haven next year."

The chances of Hill ending up in New Haven were slim. He had scholarship offers from Notre Dame, Michigan, UCLA, and seventy other schools. He had all but settled on UCLA; he dreamed of playing in the Rose Bowl. But on a day when Riverdale seniors were excused from classes if they were visiting colleges, Hill and his friends realized that by making a brief stop at nearby Columbia, they could spend the rest of the day hanging out in Manhattan. Hearing about the Columbia visit, a Riverdale assistant coach assumed Hill was interested in the Ivy League and arranged for him to tour Yale, where the coach had played on the football team. On a postcard-perfect autumn weekend, Hill walked the campus and watched Yale defeat Dartmouth before 47,533 fans at the Bowl. "I fell in love with the place," he recalled. "I always wanted to go to a college where I would play in a big stadium in front of large crowds." Yale had another factor in its favor: its football team had never had a black quarterback. Hill, who grew up idolizing Jackie Robinson, was determined to be the first.

*　*　*

In 1946, Levi Jackson became the first African-American to play football at Yale. The son of the chief steward at Pierson, one of Yale's residential colleges, and one of three black students in his class, Jackson was not only the best player on the team but one of the most respected; nineteen months after Robinson broke Major League Baseball's color line, Jackson's teammates elected him captain of the 1949 squad. The vote made the front page of the *New York Times*. (Six months later, the *Times* would report that Jackson had also become the first African-American to be tapped for a secret society, and, furthermore, that he had turned down Skull and Bones in favor of Berzelius.) But Jackson had been a fullback, and even by the mid-sixties, when Calvin Hill arrived at Yale at the height of the civil rights movement, segregation still held sway at quarterback. The conventional wisdom—at least among many whites—was that black athletes were physically gifted but incapable of handling the intellectual demands of the position: memorizing the playbook, calling the signals, making split-second decisions. Those few who played quarterback in Northern high schools were routinely diverted by their college coaches to running back, wide receiver, or defensive back. No African-American had ever started a game at quarterback in the NFL's thirty-five years; fewer than a dozen had started in ninety-six years of college football, other than at historically black colleges. By 1965, there had been only one black starting quarterback in the history of the Ivy League—at Harvard, where Yovicsin had started John McCluskey the previous season. McCluskey's presence in Cambridge was one of the reasons Hill chose Yale over Harvard: at Yale, he'd be breaking new ground.

He wouldn't get the chance. On the second day of freshman football practice, the coach moved Hill to fullback. From the coach's perspective, the move made sense. Hill and Dowling were the team's most talented players; the team would do best by deploying them both in the backfield at the same time. Hill, bigger, faster, and stronger, would likely make the better running back. But it was also true that playing an African-American at quarterback wasn't something that came naturally to most coaches at the time. (Long after he'd graduated, Dowling asked Cozza why he had made him and not Hill the quarterback, and the coach would say it was because Dowling had possessed "that something extra.")

Hill kept his considerable disappointment to himself. When several black upperclassmen approached him on campus, attributed the switch to racism, and proposed picketing the athletic department, Hill said no. He had just arrived at Yale and didn't want to cause any trouble. "Son, you can best perform where the coach needs you," his father told him. But the hurt would last. Years later

Hill told a former teammate that if he had known he wouldn't get the chance to play quarterback at Yale, he might have gone somewhere else.

Even after Hill was moved to fullback, he found himself on third string, behind Bob Sokolowski and Bob Levin. He didn't play a down on offense in the first two games, though he started (and starred) at linebacker. He felt so discouraged that he considered transferring, but decided he didn't want to lose a year of NCAA eligibility. Nevertheless, he and Ed Franklin, an African-American end who wasn't getting much playing time either, talked about quitting the team. On the morning of the Cornell game, they decided to take their time walking to Ray Tompkins for the bus out to the Bowl, figuring that if they were left behind, it was a sure sign they should quit. Along the way, they wandered in and out of the stores along Broadway, looking at clothes and flipping through record albums. By the time they arrived, the bus had departed. With mixed feelings, they turned back toward Old Campus. "You guys missed the bus?" It was Bob Kiphuth, the retired Yale swim coach, calling out his office window. "Hold on, I'll give you a ride," he said. "I'm on the way there myself."

That afternoon, late in the fourth quarter, Hill was put in on offense. On his first play from scrimmage, he ran 6 yards for a touchdown. The following week, against Dartmouth, he came in twice with plays from the bench. On one, he took a pitch from Dowling and ran 58 yards for a touchdown. On the other, he went 50 yards with a screen pass. After the game, the coaches agreed that Hill deserved a try at starting fullback. Against Princeton, not only did Hill intercept a pass, force a fumble, and block a punt, but he scored five touchdowns.

*　*　*

On varsity, Hill started at halfback from day one. With his broad shoulders, 33-inch waist, massive thighs, and long legs, Hill was so imposing it looked as if he might burst free from his uniform at any moment. (Scott Robinson, the six-foot-three, 205-pound defensive end whose locker was just to the left of Hill's during their senior year, was no 98-pound weakling, but he always felt a little inadequate dressing next to Hill.) To opponents, the sight of Hill bearing down on them in the open field inspired anxiety, if not outright fear. When Ted Skowronski, playing linebacker in the 1965 Harvard-Yale freshman game, found Hill heading right at him, his first thought was, "My God, what am I going to do?" Screwing up his courage, Skowronski hit Hill harder than he'd ever hit anyone on a football field. Hill wobbled momentarily; Skowronski looked up from the ground to see him go another ten yards before a gang of Harvard defenders finally brought him down.

Hill was not only powerful but uncommonly swift. He had been clocked at 4.5 for the 40-yard dash—fastest on the team—and usually won the wind sprints at practice. When he ran a sweep, opposing defensive linemen, moving laterally down the line of scrimmage to contain the play, would calculate where they needed to be to intersect with the runner—only to arrive there and find that Hill had turned the corner and was five yards downfield. Junior year, a Princeton kick returner was in the clear, well on his way to a touchdown, when he suddenly found himself on the ground. Hill had caught up with him.

Hill was also a prodigious leaper, as John Waldman had learned that first day of freshman practice. He had decided not to play basketball for Yale even though he held the Riverdale single-game scoring record with 54 points. He needed the time for his studies. He did, however, join the track team, largely to stay in shape for football. In his first meet, after only three days of practice, he set the Yale freshman record in the long jump. Sophomore year, he set the varsity record in the triple jump. Junior year, he set the varsity record—25 feet, 1 inch—in the long jump, breaking a mark that had stood for forty-three years. His Yale jumps easily surpassed the qualifying standards for the 1968 Olympic trials, but the Games would take place in the middle of Yale's football season, and he chose not to try out for the U.S. team. Most jumpers are lithe and sinewy; Hill was the only man on earth to weigh more than 220 pounds and long-jump more than 25 feet. On the football field, if someone tried to tackle him low, he'd vault over him; in short-yardage situations, he'd hurl himself over a wall of linemen like a stone from a trebuchet. In one game, guard Jack Perkowski, knocked to his knees by a defender, felt a cleat in the middle of his back; Hill, using him as a launching pad, took off and soared another five yards.

In his junior year, Hill, a first-team All-Ivy selection, led the Bulldogs in rushing with 463 yards. He would have gained more if he hadn't been hampered by injuries. Even when healthy, he didn't carry the ball as often as he might. On a less talented team, he would likely get twenty carries a game, but Yale's offense had so many weapons he averaged half that many. (He had yet to fulfill his long-standing goal of rushing for a hundred yards in a single game.) Furthermore, his ability to outjump any defensive back made him even more dangerous as a receiver—second on the team in receptions in his junior year with thirteen, averaging 17.5 yards per catch. And yet he was, perhaps, most dangerous as a passer; running the halfback option, the former quarterback completed six of nine attempts for 192 yards (a preposterous 32 yards per completion) and two touchdowns. If Dowling threw flutterballs, Hill threw bullets: tight spirals that stung a receiver's hands.

For all Hill's accomplishments, there were some who felt that a man blessed with such prodigious physical gifts could be doing even more. A 1967 *Yale Daily News* profile called him "a curious mixture of unmatched performances and unrealized potential." In one of the weekly memos that Dartmouth coach Bob Blackman sent his players during the summer of 1968, preparing them for the upcoming season, he observed that Hill was, hands down, the most talented player in the Ivy League, but that if the defense kept after him his enthusiasm could flag. Where Harvard's Vic Gatto was a 90 percent player who always played at 110 percent, wrote Blackman, Hill was a 110 percent player who sometimes played at 90 percent.

It may have been a matter of perception. Hill didn't conform to the ideal of the hard-running, tackle-busting big man. He "ran high," as coaches put it—body upright, knees elevated. He rarely lowered his head and plowed through tacklers, like Bob Levin. Hill could run over people, too, but with his speed and athleticism, he could just as easily go around. He was a graceful ball-carrier, pausing as he approached the line, pondering his options, and then suddenly accelerating, his choice seeming inevitable, the way water finds the path of least resistance. Like Dowling, he had a long, loping stride. But where sportswriters wrote admiringly of Dowling's "nonchalance," they criticized Hill's relaxed style ("the complaint has been voiced that he is a 'lazy' athlete," a *Yale Daily News* writer noted): criticism that seemed, however unconsciously, to contain an element of racial stereotyping. It was true that Hill moved casually, unhurriedly, on and off the field. He occasionally missed the early bus to practice, took his time getting back to the huddle between plays, and was usually last in the locker room to finish dressing after a game. But the opponents who tried to tackle Hill never questioned his toughness, and though his teammates kidded him about how he'd limp back to the huddle and then run for 20 yards on the next play, they knew how often he played through bruises and strains, giving his all until the whistle blew.

The perception of Hill as insufficiently pugnacious on the field may have been influenced by his demeanor off it. Friendly but shy and unassuming, "Cal" had a voice somewhat softer and higher-pitched than one might expect from someone his size—more tenor than bass. Sportswriters commonly referred to him as "the gentle giant." He treated everyone with respect. Levin considered him the most decent person he knew. Years later, long after Hill had gone on to an illustrious career in professional football, whenever his former Yale teammate Bob Sokolowski ran into him at reunions, Hill introduced him to friends as the man who had started ahead of him at fullback freshman year. A small but gracious gesture, it always made Sokolowski proud.

Hill's character had been molded by his faith. In Turner Station, he had attended Sunday school at the Friendship Baptist Church; at Riverdale, he had taught Sunday school at the local Presbyterian church; at Yale, he was a deacon at Battell Chapel, where he had gotten to know and admire Coffin. (He was a frequent conscript in Coffin family touch football games; the hypercompetitive chaplain always managed to arrange things so that Hill was on his team.) Sophomore year, Hill told sportswriters that he hoped to play pro football for a few years so he could earn enough money to attend Union Theological Seminary, which Coffin had attended. In the anxious minutes leading up to each football game, his teammates always knew where they could find Hill: sitting in a bathroom stall, reading passages from a well-thumbed copy of the Bible. Moments before this year's preseason scrimmage against Boston University, as the players walked through the tunnel that would lead them to the Bowl, Hill called out to his teammates in alarm: they had forgotten their pregame prayer. Turning around awkwardly in the cramped space, cleats clattering on cement, eighty football players retraced their steps and knelt in the squad room.

*　　*　　*

In September of Hill's sophomore year, while the Yale football team was in the middle of two-a-days, the Congress of Racial Equality marched through downtown Cicero, a white, working-class suburb of Chicago, to protest housing discrimination. They were subjected to racist jeers from a gauntlet of screaming whites. Television screens across the country were filled with the kind of ugly scenes many white Northerners preferred to believe were confined to the Deep South. One afternoon, during a break in practice, Hill approached defensive tackle Rich Mattas, who had grown up in the town next to Cicero, and, in a tone of voice that suggested he sincerely wanted to understand, asked, "Why do people there feel that way?" Mattas, embarrassed, didn't know what to say.

Hill had been sixteen when he went to the 1963 March on Washington and heard Martin Luther King deliver his "I Have a Dream" speech. "I remember going back to Baltimore," he would recall, "and somehow thinking when I woke up the next morning that racism was going to disappear." Two years later, he was one of twenty-three black students in Yale's freshman class, the most, by far, in history. The following year, in the first class chosen by Inky Clark, there were thirty-five. Many of them, like Hill, were the first in their family to attend college. Hill's four years at Riverdale had helped ease his transition, but for some the adjustment to Yale proved too abrupt; 35 percent of African-Americans in Clark's first class did not return after their freshman year.

Perhaps even more than Harvard, Yale could be an uncomfortable place for young African-Americans. Although the number of black students was increasing, its first black professor, a biochemist, hadn't been hired until 1966, and its curriculum was, as one student put it, "lily-white." It was a place where casual racism was embedded in the institution, in some cases literally: where a stained-glass window in the common room of Calhoun College depicted a shackled slave kneeling before John C. Calhoun, the 1804 Yale graduate and virulent secessionist who had declared that slavery improved black people "not only physically but morally and intellectually"; where a courtyard surrounded by low, whitewashed buildings in Hill's own college, Pierson—an otherwise elegant Georgian brick edifice—was known as "slave quarters"; where a course on the history of African-American music was commonly referred to, without a blink, as "Coons and Tunes"; and where black students were routinely asked by security guards to show identification before entering the colleges, even their own, while white students were never asked.

In his freshman year, Hill joined the newly formed Yale Discussion Group on Negro Affairs, whose initial deliberations largely
centered on how to improve its members' social lives at the all-male
school. The following year, renamed the Black Student Alliance
at Yale (BSAY), it began pressing the administration for change.
Like John Tyson, his friend at Harvard, Hill got involved. He
volunteered as a mentor to black students in New Haven, and was
often seen around campus in the company of his admiring young
mentees. He became a counselor for Transitional Year, a new Yale
program in which promising students from underperforming high
schools around the country spent a year in New Haven, taking
classes to help them get admitted to top colleges. He took part in a
BSAY-sponsored boycott of classes that protested the university's
insensitivity to the black community surrounding it, a community
that had boiled over in anger in the summer of 1967 and, again,
after Martin Luther King's assassination. In May 1968, he helped
out at a BSAY-sponsored symposium at Yale at which more than a
hundred educators from thirty-five colleges unanimously endorsed
the creation of black studies programs. (Prodded by BSAY, Yale
would become the first Ivy League institution to offer a major in
Afro-American Studies, in the fall of 1969.) Hill had realized while
visiting UCLA during his college search that recruits at big-time
football schools did little else but play football. He had chosen Yale
in part because that's not what he wanted. In fact, he later told a
friend that during his junior year at Yale he had been tempted to
quit football, because there were so many more important things
that needed attention.

* * *

Returning from the concussion he sustained in the opening game
of the 1968 season, Hill had one of the finest days of his career
against Brown, catching three passes for 137 yards and two touch-

downs, rushing eight times for 36 yards, and throwing a 14-yard scoring pass to Weinstein. The *Yale Daily News* observed that in his senior season Hill seemed to be running with greater authority. "By the third quarter nobody wants to hit him," said backup fullback Buzzy Potts. Each week, more scouts were showing up to watch the player the *New York Times* called "the Ivy League version of O. J. Simpson." The prospect of playing professional football seemed increasingly realistic. (That summer Hill had received one of the highest scores ever recorded on the intelligence test given by the Dallas Cowboys to prospective draftees.) Hill no longer thought of the NFL as a way station en route to Union Theological Seminary. But he still hoped to be chosen by a team in a city with a divinity school so he could attend classes at night. Though he wasn't planning on becoming a minister, he wanted to continue his theological education, believing that the church was the single most influential institution in the struggle for racial justice. He was taking as many courses in African-American history as he could. He was a member of DKE and had been tapped for St. Elmo, a secret society. He continued to make time for his work with children; after each game at the Bowl, it was common to see the massive halfback carrying youngsters on his shoulders or letting them try on his helmet. The young man for whom Coffin and King were role models had become a role model himself.

* * *

Having won thirteen straight games—at the time, the longest major college winning streak in the nation—Yale was beginning to attract notice beyond the Northeast. Its November 2 game against Dartmouth would be televised as ABC's "Game of the Week"; the network was sending its top college football play-by-play man, Chris Schenkel, just back from covering the Mexico City Olympics. Before the kickoff, Old Blues across the country had the thrill of seeing Dowling, Hill, and the rest of Yale's offense introduced on screen, each stepping forward as the announcer called his name. (*At left half, number 30, Calvin Hill.*) They would not see an incident that took place off camera a few minutes later, during the national anthem, when, seventeen days after Tommie Smith and John Carlos shocked the world on the medal stand in Mexico City, two African-American cheerleaders bowed their heads and raised their own black-gloved fists on the Yale sideline. Some of the 50,306 spectators at the Bowl, however, did. In a letter to the *Yale Alumni Magazine*, an outraged alumnus from the class of 1909 called the protest "disgraceful" and urged that the cheerleaders be expelled from the college.

Yale was favored by two touchdowns, but Dartmouth, smarting from last year's 56–15 humiliation (and stung by its loss to Harvard the previous Saturday), was primed for revenge. Adding to Cozza's concern, it was the week of midterms; each day on the bus to practice, the players' noses were buried in books.

Cozza need not have worried. By the time the slaughter was over, Yale had rolled to its fourteenth straight victory, 47–27. If the defense was erratic, the offense more than made up for it, amassing twenty-nine first downs and 561 yards. Hill rushed twenty-two times for 92 yards and a touchdown, completed two of four passes for 8 yards and a touchdown, and caught five Dowling passes for 122 yards and a touchdown. Dowling threw for 295 yards and three touchdowns, setting a Yale single-game record for total offense. (One of his only hiccups occurred before kickoff, when, for the first time that season, he lost the coin toss.) After the game, Bob Blackman came to the Yale locker room to shake Dowling's hand. "You are a great player and I want you to know how much I admire you," he said. Of Hill, Blackman observed, "He must be regarded as the most dangerous back in the history of the Ivy League." That week, Yale made its first appearance in the national rankings, placing sixteenth in the UPI Top Twenty, just ahead of Alabama and Nebraska.

*   *   *

As the Ivy League season passed the halfway point, the biggest question was whether anyone could slow down Yale's offense, which was even more potent than it had been the previous year. Sportswriters strained for ever-more-effusive superlatives: "terrifying," "stupefying," "as awesome as an Apollo launch." After beating Dartmouth, Yale ranked third in the nation in total offense, with 456 yards a game. It was fourth in scoring, with 36 points a game—a pace that tested the mettle of even the hardiest Old Blues. "We like to celebrate every Yale touchdown with a little nip," an alumnus told Charley Loftus. "But at this year's pace, you could get bombed by halftime." And the senior-laden unit did it all with a calm, confident, business-as-usual attitude. During pregame drills, most football teams engaged in a histrionic display of screaming, headbutting, and shoulder-pad pounding to work themselves into the proper state of ferocity. "When we were warming up, you would see the other team ranting and raving," Cozza recalled. "Our team looked like it was half asleep. I didn't know if they were ready to play." Then the game began, and Yale would dominate.

The lion's share of the yardage was provided by Dowling and Hill, who, over the years, had developed a connection on the field that Hill later likened to that of jazz musicians. "If one started to improvise," he said, "the other knew exactly what to do." Although Dowling received most of the publicity (it was always "Dowling and Hill," not "Hill and Dowling"), Hill never seemed to resent it. "If there was one thing that eased the bitterness of not being the quarterback, it was Brian," Hill told *Sports Illustrated* years later. "When you consider what was going on around him, you couldn't ask for a more super person." Their backgrounds were markedly different, but they were both low-key, self-effacing people who wore the mantle of stardom gracefully. They became friends, sharing a motel room for away games. Asked about Dowling's godlike qualities, Hill quipped, "I room with the guy on road trips and he certainly *seems* mortal."

* * *

"D plus H plus 20" was Yale's winning formula, according to one sportswriter. But even if D and H had been subtracted from the equation, the Yale offense might have dominated. Fullback Bob Levin was a punishing blocker and short-yardage runner; Nick Davidson was a speedy, shifty halfback who had overcome a propensity to fumble and become a dangerous runner and a reliable receiver. In Bruce Weinstein and Del Marting, Yale had the biggest and best pair of ends in the league—as well as the ones who, not all that long ago, might have been voted least likely to succeed. As a soft-spoken high school sophomore, Weinstein had found one-on-one blocking drills with juniors and seniors so frightening he asked his mother to call the coach and say he had a stomachache and couldn't come to practice. Now he was more than a little frightening himself. At six feet five, 240 pounds, "The Tree," as sportswriters called him, had become such a devastating blocker and sure-handed receiver that in its 1968 college football preview issue *Street & Smith's* had called the All-Ivy end Yale's top pro prospect.

As a Yale freshman, Marting had spent an inordinate amount of time on midweek excursions to women's colleges and Manhattan clubs with his Exeter buddies. Languishing on fifth string, he'd grown so demoralized that on his way to one game, unsure whether he'd play or not, he had stopped by the Haunt Club, an undergraduate drinking organization, and partaken liberally of a potent vodka-and-grape-juice concoction called Purple Passion. He ended up playing—and surviving—but didn't catch a pass all season. After an end-of-season pep talk by Cozza, he rededicated himself to the game and to his studies. Last year, as a junior, the six-foot-two, 210-pounder had caught a modest eleven passes, but the eleventh, the 66-yard touchdown bomb that won the Harvard game, had taken its place, alongside Albie Booth's dropkick that spoiled Harvard's undefeated season in 1931, as one of the most famous plays in Yale history. This year, Marting and Weinstein had already combined for thirty-five receptions, 496 yards, and eight touchdowns.

Yale's offense was loaded with stars, but their stardom depended on the Toads, as the hulking players on the interior line were known. The largest and most eminent Toad was the six-foot-four, 235-pound right tackle Kyle Gee, who, along with Weinstein, was the only player allowed *two* cans of Nutrament, the high-calorie drink that constituted a Yale player's lunch on game day. A starter since sophomore year, Gee was acknowledged to be the finest offensive tackle in the league. (On a double team, he and Weinstein formed an all-but-impenetrable wall of nearly 500 pounds.) The garrulous, curly-haired Virginian was also the resident wit on offense, liable to disarm the huddle at any moment with a wry aperçu. George Bass, a chess-playing, stamp-collecting, Lutheran minister's son from Minnesota, had been a freshman walk-on, but by junior year, fortified by an additional 22 pounds of muscle, he was starting at left tackle. Although just shy of six feet (Gee was always accusing him of standing in a hole), Bass had the ideal shape for an offensive lineman, a healthy portion of his 225 pounds being devoted to his posterior, making him hard to knock off his feet. He attracted less attention than the bigger, faster Gee, but after grading the 1967 Columbia game film, the coaches had given Bass a 92, the highest score they'd ever awarded. At guard, juniors Jack Perkowski and Bart Whiteman were fitting in seamlessly in their first year as starters. Center was manned by six-foot-three, 215-pound Fred Morris, a political science major from Indiana who seemed always to be rushing off to Sterling Library.

Toads toiled in anonymity, noticed only when they made a mistake: giving up a sack or whiffing on a block. The sole people in the stands paying attention to them were their parents and girlfriends. By nature, they tended to be strong, silent types—Gee was the rule-proving exception—willing to labor selflessly for the greater good. Their lone moment of glory came at the end-of-preseason barbecue, when the winner of the unofficial steak-eating contest was, invariably, a Toad. Inside every Toad, however, there was a frustrated skill player struggling to emerge. (Gee had a recurring dream in which he scooped up a Dowling fumble and juked his way into the end zone.) Before each Friday practice, the Toads lived out their fantasies, pretending to be quarterbacks and wide receivers as they threw long bombs, made melodramatic touchdown catches, and called on their coaches to admire their moves. Gee and Bass were always trying to persuade Seb LaSpina, who coached the offense, to let them handle the ball in a game. Indeed, in preseason, they had wheedled him into agreeing that if the team went into the Harvard game undefeated and then secured an insurmountable lead, he'd put them in the backfield and let them run the ball. As the team continued to win, they reminded him of his promise.

Players usually dreaded Sunday nights, when they watched film of the previous day's game, knowing their mistakes would be exposed. ("Let's run it again," a coach might say as he screened the same play over and over, "maybe you'll get him *this* time.") But after the Dartmouth game, when Coach LaSpina ran the film for the offensive line he let it roll without comment. The only sound was the whir of the projector as the players watched play after play in which the line fired out and it was five or ten yards before anyone got a hand on the ball carrier. LaSpina finally spoke. "There's nothing I can say."

*　*　*

The week leading up to the Penn game was unlike any other in Yale's 267-year history. Co-Ed Week had finally come to pass. Seven hundred and fifty students from Wellesley, Vassar, Smith, and nineteen other women's colleges across the Northeast were living in Yale dorms, taking Yale classes, eating in Yale dining halls, and participating in Yale extracurricular activities—from writing for the *Yale Daily News* to cheering at that week's meeting of Football 10a. There were panel discussions on "Exploitation in Ghetto Real Estate Transactions" and "Man and Sex at Yale" (whose provocative if androcentric title lured students of both genders to what was, in fact, a relatively conventional conversation on co-education). There was an "Abe Fortas Film Festival" of allegedly "obscene" movies the Supreme Court justice had ruled were protected by the First Amendment. There were impromptu co-ed games of frisbee and touch football on Old Campus, and late-night bull sessions throughout the residential colleges. There was an Election Day march, sponsored by SDS, to protest the "violent" and "racist" nature of the entire political system and attest that mere voting could not effect sufficiently radical change. (With characteristic Yale politeness, the leaders obtained a parade permit and promised that the demonstrators would stay on the sidewalk.) On Election Night, there were viewing parties in college common rooms, which became increasingly muted as Richard Nixon's win over Hubert Humphrey became inevitable.

Cozza had warned his team not to get distracted. For the most part, the players heeded his warning, though the week got off to an awkward start for Bob Levin. The fullback was among the hundreds of Yale students who had volunteered to give up their rooms for the guests. He had, however, neglected to inform his girlfriend of that fact. So when Meryl Streep drove down from Vassar for a surprise visit and walked in just as Levin was showing his room to a young woman from Smith, it took some fast talking to explain the situation. (Levin managed to find other lodgings for the Smithie.) In that week's installment of *bull tales*, B.D. is startled to hear giggles coming from the huddle. *"Now, hold on!"* he says. *"Girls in our classes and rooms is one thing, but a girl in my huddle is quite another!"* More laughter, as a bra and panties are flung in the air. In the last panel, as the bra settles on his head and a bare leg extends above the huddle, B.D. turns to the reader with a look of resignation and says, *"This is going to be a very long week."*

At the end of that long week, Yale was still standing. There were no untoward incidents other than a few stray catcalls early on, though the *Yale Daily News* apparently concluded that only the most attractive female students were newsworthy enough to have their photos in the paper, and it ran an ad for Quality Grocery barbecued chicken that instructed: "Keep Co-Ed Week alive . . . Take a chick back to your room!" Many of the visitors commented on the courtliness of their hosts, who stood up when they entered a classroom and helped them on and off with their coats. "I must say I'm not used to being treated by guys at Harvard with the kind of deference I get from men at Yale," said a Radcliffe student, not unhappily. Although several curmudgeonly professors (and a few curmudgeonly students) grumbled about the corruption of Yale's educational mission, the vast majority of Yalies viewed the week as an unalloyed triumph. On Wednesday evening, the Yale band, playing "Bulldog" and "Down the Field," led a group of 750 male and female students across the campus to the president's house to demand co-education at Yale. Brewster came to the front steps and, speaking through a megaphone handed to him by a Yale cheerleader, promised that the college would be co-ed by 1972. "NEXT FALL!" chanted the crowd. "NEXT FALL!"

On November 9, one day after Co-Ed Week ended, on the morning of the Penn game, the Yale Corporation approved Brewster's proposal to admit five hundred women in the fall of 1969.

*   *   *

Penn played Yale more closely than most teams that season—Yale fumbled two punts and led only 16–0 at the half—but even then, the outcome was never in doubt. The final score was 30–13. The defense turned in their strongest effort of the season, intercepting four passes, stopping the Quakers three times inside the Yale twenty, and shutting them out until the fourth quarter. After the game, the Penn coach said Yale's defense was as good as Harvard's.

Dowling had a routinely impressive day, setting, along the way, the Yale record for total offense in a season. Hill broke the hundred-yard barrier at last, running for 126 yards on nineteen carries. He also caught two passes for 77 yards. On one, he seemed to combine the talents of Nagurski and Nijinsky. Seeing that a Dowling bomb was falling short and in danger of being intercepted, Hill outleaped a Penn defender, tipped the ball in the air with one hand, snared it with the other, came back to earth, knocked the defender flat, and outraced Penn's fastest defensive back to the end zone. The following day, a Philadelphia newspaper devoted the better part of a page to a sequence of photos illustrating the play.

In the fourth quarter, a frustrated Penn linebacker piled on Dowling after the whistle. On his next carry, Hill slammed into two Penn defenders and carried them into the end zone on a 15-yard touchdown run. "I could have cut to my left and gone in, but I was so ticked off I put my head down," said Hill after the game. "I'm a nonviolent person, but there are times . . ."

There was general agreement that it had been Hill's finest game in a Yale uniform.

VIII

Coming Home

Halloween had come and gone. A football season that had started in stultifying end-of-summer heat now shivered in the chill of early November. The breeze off the Charles that had been a balm during two-a-days had become a dreaded blast, little tempered by the plywood walls that had been erected around the practice field to defend against it. Harvard Stadium, its concrete flanks veined with leafless ivy, looked exposed and vulnerable. Daylight savings had ended, the clock on Dillon Field House had been turned back, and the lights were on when practice began at five. The ground was as brown as a potato, and so hard that when you hit it, it seemed to hit back. It was the time of year when the Californians on the team wondered why they'd gone to college in New England.

*   *   *

Pat Conway was beginning to think that safety might be his natural position. His athleticism had never been in doubt—against Columbia, he had picked off a pass while lying on his back—but by now he knew the system so well that he was able to play on instinct. When he heard a teammate shout "Go east," he no longer had to conjure up the North Pole. Conway had a knack for making the big play—he led the team in interceptions, with four—and his hits were the kind that made opposing receivers hesitate before they ventured across the middle. It was a common sight to see Conway leave his feet to plant his helmet in a ball carrier's chest. Spearing, it was called, because the body, launched headfirst toward its target, resembled a spear in flight. All the players were taught the technique—"put a helmet on him!" the coaches yelled—but Conway's reckless disregard for his own body made him an artist of the form. To cornerback Rick Frisbie, the sight of Conway flying through the air, nearly horizontal, en route to a ball carrier, brought to mind a fighter jet intercepting the enemy. (In 1976, spearing would be banned by the NCAA because of the number of spinal cord injuries suffered by the spearers.) There were some players—middle guard Mike Georges, for instance—whose love of hitting seemed to spring from some inner well of disquiet or anger. Conway seemed to hit from exuberance. He lived for the perfect tackle, the kind that felt as if you were going right *through* the person, when you could actually hear the whoosh of air leaving the player's lungs. Conway didn't do drugs; hitting was his high. After the Columbia game, in which Conway had unleashed a particularly devastating blow, the Columbia backfield coach, showing film of the game to his team, ran the play over and over, saying, "*That's* the way we want you to play football—*hit hit hit!*"

Off the field, Conway was also making an impression. Some of the players hadn't known what to expect when they heard about this twenty-four-year-old marine coming back from Vietnam to rejoin the team. They thought he might be a prickly, in-your-face kind of guy. But Conway proved to be easygoing and eager to please—genuinely *nice*. Although he was one of the team's best players, he never bragged. He fit right into the locker room give-and-take, calling the defensive linemen (several of whom were premed) big dumb animals, and warning them not to let any ball carriers past them, lest he have to make a tackle and get his uniform dirty. His teammates kidded him back, calling him the

Old Man, telling him he was the oldest rookie in college football. To his fellow defensive backs, Conway was like an older brother. They looked up to him—because of his age, because of his talent, because he'd fought in Vietnam, and, perhaps most of all, because he'd stood up to their overbearing position coach, Loyal Park.

It happened at practice the week after the Bucknell game, in which Conway had injured his ribs returning a punt. The X-rays were negative, but each time Conway hit the ground during tip drill, in which Park threw the ball just out of reach of a diving defensive back, his chest felt as if it had been struck by lightning. The next day Conway went to Park before practice and told him he could participate in everything but tip drill. Park said okay. That afternoon the team didn't look sharp and the coaches made the players do some extra hitting. Before they started, Park pointedly announced, "Pat, you come over here and stand on the sideline. We wouldn't want you to get *hurt.*" Park was an excellent coach, but he played favorites and wore people down with his bullying tactics. No one dared challenge him, however, because those who displeased him soon found themselves on the bench. As Park continued to belittle him in front of his teammates, Conway, who prided himself on always giving his best, finally exploded. Park yelled back and the two of them nearly came to blows. The other defensive backs were shocked and impressed. Conway's status as hero was cemented. From then on, Conway and Park got along fine. After the season, a second set of X-rays would reveal that Conway had played much of the year with two broken ribs.

Conway never talked about Vietnam unless someone asked, and his teammates were nervous about bringing it up. But sometimes at night, after a few beers, one of the players would ask him what it had been like over there. Conway stuck mostly to the lighter stuff, like the time he and his men were on maneuvers and, hearing a rustle in the jungle, he had called in artillery fire. The next day, several Vietnamese peasants had walked into camp, pulling a wooden cart on which lay a dead water buffalo—the water buffalo whose movements Conway had mistaken for the enemy, and for which its owners now demanded compensation. Conway told his teammates that the water buffalo was his "only confirmed kill." But he also told them about the night at Khe Sanh when a mortar round had buried him upside down. He told them about the fragging at Camp Carroll, in which a grunt had pulled a pin on a grenade and rolled it under his sleeping officer's cot. Conway's teammates were riveted. While they'd been sweating over a Hum 3 essay on Sophocles, Conway had been engaging in firefights with the Vietcong. Even guys like Rick Berne, who were out demonstrating against the war, were awed. Conway's stories didn't change Berne's conviction that the war was wrong, but he had new respect for those who were fighting it. If anything, it made him even more determined to help end the war and bring men like Conway home.

Conway didn't tell them about lying in his foxhole at Khe Sanh and shaking with fear as the mortar rounds got closer and closer. He didn't tell them about hearing the movements of North Vietnamese soldiers beyond the wire and being terrified that this would be the night they launched an all-out assault. He didn't like going anywhere near those memories. Better, he told himself, to keep them in a box with the lid shut tight.

*   *   *

Pat Conway grew up in Haverhill, an old mill town on the Merrimack River north of Boston. At the turn of the twentieth century, the "Queen Slipper City," as Haverhill was known, produced one-tenth of all the shoes made in the United States. By the time Conway was born, in 1944, the shoe factories were empty hulks and, like Lawrence and Lowell, its larger, more celebrated neighbors upriver, Haverhill was struggling. Football remained a chief source of civic pride, however, and the Conways were a football family. Pat's father, who ran a small welding company, had started at guard for Haverhill High before playing semipro football and a game or two for the Providence Steam Rollers, an early NFL team. All three of his sons would be named All-State; all three would play in college; one would play in the pros.

Conway was seven when he started tagging along behind his older brother to a neighbor's yard for marathon games of tackle without pads. The other kids were all five or six years older and they made Conway play center on offense, telling him to hike the ball and then get in someone's way. On defense, they put him on the line. When the twelve- and thirteen-year-olds came at him, Conway hurled himself at them headfirst. "Look at Patty Conway," the other kids said. "He can tackle!" Conway got creamed but never let on how much it hurt. By the time his brother left for Princeton—the first in the family to go to college—and Pat was playing with kids his own age, he had become a very good football player. In his senior year at Haverhill High he scored seventeen touchdowns, five of them in one game, and was named a *Sporting News* second team All-American. Recruited by a host of colleges, Conway had his heart set on Notre Dame, one of the best teams in the country, and Catholic to boot. The Fighting Irish coach flew him out to South Bend—Conway's first trip on an airplane—and offered him a full scholarship. But his mother wanted him closer to home, and when John Yovicsin drove up to Haverhill and took Conway and his father to lunch at the fanciest restaurant in town, Conway reconsidered. It was already a week after applications were due, but Yovicsin told him not to worry—just fill out the application, send it to him, and he'd walk it over to the admissions office himself. His parents thought the transition from Haverhill to Harvard might be too abrupt, so Conway took a PG year at Exeter and arrived at Harvard in the fall of 1963.

Conway's admission to Harvard seemed something of a miracle, given that many people, Conway most of all, had worried that he'd never make it through high school. He had been in second grade when his teacher realized that he couldn't read. There followed countless Saturday mornings with a reading specialist and a seemingly never-ending series of tests with a psychologist. One day, his parents sat him down in the living room—a sure sign that something was seriously wrong—and told him he had something called *dyslexia.* Conway had never heard of it. It sounded like the name of an incurable disease, some form of cancer perhaps. His mother explained: when he looked at a word, his brain sometimes reversed the letters. The good news was that dyslexia was manageable. He just had to work extra hard.

Unlike Alex MacLean, Conway told no one that he was dyslexic. (He wouldn't tell his wife or his children until he was in his fifties.) At the time, dyslexia was considered something to be ashamed of. If you had difficulty reading—the term "learning disability" had not yet been coined—your classmates (and, sometimes, your teachers) assumed that you were "slow." But Conway found that as long as he went over his work four or five times, he could manage. Reading aloud, however, filled him with terror. When he was senior-class president at Haverhill High and had to read announcements in front of the entire school, he'd hole up in a corner, sweating with anxiety, repeating the words over and over to himself till he practically had them memorized. Throughout his life, Conway would be motivated by the fear that he wasn't as smart as other people. He'd joke about being a dumb jock, but he was determined not to be one. Every night in high school, he came home right after practice, ate his dinner, and went straight to his room to study. Each year he worried that he wouldn't get promoted to the next grade. In fact, he was named to the National Honor Society in his junior year.

*   *   *

Conway became the third sophomore ever to start an opening game under Yovicsin. But he wasn't taking his academics as seriously as his football. Instead of working extra hard, to compensate for his dyslexia, as he had in high school, he was staying up late shooting the bull with his roommates. Conway wasn't much of a drinker—his buddies called him a "two-beer screamer" because it took so little to get him buzzed—but when his friends urged him to put down the books and go for double cheeseburgers at Charlie's Kitchen, he found it hard to say no. Like many of them, he began sleeping in, skipping classes, and not paying enough attention when he did show up. But while his friends could do their work at the last minute and still manage a B, if Conway fell behind he couldn't read fast enough to catch up.

Spring term, sophomore year, Conway had a paper due for Fine Arts 13, a popular survey course commonly known as "Darkness at Noon" (the students met at 12 p.m. in the basement of the Fogg Museum and looked at slides). It was Conway's favorite course, and he enjoyed researching the paper—riding his motor scooter around Harvard and taking notes on architectural details. After writing it, Conway, on his way to the hospital to get his tonsils out, asked his roommate, who was in his section, to turn it in. When Conway got out of the hospital, he and his roommate were summoned by their Quincy House master, who pointed out that their essays were strikingly similar. Realizing that his roommate must have copied his work, Conway tried to cover for him by saying they had studied the buildings together. Unbeknownst to Conway, however, his roommate had already confessed. The master told Conway he admired him for sticking up for his friend, but the motto of the college was *Veritas*. Conway was put on probation. His scholarship was taken away and he was forbidden to play football.

That fall, Conway was a lost soul. Ever since he was seven, September had meant football. Now, instead of spending afternoons at practice, he worked in the field house, handing out T-shirt-sock-and-jock rollups to his former teammates and lugging balls and clocks here and there for intramural football games. He sat in the stands on Saturdays, but it was painful to watch when he knew he should be out on the field. Though he had more free time,

The Game

Conway found it hard to focus on his studies. He procrastinated and fell even further behind. At the last minute, with a history paper due, he resorted to plagiarism himself—only a page, and only once, but he felt he'd fatally compromised the ethical standards by which he'd been raised. He decided to leave school before he was asked to leave. In January 1966, filled with shame and self-doubt, he went home to Haverhill.

* * *

Conway knew that without his student deferment he was certain to be drafted, and if he was drafted he was almost certain to end up in Vietnam. He hadn't really given the war much thought, but he'd been brought up to believe in his country, and his country said that unless it stopped the spread of communism in Vietnam, the rest of Southeast Asia would fall: the domino theory. It wasn't that he *wanted* to go to Vietnam, but if he had to go, he might as well go on his own terms. He drove down to the Haverhill Post Office, where the service branches had recruiting stations. After talking with an Army sergeant about becoming a helicopter pilot, Conway looked in the doorway of the next office, where a crisply dressed marine sat behind a desk. "Is the Marine Corps supposed to be good?" asked Conway, whose knowledge of the Corps derived primarily from John Wayne movies. The man looked up at him with a little grin that seemed to say, "You think you're tough—but you're not a *marine*." Conway was annoyed. "This sonofabitch thinks he's better than me," he thought. "Well, if he can do it, I can."

Three weeks later, while his Harvard classmates were in Cambridge picking their spring-term classes, Conway was in South Carolina, standing in line with seventy other recruits at Parris Island, his head shaved, his body achy with injections, his shoulders bending under a duffel stuffed with gear, while a sergeant screamed in his ear that he was nothing but a maggot.

Conway had chosen the Marines because it was said to be

the roughest, toughest branch of the services. He knew he had screwed up badly at Harvard. He felt he had disappointed himself and everyone who cared about him. "I chose the Corps because I wanted to get my ass kicked," he would say many years later. "I needed that hurt. I needed to be punished for the mistakes I had made."

Conway's desire to atone drove him throughout his time in the service. He was an honor graduate out of Parris Island, one of the top five in his platoon. He made corporal in eleven months. Because of a bureaucratic error, however, he was left behind when the men with whom he had trained were shipped off to Vietnam. By the time the paperwork was straightened out, Conway had ten months left in his enlistment, and Vietnam was a thirteen-month tour. He was already seeing men from his platoon coming back wounded or in body bags, and he felt guilty he hadn't been with them. He requested permission to be sent to Vietnam. His captain told him he was crazy—he didn't *have* to go. But at a time when most of his Harvard classmates were turning themselves inside out to avoid Vietnam, Conway was determined to get there. In July 1967, a helicopter dropped him off at Phu Bai, a combat base just south of Hué.

*   *   *

Conway spent his first four months leading a fifteen-man squad on patrols in the A Shau Valley, a key entry point along the Ho Chi Minh Trail, down which North Vietnam ferried troops and supplies to the south. He had completed a week of jungle training at Camp Pendleton before shipping out, but it hadn't come close to preparing him for the real thing: the scorching heat during the day; the bitter cold at night; the elephant grass that left his body covered with pus-filled cuts; the buffalo-fouled streams from which he and his men were forced to fill their canteens; the monsoon rains that left them walking across rice paddies in water up to their hips and sleeping in puddles so deep that only the rifles on their chests stayed dry; the days at a time they went without food because resupply helicopters were unable to fly, days in which he'd see his men exhale their cigarette smoke and then, craving any kind of nourishment, suck it back in again; and, above all, the strange rhythm of war in which he and his men could go for weeks without encountering the enemy and then suddenly find themselves in a firefight that lasted thirty seconds but seemed an eternity—seconds so adrenalized it seemed to Conway as if his blood were literally boiling.

In November, shortly before his old football team ended the 1967 season with its thrilling 24–20 near-upset of Yale, Conway and his squad were sent to Khe Sanh, a Marine combat base in the northwest corner of the country, just south of the demilitarized zone. For nearly two months, there was little to do but settle in: fill sandbags, dig foxholes and trenches, lay down perimeter wire, stake out machine gun placements, establish interlocking fields of fire. Occasionally they'd go on patrol, but there was plenty of down time. Conway wrote to his Quincy House master, asking whether he could come back to school for the spring term—perhaps the only Harvard application letter that year to arrive smudged by the red clay of Vietnam. A month later, he received a reply on official Harvard stationery, inviting him to return. Conway put in for an early discharge so he could be there when classes began in February. But by the time the paperwork came through, the siege of Khe Sanh had begun, and the Marines needed all the bodies they could get.

The American military had been aware that North Vietnamese soldiers were massing in the jungle around the base. By mid-January, the 6,000 marines at Khe Sanh were surrounded by as many as 30,000 NVA troops. On January 21, 1968, those troops began shelling the base with an almost continuous barrage of artillery, mortar, and rocket fire. Even on days when the rain and fog cleared enough for planes to fly, NVA mortar fire trained on the airstrip made taking off and landing perilous. After a C-130 transport plane was blown up on the runway, killing eight Americans, the airstrip was almost always closed. At that point, even if his commanding officer had permitted him to return to Harvard, Conway wouldn't have been able to get out. Supplies had to be parachuted in on pallets, but only a fraction of the 185 tons of food, water, and ammunition needed to sustain the base each day got through. By early February, the base looked as if it had been hit by a cyclone: caved-in buildings, stumps that had once been trees, shrapnel-riddled fragments of jeeps and trucks. The field hospital where Conway had spent a week at Christmas sweating out a bout of malaria had been leveled. He and his fellow marines were forced to spend much of their time underground.

At the same time, the marines were returning fire with outgoing artillery, and Phantom jets from bases farther south were strafing enemy positions or dropping canisters of napalm that sent orange fireballs billowing into the sky—sometimes so close that Conway could feel the heat. Some nights, the ground shuddered and the surrounding hills erupted in explosions so massive that Conway and his men knew that, miles overhead, B-52 bombers from Guam had dropped their payloads. When Conway, a devout Catholic, read from the pocket Bible the Marines had issued him in boot camp, he often found himself turning to Revelation. Its predictions of the world coming to an end in an apocalypse of fire seemed almost credible.

Hunkered down on their two-square-mile base, Conway and his fellow marines felt like sitting ducks. Every so often, an NVA sniper picked off a man who had stuck his head above the sandbags at the wrong time, or a seemingly random mortar round found a target. One evening, Conway was in the trench line when a round landed just down the way; his face and arms were spattered with bits of warm flesh from a marine who had been less lucky. A few weeks later, while Conway was on the radio calling his superiors about some incoming fire, he was hit in the hand by shrapnel.

It was the second time he'd been wounded, and, like the first, he brushed it off as a "ticky-tack" injury. But if he hadn't been holding the phone to his ear, he might have lost an eye. Conway tried not to think about getting hit, because if you thought about it too much, you could become paralyzed by fear. Still, he couldn't forget the night NVA soldiers had overrun the marines on Hill 64, an outpost beyond the wire several hundred yards from Conway's position. For several hours, he and his men, unable to fire because in the darkness and fog they'd be just as likely to hit their fellow marines, had listened helplessly to the screaming and sobbing of the wounded. In the morning, trucks had driven out to retrieve the injured and the dead. Twenty-seven marines had been killed.

Night was the most terrifying. Sometimes the monsoon fog rolled in so thick that a man could get lost taking a leak five yards from his foxhole. Continuous mortar fire from the surrounding hills made it almost impossible to sleep. It was an unnerving sound: the distant boom as the shell left its tube, the attenuated whistle as it arced toward its target, the eerie second or two of silence as it reached its apogee, then the ear-splitting explosion. The NVA systematically worked the perimeter all night long, starting far to the left of Conway's position, then coming twenty yards closer, then twenty yards closer—until you knew the next one might land in your lap and you had to hustle underground. The next round would be twenty yards to your right, then forty, then sixty, and so on, until they reached the far end of the base. And then they'd turn around and start back toward you.

Conway learned to read the mortar rounds, to tell by the pitch of the whistle where each one might fall. But it was an inexact science. One night Conway's radio man called out "Incoming!" and it sounded as though the round might land right on top of them. They jumped into their foxhole and made themselves as small as possible. When the round hit, Conway was tossed in the air. He ended up upside down, buried in dirt and debris. After digging himself out, he asked his radio man, "Are you all right?" Conway realized he couldn't hear himself speak. He thought he had lost his voice; then, seeing his radio man move his lips, he realized he had lost his hearing. It would be several minutes before it came back.

The men's biggest fear was of an all-out ground assault by the soldiers who surrounded the base, hidden under thick mist and layers of green jungle. Every so often, there were rumors that tonight was the night. Conway knew how close the enemy had come. On patrol before the siege began, he had fallen into a bamboo-camouflaged spider hole less than two hundred yards from the base; fortunately, its occupants had either abandoned it or been elsewhere at the time. At night, Conway and his men could occasionally hear them out there: the revving of an engine, the singsong of Vietnamese voices, the rustle of soldiers on the move. They knew that at any moment, 30,000 enemy troops might pour across the line, and all that lay between them was a wall of sandbags, three strands of razor wire, and a bed of Claymore mines.

One morning, several bulldozers appeared and began pushing the soil behind Conway and his men into berms. A few days later, two tanks rolled up and rested their barrels on the berms, aiming directly over Conway's squad. Conway knew the tanks were equipped with flechette rounds—shells packed with steel darts that fanned out like pellets from a shotgun. If the tanks fired on the advancing enemy, their flechettes couldn't help hitting Conway and his men, too. That night, Conway and three of his men broke into the ammo dump and brought their squad as many grenades, mines, and rounds of ammunition as they could carry. But he knew that no matter how much they took, they'd never have enough.

When Conway signed up for the Marines the possibility of dying hadn't entered his mind, but that night he couldn't think about anything else. He knew that if the NVA launched an all-out attack, his unit would be overrun. He was so frightened he couldn't stop shaking. Conway thought about purgatory, the intermediate realm in which Catholics atone for their venial sins before they enter the kingdom of heaven. He looked up at the night sky, and found himself praying: "God, if this is my time, let this be my purgatory." The supplication calmed him; he found that his fear had eased. He thought of the old expression about making peace with one's maker. Perhaps that is what he had done. Then Conway thought of his men. If *he* had felt that scared, what must they be feeling? For the next hour, timing his moves between incoming mortar rounds, Conway scurried from foxhole to foxhole, talking to each of his men in turn, asking them how their parents were, how their girlfriend was, what they would do when they got home— just trying to get everyone's minds off what lay beyond the wire. Knowing his men were depending on him to keep it together helped him keep it together.

Conway had no idea that back in the States, Khe Sanh had become one of the biggest stories of the war. It was a delicate time; nine days after the North Vietnamese began shelling Khe Sanh, they had launched the Tet Offensive, a massive surprise attack on hundreds of cities, towns, and military bases extending all the way to Saigon. Americans were beginning to realize the war was not going as well as their government had led them to believe. President Johnson was terrified that Khe Sanh would become, as he put it, "another damn Dien Bien Phu"—the valley in northwest Vietnam where, in 1954, the Viet Minh had surrounded and forced the surrender of 15,000 French troops, effectively ending French involvement in Indochina. In mid-February, word leaked to the press that the Pentagon was considering using nuclear weapons rather than lose Khe Sanh.

Then one day in early March, eight months after he'd arrived in Vietnam, Conway was told that the runway had been repaired, a plane was coming in, and he had thirty minutes to get his belongings together. Conway crammed his stuff into his duffel, said good-bye to his men, and scrambled aboard the plane, which took off amid a volley of mortar fire. After clearing the plateau, the plane dipped, and Conway had a moment of terror: they were going to crash and he'd never get home. The plane banked and rose. Vietnam fell away beneath him.

When Conway landed at Travis Air Force Base, he was so happy to be back in the United States that he knelt and kissed the tarmac. Still in uniform, he walked outside the gate, where antiwar protestors spat at him.

*　*　*

Conway returned to Harvard determined to leave Vietnam behind. He wanted to be a student again, to be part of the mainstream. He resolved to do well academically, to make amends to all the people he had let down. He went back to the way he'd done things in high school. He made a point of never skipping a class, and each night after football meetings were over, he hurried to Lamont, found an open carrel, put his head down, and studied. He wouldn't cut corners this time. The Bs and Cs of sophomore and junior year became As and Bs. It helped that his old buddies were no longer around to distract him. It helped that he'd been placed in a suite with Gary Singleterry, the team's punter, a Christian Scientist and applied math concentrator who spent a lot of time doing homework. Occasionally, a friend fixed him up on a date, but for the most part, if Conway wasn't at football practice—where he had, indeed, found "his" kind of people—he was sleeping or studying. He wasn't going to screw things up again.

In some ways it was easy to put the war behind him. Only a handful of Harvard students had served in Vietnam, and few people were aware that he was one of them. It comforted him to know that he hadn't lost a single squad member, that he had never given an order that caused the death of one of his men. Some of them had been wounded, but they had all survived. And though he'd been in firefights in which enemy soldiers had been killed, he'd never known whether it was *his* bullet that had done the killing. He felt better not knowing. Conway never mentioned the war to his roommate. Singleterry asked about it once, and though Conway was polite, it was clear he didn't want to talk about it.

But the subject was difficult to avoid. When Conway left Harvard in January 1966, almost as many students supported the war as opposed it. He had returned to a campus where the vast majority of students were passionately against it. Every bulletin board he passed was covered with antiwar literature; he could hardly walk through the Square without being offered an anti-ROTC manifesto. When Conway crossed the Yard on his way to class, he occasionally heard students, standing on the steps of Widener Library, railing against the war through bullhorns. It angered him to hear them chanting, "HO, HO, HO CHI MINH, NLF IS GONNA WIN," while some of his buddies were still over there fighting. In his heart, he believed that most of them were motivated not by idealism but by fear—fear of going to Vietnam and getting shot at. Having been shot at himself, he knew they had good reason to be frightened. Yet it didn't seem right that these Harvard students were able to wriggle out of going when others less savvy, less wealthy, less lucky, had to go in their place. At bottom, he thought the protestors were draft-dodging cowards. But he never stopped to argue with them. He knew they weren't going to convince him of their beliefs and he wasn't going to convince them of his.

As the weather turned colder, Conway wore his green USMC utility jacket with his name stamped on it. It was one of the few things, other than the pieces of shrapnel that had winged him, that he had saved from Vietnam. He wore it because it kept him warm, but also because he was proud of his service and grateful to the Marines for getting him back on track.

*　*　*

Thanks, in part, to Conway, the Harvard defense, which had started out so uncertainly, was proving to be the team's greatest strength. It was something of a hodgepodge. There were returning starters, like John Emery, the defensive captain, and Tom Wynne, the safety from Arkansas who also served as the team's placekicker. (The previous year, Wynne's 51-yard field goal against Columbia had broken a Harvard record set in 1912 by Charlie Brickley, the three-time All-American who, in a publicity stunt to sell war bonds during World War I, dropkicked a football through J. P. Morgan's open office window on Wall Street.) There were seniors who, after several years on JV, were finally getting their chance to play, like Alex MacLean. There were juniors who had taken on larger roles, like John Cramer, the barrel-chested defensive end from Oregon who, after an injury to Pete Hall forced him into the lineup, played so well that he was second on the team in tackles, right behind Emery. And there were sophomores who had played their way into starting jobs, like Gary Farneti, a brash 220-pound high school All-American linebacker from upstate New York who, informed by Yovicsin before the season started that he was needed more at guard, had replied, in no uncertain terms, that he would play linebacker—and, furthermore, that he expected to start. Yovicsin was speechless.

The Harvard defense wasn't big, but it was smart, quick, and aggressive. Rarely were only one or two players in on a tackle; more often there were four, five, or six. In some of the game photos, one could hardly see evidence of the opposing ball carrier under the pile of Crimson defenders. Noting its suffocating effect on opposing offenses, a local newspaper dubbed Harvard's defense the "Boston Stranglers," an allusion to the serial killer who had terrorized the city five years earlier. Going into the Princeton game, Harvard was second in the country in scoring defense, giving up an average of 7.8 points per game. But Princeton, scoring 35.5 points a game, would present the Boston Stranglers with their biggest test thus far.

* * *

As the players entered the dinner line at the Varsity Club, a mimeographed sheet on the bulletin board asked: "When was the last time you beat Princeton?" Everyone knew the answer: not since 1963. The last two defeats had been particularly galling. Two years ago, Harvard had entered the Princeton game undefeated for the first time in forty-four years, and lost 18–14. Last year, Harvard had been humiliated on its home field, 45–6.

No one looked forward to Princeton Week. The Tigers were the only major college football team in the country still using the single wing. Primarily a running formation, the single wing was notorious for its strong-side sweep, a slow-developing play in which blockers accumulated until it could seem to an opposing defensive end as if the entire Princeton team, like an orange-and-black tidal wave, was bearing inexorably down on him. For the players, Princeton Week meant two-and-a-half-hour practices instead of two. For the coaches, it meant drawing up new defensive strategies. "All season long a coaching staff sets up its defenses against air attacks and conventional assaults," explained Harold Kaese in the *Globe*. "Then, suddenly, it is confronted by Hannibal's elephants."

Before the season began, there had been general agreement that Princeton, loaded with talent on both sides of the ball, would battle Yale for the Ivy League championship. But for reasons no one could fathom, Princeton had been wildly erratic; a dominating win over Dartmouth had been followed by losses to Colgate and Penn. Last week, facing Brown, Princeton had won by six touchdowns. Yovicsin worried that Princeton was hitting its stride just in time for Harvard. As it was, Princeton was not only the top rushing team in the Ivies but was second in the nation, behind USC. Although Princeton had lost three games, the oddsmakers—in a nod to Princeton's talent and a tacit acknowledgment that Harvard's unblemished record was still considered something of a fluke—had made Princeton, playing at home, a three-point favorite.

Built in 1914, ivy-covered Palmer Stadium, the second-oldest football stadium in the country after Harvard's, seemed an appropriate setting for what, from the start, was an old-fashioned defensive struggle, a three-yards-and-a-cloud-of-dust game largely played between the thirty-yard lines. There would be fourteen punts in the first half alone, eight by Princeton. The hitting was of biblical ferocity. In the second quarter, Ray Hornblower, speared in the chest, dropped to the ground as if shot. Doctors and trainers rushed to his side. Three decades later, Hornblower was at his thirtieth reunion when an elderly man approached him. He explained that he'd been one of the 1968 team doctors and told Hornblower that the halfback had suffered a "full cardiac arrest" in the Princeton game. The doctors had pounded his chest to revive him; they worried that he wouldn't make it. In the event, Hornblower not only made it but reentered the game two minutes later. At the half, the score was 3–0, Harvard.

Early in the third quarter, Princeton, uncharacteristically, decided to take a chance. Facing fourth and one from their own 49, they went for it. They tried their vaunted strong-side sweep. But cornerback Neil Hurley was able to snag the tailback's jersey and hang on till Conway arrived to stop him short of a first down. On the next play a Lazarus-like Hornblower, on a sweep of his own, ran 42 yards to the Princeton seven. Two plays later, he scored Harvard's only touchdown.

In the fourth quarter, after the Harvard defense forced another punt, Princeton got a break. Hurley, who had blossomed into one of the league's best kick returners—he had run the game's first punt back 47 yards—called for a fair catch. At the last second, he stepped away. The ball took an unruly bounce and grazed his calf. Princeton recovered at midfield. Fourteen methodical plays later, they scored, though even then the Harvard defense was so obdurate that it took the Tigers three tries from the one-foot line to do it. With less than nine minutes remaining, the score was 9–7. Moments later, Princeton was on the march again.

Harvard fans among the 33,874 in attendance felt a sickening sense of déjà vu. The last time Harvard traveled to Palmer Stadium, its undefeated team had led by three points with seven minutes to play, only to lose. Now Princeton was deep in Harvard territory, close enough to try for the winning field goal. Then Berne stopped the tailback a yard behind the line of scrimmage. On third and twelve, MacLean burst up the middle to tackle the tailback for an eight-yard loss, pushing Princeton out of field goal range. (The following morning, a photo of "Alex MacLean and his sidekick Rick Berne," as the caption put it, was published in the New York newspapers. MacLean would give his friend grief for months. "Come 'ere, sidekick," he'd call.)

It was a good day for Pat Conway. His interception in the game's final minute sealed the 9–7 victory.

Now all that lay between Harvard and Yale was Brown.

IX

Most Determined Guy Out There

On the rare occasions he was mentioned in the sports pages, Joseph Philip "J.P." Goldsmith was invariably described as "studious-looking." That was how sportswriters described any athlete who wore glasses, but, in fact, Yale's starting safety wasn't the likeliest of football players. He lacked the easy grace of a Dowling or a Hill. (In one of his "action" publicity photos, he looked as if he were attempting an original and painful midair version of the twist.) He wasn't a punishing hitter. ("I would *negotiate* the runner to the ground," Goldsmith recalled.) But the six-foot, 185-pound defensive back was a sure open-field tackler who was rarely fooled. He was almost always in the right place at the right time. He recognized his limits. He knew it wasn't his job to make the big play that won the game; it was his job not to give up the big play that lost the game, his job not to embarrass himself. In practice, he worked as hard as or harder than anyone else. He knew he had to, just to keep his place on the team. That's the way he went through life, on the field and in the classroom. (The studious-looking Goldsmith *was* studious.) "Most Determined Guy Out There" was the headline on his *Yale Daily News* profile. Goldsmith had always been the most determined guy out there, ever since he'd gone out for the Belle-vue Park Pee Wee football team in Harrisburg, Pennsylvania, a skinny little kid with thick black glasses, desperate to prove he was one of the guys.

* * *

Goldsmith's maternal grandparents had met halfway across the Atlantic, on the boat that brought them from Minsk to Ellis Island. His paternal grandmother had emigrated from Germany; five older siblings who stayed behind died in the Holocaust. J.P. was the only Jew in his high school graduating class of 370. "If anyone gives you any trouble because you're Jewish, let me know," his well-meaning Little League coach told him. No one ever did, but like most skinny little kids with glasses, Goldsmith had always felt different. He longed to have a flat top—the kind of crew cut the cool kids had, in which, with the aid of butch wax, the hair on top stood up straight—but no matter what he did to encourage it, his hair reverted to an unruly curl. He longed to hold his own in playground fights, but once his glasses got knocked off he could hardly see. He longed to be less nervous around girls, but in their presence he couldn't think of anything to say. Deep down, he worried that he wasn't brave enough, tough enough, man enough.

When Goldsmith started playing football, in the sixth grade, he was terrified. But he found out that when he got hit, he didn't die. He learned how to tackle. He learned how to get knocked down and then stand up and get knocked down again. Football was a way of proving himself to himself, and to everyone else. In central Pennsylvania in the late fifties, if you were on the football team, you were somebody.

Goldsmith had another reason for playing football: it was what his father wanted. J.P. revered his father, a gregarious, hardworking man who ran the family furniture store J.P.'s great-grandfather had founded in 1881. (John Yovicsin, who grew up in nearby Steelton, was a customer.) Whatever his father told him to do—get good grades, get a haircut, put on a coat and tie—J.P. did. When J.P.

wanted to quit scouting, his father, a former Eagle Scout, wouldn't let him; J.P. became an Eagle Scout himself. "You push that kid too much," his father's friends told him, but Richard Goldsmith adored his eldest child and only son, and wanted nothing but the best for him. And J.P. wanted nothing more than to win his father's approval.

Richard Goldsmith had never played football—few Jews did—but his years in the marching band at the University of Virginia had given him a passion for the game. Football, it seemed to him, was the quintessential red-blooded American sport. And he dearly wanted his son to be a quintessential red-blooded American boy. He encouraged J.P. to go out for the Pee Wee team, and though he worked long hours at the furniture store, he'd "chuck the pill," as he put it, with him in the backyard whenever he could. In the summer before seventh grade, when J.P. came home from sleep-away camp with a broken left wrist (an awkward landing while high-jumping), his father urged him to go to junior high football tryouts anyway; it would show the coach he had a good attitude. Standing on the sideline in T-shirt and shorts, his left arm in a cast, J.P. couldn't do much except throw the football with his good arm. That's how he became a quarterback. He had a strong arm and he pushed himself. When his high school started a weight program, the skinny Goldsmith became one of its most devoted lifters. At fifteen, he was six feet, 150 pounds; a year later, he was six feet, 185. Each summer, after delivering furniture all day for his father, he'd work out at the high school to prepare for the upcoming season. He knew he wasn't one of those natural athletes who could come in at the last minute and excel; he had to work harder than everyone else just to keep up. His father came to all his games. Sometimes he came to practice, too, setting up a folding lawn chair at the fifty-yard line, sipping iced tea, and cheering on his son.

Senior year, the team went 4–6, but Goldsmith was nominated for the Pennsylvania Big 33, a prestigious all-star team selected by the Harrisburg *Patriot-News*. (His father drove to the high school, knocked on the door of his son's history class, and showed him the newspaper article.) Goldsmith received more than forty scholarship offers, but his father had his heart set on Yale, which like millions of Americans of a certain age, he considered the epitome of manly sophistication. Frank Merriwell had gone there. Heisman Trophy winners Larry Kelley and Clint Frank, the toast of college football during Richard Goldsmith's years in the UVA marching band, had gone there. The presidents of the two Harrisburg banks with whom he did business had gone there. Richard Goldsmith might have liked to go there himself, but it hadn't occurred to him to apply; he assumed that Yale was intellectually and socially above his station. Even had he applied, he would have had difficulty getting in, given that Yale, like Harvard, had an unofficial quota for Jews in the 1930s—a quota that remained in effect until a few years before his son was admitted in 1965.

J.P. himself didn't know much about the place. Indeed, when he toured Ivy League schools with his father, he fell in love with Princeton and its postcard-perfect campus. But Goldsmith, primarily a passer, had no desire to play single wing football. He also liked Harvard, and had an encouraging interview. Coming out into the Square, however, he and his father were approached by a scruffy-looking student who handed them a flyer and invited them to a Socialist Workers Party meeting. The elder Goldsmith, a lifelong Republican, steered his son away, giving him a look that said, "We're not going to go to college *here*, are we?" (Goldsmith didn't even apply.) He made it clear to J.P. that Harvard students were eggheads and free thinkers, whereas Yale students were gentlemen. On their visit to Yale, after touring the campus, he suggested they drive out to the Bowl. One of the gates was open, and they walked onto the field. Goldsmith had never seen anything like it: the Bowl was half again as big as Beaver Stadium, Penn State's home field. Penny loafers sinking into the velvety green turf, Goldsmith began calling signals in front of 70,000 empty seats and one proud father. In his mind's eye, he saw himself throwing the winning touchdown pass against Harvard, on his way to becoming the greatest quarterback in Yale history.

*　　*　　*

Freshman year was one of the worst years of Goldsmith's life. There were 1,054 men in his class at Yale; he was certain he'd been the last one chosen. In high school, he'd been a star, accustomed to getting As on his papers and seeing his name in the sports section. At Yale, he had known he wouldn't be the smartest guy in the classroom, but he was studying harder than he'd ever studied in his life and getting the lowest grades he'd ever gotten. His social confidence was also eroding. Wearing the dress shirts he'd bought three for a dollar at the Gant Washington's Birthday Sale and the olive sport coat he'd gotten hand-me-down from a Harrisburg friend (his roommates dubbed it the Green Hornet), he felt out of place among the Andover grads in white Oxford button-downs, blue blazers, and Bass Weejuns trussed up with athletic tape. Passing the J. Press store on York Street, Goldsmith promised himself that before he graduated from Yale, he would buy something there. On Friday and Saturday nights, everyone around him seemed to be going on dates, whereas even when Goldsmith summoned up the courage to ask a girl at a mixer to dance, as soon as she found out he was a freshman her attention turned elsewhere. It didn't make him feel any better when his high school girlfriend wrote to say she was having the time of her life at Duke.

Everything might have been okay had things gone well on the football field. The game had always been the source of what self-assurance he possessed. But Goldsmith was one of fifteen quarterbacks on the freshman roster, and it was quickly apparent that his plans to be the greatest quarterback in Yale history weren't going to pan out. If anyone on the team was going to fill that role, it would be Brian Dowling. Goldsmith settled in at third-string quarterback and second-string safety.

In early October, Goldsmith got back his first English paper, an essay on Melville's "Bartleby the Scrivener." He had stayed up late, night after night, perfecting it; it was the best paper he'd ever written—indeed, he felt sure it must be one of the finest pieces of expository writing ever written for English 15. He got a 70. Was there *anything* he could do well at Yale? He had never felt so low. That night he called his father and said that maybe Yale wasn't the place for him. He had decided to quit school and join the Army. His father gently told his son it was only freshman year, give it some time, see what happens.

Goldsmith continued to work hard in practice, attend every class, and stay up late studying. His grades inched into the eighties. On the field, he had a brief moment of glory against Columbia when, after Dowling led the team to a big lead, the scrubs were sent in and Goldsmith scored on a rollout. (Hardly had he returned to the sideline when his father appeared, having rushed down from the stands to congratulate him.) He still couldn't buy a date. But his life at Yale, if far from Merriwellian, was becoming tolerable.

At the end of the year, Cozza called Goldsmith into his office. "You have a decision to make," he said. "Do you want to play quarterback or do you want to play football?" He told Goldsmith he had a better chance of getting on the field if he stuck to defensive back. Goldsmith was reluctant to give up his dreams, but he wanted to play. He went home as the third-string safety on the varsity depth chart. That summer, he worked on a track gang for the Pennsylvania Railroad, driving spikes with a twelve-pound sledgehammer, before heading over to his old high school to lift weights. He returned for preseason in the best shape of his life. By then, one of the safeties ahead of him had given up football to concentrate on hockey; the other had flunked out and enlisted in the Marines. When the season opened, Goldsmith was starting.

Goldsmith held on to the job until the seventh game, when he hurt his neck making a tackle against Penn. He was replaced by Ed Franklin, a ferocious hitter who had played for the Tigers of

Massillon, Ohio, the most famous high school football team in the country. In six-plus games, Goldsmith had had no interceptions; in the second half of the Penn game, Franklin had two. Even after he recovered, Goldsmith remained on the bench.

Goldsmith found other ways to contribute. He had always been a team player, brimming with pep, and in the all-male environment of Yale (and without his father around), he had developed a self-deprecating wit that, not incidentally, helped camouflage his lack of self-confidence. His wisecracks made long afternoons at practice seem a little less long, and his locker room impersonations of the coaches kept his teammates in stitches. But he wanted to play.

Senior year, Ed Franklin was needed at cornerback. Goldsmith was once again the starting safety. Except for the rain-soaked Columbia game, when he had slipped in the mud, enabling his man to turn a short pass into a long touchdown, he hadn't embarrassed himself. Indeed, later that game, he had intercepted the great Marty Domres twice, for which he was named Yale Player of the Week by the New Haven Gridiron Club ("They can't give it to Brian *every* week," he told his teammates). Yet even though he was a starter on a team some were calling the best in Yale history, even though he wore the white "Y" patch that indicated he was a two-year letterman on the blue blazer with brass buttons his father had bought him, even though he was one of the best-liked players on the squad, Goldsmith felt he couldn't let down for a second.

His father was there every Saturday, making the five-hour drive from Harrisburg to New Haven and staying at the Three Judges Motor Lodge, where he and J.P. had stayed when they first visited Yale, and which had the benefit of offering a complimentary martini to each guest on arrival. (In four years, his father missed only one game: sophomore year, when J.P.'s first varsity start happened to fall on Yom Kippur. "You play, I'll pray," he told his son.) On the day of the game, Richard Goldsmith always got to the Bowl an hour early and positioned himself over the tunnel through which the Yale players went on and off the field—exactly where Kingman

Brewster would sit an hour later. As the team returned to the squad room after warm-ups, he'd look for his son and, according to their unspoken ritual, J.P. would give him a thumbs-up, whereupon his father returned the gesture.

Off the field, too, Goldsmith was thriving. He had been named toastmaster at Book and Snake, his secret society. He was on the Dean's List and felt secure enough to skip an occasional class. By now, in the interest of rounding out his Yale education, he had even partaken of a joint or two, though never, of course, during football season. And after several years of romantic futility—his inability to find a date for Prom had become a standing joke among his roommates—he finally had a girlfriend, a sophomore from Manhattanville College of the Sacred Heart he'd met at a mixer junior year. Goldsmith, in tails borrowed from a prep school friend's father, had taken her to Prom last spring. On Saturday nights that fall, celebrating yet another Yale victory, they danced to soul bands at DKE. ("Jews got rhythm," J.P. joked.) Goldsmith was beginning to feel like a Yale man. The following June, a week before graduation, he would walk into J. Press and purchase a bow tie, Yale blue with white polka dots.

*   *   *

J. P. Goldsmith wasn't the only player on the Yale defense with something to prove. End Pat Madden had spent much of his life trying to convince coaches that he wasn't too skinny to play football. The eldest of nine children, the son of a Sears repairman, Madden grew up in Mingo Junction, Ohio (pop. 4,987), a failing steel-and-coal town in the Ohio River Valley, a region that was to football what the Tigris and Euphrates valleys were to agriculture. In four years at Yale, no matter how much he ate, the six-foot-two Madden had never managed to break the 175-pound barrier. "When you look at him, you want to give him a piece of bread," Cozza said. (In high school, his coach had done just that, taking sandwiches from the beefier linemen at lunch and making Madden eat them, to no apparent effect.) But the scrawny, boyish-looking Madden played with a frenzy that enabled him to get the better of opponents fifty or sixty pounds heavier, and his coaches knew that no matter where they put him, they could count on him to do whatever they asked. Sophomore year, they had him at offensive end; junior year, they moved him to monster back, where Madden, playing on a sprained ankle, had saved the 1967 Harvard game by forcing and recovering a fumble as the Crimson drove for the winning touchdown. Senior year, with the team running out of linemen, they moved Madden to end, where the Blade, as they called him for his resemblance to a spear of grass, was the lightest defensive lineman in the league. Madden played like a man possessed.

Linebacker Mike Bouscaren, the defensive signal caller, played with several chips on his shoulder. Like Madden and Goldsmith, he had been an offensive star in high school, an All-City fullback at a parochial academy outside Syracuse. But with so much talent in the Yale backfield, he'd been moved to defense, and the knowledge that he hadn't been quite good enough to make it on offense fueled his play. The coaches tried him first at cornerback, but he hadn't been fast enough, so they'd shifted him to linebacker, where, at six-foot-one and 195 pounds, he was undersized for the position and lacked the classic linebacker build of, say, Andy Coe, a thick-necked plug of a player whose nickname was "The Bludgeon." This made Bouscaren all the more determined. "He *willed* himself into being a linebacker," J. P. Goldsmith recalled. Junior year, Bouscaren started alongside Coe, led the team in interceptions, and made honorable mention All-Ivy. Bouscaren's father, a political science professor and noted anticommunist crusader, was another source of motivation. An intensely competitive man whose own Yale football career had been cut short by World War II, he drove his family down from upstate New York for every game and took such pride in his son's athletic achievements that Bouscaren's younger brother sensed that their father was living through Mike's stardom.

During the 1968 season, Bouscaren was dealing with another, far more serious familial pressure: his mother had terminal cancer. She would die the following June.

Whatever the reasons, Bouscaren played as if his life depended on it, flying all over the field to make tackles and throwing his body around with kamikaze abandon. As a punt returner—the only linebacker in the league who ran back kicks—he refused to call for a fair catch no matter how many defenders were about to slam into him. (In winter, his hell-bent-for-leather style made him one of the top skiers on Yale's Alpine team; in spring, he was a daredevil center on the rugby squad.) In practice, ranging behind his defensive line, he might suddenly proclaim that he was Pudge Heffelfinger "taking on the Princeton Tiger"—though not all his teammates recognized the name of the legendary Yale guard of the 1890s. In the rain-drenched Columbia game, when a Lion receiver shoved him after the whistle, Bouscaren, in the words of the *Yale Daily News*, "simply stepped back and stomped his foot in one of the puddles which covered the field, sending a spray of muddy water all over his aggressor and delighting the Eli fans who witnessed the incident." His infectious enthusiasm and forceful play made him one of the most popular men on the team; if Dowling hadn't been at Yale, Bouscaren would likely have been elected captain.

Beneath the high spirits, however, some of his teammates sensed an underlying core of anger that informed his relentlessly aggressive style. Bouscaren's reputation for ferocity, which he seemed to relish, made him the only defensive player to earn an appearance in *bull tales*. Trying to talk the ref out of giving #27 a penalty, B.D. says, "*Whadda ya mean roughing? You barely laid a hand on him, did you, Bous?*" Bous, unsmiling: "*I kicked his ass in.*" BD to ref: "*Do you think we could settle on 25 yards?*" "Bous" played on the edge, but never went over it, except for an unsettling incident that occurred during a preseason scrimmage, when, after tackling Calvin Hill, he jumped up and, yelling with triumph and overwhelmed by adrenaline, took a kick at Hill. A teammate quickly stepped in and the moment passed, but the players who had seen it were shocked.

* * *

It could be said that the entire Yale defense played with a chip on its shoulder. They were young: the starting lineup included four sophomores and a junior. They were almost comically undersized: only two starters weighed more than 200 pounds, and the line, averaging 195 pounds, was the lightest in the league. They lacked star power: while at least five players on offense were being eyed by pro scouts, only cornerback Ed Franklin, who played as if he were spring-loaded, attracted any attention. They were woefully undermanned: one of the top subs, end Scott Robinson, was a varsity basketball player who had been talked into giving football a whirl halfway through the 1967 season by his roommate Brian Dowling, who'd happened to see him play a decent game of touch on Cross Campus.

And they had a lot to live up to: the Yale offense. They felt fortunate to be playing alongside such a powerful unit, and during games they watched from the sideline, as eager as any fan, to see what Dowling and Hill would do next. But, like a proud younger brother, they wanted to hold up their end of the bargain; they wanted to show that they, too, could play.

Credit for fusing this collection of disparate parts into an effective whole was due to defensive coach Bill Narduzzi, who, like two-thirds of the coaching staff, had been imported by Cozza from his alma mater, Miami of Ohio. In contrast to offensive coach Seb LaSpina, a compact, cerebral man who radiated a Zen-like equanimity, the Doozer, as his players called him, was a lanky, slouch-shouldered, slick-haired, hawk-nosed pepperpot who seemed unable to keep still. His voice was perpetually hoarse from exhorting his players, his hands in constant movement as he talked. (Spreading his arms wide, like the wings of a heron, he'd squawk, "Contain! Contain!") In scrimmages, Narduzzi, who believed that pride and emotion were the keys to football, fired up his men by reminding them they played defense because they were tough—"not like the pussies on offense." In games, he'd get so involved that he'd light a cigarette, forget to take a single puff, and then throw it to the ground in surprise when it burned down to his fingertips; other times, he'd light up, absentmindedly hand the cigarette to a manager, and immediately light another. In the locker room after the blocked-punt loss to Princeton in 1966, when some of the players wept, Narduzzi wept, too.

Position coaches inspired a tribal loyalty from their players. Just as the offense revered LaSpina, the defense was devoted to the Doozer. Narduzzi drove his men hard; in drills, no matter how exhausted they were, he almost always called for "one more." (One afternoon, he called for "one more" seven times.) "I'm looking for three things," he told his players on the first night of preseason. "One: The ability to hit people. Two: The desire to hit people. Three: Just plain hitting people. If you don't have those three things, I'm going to have to send you over to the offense and then you'll have to develop a skill." At the same time, he was relentlessly upbeat; greeting the players as they arrived at practice, he'd crow, "It's a great day to work!"—even when it was pouring rain. Before each Friday-afternoon walk-through, he challenged the Toads to a field goal kicking contest for milkshakes. He was famous for his "Doozerisms," characteristic expressions that J. P. Goldsmith, to the delight of his teammates, imitated in the locker room, complete down to the slouched shoulders, extravagant gestures, raspy voice, and X-rated language. "Gentlemen," he'd say, "This defense is *horseshit.*"

If the offense, with its business-as-usual approach, reflected LaSpina's calm, the defense reflected Narduzzi's brio. There was Goldsmith, with his imitations of the Doozer. There was Bouscaren, with his puddle-splashing and Heffelfinger-channeling. There was Mick Kleber, the reserve tackle who serenaded the locker room with the vocal stylings of "Vincenzo Blasé," a lounge-lizard crooner of his own invention. There was Dick Williams, the mustachioed middle guard who rode a Harley, sang in Yale's Russian Chorus, performed the Ländler with Yale's folk-dancing club, and, when football practice was sagging, might call for the Fieldmouse Defense, a joke formation in which the entire defense lined up behind him—and then scattered to random positions, perplexing the offense and leaving everyone shaking with laughter. And there was Fran Boyer, the irrepressibly buoyant five-foot-nine backup linebacker and unofficial captain of the George Bush Memorial Scout Team, which he'd named for the recently graduated DKE president and devoted Bulldog fan who had come out for the squad a few years earlier. (Two days into the preseason grind, the players had been in the middle of a double-team drill when Bush, complaining of a headache, had walked off the field, never to return.)

Goaded by Narduzzi, spurred by pride, and tested against the league's best offense each day in practice, the Yale defense continued to improve. As the season went on, several of the offensive players told reporters that the finest defense they'd faced was the one they went up against in practice every day. Statistically, Harvard's was the top defense in the Ivy League, but Yale's was not far behind.

* * *

Old Blues liked to say that the first seven games on the Yale schedule were scrimmages; the *real* season began with Princeton. Last year's victory had lanced a boil six years in the making. But Princeton was still Princeton, and there was a run on oranges at New Haven produce stands that week. For the twenty-seven seniors, it would be their last game in the Bowl—the last time they'd make the long walk from Lapham Field House, down an aisle of cheering fans; the last time they'd gather in the squad room before kickoff; the last time they'd follow Cozza through the damp tunnel under the stands toward the rectangle of sunlight at its end; the last time they'd burst onto the field to the roar of the crowd and the sound of the band playing "Bulldog."

Yale was favored by thirteen points, but Princeton was a dangerously talented team, whose four losses had all been by a touchdown or less, including its epic two-point defeat by Harvard the previous week. Indeed, on a cold, overcast November 16, Princeton took the opening kickoff and methodically battered its way down the field for a touchdown. It was only the second time Yale had been behind in a game all season. Cozza wasn't overly concerned; he knew it usually took the defense a series or two to adjust to the single wing. In fact, they would hold Princeton to a field goal for the rest of the half. But Dowling threw two interceptions and Yale led by only 15–9 at the break.

In the second half, Yale scored the first four times it had the ball. The final tally was 42–17. After his erratic first half, Dowling completed seven of eight passes for 134 yards and two touchdowns, setting, in the process, four more Yale records: most touchdown passes in a season, most yards passing in a season, most yards passing in a career, most total yards in a career. He even returned a punt for the first time at Yale. After kick return specialist Bob Sokolowski separated his ribs in the first quarter, Cozza sent in Dowling. Fielding the kick at his 42, Dowling was chased back to the 30 before turning upfield and weaving his way through what seemed to be the entire Princeton team for a 32-yard return, Yale's longest of the season. (On the second punt return of his Yale career, Dowling fumbled. "We were almost glad," wrote Charley Loftus. "At that precise moment he joined the human race.") With eleven minutes remaining, Dowling left his final game at the Bowl to a standing ovation from the 52,510 in attendance.

Once again, the Yale offense was frighteningly efficient. Weinstein, who seemed always to have big games against Princeton, had five catches for 84 yards. (On one, the mammoth receiver outraced Princeton's fastest defensive back down the sideline and caught the ball with his fingertips.) Hill had what some longtime observers said was the finest game ever played by a Yale running back, amassing 169 yards of total offense and scoring three times. On a 24-yard touchdown run, he broke two tackles at the line of scrimmage, raced up the middle, ran into three defenders at the ten, and all but carried them across the goal line. (In the following week's edition of *bull tales*, B.D., congratulating #30 after a score, says, *"In all honesty, I really didn't think you were going to make it that time."* *"Oh? Why's that?"* asks #30, oblivious to the fact that three opposing players are clinging to him like remoras to a shark.) In the third quarter, Hill, who often ran with his tongue out, bit what later turned out to be five stitches' worth while tackling a Princeton kick returner, but was able to return to the field. In the fourth, Cozza was about to pull Hill from the game so he could leave the Bowl for the last time to the ovation he deserved. But Dowling knew that the halfback was only one score away from breaking the Yale records for touchdowns in a season and touchdowns in a career. He asked Cozza to let Hill stay in. Not long afterward, Hill, on a two-yard scoring run, broke both records—and, at the same time, tied the Yale career scoring mark of 138 points, set in 1931 by Albie Booth.

Goldsmith had a solid, if unspectacular, game. That night, he and his girlfriend were celebrating the victory at DKE, when, to his astonishment, Dowling told him he was going to give J.P. one of the game balls. Hill would get the other. (As captain, Dowling had the honor of awarding game balls.) Although Goldsmith suspected he was being recognized less for what he'd done on the field that day than for being so vocal in practice all week about the necessity of beating Princeton, he was thrilled beyond measure. On Monday, when Goldsmith arrived at Lapham Field House, the ball was in his locker.

X

Second String

F rank Champi didn't look like a quarterback. At five feet eleven and a blockish, broad-shouldered 195 pounds, he was about the same size and shape as Harvard's left guard, Tommy Lee Jones. With his thinning blond hair and wire-rimmed glasses, he more nearly resembled, as one of his teammates later observed, a graduate student in linguistics, albeit one in very good shape. Nor did Champi act like a quarterback, or at least like the way a quarterback in the popular imagination was supposed to act: cocky, charismatic, outgoing. ("Introverted quarterback" was an oxymoron.) He was one of the shyest people his teammates had ever met—quiet, sensitive, painfully self-conscious. He didn't belong to the Pi Eta or hang around the pool table at the Varsity Club or horse around in the locker room playing morra. He didn't drink or smoke and had never taken so much as a single experimental puff of marijuana. In high school, his friends had called him "The Old Man," because he was always asking them to lower their voices or pleading with them from the backseat of the car to slow down. He spent his spare time reading, composing poetry, and browsing the bookstores in Harvard Square. Those few teammates who knew him liked him; he was earnest and sweet, and he had an original mind. But even they had to admit that Champi was different.

Frank Champi didn't look like a quarterback until he threw

a football. Most of his teammates had never seen anyone who could throw like that, except maybe on TV. Champi could throw a football, with remarkable accuracy, more than eighty yards—and not a high, wobbly lob, but a spiral so tight and forceful it looked as though the ball might bore like a screw into the receiver's chest. (For that matter, he could throw it fifty yards lefty—farther than many quarterbacks could throw with their dominant arm.) At the end of practice, some of the players hung around just to watch him sling long bombs to the backup halfbacks. Wrapping his huge right hand around the ball, patting it once or twice with his left, Champi bided his time until the receiver had gone forty or fifty yards, and then let it fly. At the far end of the field, the ball would overtake the receiver and fall from the sky into his waiting arms.

This was Champi's favorite time of practice—his favorite time of day, really. The rest of practice—the handoffs, the footwork drills—were to be endured for the sake of those moments when he could throw the football. Champi not only loved throwing the football, he loved *thinking* about throwing, pondering the physics of throwing, and experimenting with the ideal arm angle, release point, and trajectory. When it all came together, he felt a kind of clarity. Champi remembered the time sophomore year when Mike Georges, the muscular middle guard, had challenged him to a throwing contest. That evening, they'd stood on the 35-yard line, facing the far end of the field. Georges went first. His ball landed on the goal line, sixty-five yards away—an impressive toss. Then Champi threw. The moment the ball left his hand he knew it was one of his best throws ever. The ball sailed across the goal line and, ten yards later, when it passed through the goal posts at the back of the end zone, it was a good five yards above the crossbar. Someone later told him it had gone about ninety yards. Even Champi was surprised—though he secretly believed that in game conditions, with his adrenaline pumping, he might be able to throw it a hundred.

▲ Yale captain Brian Dowling. "He has the smooth muscles and relaxed carriage of a country club athlete, the dark eyes and black, slightly curly hair of a choirboy, the poise and affable manner of a ship's purser," wrote Dan Jenkins of *Sports Illustrated.* (Yale Athletic Department)

▲ Harvard captain Vic Gatto. At five feet six, 185 pounds, he was almost always the smallest player on the field—and almost always the best. On a team of diverse personalities, in a fractious time, the equable, indefatigable Gatto was a unifying force. (Tony Ferranti)

▲ Yale coach Carmen Cozza posted a sign in the Yale locker room with his favorite quote: "Football is not only a game. It is a way of life." Many of his players chose Yale because there was something about the straightforward, no-nonsense Cozza that just felt right. (W. Mertens/Yale Banner Publications)

◄ Harvard coach John Yovicsin seemed to exemplify the out-of-touch authority figures against which young Americans were rebelling in the sixties. But his fastidious preparation—and his old-fashioned emphasis on the kicking game—would pay off against Yale. (N. C. Pei/ *Harvard Magazine*)

▲ The only returning letterman on Harvard's offensive line, Tommy Lee Jones, was also an "amateur thespian" (as the press guide put it) who, as an undergraduate, appeared on stage alongside John Lithgow, Stockard Channing, and James Woods. (Dick Raphael)

▲ Pat Conway near Hué, 1968. While his Harvard classmates were doing everything they could to avoid being sent to Vietnam, Conway was determined to get there. (Courtesy of Patrick Conway)

◄ After injuring his knee, All-Ivy safety John Tyson quit the Harvard football team and a possible NFL career to devote more time to black activism. "I want to find a way to help my people," he told a friend. (Courtesy of the Tyson family)

◄ Two weeks after American sprinters Tommie Smith and John Carlos shocked the world at the Mexico City Olympics with a black power salute, two Yale cheerleaders shocked alumni with their own silent protest during the national anthem at the Dartmouth game. (Yale Banner Publications)

► Nick Davidson, coach Carmen Cozza, Bob Levin, and Brian Dowling prepare to board a plane for Ithaca and the 1968 Cornell game. (Joe Pettis/*New Haven Register*)

◄ Bruce "The Tree" Weinstein and Calvin Hill, two of the main cogs in a Yale offense that ranked third in the nation, watch from the sideline during the rain-soaked Columbia game. (S. Hines/Yale Banner Publications)

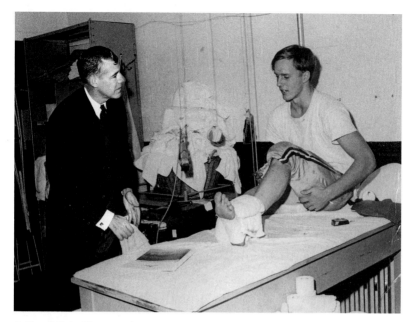

▲ Coach John Yovicsin checks on Ray Hornblower's sprained ankle a few days before The Game. The Harvard halfback, a prep school alumnus, was an anomaly: a blue-blood star on a largely blue-collar team. "The Last of the Mohicans," trainer Jack Fadden called him. (Dick Raphael/Harvard Sports Information)

▲ The *Yale Daily News* ran this *bull tales* strip the day before The Game. (Courtesy of Garry Trudeau)

◄ Dowling, on the loose, pursued by Steve Ranere, moments before throwing to Calvin Hill (30) for Yale's second touchdown. "We were like two jazz musicians," said Hill. "If one started to improvise, the other knew exactly what to do." (Yale Athletic Department)

➤ Harvard's offense watches in dismay as their Yale counterparts dismantle the Crimson defense. From left: John Ballantyne (25), Vic Gatto (40), Jim Reynolds (20), and Tommy Lee Jones (61). (Mark Statuto)

◄ Calvin Hill, Yale record-holder in the long jump and the triple jump, gains eight yards late in the third quarter before being stopped by John Emery and Rick Frisbie (14). Four plays later, on his way to an apparent touchdown, Hill would fumble after being hit from behind by Frisbie. (Julian Fisher/*Yale Daily News*)

◄ Frank Champi in the fourth quarter. Few of his teammates had ever seen anyone who could throw like Champi. But his coaches worried that he lacked the confidence to lead a team. (James Drake/*Sports Illustrated*/Getty Images)

➤ With twenty seconds left, Gus Crim (30) follows guard Bob Jannino (67) on a draw play. Yale's Bouscaren (27), Coe (67), and Goldsmith (12) move forward to meet him. Crim's only thought: Don't fumble. (Harvard Sports Information)

◄ Yale's Don Martin (45) arrives too late as Vic Gatto scores with no time left on the clock, bringing Harvard within two points, 29–27. (Yale Athletic Department)

◄ Pete Varney (80) after the game-tying conversion. Wrote Bud Collins in the *Boston Globe*: "It was a good trip if you sat on the Harvard side, a bad trip if you sat with the Yalies—but it was a mind-blower either way." Also in the picture: Yale's Franklin (15), Neville (79), and Coe (67); Harvard's Crim (30), Skowronski (50), Reed (75), and Jones (61).
(Frank O'Brien/*The Boston Globe*/Getty Images)

➤ Frank Champi gets an appreciative pat from Pete Varney in the Harvard locker room after the game. "Lightning in a bottle," a teammate said of Champi's performance that day. (*The Boston Globe*/Getty Images)

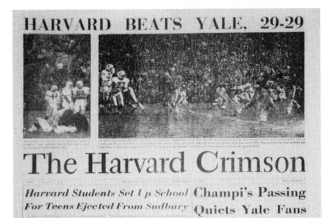

◄ The famous headline in the *Harvard Crimson* on Monday, November 25, 1968. (*The Harvard Crimson*)

◄ Dawn, April 10, 1969.
Rick Berne (in white sweater),
Alex MacLean (to his left),
and other protestors on the
steps of University Hall as
police and state troopers
approach across Harvard Yard.
(Harvard University Archives)

▲ State troopers stand guard in Harvard Yard after using their nightsticks to roust students
from University Hall. A Harvard professor called the occupation and bust "Harvard's Vietnam."
(Thomas Ittelson)

▲ Four days after the bust, Vic Gatto (hands in pockets) surveys the mass meeting at
Harvard Stadium at which ten thousand students voted on whether to continue the strike.
(Ted Polumbaum/*Life* magazine)

Second String

*   *   *

Champi savored such moments of clarity because his life off the field had been so full of gray areas. Indeed, he wouldn't learn the truth about much of his childhood until long after he had grown up. He'd been raised in Everett, a working-class town on the Mystic River named for a nineteenth-century Harvard president. Everett was only seven miles from Harvard Yard, but it was another world: tightly packed double- and triple-deckers filled with the descendants of the Irish and Italian immigrants who had poured into Boston at the turn of the century. Many of them worked in the chemical plants along the river, whose huge, mustard-yellow piles of sulfur lent the town an unpleasant smell when the wind blew from the south.

Champi's parents met during World War II, when his father was stationed in Nova Scotia on a Navy escort ship. Champi's father was in his early twenties when he married; his bride was perhaps seventeen. He brought her home to Everett, where she soon gave birth to a daughter and a son. Shortly after Frank was born, his father was diagnosed with tuberculosis. He was hospitalized for three years. During that time, Frank and his sister lived with their mother, but each Friday afternoon, she dropped them off at their paternal grandmother's for the weekend. One Friday, when Champi was three, their mother dropped them off as usual. They never saw her again. Their father and grandmother told them she was dead. A few years later, Champi picked up the phone and the woman on the other end said she was his mother. Assuming somebody was playing a cruel joke on him, he hung up.

Champi was nine or ten when he realized that his mother hadn't died. Many years later, he would piece together the story: that his mother and grandmother had never gotten along; that his mother, lonely and miserable, had considered taking Champi and his sister back to Nova Scotia; that his grandmother, getting wind of the plan, refused to give them up; that, while his father was in

213

the hospital, his mother had taken up with another man; that by the time his father was discharged, his parents had divorced; that his mother had remarried and left Everett. Champi wondered why she hadn't tried to get her children back, why she hadn't even tried to see them. It was only after his mother really *was* dead that Champi found out she had attempted to telephone them but his father and grandmother had, in every instance but one, intercepted the calls and hung up. And that each Christmas, she had sent them gifts, but their grandmother had thrown them out.

All through high school and college, Champi told people that his mother had died when he was three and that he'd been raised by his grandmother. It was easier that way. It was what he had grown up believing. It was the emotional, if not the literal, truth. "I'm your mother now," his grandmother had said.

Born in 1895, Theresa Champi had grown up near Rome, the daughter of a railway conductor. In 1911, her father put her on a ship bound for the United States and an arranged marriage to a former employee who had emigrated a few years earlier. At sixteen, she found herself in Everett, Massachusetts, married to a stranger. She hated her new country, which she found filthy and noisy. She hated her new husband, an illiterate blacksmith ten years older than she, who worked on Boston's recently completed subway system. Not long after their wedding, she wrote to her father and said she wanted to come home. By the time he sent her money for the trip, she was pregnant. A devout Catholic, she stayed in Everett and gave birth to the first of eight children, six of whom survived infancy.

Barely five feet tall, Theresa Champi ruled the small, two-story frame house on School Street with an iron hand and a shrill voice. Three of her grown children, including Champi's father, lived under her roof, but there was never any doubt about who was the head of the household. Forceful and opinionated, she constantly picked on her children, belittling them, itemizing their flaws, reminding them how disappointed in them she was. Although she loved her grandson, she couldn't help being critical of him, too. She often spoke Italian around the house, but when he tried to respond in kind, she'd tell him to speak it correctly or not to speak it at all. When he raked the yard, she'd berate him if he missed a leaf. She seemed unable to let go of the tiniest argument, unable to communicate at anything less than operatic volume. If Champi replied in a matter-of-fact tone, she wouldn't hear him until he'd raised his voice to match hers; a conversation about the weather could sound like a shouting match. Many years later, when Champi was married, his wife noticed that whenever Theresa Champi raised her voice, Frank, nearly a foot taller than his octogenarian grandmother, seemed to shrink until, by a kind of optical illusion, he somehow looked smaller than she did.

Champi was exasperated by his grandmother; at times, he feared her. But he also loved and respected her. Though she seemed unable to stop bullying her family, he knew she would do anything for them. A superb cook, she'd whip up their favorite meals at a moment's notice, feed anybody who walked into her house, and spend much of the weekend preparing her traditional Sunday dinner of roast chicken and homemade pasta with bolognese sauce. She made Champi carry the bags on Saturday shopping trips to Haymarket, but she made sure to stop in afterward at the Scollay Square candy shop that sold broken pieces of chocolate at half price. She made Champi get a paper route, but when he got up at five a.m. to do it, she had a hot breakfast waiting on the table. She instilled in her grandson the values he would hold dear for the rest of his life: *Finish the job. Be a man of your word. Do the best you can.* Neither of her sons had gone to college, and she pushed Champi to go.

For a child, the house on School Street could be a confusing place. Champi's father, who had lost his marriage and one of his lungs during his long hospitalization for TB, was physically and emotionally exhausted. A clerk at the Everett post office, he spent much of his spare time at the track, betting on the horses at Suffolk

Downs or the greyhounds at Wonderland. Champi's uncle Louis, who had taken Frank under his wing while his father was in the hospital, was a sensitive, artistic man whose bouts of depression occasionally left him unable to run his small printing shop next door. Champi's grandfather, retired from the MTA, spent all day at his workshop forge, joining his family only for meals. Whether due to Theresa Champi's hectoring or to some genetic susceptibility, or both, members of the Champi family tended to be high-strung and fidgety. Over the years, Champi would see his grandfather, father, and uncle all hospitalized with nervous breakdowns.

Sports offered Champi a way out. Uncle Louis had been a high school athlete, and each afternoon when his nephew came home from elementary school they went to the playground behind St. Anthony's Church. Uncle Louis taught Champi how to throw a football and shoot a basketball with either hand, how to hit a baseball from both sides of the plate. Champi grew up in an Italian neighborhood in which everyone knew everyone else, and whenever things got overwhelming at home he could head to the playground, where there were always enough kids to choose up sides and get a game going. As he grew older, there was Little League, CYO basketball, and then, in junior high, football. Sports also offered him a way to channel his moody, restless energy. When he hit a baseball or threw a football, he felt calm. And because he turned out to be really good at those things, sports gave him confidence. At home, he felt like a nobody; on the field, he was definitely a somebody.

At the first practice for the junior high football team, the coach asked whether anyone could throw. Champi, who in Little League had been able to hurl a baseball from center field to home plate on the fly, raised his hand. After the coach watched Champi and several other candidates pass, he called him over. Holding his hand palm out, he told the boy to place his hand against his. If the coach's was larger, it wasn't by much. "You're my quarterback," the coach said.

Second String

*　　*　　*

Champi had grown up going to Everett football games, sneaking through the fence with his friends at Memorial Stadium, where crowds of up to 10,000 cheered on the Crimson Tide. Football was a big deal in Everett. Its undefeated 1914 team had put together what many sportswriters considered the greatest season in high school football history, scoring 600 points and giving up zero. When Champi arrived on the Everett varsity, the team hadn't lost a game in two years.

Sophomore year, Champi, who had quarterbacked his junior high team to an undefeated season, was expected to start. He didn't. He was terrible. Tense and nervous, he bobbled snaps, fumbled the ball, and couldn't seem to throw. Most athletes are able to shrug off mistakes, but when Champi threw a bad pass, he'd berate himself, in a voice no less insistent than his grandmother's, for being an idiot, a failure, a bum. His next pass, not surprisingly, would be even worse.

Champi had always been hard on himself. He hated to lose. He couldn't stand it when opponents patted him on the back and said "Nice game" after they won. He'd say "Thanks," but he wanted to spit in their faces, he wanted to say, "Let's play again *right now.*" He'd go home and practice for hours, trying to make himself so good that he'd never again have to feel the pain of losing. As a quarterback in football and a pitcher in baseball, he believed that much of the burden was on his shoulders; when he threw an interception or gave up a hit, he felt he had let down not only his teammates and his coaches but his entire city. If his team lost over the weekend, he dreaded going back to school on Monday. Yet the more his team won, the more pressure he felt.

At the beginning of Champi's junior year at Everett High, the coach, Moody Sarno, took him aside. "I'm going to make you a good quarterback in spite of yourself," he told him. Champi liked Sarno, a burly, gravel-voiced, chain-smoking old-school ranter who had played at Fordham alongside Vince Lombardi. The fact that a legend like Sarno hadn't given up on him bolstered his confidence. Champi would start in both his junior and senior years. He was still terrified that he would let his team down. He still got so nervous that before every game he ducked into the bathroom and threw up. Afterward, however, he would feel almost relaxed. "I can't believe I'm getting sick over a game," he'd think. "The heck with it, I'll just do the best I can." That thought took some of the pressure off. Years later, Sarno would tell him, "As soon as I saw you throw up, I knew we were okay."

There was something else that seemed to help. Champi was a devout Catholic. Like many athletes, he prayed before each game: that the team would win, that he'd play his best. But Champi came to believe that his faith and his football were connected, that if he played poorly on Saturday it was because he'd been a bad person that week and God was punishing him. He convinced himself that if he was a *good* person that week—did all his homework, didn't swear, kept impure thoughts to a minimum—God would reward him and he would play well. The better he'd been that week, the more confidence he had going into a game. Indeed, Champi came to believe he had a guardian angel, because each week, even in the closest of contests, Everett somehow prevailed.

Champi threw twenty-three touchdown passes while leading Everett to eighteen straight wins and two state championships. "A quarterback with a golden arm," the *Globe* called him when he was named to the All-State team his senior year. He was also co-captain of the basketball and track teams (he broke the Greater Boston high school javelin record) and president of his senior class. He was sought after by colleges across the Northeast. Knowing he needed to get away from School Street, he verbally committed to Princeton. At the last minute, however, he changed his mind. The headline in the *Globe* read: "Everett's Champi Headed For Harvard." He would stay close to home.

Second String

* * *

Most freshmen, whether they admitted it or not, found Harvard intimidating; Champi, as one of his classmates observed, seemed in a state of shock. Having been brought up in a deeply conservative household by a woman whose values were rooted in the early 1900s, he arrived, like a disoriented time traveler, at the rapidly changing Harvard of the sixties. At home, his grandmother's word had been law; at Harvard, he was taught to question everything. At home, all communication had taken place at high decibel; at Harvard, displays of emotion were considered gauche. Anxious, lonely, and feeling guilty—his grandmother had wanted him to commute to Harvard from Everett—he headed home every Thursday afternoon after his last class and returned to Cambridge only after Theresa Champi's Sunday feast.

Champi had been a good student in high school, but the amount of work at Harvard overwhelmed him. And it was an entirely different *kind* of work. High school had been all about memorizing facts for quizzes and tests. At Harvard, Champi was expected to think for himself, to have a point of view. His Expository Writing instructor didn't want to know *what* the book's protagonist did, he wanted to know *why* he did it. The other students around the table jumped right in. Champi hardly said a word, terrified he'd say something stupid. Though he studied late into the night, he ended up flunking one course, getting a D in another, and being placed on probation.

Freshman football was a disaster. When Champi was recruited, he had been all but promised the job of starting quarterback. Arriving for the first day of practice, he found seven other quarterbacks—each one, like him, some kind of all-star; each one, like him, expecting to start. Everyone could tell he had talent, especially the receivers, whose hands were bruised from catching Champi's bullets. But Champi, working with tutors in a desperate attempt to stay afloat in the classroom, often missed practice, and when he was there, it was like sophomore year in high school all over again. His coaches couldn't believe this was the same Frank Champi who'd led Everett to two state titles. He started out on first string; by the end of the season he was fifth string.

Spring term was a little better. He got off probation. He got to know his roommates. He still went home every weekend, but he didn't leave his dorm until Friday night. He threw the javelin so well that he was chosen for a combined Harvard-Yale all-star track team that traveled to England that summer—the first time he'd flown—to compete against Oxford-Cambridge. While there he met a soft-spoken athlete from Yale named Calvin Hill, who won the long jump by a foot and a half and the triple jump by nearly ten feet. Champi, who had read a lot about lift versus thrust, didn't see how it was possible for someone so big to jump so far.

Sophomore year, Champi played well for the junior varsity, and the team won all but one of its games. Against Cornell, he threw a pass 45 yards on a line for a touchdown. After the game, freshman coach Henry Lamar told Champi it was the prettiest pass he'd ever seen. That spring, throwing the javelin against Princeton, Champi let go a toss in which everything came together. "I never saw a happier kid," track coach Bill McCurdy told the *Crimson*. "He knew he uncorked a beauty and ran down after his throw. The closer he got to where it landed, the more he jumped around. He was taking five-foot hops." Champi had thrown the javelin 224 feet, 1 inch, setting a new Harvard record.

* * *

Knowing the quarterback position was wide open, Champi came back in the fall of 1968 determined to win the starting job. He began the preseason fourth on the depth chart but moved up to second within two weeks. On the eve of the Holy Cross game, Yovicsin told the *Crimson* that Lalich would start, but that at the first sign of trouble Champi would take over. Champi, who thought he had played well enough to earn the position, was disappointed. Still, he figured that at some point during the season Lalich would falter and he'd get his chance.

Champi liked Lalich, and he could see how well the players responded to him. He was frustrated nonetheless. He knew the coaches doubted he had the personality to lead the team, but how could he show them he was a leader if he never got a chance to play? As it was, Lalich performed better with each passing week, and Champi got on the field only when Harvard was three or four touchdowns ahead, when the coaches told the quarterback to play conservatively and run out the clock. He was glad the team kept winning, but he knew that the better they did, the less opportunity he had to play.

Off the field, Champi felt as if his mind was opening up for the first time. He was getting better grades. He was concentrating in English, studying Shakespeare, and thinking of becoming a writer. He dreamed of reading every book in Widener Library. He explored every bookstore in the Square. One day he wandered into the Aquarian Age, one of several occult bookshops that had sprung up in Cambridge over the last few years, and found himself reading an astrology guide. Champi had always been intrigued by the forces that shape people; astrology, it seemed, was another way of understanding those forces. He drew up some simple astrological charts and taught himself palmistry. (His new talent, he found, had a fringe benefit: girls liked having their palms read.) He bought a biography of the psychic Edgar Cayce and grew curious about reincarnation, which made at least as much sense to him as the idea of living forever among harp-playing angels in a place called heaven. By now, Champi was going home to Everett only when he needed to get his laundry done.

Champi no longer went to church. His faith had brought him little more than guilt and shame. He looked back on his magical thinking in high school, when he believed that whether his team

won depended on how good a Catholic he'd been, as foolish super-
stition. Surely there had been a player on the opposing team who
was even *more* virtuous than he—and yet that guy's team had lost.
In the end, Champi concluded, a football game was just a football
game, not a contest of saint versus sinner.

When he arrived at Harvard, Champi had, like most of his
Everett friends, supported the war and dismissed the peaceniks
as nutcases and Communists. But as he began reading the history
of America's involvement in Vietnam and discussing it with his
roommates over the evening news, Champi came to believe the
war was a mistake. He knew it was being fought in large part by
working-class kids from towns like Everett. Occasionally he'd
hear that someone he'd known in high school had been wounded
or killed—and, he wondered, for what? He didn't join any antiwar groups—SDS was far too radical for him—and though he
observed the demonstrations in the Yard with sympathy, he didn't
participate. He expressed his feelings on paper, writing poems
about the senselessness of war.

Champi questioned the war, he questioned his faith, and he even
questioned football. People were always saying that the Ivy League
de-emphasized the sport, that the players were students first and
athletes second. But with taping, practice, meetings, and games,
the players spent close to thirty hours a week on football. If that
was de-emphasizing football, thought Champi, he'd hate to be in
a program that emphasized it. In high school, winning had been
everything to him; the mere *fear* of losing had made him feel sick.
Now, with assassinations, riots in the inner cities, and deep divisions
over the war tearing the country apart, who could possibly care
who won a football game? Indeed, the whole idea of winning and
losing began to seem silly to Champi. In America, winners were
showered with adulation and losers were conditioned to hang their
heads in shame. Maybe a tie, he decided, was the ideal outcome.

If Champi had been starting, he might not have indulged in
such theoretical speculation. But being a backup quarterback was

frustrating. In practice, Champi's job was to pay attention as the first-string offense went through its paces, so that if Lalich got injured he'd be ready to play. In games, Champi manned the phones, relaying instructions to the players from backfield coach Pat Stark, who was getting a bird's-eye view of the action from the press box. Whenever a halfback hit the wrong hole or a lineman muffed his assignment, Stark was enraged. "Go tell Jannino he missed that block!" he'd scream in Champi's ear. Champi would scurry over and deliver the message, but he hated doing it. He had gone to Harvard to get away from his grandmother's ranting, and now he had Stark ranting at him. In some ways, his second-string junior year was proving to be less fun than his fourth-string sophomore year; at least on JV he'd gotten a chance to throw the ball. Sometimes, when the team was warming up before a game, he'd glance at the stands and see a Harvard student with a drink in his hand and a girl on his arm, laughing and having a good time—and he'd wonder why he was spending thirty hours a week doing something he didn't enjoy anymore.

As the evening practices grew colder and Stark grew louder, Champi thought about quitting. Only one thing kept him going: he hadn't proven himself yet. He wanted to show his coaches and his teammates—and, most of all, himself—that he could do the job, that he could play quarterback, that he could lead this team.

*   *   *

Historically, the Brown game was a valley between the emotional peaks of Princeton and Yale. Each year, Yovicsin warned his team not to take Brown lightly, but it was hard not to; Brown hadn't beaten Harvard since 1959. This year, Brown was, once again, winless in Ivy League play, and with both Harvard and Yale still undefeated, Yovicsin was even more worried that the team might look past Brown to Yale. No matter how much Yovicsin fretted, however, his players couldn't imagine him resorting to the earthy motivational tactics employed by freshman coach Henry Lamar, who, three years earlier, as Gatto and company prepared to take the field against the Bears, had shouted, "What's the color of shit?"—and received, in reply, a thunderous, "Brown!"

On November 16, under a desultory drizzle at Harvard Stadium, Brown played Harvard even until the end of the first quarter, when John Emery intercepted a pass and returned it 54 yards for the game's first points, earning him yet another duct-tape football for his helmet. Gatto and Hornblower began finding holes in the undersized Brown line. The defense stifled Brown until the last minutes, when the reserves gave up a touchdown. The final score was 31–7. Champi got into the game in the fourth quarter. He threw three passes, completing one, for ten yards.

Harvard won, but its performance had been less than scintillating. A writer for the *Harvard Alumni Bulletin* likened the team to a runner who expends just enough energy in the qualifying heat to make the finals. The Harvard fans in the crowd of 16,000 were clearly looking ahead, too. Normally the mere mention of the word *Yale* over the public address system provoked boos, but each time the announcer updated the score of the Yale-Princeton game, in which Yale was crushing Princeton, a cheer went up from the Harvard side. Harvard and Yale would meet each other undefeated.

The win proved costly. In the second quarter, Conway launched himself helmet-first at a Brown running back. Both men went down. As Conway got to his feet, he was pleased to note that his neck, arms, and legs all seemed to be working. But something wasn't right. Looking around the stadium, he realized what it was: he was seeing everything in black and white. He made his way to the sideline and told trainer Jack Fadden, who walked him to the squad room. After a few minutes, he began seeing in color again. But though he was able to identify the number of fingers Fadden held up, and to name the president (Lyndon Johnson), he was sufficiently unsteady that Fadden refused to let him return to the field.

Second String

Early in the third period, Hornblower, well on his way to another hundred-yard game, was planting his left foot on ground that had already started to freeze up in the November chill when he was hit. He was carried off the field on a stretcher with a badly sprained ankle. He had finally paid the price for wearing his inch-long spikes.

After the game, the players seemed more relieved than thrilled. "A lot of the pressure is off now," admitted defensive tackle Steve Zebal. "We no longer have to sweat out each game so we can meet Yale undefeated. Now there is only one game to prepare for." The players exited the locker room sporting gangster-style fedoras that Lalich's father had brought from Chicago. On each brim, a card read RUB OUT YALE.

XI

Ballyhoo

I t was to Harvard's and Yale's everlasting chagrin that their first meeting on a football field wasn't the first intercollegiate football game played in this country. The first, between Princeton and Rutgers, had taken place in 1869. The most celebrated rivalry in college football history wouldn't get started until 2:30 p.m. on November 13, 1875, on the infield of Hamilton Park, a private racetrack on the outskirts of New Haven. In front of more than 2,000 spectators, Harvard won easily, though it must be admitted that the game was played largely by Harvard's rules, to which Yale, the younger college, had acquiesced. In a show of comity, the two teams and their fans joined forces for a festive postgame sing-along, which turned a little too festive; seven Harvard students were arrested and fined $5.29 each for what the *New Haven Register* described as "hooting and singing in the public streets."

Over the following half century, "the Adam and Eve of football," as one writer called them, came up with most of the rules and innovations that would transform the game from a semi-organized brawl into a sophisticated sport. In truth, Yale made by far the more significant contributions, of which the most valuable, some might argue, dated to 1906, when the *New York Times*, reporting on the Harvard-Yale game in New Haven, observed "small parties of automobilists eating tempting viands that had been brought in hampers spread out in picnic fashion on a table cloth laid upon the ground"—the first recorded reference to what one day would be known as tailgating.

The two schools dominated the national rankings for many years, and their annual meeting, "the most glorious event on the nation's athletic calendar," as one writer described it, frequently decided the intercollegiate champion. It also served as a focal point for the rivalry between the two schools. "We feel that Yale is at once most similar and most opposite to Harvard," wrote Harvard philosopher George Santayana after attending the 1892 game, "that she is not only a rival in those things, such as athletics, which are common to both colleges, but at the same time an embodiment of what is most hostile to our spirit." On the field, that hostility was expressed so forcefully that it seemed perfectly natural for Frederic Remington—who was a member of the Yale football team before going off to paint the American West—to spatter his jersey with blood from a New Haven slaughterhouse "to make it look more businesslike" on the eve of the 1879 contest. "Yale did not try to maim our men as much as she usually does," observed the *Harvard Advocate* after the 1881 game. "Still, there can be no excuse for the use of teeth in football." The 1894 game—the "Blood Bath at Hampden Park," as it was dubbed—was so rough that a third of the players on the field were injured (a casualty rate higher than that of Napoleon's army at Waterloo, pointed out *The Nation*), five players were hospitalized, a Yale tackle spent five hours in a coma, and the series was suspended for two years.

The rivalry resumed with less blood but no less intensity. To pump up his players before the 1908 game, it was said that first-year Harvard coach Percy Haughton strangled a live bulldog with his bare hands. (The reality turned out to be rather less gruesome; the bulldog was made of papier-mâché, and instead of strangling it, Haughton dragged it behind his car, like Hector's body behind Achilles' chariot. In any case, Harvard shut out Yale to complete an undefeated season.) In 1916, Yale coach Tad Jones told his team, "Gentlemen, you are now going out to play football against Harvard. Never again in your whole life will you do anything so important"—words that may have struck his listeners as somewhat hyperbolic, given that the country was on the verge of entering World War I, and, within a year, thirty of the thirty-three players on the field that day would be in uniform. His team responded by upsetting Harvard, 6–3, in the Bowl, before 77,000 spectators, which, the *New Haven Register* pointed out, was equal to the population of Nevada.

Harvard won its last national championship in 1919, Yale in 1927. But as the two colleges faded from gridiron prominence, the Harvard-Yale game itself lost little of its luster, even if its significance became more sociocultural than athletic. A measure of its importance on the Brahmin schedule can be inferred from the fact that Locke-Ober, the Boston culinary temple that had been serving lobster bisque to blue-blood bankers since 1875, opened its men's grill to "ladies" only twice a year. One occasion was New Year's Eve. The other was the night of the Harvard-Yale game. Over the decades, a host of cherished traditions accreted, like barnacles, to the contest. The Harvard alumnus who had attended the most Yale games was accorded the honor of waving a tattered crimson pennant embroidered with an olive "H" that had made its first appearance at the Harvard-Yale game of 1884. Like the Stars and Stripes or the Olympic torch, the "Little Red Flag," as it was known, was never permitted to touch the ground. And of course there were pranks, of which the most celebrated was the dastardly 1934 kidnapping of Handsome Dan, Yale's bulldog mascot, who was returned only after he was photographed licking the hamburger-smeared feet of the John Harvard statue outside University Hall.

That overweening sense of the game's importance was enshrined in the early 1950s, when *New York Times* sportswriters began referring to it in print as "The Game." ("As even the most backwards student knows, this naturally means the Yale-Harvard game," observed Arthur Daley.) But it would be Charley Loftus who adopted, co-opted, promoted, and enshrined the uppercase conceit. And it was Baaron Pittenger, Loftus's counterpart at Harvard, who first emblazoned "THE GAME" on the cover of the Harvard-Yale program, in 1960. It had been thus ever since, the implication being that while other football games, even a few of some consequence, might take place around the country, the Harvard-Yale game was the only game that mattered.

The Game was always the last game of the season. A Harvard or Yale team could lose every other game, yet consider its season a success with a victory over its rival. In 1960, shortly after announcing that he would run for president, Senator John F. Kennedy, who had played end for the Harvard JVs in 1937, told his guests at a Georgetown dinner party that the adrenaline rush of making decisions on the world stage would be "like playing Yale every Saturday." Three years later, when Kennedy was assassinated the day before the 1963 game, which he had planned to attend, the presidents of the two universities agreed to postpone the game a week. "They can't do that," a Harvard alumnus complained to his wife. "It's the *Harvard-Yale* game."

* * *

The 1968 game, the eighty-fifth meeting of the two teams, was the most ballyhooed ever. Both were coming into the game unbeaten for the first time since 1909, when Yale won, 8–0, to clinch the intercollegiate championship. This year, Yale was ranked eighteenth in the country. It was said that if they beat Harvard convincingly, they might break into the top ten, a feat no Ivy League team had achieved since 1950. Conversely, if Harvard won, they'd likely climb into the top twenty, where no Crimson team had been since 1948. For the first time in many years, The Game was of national consequence.

In the weeks leading up to the game, the scramble for tickets became increasingly frantic. Harvard Stadium had 37,289 seats. More than 30,000 Harvard alumni had filed requests, but after sending Yale its allotted 15,000 and distributing tickets to season ticket holders, university VIPs, and undergraduates, the ticket office had only 9,000 left. Filling orders by graduating class, oldest first, it ran out by the class of 1950, leaving nearly two decades of Harvard alumni apoplectic. The athletic department added several thousand additional seats by erecting temporary bleachers in the open end of the horseshoe and on the cinder track that ringed the field. They distributed 500 standing-room tickets for the top of the stadium, bringing the total number of tickets issued to 40,280. Even a few Harvardians admitted it was a pity it wasn't Yale's turn to host The Game. But the Bowl's 70,869 seats would not have sufficed. Harvard's ticket manager estimated he could easily have sold 100,000.

For scalpers, it was a seller's market. Harvard's final clubs and Yale's secret societies, with pools of well-heeled alumni to draw on, served as clearinghouses. By the week of the game, seats at midfield were fetching as much as $300 apiece—15 percent of Harvard's annual tuition. Few people were selling. *Crimson* classifieds grew plaintive: "2 Yale tickets can equal a lot of money. Wanted desperately. What else can I say?" One Harvard alumnus, a haberdasher, offered ten years of men's suits in exchange for a pair of tickets. Harvard players, each of whom received four free tickets, were reminded that a scalping scandal in the 1930s had cost several players their eligibility. But the profit margin made it irresistible. Defensive end Joe McKinney sold two of his tickets through a middleman at the Harvard Club of Boston for $300 the pair, a small fortune to a twenty-one-year-old father with a wife and two-month-old son. He would have sold his other two, but before the season started, he had promised his wife's obstetrician, a Harvard Medical School graduate and football fan, two tickets for each home game as part of his fee. It had seemed a good deal at the time.

Ticketless fans were disconsolate. Having missed the alumni

cutoff by two classes, a 1951 Harvard graduate who had attended every iteration of The Game since 1938 had given up on attending this one. The day before it, however, while watching the freshmen play, he happened to stand next to Victor Gatto Sr., father of the Harvard captain. He told Mr. Gatto that he admired his son so much that if he and his wife, who was nine months pregnant, had a girl, they would name her Victoria. Mr. Gatto was so moved by this declaration that he pulled two tickets from his pocket and presented them to the expectant father. Four days after the game, the baby was born, a boy: David Vicgatto Sigourney.

Harvard issued credentials to four hundred reporters, the largest press corps in Ivy League history. After filling the press box high atop the stadium, the Harvard Sports Information Office started assigning seats on the press box roof until the buildings and grounds department put a stop to it for reasons of safety. Forty-six daily newspapers from across the country planned to cover the game. The *Boston Globe* was sending six men; the *New York Times*, for the first time in its history, was sending two. *Time, Newsweek, Sports Illustrated*, and *Women's Wear Daily* would be there. CBS, NBC, and ABC would tape the game; six radio stations would provide live play-by-play. Columnists trotted out the old stories: Haughton's bulldog, Tad Jones's most-important-thing-you'll-ever-do speech. ("The ridiculous part of it all is that the impressionable kids listening to him believed every word," noted Arthur Daley in the *New York Times*. "No coach today would dare open so outrageous a can of corn.") There were daily updates on Hornblower's sprained ankle and Hill's stitched-up tongue. By the end of the week, so little had been left unsaid that one enterprising journalist hired a medium to contact the eponymic John Harvard and Elihu Yale for their predictions on the game. Each forecast a win for his college.

Dowling was the center of press attention. Charley Loftus, who had announced he would be retiring from Yale after the game, wrote and distributed a ten-page encomium titled "Biographical Data On: Brian John Dowling, Yale's All-America Quarterback

Candidate." The *Globe* published an effusive six-page profile in its *Sunday Magazine*, and each day one of its sportswriters interviewed Dowling by phone and wrote up his notes as "Dowling's Journal." The *Yale Daily News* pre-mourned the imminent end of "The Dowling Era." The *Crimson* took a characteristically tongue-in-cheek approach in a series of articles that began, "Brian Dowling walked casually across the water of Long Island Sound yesterday musing on next Saturday's game."

Once a year, during Yale Week (or Harvard Week, as it was called in New Haven), Harvard's traditional indifference to football evaporated. This year, the campus was gripped with a frenzy of Yale-esque proportions. As players made their way to class, students who'd previously ignored them now wished them luck or asked them how they thought Harvard would do. Each evening when they emerged from Dillon for practice, they were greeted by a gauntlet of alumni who clapped them on the back and shouted, "Go get 'em!" Hundreds of people ringed the field to watch them drill—including more than a few flashily dressed, gimlet-eyed strangers the players suspected of being gamblers from out of town; there was talk of "the New York element" and rumors of fortunes being wagered on the game. It had been an acrimonious fall, but the mood on campus was almost buoyant. There were even plans for a pep rally—Harvard's first since 1962—to be held the night before the game.

Though other events took place at Harvard that week, few people paid attention. On Monday night, while MacLean and Berne studied films of Yale, their fellow SDS members were drawing up demands calling on Harvard to expel ROTC from campus and announcing plans for a mass demonstration in front of University Hall. But they took care to schedule it for the week *after* the game, when students were more likely to show up. For the first time at Harvard, the Vietnam War took a backseat to football.

*   *   *

The game would represent, according to sportswriters, the meeting of irresistible force (Yale's offense) and immovable object (Harvard's defense). Yale had averaged 36 points a game, sixth-most in the country. Harvard had given up 7.6, fewest in the country. Yale was third in the nation in total offense, amassing 467 yards per game. Harvard was seventh in defense, allowing 243. Las Vegas odds-makers made the irresistible force a seven-point favorite, but few people believed the game would be that close. While Harvard had won several squeakers, Yale had dominated every opponent. The Columbia team that Harvard had edged 21–14, Yale beat 29–7. A week after Harvard barely got by Princeton, 9–7, Yale demolished the Tigers, 42–17. All week, the theme in the sports pages was mighty Yale, plucky Harvard.

If plucky Harvard was intimidated, they didn't show it. "Some of those teams have laid down and died for Yale as soon as they read their press clippings," Farneti, the feisty sophomore linebacker, told a reporter. "They're going to have to prove themselves to me personally." As for talk of Dowling never having lost a game he'd finished since seventh grade, defensive end Steve Ranere told his teammates, "Let's make sure he's standing at the end of the game so he can walk off a loser for the first time." If Big Hole was shaken by the thought of playing opposite God, he didn't admit it. Asked how Harvard would beat a player who had never lost, the insouciant Lalich, referring to his own 8-0 record as varsity starter, answered, "The way I look at it, that's Yale's worry. I'm undefeated, too, you know." Meanwhile, the quarterback's father was tacking up posters all over campus, next to flyers for rock concerts and antiwar rallies, that read, WANTED: THE HARVARD KILLERS: FOR MASSACRING YALE'S OFFENSIVE FOOTBALL TEAM ON SATURDAY NOVEMBER 23, 1968. Mug shots of the players—actually, benign coat-and-tie formal photos from the game program—were accompanied by gangster-style nicknames: John "Fingers" Emery, Alex "Trunk Job" MacLean, Pat "Knuckles" Conway.

On Monday night, when the Harvard players watched film from the Yale-Dartmouth game, the experience was sobering. The Yale offense looked big, strong, fast, and very, very good. The juniors and seniors all had memories of chasing Dowling around the backfield, and now, as they watched him elude would-be Dartmouth tacklers, they shouted "Nail him!" and "Don't let him throw!" Hill, who had thrown more touchdown passes than Lalich that season, looked like a man among boys. And then there were Weinstein and Marting. Conway couldn't believe that the shy, skinny little sophomore with whom he'd played pickup basketball on winter Saturdays during his PG year at Exeter was the same Del Marting as the six-foot-two, 210-pound end who had scored the winning touchdown in last year's Yale game.

As the players left the Varsity Club at eleven, they talked up their chances, reminding one another they'd had Yale all but beaten last year. But some of them, privately, were shaken. Cornerback John Ignacio didn't know how he and his teammates were going to stop that offense. End Bruce Freeman just hoped that Harvard could keep the score respectable. Even Farneti, who *never* admitted that anyone might get the better of him, had his doubts; back in his room, alone with his thoughts, he wondered whether Yale might be *too* good.

*   *   *

Neil Putnam, the assistant coach who did most of Yale's scouting, always painted the upcoming opponent as impossibly formidable; he could make Brown sound like the Green Bay Packers. For three weeks, Putnam had missed his own team's games in order to observe Harvard's. He made it clear that with its running attack and its gang-tackling defense, Harvard would be the best team Yale had faced that year. But as they watched the films, the Yale players weren't overly concerned. Yes, both teams were undefeated, but they felt there was a significant talent gap between them, and if they played the way they had all year, they had no doubt they'd win their seventeenth straight game. It was just a question of by how many points. They spoke diplomatically about Harvard to the press, but the possibility of losing never occurred to them. Kyle Gee didn't think twice about buying a box of cigars to hand out after the game. It was customary for football coaches to heap public praise on even the most hapless opponents, not wanting to rile the opposition, but even the circumspect Cozza, after allowing that "it should be a whale of a game," couldn't help showing his true feelings when pressed for a prediction by the *Crimson*. "I don't think Harvard can beat us," he said. "The only way we can lose is to beat ourselves."

Every year as The Game approached, Old Blues filled Cozza's mailbox with suggestions for "can't miss" trick plays, intricately diagrammed, some with twelve or thirteen men on the field. But in practice that week, it was business as usual; the coaches installed no special formations for Harvard, though Bass and Gee reminded Coach LaSpina of his promise to let them run the ball if the team got far enough ahead. Before practice began, the two tackles took handoffs from second-team quarterback Greg Lawler, just in case. Meanwhile, Cozza and his coaches, as they did each year, went over the roster and figured out which players needed to see action against Harvard in order to win their letters. Lettering in football was a big deal at Yale. Under the team's Byzantine requirements, you earned your varsity "Y" by playing in a certain number of quarters over the course of the season, with quarters against Princeton and Harvard counting double. Going into the Harvard game, the coaches kept track of who hadn't yet qualified, and as the game wound down, Cozza did his best to get them in. He wanted all his boys, from biggest star to lowliest walk-on, to be glad they had played Yale football.

One afternoon, the players arrived in the locker room to find a letter addressed to the team on the bulletin board. It had been written by Thomas Bergin '25, the Dante scholar and master of Timothy Dwight College, who had been attending games ever since he'd grown up a New Haven townie in the 1910s. Brimming with Latin phrases and references to classical myths, the letter made note of the 1937 game in which Heisman Trophy winner Clint Frank led an undefeated Yale team into Harvard Stadium only to suffer an excruciating loss. Bergin reminded the 1968 team that they had a chance at greatness, and cautioned them to keep their minds on the task at hand.

* * *

On Wednesday, Yovicsin wasn't sure who would be ready to play on Saturday. Conway, recovering from the concussion he'd sustained in the Brown game, had been on the "no contact" list all week. And the ribs he'd injured in the second game of the season still hurt. That week, the trainers made him a special, extra-large pad to protect his chest. Bruce Freeman was also out of commission. After arriving late to preseason following his father's death, the rangy sophomore had impressed the coaches enough to split time at end with junior John Kiernan. But he'd suffered a stinger against Princeton, and at practice this week could only stand on the sideline in his warm-ups, his arm in a sling. The trainers told him he could suit up for Yale but probably wouldn't play. Meanwhile, Hornblower, the league's leading rusher, discarded his crutches and ran full out at Wednesday's practice. Halfway through a drill, he limped off the field. He was beginning to realize that he should have spent the week in the infirmary with his leg up. Determined to play, however, he had minimized his discomfort to the trainers and to himself. Players went to great lengths not to miss the Yale game. Fortunately, no one on the 1968 team would have to go as far as the Harvard player who, in 1901, had suffered an attack of appendicitis two days before the contest. Telling his teammates, "I'll play if it kills me," he took the field with braces strapped around his abdomen and helped his undefeated team to a 22–0 victory and the national championship before having his appendix removed the following day.

The Game

Wednesday night, Neil Hurley was still trying to rustle up a date for Saturday's postgame parties. It had been a rough week for the Harvard cornerback. Two days before the Brown game, he had separated his shoulder in practice, and though he couldn't even lift his arm, Coach Park made him put on his pads and sit on the bench in the rain. Afterward, Hurley had been on his way to Cahaly's market to buy 7-Up for the Seven and Sevens he and his roommates planned to serve at a get-together that night, when a car pulled up next to him on Plympton Street. "Hey, do you know where there's a party?" a pretty blonde called out the window. "Yeah, back in my room," he replied—a line that Hurley, no suave ladies' man, could never have thought up unless it had been the truth. The young woman, Kathy, and her cousin, both college students from Maine in town for the weekend, came to the party. Now, on Wednesday, after practice, Hurley, whose girlfriend had broken up with him a few weeks earlier, got up his nerve, called Kathy, and asked her to the game. She sounded dubious. Hurley told her that both teams were undefeated, and win or lose there would be great parties afterward. Kathy said she had been thinking of going shopping at Filene's Basement on Saturday, but . . . okay, why not. (Years later, after they were married, Kathy would tell Neil that when he told her he was on the football team, she thought he might be exaggerating; for all she knew, he could have been the water boy.) Now Hurley had to come up with two more tickets and arrange for a friend to take Kathy to the game. Although the first National Women's Liberation conference would take place on Thanksgiving weekend in Chicago, the time when a woman could attend a football game unescorted had not yet arrived.

* * *

In New Haven, Carmen Cozza worried about the Hong Kong flu. Four hundred and fifty Yale undergraduates had come down with it, including two of his sophomore starters, cornerback Don Martin and Fran Gallagher's younger brother Jim, who were quarantined in the infirmary. Cozza usually moved his team off campus the night before a game to remove them from the temptations of Friday-night mixers, but on Wednesday, worried that more of his players might catch the flu, he sequestered the team in a motel on the outskirts of New Haven, busing them back to campus for classes and practice. Cozza also worried about Calvin Hill. The tongue he'd bitten in the Princeton game had become infected, and he, too, had ended up in the infirmary, sucking on ice cubes to reduce the swelling. (Hill had, apparently, experienced a temporary recovery on Sunday night, when he snuck out to see Jimi Hendrix play at Woolsey Hall, though his tongue throbbed every time Jimi's Stratocaster hit a high note on what the *Yale Daily News* called an "orgiastic" rendition of "The Star-Spangled Banner.")

Thursday was the final home practice of the year: the last time the seniors would ride the bus out to the Bowl, the last time they'd hear the clack of their cleats as they walked through the tunnel and onto the field, the last time they'd feel the Bowl's spongy green grass under their feet. Hill, released from the infirmary, was back at practice. His tongue was still so sore that he spoke in a mumble and had a hard time chewing his training-table steak that night. Normally, Cozza wouldn't permit a player who hadn't practiced on Wednesday to start on Saturday, believing his timing wouldn't be sharp. But this was not a normal player and this was not a normal game.

It was tradition that after the final home practice of the year, the underclassmen formed two lines and, as the seniors ran between them, pounded them on the shoulder pads. Watching what was arguably the greatest senior class in Yale football history run the gauntlet, some of the coaches got a little choked up. Cozza wondered what he'd do without Dowling and Hill. As Bob Levin felt the blows rain on his pads, he remembered doing the whacking himself in previous years, and felt a gust of emotion as he realized how much he'd miss this team.

On Friday morning, several hundred students gathered at Ray Tompkins to cheer the team bus off to Cambridge. It was a quiet ride. Dowling and Hill, sitting next to each other, tried to sleep. A few of the players talked of where the team might rank in the polls after the game. As the bus rolled down Memorial Drive past the Harvard houses, J. P. Goldsmith noticed how much earlier winter came to Cambridge than to New Haven; here, there were no leaves left on the trees.

That afternoon, players from both teams got to the fields early to watch the freshman and JV games, as well as the intramural games between Harvard's houses and Yale's colleges. Harvard fans took it as a promising sign when Harvard won the freshman game and all six intramural games. The JVs tied. In college football, there was no such thing as overtime.

At 3:30, the Yale team, wearing white sweatshirts and sweatpants, entered Harvard Stadium. As Andy Coe walked around the field, he thought of all the Harvard-Yale games that had been played there; this, he sensed, was hallowed ground. It was windy and cold. In Narduzzi's field-goal competition, George Bass won with a 40-yarder, his longest kick ever. It seemed like a good omen. Most players loved Friday practice: a short, light workout in helmets and sweatsuits. The real work had been done earlier in the week. "The hay is in the barn, the barn door is closed, and tomorrow is payday," Narduzzi liked to say. "Now go out and have some fun." They did. Toward the end of the session, the defensive players formed a straight line behind middle guard Dick Williams and then, on the whistle, scattered, harum-scarum, in one last deployment of the Fieldmouse Defense.

By the time Harvard came out for its final practice of the year, it was dark, so they drilled on the lighted practice field in the lee of the empty stadium. After sitting out Thursday's practice, Hornblower was back, his ankle heavily taped, a plastic bar fixed across the heel of his left shoe to minimize twisting. "I feel great," he told reporters. In his ongoing wager with Ballantyne and

Reynolds, Gatto had one of his best nights, making two diving sideline catches; offensive end coach Tom Stephens told him to save them for the game. At the end of practice, the scout team unveiled their most ambitious Instant Replay yet: a backward version of Yale's Dowling-to-Hill-to-Dowling pass. For the first time, the offensive unit came over to watch, and the entire team had a good laugh. Leaving the field, the players walked down a torch-lined path to the locker room, applauded by alumni and serenaded by the Harvard band.

The pep rally had been scheduled for Friday night on the steps of Widener Library; the band would play, the team would be introduced, Yovicsin and Gatto would speak. But as the day of the rally approached, Gatto had worried that it might be a distraction to the team. At his request, the rally was scaled down to a "sendoff," in which students would cheer the team as it left after dinner for the motel in Framingham where the players would spend the night. At practice on Thursday, the players had laughed at the thought of a handful of apathetic Harvard undergrads trying to make themselves heard on bustling Mass Ave as the team took off; a few of them worried that they might make a joke of the event. But on Friday evening, the players emerged from the Varsity Club to see several hundred students singing along as the band played "Ten Thousand Men of Harvard," then joining in lustily as a cheerleader led them in chants of "BEAT YALE." Boarding the bus, however, cornerback Mike Ananis couldn't help thinking that at any moment some SDS zealot was going to commandeer the microphone and start shouting "HO, HO, HO CHI MINH, NLF IS GONNA WIN!"

*　*　*

The night before the 1938 game, Harvard coach Dick Harlow led the team in singing "Fair Harvard." Shocked to find out that several of his players didn't know the words to their alma mater beyond the first verse, he declared that no one would play the next day who was not able to sing the piece in its entirety. "The eleven men representing Harvard University tomorrow afternoon are representing the greatest institution of its kind in the world," he explained, "and, in this enviable capacity, they can be expected to know the words of 'Fair Harvard,' all three verses!" The players were, apparently, quick studies, mastering "Fair Harvard"—all three verses—before mastering Yale, 7–0.

Under Yovicsin, there would be no group sing-along of "Fair Harvard" at the Framingham Motor Inn. Instead, after final meetings with their position coaches, the players settled in with milk and cookies and watched a movie. The movies were chosen by the managers and projected in 16-millimeter on a portable screen. The night before the Princeton game, they had selected *Help*, which many of the players had already seen—five or six times if you were end Pete Hall—but were happy to see again, even as John Ignacio wondered whether Yovicsin had even *heard* of the Beatles. Tonight's movie was *Von Ryan's Express*, a World War II thriller in which Frank Sinatra led a plucky group of Allied POWs through German lines on a hijacked train. The movie was intended to be inspirational, but the players couldn't help noticing that Sinatra and most of his men were gunned down in the attempt.

At the Charter Inn, the Yale managers also set out milk and cookies, which some of the players took back to their rooms. Dowling and Hill watched TV for a while, then turned in. It had been a busy week for Dowling, with queries from the press and last-minute ticket requests. He had forty-two friends and family members coming in from Cleveland to see him play his final game for Yale. Now, as he lay in bed, he was relieved to have nothing to think about but football. He was really looking forward to playing Harvard. He loved a challenge, and the Boston Stranglers, he believed, would present Yale with by far the biggest challenge the team had faced.

XII

With Almost Contemptuous Ease

A t eleven o'clock on Saturday morning, two and a half hours before kickoff, Bob Dowd crossed Anderson Bridge and made his way toward Dillon Field House. The Harvard junior was so nervous he could hardly think straight. He had never played in a game of this magnitude. Last night, he had slept fitfully, and this morning he'd been too anxious to do much more than nibble at his steak and scrambled eggs at the Varsity Club. It didn't help that yesterday's *Crimson* had published a profile of him and his fellow tackle Fritz Reed. Although it was a rare moment in the sun for the offensive linemen, it only added to the pressure. On the way down from Adams House, Dowd had stopped in at St. Paul's Catholic Church, lit a candle to Jude, the patron saint of lost causes, and prayed that the knee he'd strained against Cornell wouldn't bother him too much. But he knew that adrenaline would make him forget his physical ailments. His real fear was that he'd screw up, that Yale's defensive tackle would blow by him and get to Lalich and he'd be embarrassed in front of 40,000 people. Against a team like Yale, a single mistake could mean the difference between winning and losing, and Dowd was terrified he'd be the one to make it—and spoil everything the team had worked for all year.

Picking his way through the tailgaters who surrounded the stadium, Dowd tried to calm himself, knowing that being *too*

243

keyed up could leave him worn out before the game even started. The air, pungent with the smell of grilled meat, was filled with the sounds of laughter, the tinkling of ice cubes in martini glasses, the glad shouts of children. As he walked past the silver-haired alums tending their hibachis in fraying, too-tight old letter sweaters, the ruddy-faced dads in Chesterfield coats tossing footballs with their sons, and the well-coiffed moms emphasizing a point with their Bloody Marys, Dowd had a sudden, fierce urge to stay there with them, eating and drinking and laughing. He'd give anything to watch the game instead of play in it.

*　　*　　*

By noon, ticket-holders were streaming into Harvard Stadium. Designed by Charles Follen McKim, architect of the Boston Public Library, and built by four hundred Italian immigrants in less than five months in 1903, the cement horseshoe was the largest stadium in the country, and the first permanent one. There was worry that it might collapse when filled with spectators. Hoping to inspire confidence, its construction superintendent announced that he would stroll around under the stands while fans took their seats before the inaugural game on November 14. The superintendent and the stadium survived, but Harvard fell, 11–0, to Dartmouth. The spectators (who included two hundred of the men who'd built the stadium, cheering lustily for Harvard) were less impressed with Harvard's team than with its new home. Although McKim had taken as his model the Panathenaic Stadium in Athens, site of the 1896 Olympics, it was Rome's Colosseum of which people were reminded. A visitor from Dartmouth wrote that he would not be surprised to see "an arched gateway swing open and pour forth a flood of Gauls and Thracians, of Samnites and retarii, all crying 'Ave Caesar!'"

The oldest stadium in the country, Harvard Stadium was surely also the least comfortable. There were no individual seats, just concentric slabs of fanny-numbing concrete rising so steeply from the field that spectators occasionally experienced vertigo. It was an appropriately severe setting for a team whose mascot was a Pilgrim. On November 23, 1968, as fans climbed to their perches, an anthropologist might have noted that those on the Harvard side were, on the whole, less well equipped than those on the Yale side, who were laden like Episcopalian Sherpas with seat cushions, binoculars, plaid steamer blankets, and silver thermoses filled with hot chocolate and who knew what else. On the Yale side, Kingman Brewster was there but Charley Loftus, the subject of an effusive retirement tribute in the game program, was not; agoraphobia would have him listening to the last and biggest game of his career on radio in New Haven. On the Harvard side, John Tyson sat in the student section, attending his first game of the season, in part because he wanted to watch his friend Calvin Hill play for Yale. Farther upfield, near the fifty, Nathan Pusey sat with his wife, Anne, who was knitting another crimson scarf. The seats around them were filled with Harvard administrators, players' families, and assorted luminaries, none more august on this particular day than Allen Rice '02, a retired surgeon who, attending his seventy-second Harvard-Yale game, had custody of the Little Red Flag. Hearing a familiar Boston-accented baritone asking to borrow his program, the brother of Harvard cornerback Ken Thomas turned to see Ted Kennedy, who had scored the Crimson's only touchdown in its 1955 loss to Yale. As the senator paged through the program, people kept coming up to him to say how sorry they were about Bobby.

Outside the gates, two ticketless but enterprising Yale students donned blue blazers, borrowed a trumpet and a trombone, and fell into step with the Yale band as it marched into the stadium.

In Dillon Field House, the Yale players, many of whom were putting on their uniforms for the last time, were quiet. Pregame nerves weren't a bad thing—"If you ain't wet under the armpits, you ain't worth a shit," the Doozer liked to say—and players had different ways of dealing with them. Levin scrolled through plays in his head, picturing himself running well. Hill retreated to the bathroom to read his Bible. Goldsmith leafed through the game program, a copy of which was placed in every locker; he liked to memorize the lyrics of the other team's fight songs. By now, he knew almost all of them by heart, from Columbia's "Roar, Lion, Roar" to "Fight On, Pennsylvania!" Jack Perkowski visited the urinal every few minutes, terrified he'd get out on the field and realize he still had to go. George Bass was frantic. While putting in his contact lenses, he'd dropped one in the sink. He could hardly see without them. A janitor had to take the sink apart before the lens was spotted in the trap. Even Dowling got a few butterflies before games—more from anticipation than from trepidation. He didn't like sitting around doing nothing. Like everyone else, he just wanted to start playing; he knew his nerves would dissolve at the first hit.

A half hour before the game, the teams walked out to the stadium for their warm-ups. At 45 degrees, the day was mild for late November, and there was barely enough breeze to stir the Harvard and Yale pennants that flew from the stadium's corners. Although checking out your opponents was frowned on, lest you psych yourself out, Ted Skowronski couldn't help sneaking peeks at Dowling and Hill. They were easy to spot, not only because of their size but because of the way they carried themselves: Dowling with languorous ease as he tossed passes, Hill with casual deliberation as he took handoffs and strode a few yards upfield. In the stands, the Harvard fans, too, had their eyes on Dowling and Hill; for most it was their first glimpse of the Yale stars, both of whom had been out with injuries on the team's last visit to the stadium. All the Yale players looked impressive in their toothpaste-white uniforms with blue piping—the football version of formal dress. The Harvard players, by contrast, looked less spruce. Their crimson jerseys were smart enough, but their tan football pants accentuated their hip and thigh pads, making them appear a bit lumpy and bumpkinish.

With Almost Contemptuous Ease

Ten minutes before kickoff, the Harvard players ducked through the small door in the stadium wall that led to the squad room, a low-ceilinged, cement chamber so dank one half-expected to see a rat scurry across the dirt floor. Pep talks before the Yale game tended to be brief; the players were already so pumped up that words were hardly necessary. Now Yovicsin reiterated a few technical matters before adding, "We've worked very hard for this. There's nothing more I can tell you. Just go out there and play." The coaches left the room and Gatto spoke. When the season began, he said, no one had believed in them. Here they were, two months later, and no one believed they could compete with Yale, no one thought they would walk out of the stadium undefeated. "But we know we can and we know we will," he told his teammates. "Now let's do it."

In a similarly claustrophobic room under the stands on the far side of the field, the Yale players gathered around their coach. Cozza went over a few last details before the team knelt on the dirt floor and he led them in the Lord's Prayer. Then they poured out onto the field, where their shouts were swallowed up by the roar from the stands.

As the Harvard players filed out of the squad room, Gary Farneti was feeling even more surly than usual. Yesterday, walking from the field house to practice, passing an area where workmen were setting up restraining ropes to handle the crowds, the sophomore linebacker had stepped in a post hole and sprained his right ankle. He'd spent the night with one leg dangling over the side of his bed, immersed in a bucket of ice. He'd gotten less than an hour of sleep. All week, the upperclassmen had been telling the sophomores to be prepared, that the Yale game was different. All week Farneti had insisted it was just another game to him. All week the alumni had assured him that beating Yale was something he'd remember for the rest of his life. All week he had nodded politely. Now, as he stepped onto the field, with the stands overflowing and the fans cheering and the band playing "Ten Thousand Men of Harvard," the stadium seemed twice as big and ten times as loud as it had all season. Farneti, who prided himself on being awed by nothing, was awed. The upperclassmen had been right. The Yale game really was different.

At 1:30, Yale's Bob Bayless kicked off and the crowd, on its feet, let out a cry.

*   *   *

The first few minutes emboldened Harvard fans to believe that the game might be closer than anticipated. Backup halfback John Ballantyne, returning a kick for the first time that year (the coaches didn't want to subject Hornblower's tender ankle to the mayhem of the kickoff), raced all the way to the forty-five before he was pulled down. Although the offense failed to make a first down and had to punt, and Yale moved quickly to its own forty-five in an efficient six plays, Harvard got the ball back when a Dowling pass, tipped ten yards downfield, sailed straight into the hands of a startled John Ignacio.

For the Harvard cornerback, it was a moment of vindication. Sophomore year, he'd been hurt so often he'd never even been listed on the depth chart; junior year, he'd torn his Achilles tendon; senior year, he'd separated his shoulder, sustained a concussion, and twisted his knee. Now, in his final game, Ignacio, who would go on to win the Fadden Award for the senior athlete who had overcome the greatest physical adversity, had intercepted Brian Dowling. What's more, after evading one tackler, he could see a clear path down the field all the way to the Yale goal line. "Oh my God, I'm going to score," he thought—a moment before he was knocked out of bounds at the Yale forty.

As the Yale offense trotted off the field, tackle George Bass remained spread-eagled on the ground. Unlike Ignacio, Bass hadn't missed a game in four years. After the interception, he had been on the verge of tackling the Harvard defensive back when corner-back Rick Frisbie hit him just as he planted his right foot. As

Bass lay on the field, it was clear to him the injury was serious, not only because his knee hurt so much but because Cozza had come out to see how he was doing. The coach, gently unbuckling and slipping off Bass's helmet, stayed at his player's side until Bass was carried off on a stretcher, under the worried eyes of his parents, who had flown in from Minnesota. It was the first time they'd seen him play for Yale. Bass, who had worn a second jersey with an unused running back number underneath his usual "78," wouldn't get the chance to run the ball today. Minutes into the final game of his career he became a spectator, watching from the sideline on crutches.

Buoyed by Ignacio's interception, Harvard moved to the Yale twelve, where Ballantyne fumbled. Lalich recovered. On the next play, Lalich fumbled and Bouscaren recovered.

Dowling promptly marched the Yale offense down the field. Two plays, in particular, showed Harvard what it was up against. The first offered an initial taste of the Dowling-Hill symbiosis. With the ball on the Yale twenty-five, Dowling went back to pass. Chased by Steve Ranere, he retreated to within a step of his own goal line before turning and, seeming to know exactly where Hill would be, throwing to his halfback at the Yale twenty-eight. The second offered evidence that Yale's offensive arsenal was hardly limited to Dowling and Hill. On a center trap, Fred Morris bowled over Alex MacLean and cleared a hole up the middle through which halfback Nick Davidson sped 33 yards before he was finally tackled by Conway at the Harvard thirty-six. Six plays later, Yale had first and goal at the three.

There, Harvard's defense stiffened. Levin tried the left side of the line and was gang-tackled by Frisbie, Emery, and four other players. No gain. Hill tried the right side and was met by Farneti and Mike Georges, among others. No gain. After the ease with which Yale had traveled the length of the field, it was a relief to Harvard fans to see the Stranglers assert themselves. Which made it all the more dismaying when, on third and goal, after faking a handoff to Hill so convincingly that Ignacio ran in and tackled the halfback, leaving the corner unmanned, Dowling loped into the end zone. Yale fans roared. A cascade of toilet paper unfurled from the stands. The band launched into "Bulldog." The cheer-leaders fired their miniature cannon, which sent a plume of smoke drifting across the field.

* * *

After that first touchdown, a pattern set in: brief, failed Harvard possessions followed by long Yale drives. Harvard's defensive game plan hinged on containing Dowling in the pocket, but the quarter-back rolled out on almost every play, forcing Harvard's linebackers and defensive backs into a dilemma: whether to stay back in pass coverage or to come up and defend the run. Whenever Harvard managed to break into the backfield, Dowling was able to stay just out of reach of his straining, panting pursuers. He was faster than he had looked on film, and his passes, contrary to reputation, were dismayingly tight spirals. Dowling was doing exactly what the coaches had warned them against, and they couldn't stop him. They had read all week about Dowling's "magic." Defensive end John Cramer had the strange sensation that maybe it was true: maybe Dowling really *was* a magician.

Hill, too, was quicker than his unhurried style had made him appear on film. Pete Hall, Harvard's fastest lineman—his team-mates called him "Greyhound"—felt he was always lunging for Hill's ankles and grasping nothing but air. The Harvard defenders had talked all week about softening up Hill with some big hits, but Hill was the one doing the hitting. On one play, he literally ran over cornerback Neil Hurley (who, at five feet ten, 170 pounds, was smaller by five inches and 50 pounds); Hurley was credited with the tackle, but only because he managed to hang on to Hill for dear life on his way to the ground. MacLean, too, was getting creamed. Whenever Dowling faked a handoff to Hill into the line, it was MacLean's job to tackle Hill before he could drift out for a pass. MacLean was carrying out his assignment, but each time he hit the Yale halfback, he felt as if he'd been hit by a truck.

From the stands, one had the sense that Dowling and Hill were toying with Harvard, like grown-ups taking on a gaggle of children in a backyard game of touch. Indeed, after Dowling's score, when Harvard was unable to move the ball, and Gary Singleterry's punt, a line drive that traveled only 29 yards, was returned by Bouscaren to the Harvard thirty-three, Dowling and Hill took turns running the ball down to the Harvard nine, where it was first and goal.

Once again, however, the Harvard defense dug in, holding Yale to six yards on its first three plays. Fourth down. It appeared that Harvard, to its relief, would limit Yale to a field goal. Against this offense, that seemed a major victory.

It was, however, a tenet of Dowling's play-calling philosophy that one didn't settle for field goals. (Bayless, the team's talented placekicker, had attempted only three all year.) On fourth down anywhere near the opponent's goal line, Yale almost always went for it, and almost always made it. This time, when Dowling rolled out to his left, he found his path sealed off by Steve Ranere and Lonny Kaplan; it appeared that Harvard finally had him cornered. But Dowling swerved, reversed field, and, seemingly without looking, lofted a pass to the far right corner of the end zone, where Hill was waiting without a Harvard player within five yards. With that touchdown—which triggered another cannon salute, another chorus of "Bulldog," and another toilet-paper fusillade—Hill scored the 144th point of his Yale career, breaking Albie Booth's all-time record, a mark that had stood for almost four decades. It would, it seemed, be a day of record-setting at Harvard's expense. Less than two minutes into the second quarter, the score was 14–0.

The Harvard defense was shaken. No one had moved the ball on them like this all year. They knew Yale had a great offense, but they hadn't known how great it really was. The confidence they'd carried into the game was fraying. Why couldn't they stop Yale? *Could* they stop Yale?

They weren't getting much help. Special-team mistakes kept giving Yale great field position, and the offense couldn't seem to make any headway. Each time the Harvard defenders went to the sideline, they felt as if they barely had time to take their helmets off before the coach yelled, "Defense back in." After the offense went three and out yet again, Emery, fastening his chin strap, muttered, "Can't you guys just get a first down and give us a break?"

For the Yale offense, it was business as usual. Everything was unfolding the way they'd imagined. The Harvard defense hit hard, but didn't seem nearly as good as advertised. The Toads were moving Harvard's smaller defensive linemen off the ball. After the first touchdown, it seemed this game would be no different from any other. After the second touchdown, some of the reserves on the Yale sideline began to gloat—no one had expected things to go *this* smoothly—but a few of the older players shushed them, saying there was still a long way to go.

The ease with which Yale's offense was able to pierce Harvard's vaunted defense was surprising. That Harvard's offense was unable to dent Yale's unheralded defense was no less surprising. Coming into the game, Yovicsin had believed that his team's only chance to win was by controlling the ball with its ground attack, thus keeping it out of Dowling's hands. That plan had fizzled when, on Harvard's second series, Gatto accelerated through a hole and felt the familiar twinge in his left leg that meant his hamstring had given way—the same hamstring that had bothered him on and off ever since he'd pulled it running indoor track freshman year. The Harvard captain limped off the field to the squad room, wondering whether his college football career was over. Bending Gatto's leg at a fifteen-degree angle, trainer Jack Fadden bound his calf and quad with tape. Known as a "check rein," the tape job would protect Gatto's tender hamstring but leave him unable to extend his leg. Gatto could run—sort of—but he couldn't sprint. He was crushed. Fadden, who had been taping athletes and dispensing wisdom at Harvard since 1920, reminded him there was a lot of game left, and one way or another his team would need him. But the greatest running back in Harvard history would spend much of the first three and a half quarters next to Yovicsin on the sideline.

With Gatto hardly playing and Hornblower, his ankle numb with cortisone and heavily taped, unable to perform with his usual panache, Harvard's running game couldn't get traction. Harvard's passing game was no more successful. Lalich, who had played through a variety of ailments all fall, hadn't been throwing well the past few games, but with Gatto and Hornblower running wild, it hadn't mattered. Today Lalich felt fine for the first time in weeks. Yet whether his injuries had taken their toll or whether, in the biggest game of his life, his nerves had finally gotten the best of him, the quarterback seemed a little off to some of his teammates in the huddle. When he came to the sideline, Yovicsin asked him what the problem was. "I'm trying," said Lalich, "but things just aren't going." Offensive football was all about chemistry and timing, and Harvard was out of sync, struggling in a way it hadn't since the first half of the Holy Cross game. The coaches were making adjustments and the players were trying to get back on track, but nothing was working. "What the hell's going on?" offensive line coach Jim Feula shouted on the sideline. Harvard gained only nineteen yards in the first quarter.

After Yale's second touchdown, just when Harvard fans were beginning to despair, Ballantyne brought them to their feet with another fine kick return, streaking down the right side to the Harvard forty-nine. Once again, however, the offense was unable to move the ball. On second down, Lalich's pass was on target, but the normally sure-handed Pete Varney dropped the ball. On third down, Yale end Pat "The Blade" Madden fought through two blocks and chased down Lalich for a seven-yard loss.

Singleterry went back to punt. Long snapper Bob Teske sent the ball back on the ground. Singleterry bobbled it, dropped it, picked it up, dropped it again, and, with Yale players swarming toward him, fell on it. Yale ball at the Harvard thirty-seven. Harvard, it seemed, could do nothing right. By contrast, even when the Harvard defense stopped Yale on the next possession, Bayless, punting for the first time in the game, angled his kick toward the sideline and landed the ball on the four, where it veered left and bounced out of bounds at the Harvard one-foot line. A perfect coffin corner.

Harvard, in the shadow of its own goal, couldn't get a first down, even with the help of a penalty on Yale that gave them an extra five yards. Three runs gained a total of two yards, and Singleterry had to punt from deep in his end zone. Having stifled its offense and pushed around its defense, Yale now dismantled Harvard's kicking game, as cornerback Ed Franklin, whose blocks of two Penn punts last year had set a Yale record, raced past a diving Gus Crim, leaped three feet in the air, and got a hand on the ball. The ball shot straight up, returned to earth, and bounced into the arms of Yale tackle Tom Neville. It was the first blocked punt of Singleterry's Harvard career. When Crim got off the field, Coach Stark, on the phone from upstairs, was so furious that the Harvard fullback worried he might be benched.

Yale's offense took over on the Harvard eight. On second and goal, Dowling rolled left. Frisbie, evading a block, dogged him all the way back to the twenty-one, where Dowling spun 270 degrees, headed right, and—almost as if he were trying to make things more challenging—threw back across his body to Del Marting in the far left corner of the end zone for the touchdown. After the whistle, a late-arriving Pat Conway hurled Marting to the ground in frustration.

It hadn't been a good day for the Harvard safety. Coming into the game, he had been confident that he'd intercept one or two of those wobbly Dowling passes, that he'd get in a few good licks on Hill. But he had yet to do either, and now his man had scored. Conway sat on the ground for a moment, as smoke from the Yale cannon wafted by and a Yale cheerleader scurried over to taunt him through his megaphone. Conway felt bad about what he'd done to Marting, his old pickup basketball buddy at Exeter. He got to his feet and ran across the field to where the Yale huddle was forming. The Yale players looked up, confused to see a Harvard player approaching. Conway tapped Marting on the shoulder. "I'm sorry, Del," he said, though he wasn't sure Marting heard him in the noise.

Instead of kicking the extra point, Yale went for two. Cozza figured it would put the game out of reach. The Harvard players thought it arrogant; Yale, up 20–0, was rubbing it in. Even the go-for-broke Dowling was a little surprised the coach didn't send in the kicking team. But he was perfectly happy to roll out, reposition his receivers with a wave of his left hand, and toss another strike to Marting. From the Yale side, a chant only recently beginning to be heard at American sporting events was audible: "WE'RE NUMBER ONE! WE'RE NUMBER ONE!" It was awfully early in the game for such a proclamation. On the other hand, Yale had scored three touchdowns with what a *New Haven Register* writer would describe as "almost contemptuous ease," and midway through the second quarter it was 22–0. At that rate, the final score would be something like 50–0. The only question seemed to be whether the Yale fans would run out of toilet paper.

*   *   *

Yale was dominating not only on the field but in the stands. From the first series, when the Yale side, prompted by its cheerleaders, had erupted in a vigorous and surprisingly well-enunciated rendition of "HOLD THAT LINE!" it was clear that Yale fans, pound for pound, were capable of making far more noise than their Harvard counterparts. Each Yale touchdown set off a roar as sudden and percussive as thunder, followed by a fortissimo rendering of "Bulldog" that sounded as though its singers had been rehearsed by Glee Club conductor Fenno Heath. Their repertoire of chants was impressive. Over the course of the first half, they produced high-decibel versions of "GET THAT BALL!" "GO, GO, GO!" "BLOCK THAT KICK!" "FIRST AND TEN, DO IT AGAIN!" and "Y-A-L-E YALE! YALE! YALE!" At one point, as their offense drove downfield, they began chanting something that sounded suspiciously like "WE WANT SEX!"—a demand that even in the Age of Aquarius seemed somewhat forward—but that on further listening turned out to be "WE WANT *SIX!*" Harvard fans, by contrast, cheered lustily on an à la carte basis but seemed reluctant to express their feelings en masse. And when several Yale students held up a sign that read FUCK HARVARD—surely a first in the annals of The Game—Crimson rooters were shocked into silence until it was confiscated by police.

Finding the game painful to watch, Harvard fans sought solace in their hip flasks, disappeared under the stands to buy popcorn, watched stray seagulls wheel above the stadium. Anything to take their minds off the carnage on the field. At one point, Fritz Reed's girlfriend, who was sitting with his parents, noticed that Mrs. Reed's binoculars were trained not on the field but on someone a few rows in front of them. What was she looking at? "I'm trying to figure out if Joan Kennedy is a natural blonde," she explained, "or whether those are black roots I see."

Yale's only sign of vulnerability, aside from the injury to Bass, had come at the end of the first quarter, when its cheerleaders, looking far sleeker than their Harvard counterparts in their white letter sweaters and white ducks, sprinted onto the field and performed their signature routine. In it, a single cheerleader stood on his head with his legs spread, in the shape of a Y, and, one by one, the others took a running start, somersaulted over the Y, and stood on *their* heads to make an ever-lengthening letter. This time, the final cheerleader couldn't quite clear the formation and crash-landed on his peers, reducing the entire structure to rubble and eliciting a round of applause from the Harvard fans. Finally, something to celebrate.

*   *   *

The suspicion that Yale was rubbing it in was reinforced after Marting's touchdown, when Yale attempted an onside kick—a tactic usually employed by a team trying to catch up near the end of a game. Cozza had never been one for running up the score, but with all the emphasis on both teams being undefeated coming into the game, it seemed possible that Yale wanted to leave no doubt in anyone's mind as to which undefeated team was superior. In any case, though Harvard was taken by surprise, guard Bob "Aminal" Jannino fell on the ball at the Crimson forty-two. But the point had been made: Yale felt it could do whatever it wanted. Indeed, Harvard couldn't take advantage of its good field position and once again went three and out, not before producing a moment of futility that might have been comic were it not so emblematic of Harvard's ineptitude. Lalich pitched to Gatto on the option—the coaches hoped that even at half-throttle, the captain could get the offense going. When Gatto saw that the ends were covered, he threw to Hornblower, but the halfback wasn't expecting it, and the ball hit him in the heels. For the fifth time, Harvard was forced to punt. This time Singleterry got the kick off cleanly, but on the ensuing return a frustrated Fritz Reed piled on Bouscaren after the whistle, and Harvard was penalized fifteen yards.

Once again, Yale was on the move, gobbling up yardage in chunks. On one play Hill dove over the line and gained four yards, nearly all of them airborne. On the next, Dowling handed off to Levin. Harvard fans, grateful for any play in which the ball didn't end up in the hands of Dowling or Hill, felt they'd been granted a momentary reprieve. But Levin ran off tackle for six yards before he was hit and spun around by Farneti—whereupon the 220-pound fullback, legs churning, ran *backward*, dragging three Harvard defenders another five yards before he was finally brought down.

Yale was on the Harvard thirty-four when, on third and three, Dowling pitched left to Hill. Turning the corner, Hill had yet another first down—and looked, in fact, as if he might be headed for Yale's fourth touchdown—when Conway, coming from the side, launched himself helmet-first at the halfback and jarred the ball loose. In the ensuing scramble, Harvard's Lonny Kaplan latched on to it. On the sideline, John Yovicsin shouted, "Where's Champi?"

XIII

Handkerchiefs

Half a century later, Harvard fans still disagree on whether Yovicsin was looking for a spark or throwing in the towel when he turned to his second-string quarterback and said, "Okay, you try it for a while." Certainly, a change couldn't hurt. Lalich had completed two passes for 22 yards and looked overwhelmed. On the other hand, Champi had thrown only twelve passes for the varsity all year. Yovicsin was loyal to his seniors and extremely fond of Lalich. He hated to bench the quarterback who'd gotten them this far, in what should be the crowning game of his college career. He knew Lalich wasn't the only one playing poorly, but he had to try something. It was, he said later, the most difficult coaching decision he'd ever had to make.

When Yovicsin told him he was going in, Champi was ticked off. He wanted to play, but not under these circumstances—not with five minutes left in the half and Harvard trailing by 22 points. Yovicsin hadn't played him all year and *now* he was putting him in? He felt he was being thrown to the wolves. He worried he'd make a fool of himself. But then he decided, the hell with it, he didn't really give a damn. He'd just do the best he could.

As Champi trotted onto the field, Yale fans (and all but the most knowledgeable Harvard fans) flipped through their programs to find out who #27 was. The Yale players had never heard of

Champi—he hadn't been mentioned in the scouting report—and they had no idea what to expect. It was hard not to interpret the switch as a sign of desperation, a waving of the white flag. There was, however, one man on the Yale sideline who didn't necessarily welcome the sight of the backup quarterback. Calvin Hill had been Champi's teammate on the Harvard-Yale track team that had beaten Oxford-Cambridge in the summer of 1967. Hill had seen Champi throw the javelin. He knew Champi had an arm.

Champi's teammates were surprised to see him in the huddle. Some of them assumed that Lalich had gotten banged up and would be out for a few plays before returning. They knew Champi was the best passer on the team. But he had never taken snaps in practice with the first string, and the few times he had played with them in games he had seemed a little antsy. How would he handle playing in front of 40,000 people in the Harvard-Yale game? As Champi stood in front of them, kneading his hands, Tommy Lee Jones thought he looked scared to death. Whether it was Champi's nerves or his thick Boston accent, when he called the first play, it came out sounding something like *fawdy wawdy on one*. Locals like Dowd and Jannino understood that he was calling "Forty-one on one," a pitchout to Hornblower. But Jones and everyone else who'd grown up beyond Route 128 looked at one another, bewildered, and Champi had to repeat the call.

Sometimes merely changing a quarterback can give a team a lift, and if at first all Champi did was hand the ball off, Harvard's offense nonetheless began showing signs of life. Crim, who had *not* been benched after the blocked punt, ripped off a few good runs, and though Champi's initial pass was incomplete, J. P. Goldsmith hit the receiver, Bruce Freeman, before the ball arrived, and was called for interference. With forty-four seconds left in the half, Harvard had moved to the Yale fifteen, third and six. If nothing else, as long as Harvard had the ball, Yale couldn't score.

Few people noticed that when Yovicsin put in Champi for Lalich, he had also put in Freeman for end John Kiernan. Harvard had a running offense, and Kiernan, a solidly built junior who loved getting hit almost as much as he loved to hit, was the better blocker. But the running game wasn't working, and Freeman, the six-foot-three sophomore from California who hadn't played since getting the stinger in the Princeton game, was the better receiver. Now, in the huddle, he told Champi he thought he could get open behind the linebacker on the far side of the field. On the twelfth play of the drive, Champi dropped back and threw a dart to Freeman at the seven, whereupon the end turned and ran untouched into the end zone. Harvard flubbed the extra point when the long snapper bounced the ball back to the holder, but it didn't seem important; Yale had been so dominant that Harvard's touchdown was more about saving face. At least Harvard wouldn't get shut out. Thirty-nine seconds later, the half ended with the score 22–6.

*   *   *

In the Yale squad room, the players were loose and confident. That they were handling Harvard was nothing unexpected—after all, they had done the same thing to every other team they'd faced that fall. The ease with which they were doing it, however, was a little surprising. Cozza, who never had to say much to this team, told them not to let up, to keep playing their game.

In the Harvard squad room, the players sat on their benches, gnawing on orange segments, staring at the floor. They knew how poorly they had played. They knew they were fortunate to be down by only sixteen points. The offense had done nothing till the end of the half; the defense had never been pushed around like this. The only time Harvard had trailed by more than a touchdown all year had been in the opening game of the season. No one was giving up, but Yale was head and shoulders above any other team they had played. Yovicsin told his team that they were still in it; all they had to do was shut out Yale while getting two touchdowns and a field goal. But the players weren't really listening to him. A few of the seniors spoke up. It was their last game and they didn't want to go out this way, they said. Let's not embarrass ourselves. Let's show them we're a good team. Then Gatto spoke. It isn't over yet, he said. Let's go out there and play our game and who knows what could happen.

* * *

Harvard got off to a good start in the second half. The defense held Yale to a quick three and out, forcing them to punt for only the second time that day. After Conway spun away from a Yale tackler and returned the kick nine yards, Harvard had the ball at its forty-three.

Hoping that another chance might bring him back to life, Yovicsin reinstalled Lalich at quarterback. But after two Ballantyne runs gained only four yards and Lalich threw a pass that landed at Crim's feet, Harvard had to punt. Bouscaren fielded the kick and spun away from Freeman only to be hit by Jannino, a former linebacker who relished his infrequent opportunities to tackle someone. Bouscaren fumbled; Freeman recovered on the Yale twenty-five. When the Harvard offense took the field, Champi was at quarterback.

Champi had been disappointed and a little peeved when he was told that Lalich would start the second half. But his annoyance helped him forget his nervousness. In high school, vomiting before games had eased the pressure; today anger served the same function. After a pitch to Gatto lost two yards, Champi threw a short pass to Varney. The sophomore end, who'd been in bed most of the week with the flu—and lost fifteen pounds—had dropped the only pass thrown to him in the first half. But now he raced down to the six, where he knocked Goldsmith aside before Coe brought him down at the one. On the next play, Crim piled into the end zone behind Jones and Reed. This time the extra point was good. Less than three minutes into the third quarter, it was 22–13. Harvard fans felt a sliver of hope.

The rest of the third quarter settled into the game most people had expected to see. Yale still got the better of things, but it was a little more even. Dowling continued to bedevil the Crimson linemen. One play, a scramble from the Yale twenty-five, brought to mind the kind of comic-book sequence in which a succession of villains takes on the superhero only to meet defeat. First, Kaplan dove at Dowling's feet but couldn't grab him; then MacLean forced him to retreat but was blocked by Whiteman; then Kaplan, resuming his pursuit, almost got to him, but Dowling wriggled out of reach; then Zebal chased him toward the Yale goal line until Dowling planted his feet at the nine—sixteen yards behind the line of scrimmage—and, just as Zebal and two other Harvard players were about to engulf him, threw all the way back across the field to Levin on the thirty-one. The play gained a mere six yards, but if the path Dowling had followed during his ten-plus seconds of curlicue scrambling had been laid out in a straight line, it would be at least forty yards long. Even Harvard fans, squirming during the play as if they were the ones chasing him, had to admit all that Merriwell talk didn't seem so far-fetched.

The score would have been more lopsided if Yale hadn't kept fumbling. Their second of the quarter occurred on third and less than a yard from the Yale forty-four, when Levin leaped over the line. He made the first down but lost the ball when Conway flew in at the end of the play, helmet first, and knocked it loose. Cramer recovered on the forty-two. Their third took place on Yale's next possession, after they had driven from their own ten to the Harvard thirty-five. Dowling pitched to Hill, who was all the way down to the seventeen and headed for the goal line when he cut outside. He never saw Frisbie, who had fought off a block to chase him down from behind and wrench the ball free. Tom Wynne dove on it at the ten. Yet even these gaffes seemed a kind of noblesse oblige, as if Yale's offensive gifts were so extravagant that the team could afford to waste a few touchdowns. The third quarter came to an end with the score 22–13. Yale was still firmly in control, but reporters in the press box noted that it was the first time in twenty-three straight quarters, dating back to the Brown game, that Yale had failed to score.

Harvard's slim hopes seemed to evaporate on the first play of the fourth quarter, when Hornblower, a step slower on his gimpy ankle, was unable to turn the corner on a sweep. Tackled around the legs by Jim Gallagher, he felt a searing pain. He knew immediately that his day was done. He tossed the ball away and hopped off the field on his good foot. It had been a frustrating afternoon for Hornblower. He and Gatto had come into the contest rushing for a combined 163 yards per game; against Yale they would total 23 yards on fourteen carries.

Two plays later, however, Harvard hopes flared anew when Champi rolled to the left, slipped on the chewed-up turf, regained his footing, and fired the ball to Freeman at midfield. Breaking two tackles, Freeman staggered all the way to the Yale twenty-seven. But the 49-yard gain was called back; Champi's knee had touched the ground.

Back to punt yet again, Singleterry got off a low 35-yard line drive. Fielding it on the bounce, Bouscaren evaded a tackler and headed upfield, where he encountered Bob Dowd. Dowd was simmering with frustration. Each time they came to the line, the Harvard offense was taking guff from some of the Yale defenders about how badly they were being beaten. The linebacker on Dowd's side had been particularly annoying, and now, as he saw #27 approach, Dowd grabbed his jersey, whipped him around, and slung him to the ground like a lassoed calf.

Dowd may have vented his spleen, but, once again, Yale was starting in Harvard territory, this time at the forty-five. Mixing plays adroitly—a pass to Weinstein, runs by Hill and Davidson, an impromptu quarterback scramble—Dowling soon had his team at the Harvard five. On third down, he called for a square out to Weinstein. Rolling to the right and seeing no one in his path, Dowling, as if refusing to chance another turnover, kept the ball himself and ran it easily into the end zone, triggering yet another broadside from the cannon, another chorus of "Bulldog," another toilet paper salute. A strand settled on the arm of Tom Wynne, who slapped it away angrily. On the sideline, the Yale coaches discussed whether to go for two again. This time Cozza decided against it, reasoning that the safer one-point kick would still leave the game beyond Harvard's reach. "I figured, what difference does it make?" Cozza would say later. "There was no way they could come back."

With everyone's attention on Dowling as he crossed the goal line, few people saw what befell in his wake: Weinstein peeling back and obliterating Gary Farneti with a block so square and forceful it seemed it should have its own cartoon balloons attached, *Batman*-style, reading POW! and SPLAT! Farneti, usually the one doing the obliterating, had never been hit so hard. Weinstein had executed the most satisfying block of his career, an exclamation point on what appeared to be the game-clinching score.

The extra point provided its own humiliating coda when Hurley and Frisbie, sprinting from opposite sides in an attempt to block the kick, ended up blocking each other, leaving Hurley facedown, out cold, as his helmet rolled eight yards upfield, like a crimson pumpkin, before coming to rest. Taught since Pee Wee football to get right up after being knocked down, Hurley, who had been kneed in the temple, attempted to do so, but crumpled to the ground, wobbly as any movie drunk. He struggled to his feet again. He fell down again. With the help of a trainer, Emery half-carried, half-dragged his teammate off the field. Although Hurley, who had suffered a concussion in the first game of the season, was able to touch his nose with his finger and tell the team doctor who the president of the United States was, it was clear he couldn't play again that day. In the temporary stands in the end zone, his last-minute date, Kathy, partly watching the game but mainly thinking about how cold it had gotten, didn't see the play. "I think Neil got knocked out," said her escort, Hurley's high school friend. "Oh, *great*," thought Kathy, who had gotten dressed up for the game in a sleeveless wool dress whose plaid miniskirt matched her coat, not to mention her special alligator shoes. "Not only am I freezing to death but there goes my date for tonight." The extra point made it 29–13. There were ten minutes and forty-four seconds left.

The first of several thousand Harvard fans started leaving now, muttering something about beating the traffic as they made their way, a little embarrassed, past their neighbors to the end of the row and down the steps, taking a last look at the field before they ducked under the stands. Some would listen to the rest of the game on their car radios as they headed back to the suburbs; others were too disheartened. Clumps of alums trudged across the Charles to drown their sorrows at their final clubs, the sound of cheering Yale fans mercifully fading as they approached the Square. In the press box, reporters began tapping out ledes: "Brian Dowling completed a spectacular Yale football career today by passing for two touchdowns and running for two more," wrote Steve Cady of the *New York Times*. Red Smith packed up his typewriter and left for his hotel room to finish up his column. Heywood Hale Broun made his way to a waiting limousine and headed to the studio to tape his story on Yale's victory for the *CBS Evening News*. A *Crimson* editor hurried back to 14 Plympton Street to help get out the postgame extra with word of the defeat. The mother of Harvard defensive end John Cramer, who had flown in from Oregon—it was the first time she'd seen him play college football—started thinking of what she could say to console her son.

By now, the sun was dipping behind the west side of the stadium, leaving the Harvard fans in shadow while the Yale fans sat in what remained of the sunlight. But the shadows were slowly reaching across the field. The wind had whipped up off the river, rippling the Harvard and Yale pennants on the corners of the stadium. Yale end Lew Roney shivered on the sideline. He was from Wyoming and he knew what cold was, but this strange, damp chill seemed to seep into his bones. In the fading light, the color on the players' uniforms seemed to fade, too, as if the game itself were now being played in black and white. Held on the Saturday before Thanksgiving, the Harvard-Yale game traditionally marked not only the end of the football season but the end of autumn. Winter was on its way.

Harvard's next possession began promisingly, with a nine-yard Ballantyne run to the thirty-one. On second and less than a yard, Champi threw a long pass to Freeman, who had gotten behind the cornerback. Goldsmith arrived just in time to bat the ball away. On third down, Champi burrowed into the line on a quarterback sneak and met a wall composed of Williams, Bouscaren, and Coe. A measurement found he had gained a foot or so. Fourth down. With less than ten minutes left and about two inches for a first down, Yovicsin decided to go for it. Harvard's chances, however minuscule, might well come down to this play. As Yale fans launched into a thunderous chorus of "HOLD THAT LINE!" Champi tried another sneak. Again, he was met by Williams, Bouscaren, and Coe. The officials called for another measurement. Eyeing the evidence, the referee reared back, and, in the manner of a Hollywood movie general urging on his troops, threw his arm toward the Harvard goal line. The Yale fans let out a roar. Cozza jumped in the air and punched the sky in delight. Yale ball, first and ten at the Harvard thirty-one.

Once again, Yale was on the move. In the stands, their fans began to wave white handkerchiefs at the Harvard side, in the traditional Ivy League victory taunt; it looked as if the Yale side was experiencing a sudden, extraordinarily localized snow flurry. The "WE'RE NUMBER ONE" chant started up again and gathered force until it was almost deafening. The trickle of Harvard fans leaving the stadium became a small river. On the bench, Rick Berne, who had played little since aggravating a pinched nerve in his neck early in the second half, turned to his best friend from high school, for whom he'd wangled a sideline pass, and said, "Let's get this shit over with and start partying."

As the game wound down, the sidelines grew ever more chaotic. Despite its size, Harvard Stadium was a surprisingly intimate place to play. The Yale Bowl was much larger, and its stands were farther from the field and leaned back at a gentler angle. At Harvard Stadium, the seating started precipitously close to the action and climbed so steeply that players often felt as if the spectators were on top of them. It was not uncommon for players standing on the sidelines to hear fans behind them shouting, "Down in front!" Today, it was so loud that Cozza wore headphones most of the game, as much to hear himself think as to communicate with his coaches in the press box. So many passes had been handed out to alumni, former players, and players' friends that the sidelines were as congested as the Park Street subway platform at rush hour. At one point Cozza yelled into his headphones, asking the coaches upstairs what yard line Yale was on, only to have four or five nearby alumni answer him. Spectators stood within inches of the field; when Dowling ran wide for his first touchdown, he ended up in their arms. And now, with Yale driving for another score, Bulldog fans were swarming down from the stands to join their team on the sideline. J. P. Goldsmith heard his name called; the Yale administrator for whom he worked part-time at the bursar's office came over to shake his hand and congratulate him on a great season.

On second down, Dowling went for the kill. He pitched to Hill, who rolled right and sent a perfect spiral into the end zone, where Davidson, arms extended, prepared to gather it in. At the last moment, Tom Wynne batted it down. Oohing over the play, fans didn't immediately notice that behind the line of scrimmage, both Dowling and Hill lay on the ground, motionless. Then the stadium went quiet. It was a heart-stopping sight: two of the greatest players in Bulldog history surrounded by trainers and doctors on their hands and knees. Cozza came out to check on them, while the other Yale players looked on, aghast.

Eventually, Dowling (hit from behind by middle guard Mike Georges after he pitched to Hill) got to his feet; he had retwisted a sore foot but was okay. Hill (hit by linebacker Dale Neal just after he let go the pass to Davidson) was shaken up. He stumbled to the sideline, where Narduzzi turned him around and sent him right back in, to an ovation from relieved Yale fans.

After another long scramble ended in an incompletion, Yale faced fourth and eight from the twenty-nine—too far for a field goal, too short for a punt. Once again, they went for it. This time, Dowling's pass was nearly intercepted, and Harvard took over on downs. There were eight and a half minutes left.

On the field, the Harvard players sensed they were not going to be able to overcome the deficit. But even if they couldn't win the game, they were determined to finish it the right way. Fritz Reed told himself it was important to keep playing hard; Harvard had to let Yale know they had shown up for the game.

Whatever Harvard was going to do, it would have to do it with a backfield composed almost entirely of second-stringers. Hornblower, of course, was out, and Gatto had spent much of the game on the sideline, trying to loosen up his hamstring while discussing strategy on the phone with Pat Stark and going over plays with Champi on the bench. He had played in spots, but his teammates could tell he was getting by largely on guts. Midway through the fourth quarter, believing that his presence on the field was only hurting the team, Gatto asked Yovicsin to take him out. In a season during which he'd repeatedly shown his players how to put the team before themselves, this was perhaps his most captainly moment.

With Gatto and Hornblower out, Yovicsin was forced to rely on juniors John Ballantyne and Jim Reynolds at halfback. The five-foot-nine Ballantyne, who had won Harvard's freshman boxing tournament in the 155-pound weight class, was one of the smallest players on the team, a quick, shifty runner with a feisty streak. He hadn't played much this season until the Brown game, when, after Hornblower sprained his ankle, he had carried seven times for 126 yards and two touchdowns in little more than a quarter.

Today, his two long kickoff returns had given Harvard what little early hope it had had. Reynolds, also five foot nine but of sturdier build, was a determined blocker, relentlessly cheerful, and willing to do whatever he was asked—although prior to the Yale game his most notable contribution may have been that he held for extra points. Ballantyne and Reynolds knew they were no Gatto and Hornblower, but they wanted to show they weren't there just to play out the string.

After a nifty 15-yard run for a first down by Ballantyne, however, the offense stalled, and Harvard was forced to punt. Bouscaren, displaying the moves of the running back he had once been, made a twisting, leaping 18-yard return to set up Yale at its own forty-five. Six and a half minutes remained. A Yale trainer told the injured George Bass that he should start making his way to the locker room, so he wouldn't get knocked down by exuberant Yale fans when the game ended. Bass picked his way on crutches down the crowded sideline toward the open end of the stadium.

On the Harvard sideline, as the offense watched Yale drive toward another touchdown, it started to sink in that the game was out of reach. Skowronski was heartsick, realizing that his football career was coming to an end. Even Gatto, the irrepressible optimist, couldn't help feeling a little gloomy. Harvard hadn't given up—Goldsmith, on the Yale sideline, could hear how hard its defense was hitting—but as the seconds ticked away, its hitting took on a whiff of desperation. On a short Dowling-to-Weinstein completion, Ignacio wrapped his arms around the receiver's middle, but couldn't bring down the towering end. Even after the whistle blew, Ignacio kept tugging, determined to get him to the ground—to no avail. Kaplan stepped in and shoved Weinstein. Weinstein shoved back. The crowd roared, the officials jumped in, and their teammates herded the two players apart.

On the Yale sideline, Cozza and his coaches began sorting through how and when to insert some of the reserves into the game so they could win their letters. In a two-birds-one-stone maneuver, while putting in his subs he'd take out his star seniors, one at a time, giving fans a final chance to cheer the men who had made these last few years so memorable: Levin, Marting, Weinstein, Hill. Dowling, of course, would be saved for last.

Yovicsin, too, began putting in a few senior reserves, like linebacker Gerry Marino. Marino had been expected to start this year but had been sidelined by a series of injuries. By the time he'd recovered, Farneti was ensconced in his position. Now, in the final quarter of his final game, Marino was playing again, and though it was only mop-up time, and though both knees, both ankles, one hamstring, and one elbow were cocooned in tape, it felt good to be back on the field, to be in on a few tackles.

With six minutes left, Yale faced third and half a yard from the Harvard forty-five. To have any chance at all, Harvard had to make this stop. Expecting a plunge, the Crimson linemen submarined, diving low to take the Yale line's legs out from under them—only to see Levin skip over the heap of fallen players for three yards and another first down.

In the Harvard stands, a professor of sociology turned to his neighbor, a professor of statistics, and asked him what the probability was of Harvard's coming back to tie the game. "Infinitesimal," the statistician replied. The sociologist decided to beat the crowds and left. Half a minute later, the statistician left, too.

A team that is ahead in the fourth quarter usually tries to "milk the clock" by running the ball, rather than risk stopping the clock with an incomplete pass. Yale, however, was still throwing; four of their last six plays had been passes, a few of them bombs into the end zone. In the Harvard huddle, no one said anything, but Pete Hall was not the only player who felt Yale was rubbing salt in the wound. In the press box, the Boston writers agreed that Yale was trying to run up the score in hopes of moving up a notch or two in the national rankings. But Dowling had never been one for sitting on a lead, and Yale was simply playing the same pull-out-the-stops way it had played all year. Too, there was an unspoken feeling among the players that they had squandered numerous scoring opportunities, that they really were three or four touchdowns better than Harvard, and that they wanted to show the world how good they were. All this speculation, however, was moot. Dowling was passing, but he was completing his passes, and the clock continued to move.

On first down at the Harvard thirty-two, with four minutes and five seconds left, Dowling called for another long pass. As three Harvard defenders broke through the Yale line, he hurled the ball toward Hill at the goal. But Frisbie stayed with Hill, step for step, and, as both players leaped, the ball flew inches above the Yale player's outstretched fingertips. Trotting past Frisbie on his way toward the huddle, Hill tapped the Harvard player on the back, acknowledging his good coverage.

Cozza called Bill Primps and Greg Lawler to his side. Primps, a sophomore fullback who would likely be a key contributor next year, needed to play to get his letter. So did Lawler, a senior quarterback who was talented enough to have started for many Yale teams but in four years had played only when Dowling was injured. Cozza put a hand on Primps's shoulder and told him to go in for Levin after the next play. He would keep Lawler next to him until the right moment came to pull Dowling, who would no doubt walk off the field to one of the biggest ovations in the history of Harvard Stadium.

With less than four minutes left, Dowling came up with another unexpected call, a screen pass. Yale hadn't practiced the play that week, but it unfolded perfectly. Dowling dropped back, luring in all five Harvard linemen, who seemed certain to tackle the Yale quarterback behind the line of scrimmage for the first time all day. Just as they were about to smother him, he lofted the ball over their heads to a waiting Bob Levin. Preceded by a chevron of blockers—Morris, Gee, and Perkowski—the Yale fullback took off down the sideline. Usually limited to short-yardage work, Levin now did some fine open-field running, brandishing the ball in one hand with Dowling-like abandon as he cut back inside. He had gone almost twenty yards when, encountering several Harvard defenders, he heard Hill behind him, calling for the ball. Turning to lateral, Levin was hit by Mike Georges, who, after failing to get his hands on Dowling, had sprinted nearly thirty yards downfield to catch Levin from behind. The ball squirted loose. Harvard's Steve Ranere fell on it. Spectators and players alike couldn't help taking a peek at the scoreboard clock: There were three minutes and thirty-four seconds left. Some of the fans making their way out of the stadium paused on the steps.

Levin and Hill jogged off the field together. When they reached the sideline, Cozza gave them a what-were-you-thinking look. Levin was annoyed at himself. He almost never fumbled. It was his second fumble of the day, the team's fifth. But what did it matter? The score was 29–13. Yale was still up sixteen points with only a few minutes to go.

* * *

Harvard had the ball at its own fourteen. Eighty-six yards lay between them and a touchdown. To a spectator in the stands, eighty-six yards looks like a very long way; to a player on the field, the opponent's goal line, at that distance, can seem as remote as the horizon line in a desert.

No one in the Harvard huddle was thinking about sixteen points. The players just wanted to finish the game right, just wanted to remind Yale that they were still there. Even so, it seemed strange that Harvard, acting as if it had all the time in the world and not three minutes and thirty-four seconds, came out running. A pitch to Ballantyne lost two yards. And though a Ballantyne reverse gained seventeen yards and a first down at the twenty-nine, the two runs consumed forty-four precious seconds. Two minutes and fifty seconds left. Champi, under pressure, threw incomplete. On second down, Champi, dropping back to pass, was quickly buried under a veritable pigpile of Yale players composed of Madden, Kleber, and the Gallagher brothers. The twelve-yard loss made it third and twenty-two. The chant of "WE'RE NUMBER ONE!" swelled anew from the Yale stands. The TV camera panned to the Harvard sideline. "There you see Captain Vic Gatto, number forty," said announcer Don Gillis. "A sad ending to his final game as a collegian."

Gillis was one of many people in the stadium who hadn't noticed that, twenty yards downfield from the pigpile, a red flag lay on the ground. The crowd quieted and the players milled about uncertainly as the officials conferred. Then the referee, clutching the ball, began walking toward the Yale goal line as purposefully as a Boy Scout leader setting off on a hike. The players trailed behind in some confusion. The referee crossed all the way into Yale territory before carefully placing the ball on the forty-seven. A holding call in the Yale secondary. As he arrived on the scene, Gus Crim thought it had to be the longest penalty in the history of football. Indeed, because the penalty was marked from the spot of the foul, it represented an almost unimaginable reversal of fortune. Instead of facing third and twenty-two from their own fifteen, Harvard had first and ten on the Yale forty-seven—a 38-yard swing in Harvard's favor.

Four plays and sixty-seven seconds later, however, after Neville dropped Champi for an eight-yard loss, Harvard faced another daunting task: third and eighteen from the Yale thirty-eight. Yale called time-out, an unusual decision given that it stopped the clock with one minute and thirteen seconds left in the game. The Yale band struck up the *Mickey Mouse Club* theme song, and the Yale cheerleaders fired their miniature cannon over and over. The flurry of white handkerchiefs in the stands thickened to a blizzard. (Meant to taunt the fans on the far side of the stadium, the hankies acted on the Harvard players like a red flag on a bull, making them all the more determined to finish the game strong.) To their chant of "WE'RE NUMBER ONE!" Yale fans now added a humiliating addendum: "YOU'RE NUMBER TWO!" repeated over and over at a volume that seemed to make the stadium throb. A fresh wave of Harvard fans headed for the exits. On television, Don Gillis pointed out that Champi was "getting some great experience" for next year. Two Yale coaches left for the locker room to get the champagne and cigars ready.

The "YOU'RE NUMBER TWO" chant reverberated as Champi brought the team to the line. Once again, he dropped back to pass. Once again, the Yale line was in on him. Champi cocked his arm to slow them down, but the pocket crumbled and he was buried by Fran Gallagher and Tom Neville and backup middle guard Milt Puryear. As he went under, Champi, thinking he saw Crim to his left, tried to lateral the ball, which coughed clumsily out of the scrum and dribbled toward tackle Fritz Reed.

That of all Harvard's offensive linemen it was Reed toward whom the ball made its way was fortuitous. Offensive linemen are not known for their manual dexterity or their speed afoot; the adjective *lumbering* is routinely applied to them. If they see a ball on the ground, they are taught to fall on it. But Reed, the former end who, to his dismay, had been switched to tackle in preseason, had the presence of mind to pick up the ball and take off down the field. The Yale players seemed momentarily paralyzed; some of them thought they'd heard a whistle. And because Yale's defensive backs were playing deep to prevent the long pass, Reed found a prairie's worth of open space in front of him. Pat Madden, himself a former offensive end, raced diagonally across the field toward Reed, but, perhaps assuming the Harvard player was a tackle of the lumbering variety, took the wrong angle and just missed him. Reed made it to the Yale twenty before, like a boy running downhill whose legs start to go too fast for his body, he began to stumble, finally pitching forward into the arms of safety Ed Franklin at the fifteen-yard line. Reed had picked up twenty-six yards, Harvard's longest run of the day. Instead of fourth and eighteen from the thirty-eight, it was first and ten from the fifteen.

Hearing the roar from the Harvard stands, George Bass paused at the far end of the field on his way to the locker room. He was joined there by Madden's girlfriend, who had arranged to meet Pat at the open end of the stadium after the game and had left her seat a few minutes early to get there in time. Only five feet three, Debbie couldn't see what was taking place at the far end of the field. "What's going on?" she kept asking Bass. "What's happening?" But all Bass, a minister's son who almost never cursed, could say was, "Oh, damn. . . . Oh, damn. . . . Oh, damn."

The Yale defense began to pep one another up in the huddle. They weren't overly worried. The team was still ahead by sixteen points with one minute to play, and they knew that even if they gave up another touchdown, the offense would get the ball back and run out the clock. But they were a proud group of men and they were determined to keep Harvard from scoring.

On the next play, Champi fired the ball to Freeman, who caught it at the Yale five, turned, and shoved his way into the end zone. The score was now 29–19. There were forty-two seconds left.

By this point, everyone in the stadium was standing. The Harvard band struck up "Ten Thousand Men of Harvard." On the Harvard sideline, defensive end Joe McKinney noticed that the Yale fans had put away their handkerchiefs. In the press box the Boston sportswriters nudged one another and said that losing 29–19 wasn't so bad. But the players were hastily doing the math: If Harvard made its two-point conversion and then recovered an onside kick, they had, in theory, a chance to tie the game. Someone on the Harvard sideline reflexively tossed a kicking tee onto the field. Ballantyne stepped from the huddle and fired the tee back toward the bench; everyone knew Harvard had to go for two.

Cozza took this opportunity to insert two more seniors into the game so they could earn their letters: linebacker Fran Boyer, inspirational leader of the George Bush Memorial Scout Team, and cornerback John Waldman. A converted halfback, Waldman had hoped to start for the varsity this year, but two talented sophomores, Don Martin and Kurt Schmoke, had moved ahead of him on the depth chart during preseason. Waldman considered quitting; he wanted to be a neurosurgeon, and he could use the time for his premed studies. Narduzzi talked him out of it. Though he had played mostly JV, Waldman was glad he had stuck with it. Pleased to realize he'd be getting his letter, he ran toward the Yale huddle.

At five feet nine and just shy of 150 pounds, Waldman was the smallest player on the Yale team, other than the second-string kicker. The man he would cover, Pete Varney, was the largest player on the Harvard team. Even without the fifteen pounds he'd lost to the flu that week, the Harvard end outweighed the Yale defensive back by nearly a hundred pounds and was a good five inches taller. Nevertheless, as Varney ran five yards into the end zone and cut inside, Waldman made a deft play, reaching around the larger man from behind and swatting at the ball before the Harvard player could gather it into his belly. Yale fans roared. On his only play of the game, Waldman, it appeared, had done his job. But there was another flag. Pass interference. Goldsmith, incensed—yet another iffy call had gone Harvard's way—went momentarily berserk, shaking his head vigorously and kicking the turf like an irate baseball manager.

Harvard would get a second chance—this time from the one-and-a-half-yard line. In the huddle, Champi suggested a quarterback sneak. Reed, recalling the two failed sneaks earlier in the quarter, urged Champi to give the ball to Crim. Reed wanted to block for his fellow Ohioan. (When the team needed to pick up a particularly tough yard, they often ran over the left side, behind Reed and Tommy Lee Jones.) "Okay, but it better go," said Champi. "We've come this far, it would be a shame not to get this." Reed and Jones parted the Yale line, and Crim got it. 29–21.

Forty-two seconds left. It dawned on a great many people that it was in the realm of possibility that Harvard could tie this game. In the stands, a Harvard junior turned to his friends and announced, "If Harvard pulls this off, I will leave the stadium naked." On Storrow Drive, a Harvard administrator who had left early to beat the traffic was listening to the game on the radio as he drove home to the North Shore. He was about to enter the Callahan Tunnel. Knowing he'd lose reception, he pulled over and stopped in the right lane. With cars honking angrily as they swerved around him, he listened to the rest of the game. In Harvard Square, hundreds of fans who had left the game early, seeking comfort in bars and restaurants, rushed outside and began running down Boylston Street toward the stadium, from which issued, every so often, a mighty roar.

XIV

Forty-Two Seconds

Ken Thomas was shaking inside. Until a few minutes ago, he had been sitting on the Harvard bench, just waiting for the game to be over. It had been an awful season for the junior cornerback. Last year, he had been a top backup, a favorite of defensive backfield coach Loyal Park, who called him "Rabbit" because the five-foot-seven, 180-pounder was so quick. Thomas had also returned an occasional punt, played on the Headhunters, and handled onside kicks: special short kickoffs, used in extremis by trailing teams, that gave the kicking team a chance to recover the ball. Though he had never kicked before, Thomas had learned how to strike the top of the ball, driving it into the ground and producing a series of bounces, the third of which (djjj djjj *boom!*) leaped high in the air, allowing his teammates time to get to it. Onside kicks were exceedingly rare, but Yovicsin, who had been a kicker himself in college, made his team practice them every day. Thomas took his assignment to heart and got so good at them that he could produce that ideal high bounce four out of five times. By the end of the 1967 season, he felt he had a decent chance of starting at cornerback the following year and could hardly wait for the 1968 season to begin.

In the spring of 1968, Thomas's girlfriend told him she was pregnant. They would, of course, keep the baby; they were devout

Catholics, they'd been dating since they were high school sophomores, and they had planned to marry someday. But at the age
of nineteen, Thomas saw his life turn upside down. In a matter
of weeks he went from hanging out with his roommates at the
Quincy House grill to being married, living in a small apartment in
North Cambridge, and trying to keep up with his premed studies
while working part-time as a dishwasher at the Faculty Club—and
wondering how he could possibly afford a child.

Thomas had reported for the 1968 preseason in less than top
condition. A few of his teammates had been allowed to play their
way into shape. But they weren't coached by Loyal Park. Thomas
soon found himself on the bench. Park no longer called him Rabbit.
After a while, he rarely called him anything at all; Rick Frisbie was
Park's new favorite. Thomas grew increasingly bitter. His father
was a career Army man, and the family had moved a lot. Sports
had given Thomas an identity; sports had gotten him through high
school; sports had gotten him to Harvard. If he wasn't succeeding
in sports, he felt he was a failure.

The baby had arrived three days before the Penn game. At practice that afternoon, his teammates whooped and clapped him on the
back. Equipment manager Jimmy Cunniff bought a box of "It's a
Girl!" cigars for Thomas to pass out. Several of the assistant coaches
gave him their children's outgrown baby clothes. That everyone was
so wonderful almost made things worse. Thomas felt he was the one
bad apple who couldn't enjoy this extraordinary season. Living two
and a half miles from campus meant he hardly saw his teammates
after practice. Unless there were team meetings, he skipped training
table and caught the number 79 bus back to his wife and daughter.

Thomas never considered quitting—he had started the year
and he would see it through. But he was miserable. In games,
when his fellow reserves were on their feet, cheering for their
teammates, Thomas sat on the bench, stewing. He still played on
the Headhunters, he was still the team's onside kicker, but he no
longer stayed late to practice on his own. He didn't see the point.

He knew this would be his last football game. He'd already decided not to play next year; he never wanted to play for Loyal Park again. But after Fritz Reed's improbable run, it occurred to him that he might have to execute an onside kick. He had never tried one in a game. And this wasn't just any game. It was the biggest Harvard-Yale game in history. He was terrified. Like the student who sits down to an exam, looks at the questions, and realizes he should have studied harder, Thomas began to wish he'd practiced more. Not to mention that he'd been sitting the entire game and his foot was cold. He stood up and frantically began to swing his leg.

Across the field, the Yale sideline was in some confusion. On a normal kickoff, a receiving team's front line consisted of five or six beefy linemen, who blocked for the lighter, faster players behind them. For an onside kick, the receiving team often inserted what, years later, would be called a "hands team": not only putting more players on the front line but stocking it with halfbacks, receivers, and defensive backs—players accustomed to fielding the ball. Yale, however, had no special onside kick return team, and had never practiced defending them, presumably because they hadn't seen the need. Only once had an opponent (Cornell) been close enough in the fourth quarter to try one, and Yale had recovered the ball just fine. Now Kyle Gee went to Coach LaSpina and suggested they put some people on the front line who were used to handling the ball. LaSpina took the idea to Cozza, but the coach said no. He didn't like to try in games things they hadn't practiced during the week.

Cozza sent out their usual return team, with five big men up front. Weinstein and Hill were stationed ten or fifteen yards farther back. Bouscaren and Levin were ten yards behind them. All four would have been ideal candidates for the front line but could be of little use where they were. Cozza did make one substitution. Mindful of the promise he'd made in preseason, when he'd told Dowling that if he stayed healthy all year he'd let him return a kickoff against Harvard, he sent in the quarterback as one of the deep men, alongside Davidson. Standing on the fifteen-yard line, Dowling could only watch from afar what would be his last play in a Yale uniform.

An onside kick is a bit like a bunt in baseball. The ball must be hit just right. It has to travel ten yards or it isn't legal, but if it goes much farther, the kicking team can't get there in time to recover it. Even a well-executed onside kick is a long shot; only one in seven tries succeeds.

On the whistle, Tom Wynne, Harvard's regular placekicker, strode toward the ball as if to boom it downfield, then veered away, allowing Thomas to come from his right and strike the top of the ball with his foot. In the event, Thomas's worst fears came to pass. He mishit it, and instead of the customary end-over-end trajectory culminating in a high third bounce, the ball skittered crabwise on the ground toward Yale's Brad Lee.

If Cozza could have chosen an offensive lineman to field the onside kick, it might have been Lee. Although a well-muscled 220 pounds, the junior guard was no lumbering oaf; in high school he had played offensive end, and as a relief pitcher on the Yale baseball team he was accustomed to fielding ground balls. It was Lee who had recovered the onside kick in the Cornell game. Like Thomas, Lee had not had the year he'd expected. He had hoped to start; in preseason, when it became evident that Bart Whiteman would beat him out, he'd been so disappointed he'd nearly quit. He had gone so far as to walk to the corner phone booth one night to call his mother and tell her he was coming home, before realizing he couldn't do it. Unlike Thomas, he was glad now to be on the team; as the first guard off the bench, he had ended up playing almost as much as he would have had he started, and he was thrilled to be part of this unforgettable season.

As the ball skittered toward him, closely followed by a horde of Harvard players, Lee had to make a split-second decision. He knew his task was to fall on the ball, but he could either go forward to meet it or he could wait until it came to him. As a baseball player, he had been taught to be aggressive, to charge grounders, to play the ball instead of letting the ball play him. Waiting, however, would give him a chance to set his feet so that when he got hit he wouldn't fumble. He chose the latter option. As the football came toward him, it seemed to veer slightly upfield. The ball caromed off his chest. As Lee lunged to retrieve it, Harvard's Joe McKinney crashed into him. When second-string safety Bill Kelly arrived on the scene a split second later, the sophomore was astonished by what he saw: the football, lying on the ground, unattended. Kelly was a superb athlete—all-league in three sports in high school, drafted as a pitcher by the St. Louis Cardinals, first-string Harvard freshman quarterback—but all he had to do was fall on it. Thomas may not have kicked it the way he'd wanted, but the result couldn't have been better. Harvard ball on the Yale forty-nine. Forty-two seconds.

In the Harvard huddle, no one was thinking any longer of just trying to make a creditable showing. To a man, they believed they were going to score. "Now we *have* to do it," someone said. As a sophomore, Bruce Freeman hadn't spent much time with the juniors and seniors around him in the huddle. They had always seemed so much older, their concerns so different from his. But at that moment, for the first time, he felt an unshakable bond with them. He felt that he knew them now, and they knew him.

In sports, sudden changes of fortune are commonly called momentum shifts, but the phrase hardly seemed adequate to account for what was happening. As Yale tackle Tom Peacock, who had replaced the injured George Bass only to be injured himself, put it, "You just got the feeling that the universe had shifted somehow and that something significant—portentous—was taking place. Some kind of weird force that had descended upon the stadium."

Yet such was Harvard fans' belief in the omnipotence of Yale's stars that even with forty-two seconds left and Yale's offense on the sideline, many of them worried that Dowling and Hill, as a kind of gridiron dei ex machina, would somehow step in and save the day for Yale. Indeed, as Champi and the Harvard offense huddled, Dowling and Hill were pleading with Cozza to put them in on defense. It was not such a far-fetched idea: Dowling had made thirty-three interceptions as a high school safety, Hill had been the top linebacker on the freshman team. Most big-time college coaches wouldn't have thought twice about okaying such a move if they thought it might help their team win. But Cozza said no. "I'm sorry, I can't do that," he told them. "Think of what it would do to those young men who have played those positions all year long." His two stars could only stand on the sideline, Hill with his hands on his hips, Dowling with his arms folded, and watch.

In the week leading up to the game, all anyone had talked about was Yale's offense and Harvard's defense. Now it was Yale's defense and Harvard's offense that would decide the game. On the Harvard sideline, Emery and some of his teammates stood on the bench so they could see better, sneaking looks at the scoreboard clock, which seemed to be going impossibly fast. Ten minutes earlier, Steve Zebal had been walking from teammate to teammate, shaking their hands and telling them it had been a hell of a season and they had nothing to be sorry for. Now he was on his knees, praying.

On the Yale sideline, some of the coaches, stunned by the turn of events, seemed to be in a state of shock. Others were frantically yelling instructions that no one on the field could hear. The offense shouted encouragement to the defense; there was nothing else they could do. Weinstein felt as if he were in a slow-motion nightmare from which he was unable to awake. Perkowski kept looking up at the scoreboard; the clock seemed hardly to move. The Harvard cause was aided by a new NCAA rule, instituted that year, that stopped the clock whenever a team made a first down, so the chains could be moved. If it hadn't been for the new rule, time would have long since expired.

On the field, Mike Bouscaren decided he had to make something happen. The leader of Yale's young defense had played well that day; he had recovered Lalich's fumble in the first quarter, he had made several fine punt returns, he had batted away a key third-down pass. But in the third quarter his fumble had led to Harvard's second touchdown. And in the fourth quarter it was Bouscaren who had been caught holding on the long penalty. He was determined to atone for his mistakes, to do something extraordinary, to make a big play that would stop Harvard. And it was clear to him that to stop Harvard, he had to stop #27, its second-string quarterback. One way to stop him would be to hit him hard enough to put him out of the game.

Bouscaren saw his opportunity on the first play after the onside kick, when Champi dropped back to pass. Almost immediately, Neville broke past Dowd into the backfield. (It was the moment of humiliation Dowd had dreaded when he had prayed to Saint Jude that morning.) Chased from the pocket, Champi barely eluded Neville, and then a lunging Williams, as he took off down the field.

Racing across the turf, Bouscaren leaped at the Harvard quarterback near the Yale sideline, extending his left arm in a clothesline tackle—so named because the recipient's forward progress is arrested as suddenly as if he'd run full speed into a clothesline—and dropping him, as it happened, at the feet of Coach Narduzzi. The Doozer applauded vigorously. But, as Bouscaren would observe many years later, in trying to make up for a mistake, you can sometimes try *too* hard. There was another flag. In getting Champi to the ground, said the referee, Bouscaren had grabbed his face mask. It was the third of three close, crucial calls, all of which had gone Harvard's way. Narduzzi, shaking both fists and screaming at the officials, had to be restrained by Cozza.

Combined with Champi's fourteen-yard run, the fifteen-yard penalty gave Harvard a first down at the Yale twenty with thirty-two seconds left. The Yale defense, which had outperformed the Boston Stranglers almost all afternoon, looked tired. They weren't used to playing an entire game—they'd never had to, because by the fourth quarter Yale was always so far ahead that Cozza could send in the scrubs. Furthermore, though Harvard had been in several close games that year, Yale had trailed only twice all season, both times early in the first quarter and then for only a few minutes. They had never entered the fourth quarter with less than a twelve-point lead. They had never faced pressure like this. Meanwhile, every official's call, every bounce of the football, seemed to be going against them. The players weren't panicking, but they had lost some of their certitude. In the huddle, they tried to buck one another up: "Come on, let's *go.*"

For the Harvard offense, everything was going right. As discombobulated as they had been in the first half, they were now in perfect sync. Each time Skowronski broke the huddle and headed to the line, he felt as if his feet weren't even touching the ground. He had the eerie feeling that no matter what Harvard did, it was going to work. Tommy Lee Jones, sensing that Yale was getting flustered, reminded himself to stay cool, to stay focused, to do his job, to *think.* Champi, meanwhile, had entered the kind of exalted state that Dowling seemed always to inhabit—the kind of state in which time seemed to slow down, the kind of state that a later generation of athletes would describe as being "in the zone," the kind of state Champi hadn't been in since his senior year in high school. He would never be the charismatic type, but there was no doubt who was leading this team.

Harvard's good fortune seemed to come to an end, however, when a long pass to Freeman at the right corner of the goal line was broken up at the last moment by defensive back Don Martin. On second down, Champi threw again to the right corner of the field. This time, the pass was intended for Reynolds. Again, Martin batted it down. Third and ten from the twenty. Twenty seconds left.

By now it was getting dark. It was the time of day when mothers begin calling their children inside for supper, and the children, though they can barely see the ball, beg to stay out and play a few minutes more. The word *gloaming* would appear in the accounts of several Boston sportswriters the following morning.

In Dillon Field House, Hornblower sat in the trainer's room, his foot marinating in a bucket of ice. With four minutes left in the game, the trainers had told him he might as well go in and get his ankle taken care of. There was no radio in the room, but every so often, he'd hear a roar and he could feel the building tremble. He had no idea what was happening—was Harvard coming back or was Yale sealing its victory?—but clearly *something* was.

Champi had tried to pass on ten straight plays. With so little time left and so many yards to go, everyone expected another pass. "Whattya think about a draw?" said Gatto, on the phone to Pat Stark. Running the ball would be an enormous gamble. If the play failed, Harvard would face fourth and long with almost no time left on the clock. On the other hand, Harvard hadn't tried a draw all game and might catch Yale off guard. Stark gave Gatto the go-ahead. His right thigh swaddled in tape, the Harvard captain limped onto the field. He had thought that when he'd asked to come out of the game, that was that. But there were still twenty seconds left in his college football career.

In the huddle, the call met with a fraught silence. Everyone was flashing back to last year's Yale game, when, with less than a minute to go, driving for the winning touchdown, Harvard had run the draw. After a sizable gain, fullback Ken O'Connell had fumbled on the Yale twelve. He'd been in Stark's doghouse ever since and was on the sideline today. Crim, whose rugged running had helped Harvard back into the game, was the fullback. All Crim could think was: *Don't fumble.*

On the Yale sideline, Narduzzi, suddenly suspecting, bawled, "Draw! Draw!" but there was so much noise that the players on the field couldn't hear him. Expecting a pass, Yale's linebackers retreated into coverage, and their ends stormed ravenously upfield. Champi dropped back as if to throw, then tucked the ball into Crim's belly. Dowd had struggled all day with Neville, Yale's superb sophomore tackle, but this time, he moved a little to his left, inviting Neville to loop outside, which left a hole where he had been. That hole was enlarged by Skowronski, who'd had his hands full with Williams but was able to seal off the middle guard. For a moment, as Crim approached the line, all he could see was the fans in the stands behind the end zone. He rumbled a dozen yards before bulling into Goldsmith, who held on as monster back Ron Kell arrived to help bring down Crim at the six.

As soon as the whistle blew, everyone on the Harvard offense signaled frantically for time-out. First and goal, fourteen seconds left. While Champi conferred with Yovicsin on the sideline, policemen herded a few hundred overzealous Harvard fans, who had spilled onto the field, back behind the end zone. By the time Harvard came to the line, however, the fans had edged onto the field again, and the officials had to stop play until they had shooed back the trespassers. Yale fans who not long ago had been screaming "YOU'RE NUMBER TWO!" were now pleading "HOLD THAT LINE!"

With everyone in the stadium standing and howling—Harvard fans for their offense to score, Yale fans for their defense to stop them—Champi dropped back to pass. He moved to his right, but was unable to find an open receiver. He feigned a throw; Coe and Neville leaped in the air, arms outstretched, to block it. He scurried left, chased by Fran Gallagher. He looked right and left, but could find no one open before Jim Gallagher pulled him down at the eight for a two-yard loss. Champi called Harvard's final time-out. Everyone in the stadium looked at the clock. There were three seconds left. Time for one more play.

Again Champi trotted to the sideline to confer with Yovicsin, who called for a curl-in to Varney, the same play they'd tried on the two-point conversion attempt. Champi dropped back, but once again Yale's linemen broke through, and he couldn't find his big end. Champi pump-faked to slow the pass-rush, then ran to an unoccupied area near the line of scrimmage. There, unable to spot an open receiver, he came to a stop. As bodies bobbed and lunged around him, Champi had the strange sensation that nobody could get to him, as if he were surrounded by a force field. And then, after what seemed an eternity but might have been a second, the sensation ended and he knew he had to move. Turning right, he nearly ran into Neville, who swiped at him as Champi fled all the way back to the sixteen, where he circumnavigated the fallen Dowd. By now the game clock had long since run down to 0:00, but the play, by rule, would be allowed to run its course. (The average play lasts four seconds; Champi would scramble for a Dowling-esque eight, a lifetime in football terms.) Champi looked right—nothing there—then looked left, and suddenly, as if he just had to find the proper angle for everything to come into focus, it seemed as if he were looking down a tunnel of players, at the end of which he saw Gatto. A split second before he was clobbered by Bouscaren, Champi, throwing off his back foot, hurled the ball toward his halfback.

Gatto, like Varney, had been running a curl. When he saw that the play had broken down, he moved, as well as he could on his injured hamstring, across the back of the end zone, trying to find open space. By the time he got to the far left corner, he found himself alone, and, not wanting to draw Yale's attention to that fact, had, like a shy student who knows the answer and wants to be called on but doesn't want to make a fuss, raised a tentative hand. As the ball came toward him, it looked as big as a watermelon. It is a truism in football that the easiest pass to drop is the one that arrives when you are wide open. But after four years at Harvard, three years at Needham High, and countless tutorials with his father in the Gatto backyard, there was no way he was going to drop this one. The Harvard captain caught the ball in his gut, and, after a moment's pause—like the delayed reaction of a cartoon character who gets knocked over by a feather—toppled over.

For a moment, there was silence. Then a roar rose from the Harvard side. Toilet paper rained down. Several hundred delirious fans rushed onto the field. Some lifted Gatto into the air, others ran in all directions. A middle-aged couple—he in a suit, she in a fancy coat, heels, and black gloves—tiptoed onto the field, tentative smiles on their faces, looking as if they were venturing onstage at one of those newfangled theater productions in which audience participation was encouraged. But the celebration was premature. Although there was no time left on the clock, Harvard, down 29–27, was entitled to a two-point conversion attempt. This time, no one threw the kicking tee onto the field.

It took the police several minutes to clear the field, and even then, they could corral the crowd only to the fringes of the end zone, where they stood ten deep. "Quiet, please!" the P.A. announcer implored. As an official tried to tidy the end zone of stray toilet paper, Gatto got on the phone with Stark. There was no question what the call would be: Varney and Freeman running curl-ins. The same play they'd run for the last two-point conversion attempt. The same play they'd just tried on the Gatto touchdown. On a curl-in, the quarterback usually has time to look for only one of his receivers. In the huddle, Champi turned to Varney, the bigger of his two targets, and said, "I'm coming to you." At the line, Champi raised his hands in the quarterback's universal appeal for quiet—it looked as if he were blessing the crowd—but so briefly that the gesture seemed almost pro forma, as if he were eager to get on with things. As he bent over center, Champi felt a sense of inevitability, almost as if what was about to happen had already happened and he was merely repeating it. It seemed almost anticlimactic when he rolled right, pulled up, and threw. After all those years of anxiety, it was like playing catch with his uncle at the playground behind St. Anthony's. The moment Varney turned, the ball was there.

On the Harvard sideline, Mike Ananis had no idea what was happening. The Yale end zone was fifty yards away in the dusk, and at five feet nine, he wasn't tall enough to see over everyone in front of him. Before the last play, he turned around and looked up at the Harvard stands. Twenty thousand faces were peering toward the closed end of the stadium. For the last half hour the fans had been yelling their lungs out, but now they were strangely quiet. Then hats, programs, and scarves flew into the air, there was an enormous explosion of sound, and Ananis knew that Harvard had done it: 29–29.

XV

Pandemonium

In a photo taken a split second after the catch, Varney, his back to the camera, is in mid-jump, arms overhead in triumph, right hand squeezing the ball like a grapefruit. Yale cornerback Ed Franklin has his arms around Varney's midsection, as if the massive receiver were about to rise aloft like a Macy's Thanksgiving Day balloon and he was gently trying to keep him earthbound. The referee, facing Varney, is bending slightly backward from the waist, arms overhead in a mirror image of Varney's, signaling the score, wearing the startled expression of someone who has just been ordered to surrender. In the background, Crim and Reed are jumping for joy, while Skowronski is getting to his feet. Yale linebacker Andy Coe, arriving too late, is slowing to a walk. In the distance, the Harvard stands are beginning to blossom with white handkerchiefs.

The moment Varney caught the ball, Harvard fans stormed the field. From the stands, it looked as if a dam had burst. Varney tried to find Gatto to give him the ball, but before he could, the massive end was hoisted overhead by ecstatic admirers. Gatto and Champi, too, found themselves on the shoulders of strangers. Skowronski was knocked over in the delirium, and the crowd was so dense he had to struggle to stand up. Conway was kissed by women he'd never met, hugged by professors whose courses he'd never taken.

Some fans danced on the fringes of the throng; others staggered around aimlessly, shaking their heads and shouting "I can't believe it" and "Oh my God!" Students thrust two fingers in the air, a gesture that in this tumultuous year almost always indicated a desire for peace but now signified victory. Fans smacked Harvard players on the shoulder or pounded them on the back, wanting some kind of physical contact, as if the players possessed a talismanic power that might be transferable. Children begged them for chin straps, elbow pads, autographs. Fans of a more mature age dug up chunks of the chewed-up turf to preserve as relics, as if the field had become sacred ground. Watching from the press box, the *Globe*'s Harold Kaese wrote, "A stranger might have thought that Hubert Humphrey had been elected President, or the Vietnam War had ended." If any spectators noticed a naked young man darting through the crowd on his way out of the stadium, they took it in stride. They had just witnessed something far more improbable.

Standing here and there in the melee, the Yale players, in their white uniforms, were as still as marble statues in the gathering dark. Dowling, arms crossed, watched the celebration in silence. Cozza somehow found Yovicsin at midfield and shook his hand. Yale fans hurried, grim-faced, from the stadium. Some remained in the stands in a state of shock, dabbing their eyes with the handkerchiefs they'd been waving minutes earlier. Some tried to console the players, but it was hard to know what to say. An alumnus reminded the sophomore Neville that he had two years to get back at Harvard. It was no comfort. On his way to the locker room, Weinstein ran into a friend who had left a few minutes before the end because she wanted to congratulate the players as they exited the stadium. Now she ran up to him, exultant, calling, "We won, we won!" The normally sweet-tempered Weinstein said, "No, we didn't," more gruffly than he'd intended, and walked on.

Goldsmith, swept along in the human tide toward the open end of the stadium, was in a daze. He had known agony on the football field, but *this* had been too strange to be painful. He didn't feel sad;

he felt bewildered. What had just happened? He saw Narduzzi, who looked no less stunned. "God damn it," Goldsmith said. "You deserve better." Center Fred Morris felt as if he'd been transported to a foreign country where everyone around him was going crazy in a language he didn't speak for a reason he couldn't understand.

It took some Harvard players half an hour to make their way through the fans to Dillon Field House. Others lingered on the field, soaking it all in, as if fearing that if they left the scene of the miracle, they might find out it hadn't really happened. Players and fans alike kept looking up at the scoreboard, as if they just had to see the evidence again—HARVARD 29 YALE 29, in yellow bulbs that shone ever brighter against a sky that was now almost dark. As people left the stadium, *Crimson* staffers handed them one-page extras: "HARVARD-YALE DRAW, 29–29." The paper's Monday edition would more accurately capture the emotional gist of the game, in what would become one of the most famous headlines in sports history: "HARVARD BEATS YALE, 29–29."

*   *   *

After each victory, the Yale team gathered around Cozza in the locker room to belt out the Yale fight song: *Bulldog! Bulldog! / Bow, wow, wow / Eli Yale!* It was a moment that always left Cozza a little choked up. But today the cramped dressing room on the second floor of Dillon Field House was so quiet that the plunk of a dropped soda can was startling. The players could hear the muffled sounds of Harvard whooping it up in their locker room downstairs. For fifty-seven minutes, Yale had dominated the game, but its historic season had ended in a tie that felt worse than any defeat. Some of the players showered and dressed as quickly as possible; others sat at their lockers, gazing into space, still wearing their helmets, as if they might be summoned out onto the field and given another chance. A few wept silently.

On his way to the Yale locker room, Calvin Hill stopped by the Harvard locker room and found Gatto. "Good game," said Hill, as they hugged. Hill congratulated a few other Harvard players, who would remember his sportsmanship years later. Then Gatto, one arm across Hill's back, accompanied him to the Yale locker room to see Dowling. "What a way to go out," said the Yale captain to his Harvard counterpart.

Even the most hard-boiled members of the Boston and New York press waited nearly thirty minutes before entering the Yale locker room, wanting to give the players time to collect themselves. Then they began to circulate, asking questions in the muted, respectful tones reporters use at crime scenes and funerals. Asked what the tie felt like, Marting said, "Nothing. A tie feels like nothing." About his knee, Bass said, "It's just a sprained knee. The knee will get better before I do." Dowling and Hill answered questions patiently. They neither made excuses nor blamed the officials. Hill praised Gatto's grit and Champi's arm. "I still think we had the better football team," he said, "but you have to give Harvard credit." Dowling—who had run for two touchdowns, passed for two more, and "put on perhaps the most thrilling and spectacular one-man show in the 65-year history of the Allston horseshoe," according to the *Boston Sunday Advertiser*—was as gracious as ever, though when a reporter asked him how it felt to lose his first game since seventh grade, he pointedly observed, "I thought it was a tie." He signed a few autographs, then gathered up his football gear and started toward the door, where Cozza caught up to him. "Buddy," the coach said, "you're still an All-American to me."

Downstairs, so many people crammed into the Harvard locker room that it was difficult to move. "Where's George?" shouted a hoarse John Yovicsin as he entered. He fought his way through the crowd and found Lalich. It had been a bittersweet afternoon for Harvard's first-string quarterback. He was glad the team had come back, but he had been heartbroken not to be out there with the guys he'd played with all season. At the end of the game, as fans poured past him onto the field, he had sobbed uncontrollably in his wife's arms. He felt he'd failed his teammates. Now Yovicsin put an arm around him and reminded him that if it weren't for him, the team would never have gotten to this point: "The 1968 season was yours—you brought us here."

Across the room Champi was pinned up against his locker by reporters, who seemed surprised to find someone who resembled Clark Kent more than he did Superman. As Gerald Ezkenazi of the *New York Times* wrote, "Frank Champi, the junior quarterback who came off the bench to lead the Crimson, turned out to be a chunky, moonfaced boy who is baldish." The moonfaced boy also turned out to be a highly quotable interviewee—if somewhat more metaphysical than most. "It's been a strange day from the beginning," he said quietly, pausing as teammates came by to shake his hand, pound him on the back, or muss his thinning hair. "I'm an intuitive guy, and when I woke up this morning I was sort of in a dream. It felt like something great was going to happen to me. Then when I got here, I still felt strange. It didn't feel like I was here but someplace else. I still don't feel like I'm here."

Not far away, Pat Conway turned toward his locker for a moment, unable to keep the tears from coming. At the beginning of 1968, he'd been under fire in Vietnam, wondering whether he'd even be alive by the end of the year. Now 1968 was almost over, and here he was, back at Harvard, part of what had to be one of the most unbelievable football games ever played. He shook his head, and, letting out a whoop, rejoined his teammates.

At the press conference, reporters could tell Yovicsin was doing his best to avoid saying anything that might add to the pain of the man sitting next to him, who seemed as stunned as his players. "It was almost like a nightmare, really," Cozza said. "I don't know how else to explain it. We feel like we lost it, even though we didn't. Something like that won't happen again in a thousand years."

Outside Dillon Field House, several thousand Harvard fans— long-haired undergrads side by side with gray-haired alums—stood in the darkness and belted out "Ten Thousand Men of Harvard." No one wanted to leave.

Then the band played "Fair Harvard." *First flower of their wilderness, star of their night / Calm rising through change and through storm.* Not a few old grads were forced to resort, once again, to their handkerchiefs.

* * *

Because it was the last game of the season, the Yale players didn't have to go back to New Haven that night. Many of them had made plans to celebrate with friends and family in the Boston area. Eight or ten players, the majority of them sophomores and juniors whose families hadn't been at the game or who hadn't been able to line up dates for the evening, returned on the team bus with Cozza, who made it a point always to travel with his players. Most of them sat alone. The driver had the radio on, and the big story was the game (*an incredible Harvard comeback . . .*). The players asked him to turn it off. The rest of the two-and-a-half-hour trip passed in silence.

Yale players who stayed in Cambridge wished they hadn't. Kyle Gee and his girlfriend went to a Harvard party. When they found out Gee played for Yale, the Harvard students assured him Yale was the better team and should have won. They were trying to be nice, but it was the last thing Gee wanted to hear. Brian Dowling went to a reception his mother had organized at the Sheraton Commander Hotel for the Dowling entourage from Cleveland, before heading back to New Haven, where he watched a replay of the game on TV. He turned it off at the half, unable to watch any longer. George Bass limped to dinner with his parents. An elderly man came up to their table and said, "Don't worry, son, it'll all go away eventually." Bass wasn't sure whether he meant the physical or the emotional pain. Bob Levin and Meryl Streep had planned to go to Durgin-Park, the Boston restaurant legendary for its no-nonsense food and its equally no-nonsense waitresses, but they didn't have much of an appetite and ended up getting a quick bite in Cambridge. Streep was upset about the game, too, but did her best to cheer up Levin. They decided to go to a party they'd heard about. Surrounded by deliriously happy Harvard students, they lasted about ten minutes before heading back to New Haven in Streep's wheezing Nash Rambler.

As Brad Lee walked off the field, a Harvard lineman had caught up to him and told him not to worry about the onside kick; it could have happened to anybody, and it had been a great game. But Lee was distraught. All he wanted to do was shower and dress and get out of the locker room as quickly as possible. He spent the night with his girlfriend, a Tufts junior, at the Sheraton Commander. Next morning, on the train back to New Haven, he could tell he was coming down with the flu. That afternoon, lying in his bed at Saybrook with a 103-degree temperature, replaying the kick over and over in his mind, he got a call from a *Globe* reporter. In the course of their conversation, Lee told him that he had returned alone on the train. In the article published the next day—and reprinted across the country—the reporter wrote that Lee had been so devastated by his fumble that he'd refused to go home with the team. Over the following weeks, Lee would receive more than a hundred letters and telegrams, some from senators and congressmen, offering words of consolation. A few cited the California tackle who had run sixty-five yards the wrong way with a fumble in the 1929 Rose Bowl. It was of little comfort to Lee that, as one letter-writer assured him, the player had overcome his gaffe to become a successful businessman.

Bruce Weinstein went to a small party at his father's hotel room in Boston. His father had been coming to his games ever since Bruce was a boy. But for more than a year he had been suffering from excruciating leg pain. He managed to attend one or two games early this season, but by Princeton he was bedridden. He had summoned up all his strength to get to Harvard Stadium, and to invite a few relatives and friends back to his hotel for what he had assumed would be a celebration of Yale's remarkable season. Bruce showed up, but was feeling so depressed that, after ten minutes, he excused himself and drove back to New Haven. He couldn't know that today would be the last time his father would ever see him play. What the doctors thought was sciatica turned out to be liver cancer. His father died in March. For the rest of his life, Weinstein would wish he'd stayed longer at the party.

J. P. Goldsmith and his girlfriend had a quiet dinner with his parents at Anthony's Pier 4. It was hard to say who was more downcast, J.P. or his father. Back at Yale on Sunday, J.P.'s girlfriend, taking pity on him, stayed the night and allowed him "certain liberties": a silver lining of sorts.

Walking out of the locker room and into the Cambridge night, Mick Kleber was surprised he didn't feel worse. After the initial shock wore off, it came to him, almost as an epiphany, that he had been incredibly fortunate to have been part of this game. Old Blues might be rolling over in their graves, but this was a game that would never be forgotten. He went off in search of a bottle of Wild Turkey.

Calvin Hill had planned to take the team bus back to New Haven, but was so upset about the game that he just couldn't do it. He decided to check out a party at Radcliffe he'd gotten wind of. There he met a Wellesley senior from New Orleans. Though his infected tongue hampered conversation, Hill made enough of an impression that they agreed to see each other again, and he returned to New Haven feeling that the weekend hadn't been a total loss. (In the years to come, whenever Hill told the story of how he'd met his wife, he would note with satisfaction that he had taken her away from a Harvard man.) Back at Yale, Hill found another measure of consolation. Because the game *felt* like a defeat—Harvard so exultant, Yale so miserable—he had been under the impression that his team had lost by a point. It wasn't until he read Monday's *Yale Daily News* that he realized the game had ended in a tie and the teams had shared the Ivy title.

Pandemonium

* * *

There were parties all across the Harvard campus that night. Many of the players ended up at the Pi, whose three floors were so packed that people were lined up around the corner, hoping that someone would leave and they could squeeze in. Pat Conway was there with a date, a Cliffie with whom his roommate had fixed him up. He told her he'd get them some drinks and headed toward the bar. But so many alumni and former players stopped him to offer congratulations that it took him thirty minutes to get back to her. A half hour later, when he left to get another round, the same thing happened. "Pat, this is your day," she finally told him, "I think I'll just go home." He never saw her again. Neil Hurley was there with Kathy. Taking into account his concussion, which had left him unable to sign autographs after the game because he was seeing double, Kathy had assumed their date was off and he'd be heading to Mass General. But Neil had rallied and, though he still had a brutal headache, they danced into the night. Five years later, they were married.

Not everyone celebrated. Bob Dowd was so tired he went right back to his room and slept. Ray Hornblower, disappointed not only that had he been knocked out of the game but that he hadn't even witnessed the comeback, didn't feel up to partying with his teammates. He had dinner at Eliot House, stopped by the Owl Club, and spent the rest of the evening with friends at the Hasty Pudding bar. Ken Thomas had been one of the first to shower, dress, and leave the locker room. He was happy the team had come back to tie the game, but despite the crucial role he'd played with his onside kick, he didn't really feel a part of things. He walked home to his wife and daughter in North Cambridge.

Frank Champi was in a daze. Gary Singleterry's girlfriend had arranged a blind date for him with a Wheelock College classmate, and the four of them went out to dinner. Later, they stopped by the Pi, where the quarterback was greeted with a roar. The following day, Champi, whose picture was on the front page of the *New York Times* sports section, went back to Everett for his grandmother's Sunday feast. The *Boston Herald Traveler* arrived to do a story on the hero of The Game at home with his family. His father and aunt and uncle and sister were there, as well as a passel of cousins who had shown up to help celebrate. His grandmother, who had listened to the game on the radio, didn't really understand football, but with forty-two seconds left, had prayed to St. Anthony. Although she wasn't sure what all the fuss was about, she was proud that so much attention was being paid to her grandson, and she made sure the reporter and photographer went away well-fed.

* * *

Seven thousand miles away, a thirty-eight-year-old Yale alumnus named John Downey was sitting in a five-by-eight-foot Chinese prison cell, wondering who had won The Game. Downey had played guard for the Bulldogs twenty years earlier. After graduating in 1951 he had joined the CIA; the following year, his plane was shot down over Manchuria. Convicted of spying, Downey was given a life sentence. By 1968, he had spent sixteen years in prison, much of it in solitary confinement. To pass the time, Downey, among other things, mentally replayed the Yale-Harvard games in which he had participated. Downey was permitted to receive mail, and Charley Loftus sent him football programs and newsletters to keep him updated on his old team, though they took some time to reach him. Having followed Yale's 1968 season as closely as he could, Downey was eager to know the result of the Harvard game. In mid-December, he received a card from a family friend: "Jack: Yale undefeated, champions 29–13!" Downey was overjoyed. He had no idea his friend had left the stadium early. On Christmas Eve, he received several clippings from Loftus that told the real story. In his cell, Downey, who would not be released until 1973, a year after Nixon went to China, let out a howl of disappointment.

Pandemonium

*   *   *

When President Nathan Pusey spoke at the end-of-season banquet for the 1968 Harvard football team, he called their last-minute comeback against Yale "a triumph of the human spirit." But, he said, it was something more. Obviously thinking about the generational conflicts that had rent his campus that fall, he added, "In our troubled society, a lot of people wonder about whether young people have got it, or what's wrong with them. And young people don't have any use for older people. But at that point, we felt we were all part of the same group, rooting for the same thing. And I think the older people will always feel grateful for the way that game came out, because their faith in the young people was restored."

XVI

Strike

S hortly after noon on April 9, 1969, a little more than four months after the game, about fifty members of SDS, chanting "FIGHT! FIGHT! FIGHT!" rushed into University Hall, the four-story granite building in the center of Harvard Yard that had housed the college's main administration offices since 1815. Hustling the startled deans and their secretaries down the stairs and out the door, they hung the black-and-red SDS banner from a second-story window and announced they would stay until their demands—the abolition of ROTC chief among them—were met.

* * *

The move was shocking but not wholly unexpected. The number of U.S. troops in Vietnam had reached an all-time high of 543,000. More than 30,000 Americans had been killed in the fighting since 1965, and each month another 500 were added to the toll. Nixon had taken office in January, promising to restore "law and order," which was understood to be a euphemism for clamping down on campus radicals and militant blacks. That spring, three hundred colleges and universities would be hit by student demonstrations— some for ending the war, some for Black Power, some for greater student autonomy, some for all three. A quarter of them ended in strikes or building takeovers; on a single day in April, students were occupying buildings on seventeen American campuses. At Harvard, 150 SDS members staged a sit-in at a faculty meeting on ROTC, forcing its cancellation, in what the faculty dean called "the most serious offense of its kind I have seen at Harvard." Six hundred and thirty-three students were enrolled in Social Relations 149, "Radical Perspectives on Social Change," the sequel to Soc Rel 148, making it the second-most popular course at Harvard. Though back-to-back blizzards quieted the campus in February and March, there was a growing sense that when students returned from spring break, Harvard might have its Columbia.

* * *

The night before the takeover, more than four hundred students had attended an SDS meeting in Lowell Lecture Hall. After agreeing on a list of six demands to present to the administration, they discussed the possibility of militant action. The Progressive Labor faction proposed occupying University Hall as soon as the meeting adjourned; the New Left wanted to wait until they had more student support. During an acrimonious four-hour debate, a PL motion to occupy the building right away was defeated three times. After the meeting ended near midnight, several hundred students walked up Quincy Street to the President's House, a red-brick mansion just inside the Yard, chanting "ROTC MUST GO!" Getting no response to his knock, an SDS leader affixed a copy of the six demands to Pusey's front door with a pocketknife. Then the crowd roamed among the Harvard houses, calling for a rally at noon in front of Memorial Church, before they dispersed. Unbeknownst to rank-and-file SDSers, however, a cadre of PLers, plotting through the night, decided to ignore the vote and take action. At the noon rally, shouting "LET'S GO RIGHT NOW!" they hurried up the steps and into University Hall.

Alex MacLean and Rick Berne had been at the meeting the

night before. They had voted to postpone the occupation. At the noon rally, they'd been taken by surprise when the protestors went in. The group included MacLean's Soc Rel 148 section man, Jamie Kilbreth, as well as MacLean's girlfriend, Delia O'Connor. MacLean was conflicted. He still felt deeply indebted to Harvard—one of the deans ejected from University Hall had helped get him admitted—and he didn't want to be kicked out two months before graduation. But he also believed that something dramatic needed to be done to get Harvard's attention; the war showed no signs of slowing down, the administration continued to sanction ROTC's presence on campus, and "business as usual" just had to stop. At some point in the afternoon, as more and more people joined the demonstrators inside the building, MacLean, thinking there might be safety in numbers, walked up the stairs and went in too. Not long afterward, Berne joined him.

Inside, the plastic letters on the first-floor directory had been rearranged to read CHE GUEVARA HALL and LIBERATED AREA and POWER TO THE PEOPLE and SMASH IMPERIALISM. On the second floor, SDS held planning meetings in the Faculty Room as three centuries of Harvard presidents looked down from their portraits on the wall. Committees on political action, food collection, mimeographing, and sanitation were appointed; after several people lit up joints, it was voted that no drugs were to be used. (The demonstrators were well-behaved, for the most part. Finding that someone had scrawled FUCK AUTHORITY on the wall of the college dean's office, others spray-painted over the words and taped up a note: "Dear Sir—We apologize to you for whoever did this. This vandalism is not a purpose of our protest.") There was a discussion of what to do if Pusey sent in the police. Some PLers, veterans of the street battles at last summer's Democratic National Convention, argued for fighting back, but the vast majority voted for nonviolent resistance: linked arms and chants. Elsewhere in the building, people milled around, a little giddy; it was hard to believe they were actually, finally, doing this. It was, thought MacLean as he wandered from room to room, a little like a be-in, but without the dope.

Most students had been at lunch when the first SDS members had gone in, but word spread quickly through the house dining halls, and by early afternoon, several hundred people stood outside University Hall, some cheering, some jeering, most just watching and waiting to see what would happen. Pat Conway, walking through the Yard on his way to class, stopped to watch with Vic Gatto, who had come up from Quincy House. Conway was infuriated by the takeover; Gatto, who was friends with some of the occupying students as well as with some of the ejected deans, sympathized with the occupiers' goals but felt they had no right to seize the building. When an SDS spokesman with a bullhorn stepped outside and urged onlookers to join them in their "fight against imperialism," there was hooting. "If you're so democratic, put it to a vote," someone called.

The cry "VOTE!" "VOTE!" was taken up. The SDSer asked how many opposed the takeover. Conway and Gatto were among hundreds to voice their disapproval. How many in favor? A noticeably smaller number of voices was heard. "Be quiet," the SDSer said. "You've had your silly vote." The crowd booed. "As long as one person wants us to stay, we'll stay," he shouted before disappearing inside. After Conway went to class, Gatto watched for a while with Tommy Lee Jones. Elsewhere in the crowd, John Tyson and a group of his friends from Afro discussed how the occupation would affect the chances of getting the administration to accede to *their* demands.

It was a warm, sunny day, the first springlike weather of the year, and the crowd outside University Hall continued to grow. By mid-afternoon, there were several thousand onlookers. A stereo system poured music into the Yard from a window in Weld Hall, a nearby freshman dorm. From time to time, an SDS member emerged to make an announcement or pass out flyers stating the group's position. Faculty members spoke from the steps of Widener

Library, urging the students to leave the building. At one point, several students appeared with a stuffed dummy wearing a sign saying SDS GET OUT, which they burned in effigy. But as the afternoon went on, it seemed to Alex and Delia, peering through the Palladian windows on the second floor, that the crowd was increasingly supportive—or, at least, increasingly tolerant. In any case, it was comforting to have so many witnesses.

By now there were several hundred people inside University Hall. Some were there from curiosity—rubberneckers checking out the scene and then moving on. Some were there to see friends. Some, like Tony Smith, the reserve end on the football team, were trying to decide how committed they were. Though Smith had come to believe the war was wrong, he had never taken part in a protest. He sat on the Faculty Room floor for several hours, listening to the discussion. He was impressed by how thoughtful the students were. He admired their courage. He was tempted to stay. But when a rumor went around that if you were arrested, Harvard would expunge your record, erasing all trace of your having been at the college, Smith—a class marshal, Rhodes candidate, and varsity football player—realized he wasn't willing to pay that price. He left, telling a friend he'd be back in the morning.

MacLean grew more comfortable as time went on. At some point, he and Berne wandered into a room where people were rummaging through file cabinets. "Listen to this shit!" someone said, reading aloud a letter from Dean of the Faculty Franklin Ford to President Pusey deploring the faculty's liberal position on ROTC. When someone came across several drawers full of student records, MacLean and Berne took a look at their folders. Both were surprised to find they had been slated for Group Five. (When a student applied to Harvard, the admissions office, taking into account high school rank and SAT scores, predicted his likelihood of academic success by placing him in one of six Rank List Groups. Group Five was the second-lowest.) Berne, who, after a rough freshman year, had become a Dean's List student, was chagrined that he'd been considered such poor academic material. But then, given the circumstances in which he'd learned this, he had to laugh.

At 4:15 p.m., Dean Ford mounted the steps of Widener with a bullhorn and announced that the students had fifteen minutes to leave University Hall: "Anyone failing to observe this warning will be subject to prosecution for criminal trespass." About a dozen people left the building. At 4:30, all but one of the gates to the Yard were locked. Some two thousand people remained in the Yard. At 4:45, the stereo in Weld Hall blasted out the Beatles' "Revolution."

*　*　*

By the time the sun went down, the crowd outside had dwindled to fewer than a thousand, as students returned to their houses for dinner. Although the police had padlocked the gates to the Yard, people climbed the wrought-iron fence and continued to drift in and out of University Hall, which, in the early evening, had an almost festive atmosphere. Some students made sandwich runs to Hazen's and Elsie's Lunch; others were dispatched to Cahaly's for bread, bologna, peanut butter, and jelly. A few people played guitars. By nine, there were more than five hundred people inside. A group of tipsy young men in tuxedos stopped in after a formal dinner at the *Lampoon*, Harvard's humor magazine. A few members of the final club to which one of the PL leaders belonged came by with a case of champagne.

All day, there had been talk of how the administration might respond. But after Pusey released a statement at eight o'clock, dismissing most of the demands—"Can anyone believe the Harvard SDS demands are made seriously?" it began—there was no further communication. Everyone had agreed that Pusey wouldn't send in the police during daylight, with so many people watching. But as the hours passed and things quieted down, the undercurrent of apprehension that had lain beneath the exhilaration all day moved closer to the surface. More people were leaving the building, going back to their dorms for the night, than were coming in. By midnight, several hundred students remained. Some played cards, some read magazines, some talked quietly, some curled up on the floor of the Faculty Room and tried to get some sleep.

At three a.m., student lookouts returned to University Hall to report that policemen were gathering near Memorial Hall, just outside the Yard. It was clear there was going to be a confrontation. Reminding people that resistance should be nonviolent, SDS leaders suggested that anyone who didn't want to remain inside could help by staying on the flights of steps that led into the building, as a kind of protective buffer between occupiers and police.

MacLean and Berne talked things over. They had never been hard-core radicals like their friend Jamie Kilbreth, and they had no desire to be arrested. But they believed in the cause and wanted to show their support. The steps seemed like a good compromise. Alex said good-bye to Delia, who was staying inside. Feeling a little guilty and a little cowardly, he and Berne went outside and sat among a knot of students on the steps closest to Widener. Inside, the protestors locked the doors with bicycle chains.

It was a surprisingly chilly night. MacLean felt a mix of fear, exhaustion, and adrenaline. He was glad he had been part of the takeover. He and Berne joined in as the group on the steps began singing the old spiritual "We Shall Not Be Moved."

Shortly after four, runners dispatched from University Hall began pulling fire alarms in the houses and freshman dorms, and yelling "BUST!" Hundreds of students, some in pajamas and bathrobes, rushed up to the Yard.

A few minutes before five, as the details of Widener Library and Memorial Church began to show in the approaching dawn, MacLean and Berne heard a roar from the direction of Broadway. They stood and watched a convoy of MBTA buses drive into the Yard, followed by a long line of policemen, two abreast, on foot. The buses pulled up in front of Sever Hall, home to most of the college's English classes, where they disgorged two hundred twenty-five state troopers in riot gear. MacLean and Berne watched them form ranks. The troopers, in their jodhpurs and black boots, carried riot shields and black nightsticks. Some wore gas masks. Berne couldn't help thinking that in their padded uniforms and Columbia-blue helmets, they looked like 250-pound linemen. As the policemen, followed by the troopers, moved smartly across the Yard toward them, MacLean and Berne and the others on the steps linked arms. Years later, Berne would note with pride that as the tightly massed students watched them approach, nobody ran—at least until the police began clubbing their way up the steps. At that point, as another protestor recalled, "we broke before them like water before the plow of an icebreaker."

After the police cleared the steps, the state troopers used bolt cutters and a battering ram to force their way into University Hall, where the protestors were packed in the first-floor hallway, arms linked, singing "Solidarity Forever." Setting off tear gas, swinging and jabbing their batons with gusto, the troopers routed the students from the building and, pulling some by the hair, shoved them into waiting patrol wagons.

After being chased from the steps, Berne and the other students had scattered into the Yard, some with the police in pursuit. Tripped by a policeman, Berne fell. A nightstick whacked him in the groin. Berne's instinct was to fight back, but he immediately thought better of it. The policeman hit him a few more times before Berne was able to get up and run.

MacLean, too, had fled into the Yard, where he and Delia found each other in the crowd. Delia was shivering and crying. As the troopers charged into University Hall, she had been one of dozens of students to leap from a first-floor window. The window was ten feet above the ground and the woman who jumped before her had broken her back. Delia waited until the woman had been helped away, and then, reminding herself to bend her knees, jumped. She landed next to the bronze statue of John Harvard. A sympathetic campus policeman hurried her to safety before the Cambridge police could put her on a bus for booking.

By now there were about five hundred onlookers in the Yard, watching in disbelief as the police dragged their fellow students from the building. It seemed impossible that what they saw could be taking place at Harvard, in the Yard, in the very heart of the university. Some booed, some wept, some watched in silence, some shouted "FASCISTS," "FUCKERS," "SIEG HEIL," or "PUSEY'S PIGS." Every so often, angered by the taunting and fueled by years of resentment of antiwar protestors in general and privileged Harvard longhairs in particular, policemen charged into the crowd and threw people to the ground, clubbing them. (In the end, when it came to using their batons, there would be little distinction made by the police as to whether someone had been in the building, on the steps, or in the crowd.) From the second floor of the President's House on the far side of the Yard, Pusey, who had authorized the police action but not the violence, watched through binoculars, aghast.

Bob Dowd had rushed up from Adams House with his roommates in time to see the troopers enter University Hall. Although he was sympathetic to the antiwar cause (he was taking Soc Rel 149 that semester; Delia O'Connor was his section leader), he had opposed the takeover. But now he was appalled by what he saw. Dowd, whose father was a fireman, came from the kind of working-class Boston background that furnished much of the metropolitan police. He had great respect for the police. But there was no doubt that some of them were clubbing students not because they had to but because they wanted to: they were enjoying it. He was even more upset when, after it was all over and the police got back in their buses and drove out of the Yard, they giggled and waved at the Harvard students through the windows, like schoolchildren heading home from a field trip.

As Alex and Delia made their way back to Alex's apartment, Berne ran to Adams House and called his father, a radiologist who was about to leave for his job at the hospital. "Dad! This is it! The revolution has begun!" His startled father tried to calm him down. In Berne's view, however, this was no time for calm. "You're either with us or against us," he said. He started telling him about finding his academic file, about being pigeonholed for Rank Group Five. He thought his father would find it amusing. He didn't: "You did WHAT?" Berne tried to explain but realized his father had hung up on him. (Al Berne, who was against the war, could understand occupying a building for a cause, but the opening of confidential files was, for this scrupulously honest man, an unpardonable breach.) Berne thought his father was nuts for getting bent out of shape over a few files when the revolution had begun.

* * *

The revolution had not begun, although for a few adrenaline-fueled days it seemed as if it had. Pusey's decision to send in the police, in hopes that Harvard could avoid the kind of stalemate that had paralyzed Columbia, radicalized the campus overnight. Even those who had opposed the occupation were outraged by the bust. One undergraduate said that on Wednesday he hated SDS; on Thursday he hated Nathan Pusey. Later that day, more than two thousand students packed Memorial Church to debate the SDS demands and express their rage at the Harvard president and his administration. Offensive tackle Joe McGrath, sitting in the balcony, stood and asked to speak, but, seeing his green ROTC uniform, the crowd hooted him down before he could say what he wanted to say—that the right of *all* students to be heard should be protected. At the end of an emotional four-hour meeting, the students voted to boycott classes for three days. It was the first student strike in Harvard history.

There followed a fortnight of teach-ins, alternative classes, emergency faculty meetings, and so many demonstrations and counterdemonstrations that Harvard Yard turned as brown as a football practice field in November, criss-crossed by the still-visible treadmarks of the state troopers' buses. The Yard's elms, which five months earlier had been festooned with posters of the Boston Stranglers, were covered with posters of red fists silkscreened above the word STRIKE. The ground was littered with discarded leaflets, broadsides, and position papers. Bedsheet banners endorsing the strike hung from dorm windows. Picket lines formed in front of classroom buildings, inspiring Pat Conway to conduct his own one-man counterprotest. Each morning, he donned his Marine utility jacket, sought out a building that was being picketed, and walked through the line. When the strikers tried to talk him out of it, he was polite but firm: "I'm going in there," he told them. "If you don't move, I'm going to move you." Conway strode into the building to a chorus of jeers, had a quick look around, then headed out the back door and found another picket line to cross.

Berne, wearing the red armband and red-fist-on-white T-shirt that identified him as a strike supporter, plunged into the fray: boycotting classes, attending rallies, and handing out leaflets. One afternoon, he was surprised to get called down to Dillon Field House. Yovicsin was there with freshman coach Henry Lamar. They were worried. They had heard he'd been hanging around with the radicals and urged him to be careful. Did he understand that getting involved with "the Communist element" could ruin his future? Years later, Berne would appreciate that Yovicsin had been looking out for him. At the time, he thanked him, then went back and told Alex and Delia the story, and they all had a good laugh.

Four days after the bust, more than ten thousand students filled the bowl end of Harvard Stadium out to the thirty-yard line. At the end of a four-hour meeting, they voted to endorse eight demands similar to those of SDS, and to extend the strike for another three days. MacLean, sitting with Delia and Rick, remembered back to the Dow sit-in, and marveled at how the movement had grown. It seemed entirely possible that they could end the war, that they could change the world. They were no longer just pissing in the wind. Tommy Lee Jones was in the stands, as were many others from the football team, looking down at the field where, five months earlier, Harvard had tied Yale in a game that seemed to have taken place in another life. In a photograph of the mass meeting published in *Life* magazine, a short, muscular young man with closely cropped hair stood prominently in the foreground, hands in pockets, looking around in apparent wonder. The student wasn't identified in the caption, but fans of Harvard football recognized Vic Gatto. It was said that after seeing the photo, more than a few conservative older alumni wrote letters to the administration suggesting that the presence of the football captain at a gathering of "radicals" was a measure of how far along the road to perdition their alma mater had traveled.

To some, it seemed that Harvard's very existence was at stake, although as Dean Ford said, "It's hard to believe that something put together over a third of a millennium by Harvard men can be destroyed in a few days in April." The crisis sent shock waves across the country. "If Harvard—paragon harbor of rational doers and thinkers—cannot govern and restructure itself without violence," worried the *Christian Science Monitor*, "what lies ahead for the rest of the nation?" But the stadium rally proved to be the high-water mark of the revolution. The disparate groups that had united in their outrage over the bust began to fracture, SDS's schisms reasserted themselves, and Harvard's moderates drifted back to more practical concerns. The momentum was lost. The moment had passed. A day after the faculty voted to reduce ROTC to extracurricular status, a second mass meeting in the stadium produced a two-to-one vote ending the strike. People's attention turned to exams, the draft, graduation, summer plans. Harvard had survived, but the occupation and the bust left scars from which it would take the university decades to recover. A faculty member called it "Harvard's Vietnam."

*   *   *

After the events of April, there were rumors that for the first time since the Revolutionary War, Harvard would hold no commencement exercises. But on June 13, fifteen thousand students, parents, and alumni gathered in Tercentenary Theatre, the quadrangle just east of University Hall, where, two months earlier, students had been chased and clubbed by police. For weeks, there had been discussions among the graduating seniors about how to express their anger at the university: some favored burning their diplomas ("If you burn your diploma, be sure to get it photostatted first," the Ivy Orator suggested in his Class Day speech), others voted for a walkout. As Commencement Day dawned, there were reports that radicals might attempt to storm the platform during the ceremony. In hopes of avoiding such a scene, at the last minute—even as the traditional procession, led by members of the Corporation and the Board of Overseers in top hats and tails, wound its way into the quad—President Pusey was persuaded to let someone from SDS speak for five minutes following the national anthem. Puffing on a cigarette and pacing the dais, the speaker, one of six seniors suspended for their part in occupying University Hall, read from a 1,500-word diatribe that called Pusey a criminal, Harvard a racist institution, and the commencement ceremony an atrocity. The audience began to hiss and boo; nine minutes in, senior class officers escorted the speaker from the stage. Shouting "Let's get out of here!" he headed down the center aisle. Thirty or forty seniors, wearing red armbands over their black academic robes, rose from their seats and, chanting "SMASH ROTC—NO EXPANSION," followed. They were joined by about a hundred friends and supporters.

As he made his way through the crowd, Alex MacLean, accompanied by Rick and Delia, felt almost physically ill. He had committed himself to the walkout, but he was mortified that his four years at Harvard were ending this way. He was grateful for his time there. He was proud—and amazed—that, despite his academic struggles, he was graduating. He knew how much this ceremony meant to his parents, who had sacrificed so much to help him get to this point, and how anguished they must be as they watched him leave. After the exhilaration of the stadium meeting, the walkout seemed almost pathetically anemic. The audience had already redirected its attention to the dais, where the commencement ceremony resumed with the traditional Latin Oration (*"Gratissimi te primum salutamus,* Nathan Marsh Pusey . . ."). As MacLean passed near where his parents were sitting, his younger sister jumped up and joined him. And then, as Harvard graduates had been doing for more than three centuries, he walked out of the Yard and into the rest of his life.

*　　*　　*

At Yale, anti-ROTC feeling intensified that spring. Before it could boil over into a Harvard-like uprising, Kingman Brewster called for a mass meeting of students, faculty, and administration to discuss the issue. On the night of May 1, more than four thousand people packed into Ingalls Rink. At the end of a four-hour session one reporter described as "filled with fiery speeches, ovations, boos, cheers, a few hearty insults, and great goodwill," a nonbinding vote was taken on whether to expel ROTC from campus. When the results were announced—1,286 for, 1,286 against—there were gasps and then a great roar of laughter. Another tie.

Epilogue

My family stayed until the end of the game, of course. It wouldn't have occurred to us to leave, not because we thought there was any chance of a Harvard comeback, but because we *always* stayed till the end; to do otherwise would make us that most despised of creatures, what my father called "fair-weather fans." But as the sun went down and I shivered on the cold concrete, I couldn't help hoping that the game would be over soon and we'd be put out of our misery. And then—play by unlikely play, second by unbelievable second—the impossible took shape before our eyes. My brothers and I, crossing two pairs of fingers on each hand, stood on our seats, craning our necks to see what was happening in the murk at the bowl end of the stadium. By now it seemed almost dark enough for stars to appear.

Suddenly we were jumping up and down, pummeling one another. As fans around us streamed down to the field to celebrate, I turned to look at my parents: my mother, who came to the games only because that's what loyal Harvard wives did in those days, was radiant at having witnessed what even a nonfootball person like her knew to be a miracle; my father, face flushed with emotion and possibly a little tailgate bourbon, had fished out the handkerchief he always carried in the pocket of his gray flannel pants and was waving it wildly over his head.

I still have the ticket.

*   *   *

Furred with dust, the football sits on the top shelf behind the counter at Leavitt & Peirce, the tobacconist on Mass Ave that since its opening in 1883 has served not only as a purveyor of pipes, cigars, and backgammon sets but as a reliquary of Harvard sports memorabilia. It is one in a row of twenty-three footballs, each of which bears, in fading white paint, the date and score of a signal Crimson victory. The oldest, its leather cracked with age, dates from the 1898 Yale game, a 17–0 Harvard win. This ball, a time-softened Wilson "The Duke" model, bears the words:

NOV. 23, 1968
HARVARD 29
YALE 29
STADIUM
UNDEFEATED SEASON

Even as fans walked off the field that day, whether in agony or ecstasy, they knew they had witnessed something extraordinary. The following year, *Sports Illustrated* ranked the game among the ten most exciting in college football history. But as time went on, it would be remembered as more than just an exciting game. It would be remembered as a rare moment of grace in a tragic and turbulent year. At an intensely polarized time, in which the country seemed irrevocably divided—dove vs. hawk, black vs. white, young vs. old, student vs. administrator, hippie vs. hard hat—the tie between archrivals seemed a kind of truce. Indeed, the teams had unwittingly combined to create something like a work of art that would take its place in the iconography of the era. Not long ago, the former Yale linebacker Andy Coe happened to visit *The 1968 Project: A Nation Coming of Age* at the Oakland Museum, an exhibition examining that watershed year. There, not far from photos of a busboy attempting to comfort a dying Robert F. Kennedy and of Vietnamese civilians massacred at My Lai, was the image of Pete Varney holding the ball aloft in the Yale end zone, with Coe himself in the background, looking stunned.

Today, as they watch film of the game, some of the players still can't believe it will end in a tie. Certainly, Yale's school-record-tying six fumbles—three inside the Harvard twenty—were a primary factor in Harvard's comeback. Certainly, too, the series of calls against Yale in the game's chaotic final minutes played a role. (Cozza wrote in his autobiography, "There's no doubt in my mind that the officials got caught up in the emotion of the game.") And yet for the game to end the way it did required an almost otherworldly confluence of timely plays, questionable decisions, debatable calls, fortuitous bounces, and the kind of blind luck usually encountered only in fairy tales. And that was just the last three minutes. Tommy Lee Jones mischievously points out that if Harvard hadn't botched the extra point after their first touchdown, they would have won the game, 30–29. Indeed, it is tempting to wonder: What might have happened if Yale had fumbled *five* times instead of six? If Gatto and Hornblower had been at full strength? If Bass hadn't been injured? If Dowling had passed one less time on Yale's final drive? If Yale hadn't called time-out with a minute to play? If Cozza had put in Dowling and Hill on defense for those last forty-two seconds? (Cozza, for one, maintained that if he *had* put them in, they would have found a way to stop Harvard.)

Perhaps nothing would have made a difference. Many of the players have concluded that larger forces were at work during the game's final minutes. Yale's Brad Lee likens it to "a Greek tragedy unraveling." Pat Madden talks of "the hand of God." Harvard players use words like *destiny*, *fate*, and *divine justice*. Rick Berne has another theory. "It was karma," he says. "That sounds silly, but

I really think that the student movement and everything else that was going on at the time contributed to the camaraderie, to the vibe, to the success of our team. It gave us some perspective. Most of us weren't focused single-mindedly on football. Which isn't to say we weren't just as dedicated to the team. But looking at what was going on in the world was part of the picture, and maybe part of the reason the game turned out the way it did."

* * *

Each November, as The Game approaches, highlights of the 1968 game appear on TV, the film looking as grainy and old-fashioned now as film of Albie Booth looked in 1968. Each November, the players get calls from sportswriters, asking the same questions. Each November, when alumni gather and talk of games gone by, the conversation inevitably turns to 1968. Harvard people refer to it as "the famous tie," Yale people as "the infamous tie." Neither side, of course, thinks of it as a tie. Former New York governor George Pataki (Yale '67) writes, "I take some solace in the knowledge that Harvard considers a tie with Yale to be its greatest 'victory,' while Yale considers the tie with Harvard to be its worst 'defeat.'" Fifty years later, Harvard players reflexively use the word *win* when they talk of the game; Yale players use the word *loss*.

For Yale, the imperfect end to their perfect season took time to absorb. A few days after the game, the Harvard team invited their Yale counterparts to a joint Ivy League championship banquet. The Yale players voted, overwhelmingly, to decline the offer. There was nothing to celebrate. The wound was too fresh. Their own annual banquet, held that same week, was a somber gathering. It didn't seem fair that a game they dominated for fifty-six-and-a-half minutes hadn't resulted in a victory. Some of the players say that if the teams had played ten times, Yale would have won nine. Many Harvard players agree; Yale, they admit, was a far more talented team. "We were lucky to be on the field with them," says Gus Crim.

Epilogue

For some Yale players, the sting lingered. "My friends joke that if I had an MRI right now, there would be a little lesion up there that reads '29–29,'" says Kyle Gee. Over the years, however, most of them have made their peace with it. Indeed, Yale and Harvard players alike admit that if either team had *won*, they'd be the only ones who would remember the game. Almost everyone agrees that the chance of any future Harvard-Yale game eclipsing the tie of 1968 is impossible—and not just because in 1996 the NCAA changed its rules to permit overtime.

Although no one realized it at the time, the 1968 game would be the last hurrah in the history of big-time Ivy League football. In 1982, the NCAA demoted the league from Division I-A, college football's top stratum, to the less-competitive Division I-AA. Harvard and Yale continued to recruit talented prospects—since 1970, fifty-one of their players have gone on to play in the NFL—but would never again compete in the rankings with Alabama and Nebraska. These days, they fight for standing in the polls with Lafayette and Central Connecticut State. With the demotion to I-AA and the meteoric rise in popularity of professional football, game attendance has fallen precipitously. In the 1990s, faced with a dwindling fan base and a deteriorating physical structure, Yale considered tearing down the Bowl. Although in the end the decision was made to renovate, the Bowl—and Harvard Stadium—can look almost deserted on Saturday afternoons in the fall. Newspaper coverage, too, has shrunk. Five decades after devoting half the front page of its sports section to the 1968 game, the *New York Times* (which, like Harvard and Yale themselves, has become more meritocratic) relegates the annual contest to a few short paragraphs on page two.

The game, however, remains The Game—"the last great nineteenth-century pageant left in the country," as former Yale president A. Bartlett Giamatti called it. It still sells out Harvard Stadium and nearly fills the Bowl. It is the one game students still attend, the one game around which alumni schedules still revolve. As a sophomore linebacker in 1968, Gary Farneti couldn't understand why the alums made such a fuss about it. These days, Farneti, a trial attorney in Binghamton, New York, wouldn't miss it for the world. He gets goose bumps when the band plays "Ten Thousand Men of Harvard."

* * *

In the weeks after November 23, 1968, it was hard for the players to think of anything but The Game—whether they were eagerly reliving it, or trying, without much success, to forget it. Eventually, however, as the calendar moved on, they realized that they needed to move on as well.

But before they could figure out what they were going to do with the rest of their lives, the players, like all young men in the United States, had to figure out what they were going to do about the draft. Some of them had med-school deferments. Some got occupational exemptions by going into teaching. More than a few found that their football injuries, especially when combined with a persuasive letter from a sympathetic physician (often one of the team doctors), had a silver lining. Ray Hornblower's ankle, Gerry Marino's knee, and Jim Reynolds's shoulder got them medical deferments—not without some feelings of guilt. Brian Dowling was classified 4F when X-rays revealed bone chips in the back he'd injured in the city championship game his junior year in high school. J. P. Goldsmith was saved by his abysmal vision. ("Man, you can't see shit!" was the draft board doctor's diagnosis.) John Emery was shocked to be told he'd flunked the physical because he was "obese"—with 210 muscular pounds on a five-foot-eleven frame, he exceeded the acceptable body mass index. The process seemed to be something of a crapshoot. When Mike Ananis reported to the Boston Navy Yard for his physical twenty-six days after graduation—and twenty-four days after getting married—he assumed the shoulder that had kept him off the field most of the season would be more than sufficient for a deferment. He was horrified when the doctor told him the shoulder was "no problem." He was certain he was headed for Vietnam. "I looked out the window and saw a Navy ship anchored in the harbor," he recalls. "I thought, 'Oh my God, they're gonna put me on that ship today—I'm not even gonna be allowed to go home and say good-bye to my bride.' Next thing I knew, they had ten of us in a room, in our skivvies, doing deep knee bends. I was still in shock and nearly fell over trying to do them. The guy looked at me more closely and said, 'Jesus, you've got flat feet.'" Ananis was classified 4F.

Many of the players' immediate futures were determined shortly after eight p.m. on December 1, 1969, when the nation's first draft lottery since World War II was held at Selective Service headquarters, in Washington, D.C. That evening, Bob Dowd, Fritz Reed, and their three roommates gathered around the radio in their Adams House living room with a few cases of beer. It was said that if your birthday was among the first third chosen, you were almost certainly headed to Vietnam. If it was in the last third, you were almost certain not to be. If it was in the middle third, your chances were fifty-fifty. As the first dates were read out, screams reverberated in the entryways of Harvard houses. In Dowd's suite, four of five roommates—everyone except Reed—were called by the time number 30 was reached. Dowd was number 21. As each man's number was called, he walked silently to his bedroom. None of the beer was drunk.

Dowd was leaning toward joining the Army Reserves when, two nights after the draft, playing handball on the Adams House court, he went hard for a shot off the back wall and blew out his knee. He had surgery three weeks later. Classified 4F, he enrolled in Boston College Law School.

By then, the war had become so unpopular that when Rick Berne (number 44 in the lottery) rode the yellow school bus that ferried potential draftees from Cambridge City Hall to the Boston Navy Yard for their physicals, everyone on board was chanting, "HO, HO, HO CHI MINH, NLF IS GONNA WIN!" At the Navy Yard, the man next to Berne gave the same answer to every question. What's your name? *Fuck you.* Give us a push-up. *Fuck you.* Berne, armed with letters from doctors about his injured knee and his asthma, got his 4F.

Harvard's Neil Hurley and Yale's Pat Madden managed to get places in the National Guard. Yale's Fred Morris and Bob Sokolowski joined the Army Reserves; Scott Robinson spent two years in the Army. Mike Bouscaren spent two years in the Navy, working in military intelligence. Harvard's Joe McKinney fulfilled his ROTC commitment on an Army base in Germany. By the time he was slated for a tour of duty in Vietnam, the Pentagon was beginning to bring troops home. After three years as a Navy SEAL in Virginia, Yale's Del Marting, too, was scheduled for deployment, as part of a four-man SEAL advisory team. He was in the middle of language school, learning Vietnamese, when the mission was called off. The war was winding down.

Three of the players on the field that day, in addition to Pat Conway, served in Vietnam. As a platoon commander operating out of Da Nang, former Yale tackle Mick Kleber had little time to ponder Hemingway's definition of heroism as he led his men on search-and-destroy missions in the mountains; he needed all his wits about him just to survive. Near the end of his tour, when he and his men were ordered to find and dismantle Vietcong booby traps, he felt almost unbearable stress. "It got to a point where I was too frightened to eat," he recalls. Kleber weighed 235 pounds when he played in the 1968 Harvard game; after basic training he weighed 195; when he returned to the States he weighed 155. He spent two and a half more years in the Marines, some of them as a White House aide during the Nixon administration. He was on duty in the East Room when the president, with impeachment proceedings under way for his involvement in Watergate, bade a tearful farewell to his staff. In 1976, Kleber, who at Yale had dreamed of directing musical comedies on Broadway, resigned his commission and moved to Los Angeles, where he became an executive in the fledgling music video business.

Harvard offensive tackle Joe McGrath spent much of his ROTC commitment on a NATO base in Turkey. Toward the end of his time, he was sent to Vietnam. Although he worked primarily as an administrative officer on a base near Saigon, it was impossible not to be affected by the sight of the wounded and the dead coming back through the base, or by the poverty and disillusionment of the Vietnamese people. Shortly before Christmas, he received a letter from an attorney informing him that his wife was suing him for divorce. A few weeks earlier, a soldier on the base who received a similar letter had put a bullet in his head. Lonely and despairing, McGrath considered doing the same. A friend talked him out of it. Back in the States, McGrath, who wanted to be a teacher, had trouble finding a job. At every school to which he applied, he got the same response, often from young men who had gone into teaching to avoid the draft: "What have you done other than spend three years in the military?" He worked in banking before taking a job at Grantham University, which offers online degree programs geared to veterans. From 2011 to 2014, McGrath served as Grantham's president.

Yale linebacker Fran Boyer, erstwhile leader of the George Bush Memorial Scout Team, decided it was his responsibility to serve. He enlisted in the Marine OCS. As a first lieutenant, he led a platoon in combat in Vietnam. On December 3, 1972, not long after returning from his tour of duty, and not long before he was due to be discharged, he died in a motorcycle accident at Camp Pendleton.

*　　*　　*

Two weeks after graduation, Alex MacLean, his girlfriend Delia O'Connor, and several dozen other Harvard leftists took an all-night bus to Chicago for the SDS national convention. The proceedings made Harvard SDS meetings seem as decorous as tea parties. On one side of the cavernous Chicago Coliseum, the New Left screamed, "HO, HO, HO CHI MINH, NLF IS GONNA WIN!" On the other, the Progressive Labor Party screamed, "MAO, MAO, MAO TSE TUNG, DARE TO STRUGGLE, DARE TO WIN!"—each trying to drown out the other, like fans of opposing football teams. A third faction, the Revolutionary Youth Movement, led by Bernardine Dohrn and former Columbia SDS president Mark Rudd, staged a walkout. (Over the next several years, as the Weather Underground, they would bomb banks and office buildings in an attempt to overthrow the federal government.) When a contingent of Black Panthers showed up, ranting about "offing the pigs," Alex and Delia realized they might be in over their heads. In any case, by that time they and the half-dozen other Harvardians staying in the basement of a hospitable elderly leftist had worn out their welcome; the last straw came when the toilet backed up from overuse and the elderly leftist's husband, less committed to the cause, all but ordered them out of the house. The convention, for all intents and purposes, marked the end of SDS.

That summer, Alex, Delia, Rick, and two other activist friends lived in a ramshackle house on Fort Hill in Roxbury, next door to a commune-turned-cult run by Mel Lyman, the editor-publisher of *Avatar*. Progressive Labor had instructed its followers to get blue-collar jobs at which they could indoctrinate their fellow workers for the revolution. Neither Alex nor Rick, who worked in construction, did much indoctrinating, but Delia, making The Hot One shaving cream dispensers on an assembly line at the Gillette plant in South Boston, proselytized to her linemates about Vietnam, capitalism, and seizing the means of production. "Some responded angrily, saying their brothers were over there fighting and I was no patriot," she recalls, "but for the most part they responded with good-natured tolerance. They were just trying to make a living and couldn't have cared less about the revolution. They didn't understand why I would jeopardize my college education. They told me I was ruining my life and my mother must be horrified, and they were going out for sandwiches and what kind did I want?"

It was a strange summer. In July, they watched Neil Armstrong walk on the moon. They had recently brought back some smooth stones from the beach; Alex arranged them on top of the television set, and whenever he was high, he was convinced they were moon rocks. A few days later, they were shocked to hear that Ted Kennedy had driven off a bridge in Chappaquiddick, an island on the eastern end of Martha's Vineyard. The senator had swum to shore, but his passenger, Mary Jo Kopechne, an office worker on his brother Bobby's 1968 presidential campaign, had drowned. In August, Alex and Delia heard about a music festival in upstate New York at a place called Woodstock but decided it was a long way to go and probably wouldn't be worth it.

One night, burglars broke into the house, robbing one of their leftist friends at knifepoint. After it was over, Alex, who, like Delia and Rick, had slept through the whole thing, said they should call the police. Their friend insisted they shouldn't, because the police were pigs and the burglars weren't to blame because they were victims of an oppressive system—a point of which she had endeavored to convince her knife-wielding assailants. In the end, they called, but the intruders were never caught. After that summer, Alex and Delia's involvement in radical politics began to fade. As did, more slowly, their romance, though they would remain lifelong friends.

MacLean, whose application for conscientious objector status was successful, attended the Harvard Graduate School of Design. He took flying lessons. He combined his interests to become a renowned aerial photographer with a focus on environmental issues. His concern with global warming has led him to reflect on his days as an antiwar protestor. "At the time, I didn't fully appreciate the connection between taking local action and changing something on a larger scale," he says. "Our efforts seemed ineffectual. Now I look back and think that the student movement in the sixties was a huge factor in helping slow down the war." He is still close to Berne, a criminal defense attorney in Portland, Maine, whose reconstructed knee held up through twelve marathons before it had to be replaced—not long before both of Berne's hips were replaced as well.

Though many of the players have dealt with damaged joints, they are all far more concerned about damaged brains. Whenever they forget a word, a name, or a face, they can't help worrying that their absentmindedness may be a symptom not of the aging process but of chronic traumatic encephalopathy (CTE), which, of course, none of them had heard of during the years when they were repeatedly "getting their bell rung" on the field.

*   *   *

As Harvard and Yale graduates have done for centuries, many of the players went on to work in business or finance. Rick Frisbie, the Harvard sophomore who caused Calvin Hill's second fumble in the 1968 game, became a venture capitalist and a major donor to Harvard athletics. Yale guard Jack Perkowski became one of the first Western businessmen to operate in China after it reopened for foreign investment, an experience he wrote about in *Managing the Dragon: How I'm Building a Billion-Dollar Business in China.* Yale's Del Marting spent twenty years in banking, then headed up a gold-mining company in Nevada before getting into health-care financing. His fellow end Bruce Weinstein, drafted in the eighth round by the Miami Dolphins, played semipro football before working as a substitute teacher, a tugboat crewman, a race car driver, and, for the last twenty years, president of a real estate syndication business in Connecticut. J. P. Goldsmith, one of four Yale starters to attend Harvard Business School, worked in investment banking for forty years before retiring with his wife to Florida. ("I think I may have been the only person who was at Salomon during the bank scandal *and* at Lehman Brothers during the meltdown," he says.) The Princeton game football Dowling awarded him sits on a shelf in his library. His father, Richard Goldsmith—who, many years after J.P. graduated from Yale, told him, "Everything I wanted to be, you were"—died in 2017, two months short of his hundredth birthday.

A number of players, including Harvard center Ted Skowronski and Yale tackle Kyle Gee, became lawyers. Harvard linebacker John Emery became a district court judge in New Hampshire. Four players became doctors, including John Waldman, the Yale cornerback called for pass interference while covering Pete Varney, who is a pediatric neurosurgeon in Albany, specializing in hydro-cephaly, craniofacial disorders, and brain tumors.

*　*　*

Several players followed career paths more directly influenced by the era. A few months after intercepting Brian Dowling in the 1968 game, Harvard cornerback John Ignacio read Jonathan Kozol's *Death at an Early Age* for an education course. Inspired by the young Harvard graduate's description of his experiences teaching elementary school in Roxbury, Ignacio spent his career as an assistant principal and principal in San Francisco public schools.

Tackle George Bass, whose last play in a Yale uniform left him spread-eagled on the Harvard Stadium grass, spent two years in inner-city Philadelphia teaching fifth grade: nineteen children whose reading levels ranged from pre-primer to second grade in a windowless room so small there was no space for a teacher's desk. There were days when Bass found himself thinking that two-a-days had been less grueling than teaching. He realized that, even more than teachers, the country needed people to *prepare* its teachers. He went back to school in educational psychology, and taught the subject for twenty-six years at the College of William and Mary.

Yale linebacker Andy Coe applied for and was granted consci-entious objector status. (Cozza wrote him a letter of support.) He drove his VW Beetle across the country to Los Angeles, where he worked as a union organizer for Cesar Chavez's United Farm Workers for five dollars a week plus floor space in a house with twenty other workers. He would spend much of his career in community relations for nonprofit organizations.

Yale fullback Bob Levin worked for a program that sent recent college graduates into inner-city schools. He hoped for an assignment in Harlem, to be closer to Meryl Streep, who was still at Vassar, but was sent to Chapel Hill, North Carolina, to teach high school history. (He and Streep broke up a year later, not long before she entered the Yale School of Drama.) A week before classes started, the special-education teacher quit and Levin was asked to take her place. He went on to a career teaching special-needs students and coaching high school football in Winnetka, Illinois. "I try to instill in these kids the hope that somewhere out there, 'even for them,' there is the possibility of something better, of someone who is good to them," he wrote in his Yale twenty-fifth-reunion report.

Harvard end Tony Smith, who had contemplated joining the University Hall occupation, embarked on something of a counter-cultural odyssey: teaching in inner-city Worcester, studying under a charismatic rabbi "capable of certain psychic phenomena," building a post-and-beam farmhouse on thirty-five acres in New Hampshire, working with drug-addicted Vietnam veterans in a naval prison, taking Erhard Seminars Training (EST), using mind-body techniques to treat people with AIDS, attending men's consciousness-raising weekends, and reading Herman Hesse. Smith has spent the last thirty-three years as a motivational coach, helping public leaders and corporate executives achieve "performance breakthroughs"—work, he says, inspired in part by the 1968 game, in which Harvard achieved a performance breakthrough of its own.

As a Yale senior, defensive back Kurt Schmoke co-founded the Calvin Hill Day Care Center to help low-income Yale employees, especially those working in dining halls and maintenance. After studying at Oxford on a Rhodes Scholarship, he went into politics. In 1987, he became the first African-American mayor of Baltimore. During his three terms, he worked to improve public housing, promote adult literacy, and establish a needle-exchange program for addicts. In 1989, he was named to the Yale Corporation.

John Tyson, who quit the Harvard football team because he wanted to "do something for my people," earned master's degrees in theology and divinity. During that time, he worked in Boston-area prisons, helping young black men get their lives back on track. He spent much of the rest of his career running an import-export business in Kenya. Along the way, he sponsored more than a dozen young African men to enroll in American colleges. In 2000, on the thirtieth anniversary of the founding of Harvard's Afro-American Studies department, he and his fellow members of Afro's Ad Hoc Committee were awarded the W. E. B. Du Bois medal for their role in its creation.

Several years later, Tyson was diagnosed with early-onset Alzheimer's. Friends and former teammates can't help wondering whether CTE may have been a factor. He spent six years in assisted-living facilities. For much of that time, Tyson was in his own world. Visitors were never sure whether he'd recognize them, though one afternoon, when his friend Ron Burton brought him his old high school football jersey, tears filled Tyson's eyes. Among his visitors was Al Gore, with whom he had remained friends and whose nomination for president he had seconded at the 2000 Democratic National Convention. At the end of one visit, the former Dunster House roommates could be seen walking slowly down the hall, arm in arm.

Tyson died on April 6, 2017, at age seventy. His former teammates recall his play with awe. "He was better than all the players who played in the 1968 Harvard-Yale game," says John Ignacio.

* * *

Epilogue

Several men who played in the 1968 Harvard-Yale game have also died. Yale guard and antiwar activist Bart Whiteman, who founded the Source, a small, idiosyncratic nonprofit theater in Washington, D.C., died of a heart attack in 2006, at fifty-seven. Fritz Reed, the end-turned-tackle whose impromptu run spurred Harvard's comeback, became a bankruptcy lawyer in Ohio, and died of a heart attack in 2007, at fifty-nine. Harvard placekicker Richie Szaro, who missed a botched-snap extra point in the game, passed Charlie Brickley to become the leading scorer by kicking in Harvard history. He kicked for five years in the NFL, leading the league in field goal percentage in 1976. In 2015, he died of cancer at sixty-seven. Yale tackle Rich Mattas, whose grad-school work on semiconductors earned him an occupational deferment, became a nuclear physicist, conducting fusion research at the Argonne National Laboratory outside Chicago. He died of cancer in 2016 at sixty-nine.

*   *   *

After the 1968 game, John Yovicsin coached two more years before the Harvard athletic director decided a fresh approach was needed—a decision that dovetailed with his cardiologists' recommendation that he give up coaching. In 1970, Harvard went 7-2, upsetting Yale, 14–12, in Yovicsin's final game. Named top coach in New England for the fourth time (he also won in 1968), Yovicsin retired as the winningest football coach in Harvard history, having eclipsed the alleged bulldog strangler, Percy Haughton. After he moved to Cape Cod in 1979, there were rumors that Yovicsin had become a hippie. These proved unfounded, though fans who spotted him at Harvard football games were shocked to see that the famously fastidious coach had let his hair grow as shaggy as that of the players on his 1968 team. In 1989, Yovicsin's heart finally gave out. The *Globe* obituary began: "John Yovicsin, the former Harvard football coach who died yesterday at the age of 70, was a true gentleman."

Epilogue

Carmen Cozza became the winningest football coach in Yale (and Ivy League) history long before he retired in 1996. In thirty-two years, his teams won 179 games and ten Ivy titles. In 2002 he was inducted into the College Football Hall of Fame. It was said that he could recognize all of the nearly two thousand men who played for him, many of whom, like Brian Dowling, describe him as a second father. Five of his players were Rhodes Scholars, including two who played in the 1968 game: Kurt Schmoke and tackle Tom Neville. Only seven of his players failed to graduate. Mention of the 1968 Harvard game, "the game that no one will ever let me forget," always brought a pained look to his face. In 2018, Cozza died of leukemia at eighty-seven.

In 1973, with the help of a recommendation from Cozza, twenty-six-year-old Vic Gatto became the youngest college head football coach in the country, at Bates. He went on to coach at Tufts (his 1979 team went undefeated) and Davidson. In 1989, he left coaching to work in the business world, primarily in renewable energy. Gatto is one of five players from the 1968 team, along with linebacker Gary Farneti, punter Gary Singleterry, safety Bill Kelly, and end Pete Varney, to be elected to the Harvard Varsity Club Hall of Fame. Although Kelly, who recovered the onside kick, and Varney, who caught the game-tying conversion, are remembered for their contributions in the 29–29 tie, they were inducted for their achievements in baseball. After playing catcher in the major leagues for parts of four seasons, Varney, like Gatto, went into coaching. By the time he retired in 2015, his Brandeis baseball teams had won 705 games, more than any coach in any sport in Brandeis history had ever won.

Gatto's backfield mate Ray Hornblower, who graduated as the third leading rusher in Harvard history, eschewed the family banking business for law school. After five years in the Justice Department, primarily as a trial attorney in the Civil Rights Division, the former Saint Paul's Glee Club member embarked on a second career, as an opera singer. In twenty years as a lyric tenor, he sang in more than three hundred performances, most of them in Europe. (A critic for *Paris Normandie* praised his "valiant voice.") "Opera is similar to football," says Hornblower. "Both are out-of-body experiences that trigger all sorts of wonderful endorphins. I challenge you to find anything as sublime as making a fifty-yard run at Harvard Stadium or singing Verdi in a packed opera house."

In the spring of their senior year, Tony Smith asked his teammate Tommy Lee Jones what he planned to do after graduation. Jones responded with characteristic brevity: "Act." He made his first screen appearance, wearing a Department of Harvard Athletics sweatshirt, as one of Ryan O'Neal's roommates in *Love Story*. (Screenwriter Erich Segal '58 modeled O'Neal's character on an amalgam of Jones and his suitemate Al Gore, both of whom Segal got to know in the fall of 1968, when he was a visiting fellow at Dunster House.) Since then, Jones and his flinty demeanor have been featured in more than sixty films, including *The Fugitive*, for which he earned an Academy Award for Best Supporting Actor, and *Hope Springs*, in which he played the dispirited husband of Bob Levin's former girlfriend Meryl Streep. Every other year, when The Game is played in Cambridge, Jones hosts a dinner for his old teammates at the Signet Society. A while back, Gary Farneti was watching *Inside the Actors Studio*, a television show on which the host happened to be interviewing Jones. Jones was asked to describe a turning point in his career. Farneti assumed his former teammate would cite a particularly challenging role, perhaps something from Shakespeare. Jones said it was a football game played by Harvard and Yale in 1968.

* * *

For some, it would take time to put the game in perspective. Despite playing a pivotal role in the most famous game in Harvard football history, Ken Thomas, the junior cornerback who executed the onside kick, was so upset about his treatment by defensive backfield coach Loyal Park that when the team picture was taken two days later, he didn't show up. "I look back now and I realize that it wasn't all Loyal's fault," says Thomas, a doctor in Manchester, New Hampshire. "I was a nineteen-year-old kid who couldn't see the big picture. I understand that now. But I have bitter feelings to this day. Awful, isn't it? And it's a *game*, for God's sake." For four decades, Thomas couldn't bring himself to go back to Harvard. Then in 2008, when a documentary film about the 1968 game premiered at the Brattle Theatre and the players were invited, Neil Hurley persuaded his former teammate to attend. Thomas has been going to Harvard reunions and football games ever since. "It has been a kind of rebirth for me. I should have realized a long time ago that it's not about Loyal Park, it's about the friendships with my teammates. But better late than never."

Brad Lee, the Yale guard who fumbled Thomas's kick, spent eight years as a professor of history at Harvard. Despite excellent credentials, he wasn't granted tenure—"the second time he got screwed by Harvard," observes J. P. Goldsmith—and went on to teach military strategy for twenty-seven years at the U.S. Naval War College in Newport, Rhode Island. At Harvard, Lee never told his colleagues he'd played football for Yale. "I didn't want them to find out I was a dumb jock," he says with a chuckle. One day, he was crossing the Yard with a friend, an eminent professor of Victorian history and literature who suffered from depression. The friend told Lee that he was slipping once again into despair. Lee commiserated. His friend said that sometimes when he felt really down, he put on a record album made from the radio broadcast of a certain Harvard-Yale football game; listening to it, especially to the last few minutes, lifted his spirits. "Was that the twenty-nine–twenty-nine tie?" Lee asked. It was. Lee told him that he was the Yale player who had fumbled the onside kick. The revelation, for some reason, had an immediate cheering effect on his friend. (These days, Lee himself is philosophical about his misplay. "I choked," he admits. "Brian Dowling would have *charged* the ball.")

Epilogue

Two days after the game, Harvard quarterback George Lalich, mortified by his benching but determined that no one feel sorry for him, summoned up his resolve and gave the keynote speech at the football banquet. He received a standing ovation. After teaching elementary school in Chicago's South Side projects for four years, Lalich became a lawyer for the gaming industry in Las Vegas. For decades, he was just as happy not to bring up the fact that he'd played football at Harvard. Then, in 2008, around the time of the game's fortieth anniversary, he began having two recurring dreams. In one, he wandered the banks of the Charles dressed in his football uniform, looking for Harvard Stadium but unable to find it. In the other, he stood outside the stadium in his uniform; he could hear the crowd cheering but couldn't get in. One day the dreams stopped, and Lalich felt a weight had lifted. In recent years, he has been diagnosed with Parkinson's disease. His ebullience remains undimmed.

"I'm glad that we lost," says Mike Bouscaren, whose fourth-quarter penalties inadvertently enabled Harvard's comeback. "Because if we had won I probably would have had more difficulty becoming a regular person, a person who understands that all in life is not fair, that you can't win all the time and it's good to be humble." During thirty-five years in investment banking, Bouscaren had his professional and personal ups and downs, including finding sobriety, which he touched on in *Ultrarunning: My Story*, a book that describes the competitive and spiritual rewards of testing himself in races of up to 100 miles. In retirement, Bouscaren teaches yoga, meditates, and works as a hospice volunteer. "I practice gratitude, forgiveness, selflessness, and compassion," he says, qualities he brings to bear when he looks back on the 1968 game. "The fact is that everyone was out there, twenty-two people on the field at a time, trying to do the best they could."

*   *   *

By the end of the 1968 season, Brian Dowling held nine Yale records, including season and career marks for yards passing, touchdown passes, and total offense. (Fans wonder how many more records he might have set had he not missed almost half the games in his varsity career to injury.) He was an honorable-mention All-American and finished ninth in the voting for the Heisman Trophy, won that year by O. J. Simpson. A generation after he graduated, *Sports Illustrated* named Dowling the sixth-best college quarterback of all time.

Drafted in the eleventh round by the Minnesota Vikings, Dowling spent nine years playing sparingly for various NFL, WFL, and minor league teams, never finding the success that had seemed to come so effortlessly in high school and college. In the years since, he has taught high school algebra; sold real estate; written for newspapers; with Vic Gatto, announced Ivy League football games on TV; served as executive director of a sports museum; and held a variety of jobs in sales, marketing, and insurance. If his post-Yale career has seemed less touched by magic, Dowling himself has maintained the equanimity that served him so well on third and long. "I remember seeing him in New York when he was between jobs," recalls a former teammate. "He was clearly not having what most Yalies would think of as great professional success. But he was totally unfazed. He dealt with it in the same graceful way he dealt with his success on the field." After frequent moves around New England for his work, Dowling has settled with his family in Westville, a New Haven neighborhood less than two miles from the Yale Bowl. In 2014, on the Bowl's hundredth anniversary, Dowling was one of four players from the 1968 squad, along with Hill, Weinstein, and Gee, named to the All-Yale-Bowl Team. In the pantheon of Yale gridiron gods, Dowling has taken his place, as Charley Loftus hoped he would, alongside Heffelfinger, Booth, Kelley, and Frank. "To this day, when I'm around Brian Dowling, I feel like I'm twelve and he's a rock star," says his former teammate John Waldman. "It's as if he has some aura or energy field around him."

Dowling's pen-and-ink alter ego has traveled his own path in *Doonesbury*, the Pulitzer Prize–winning comic strip by Garry Trudeau that got its start in 1968 as *bull tales*. When a former teammate saw a *Doonesbury* strip in which B.D. lost his leg to a rocket attack while serving with the National Guard in Iraq, his initial reaction was to call Brian and find out if he was okay—before he remembered it was just a cartoon.

In the spring of 1969, when Calvin Hill got a phone call from the Dallas Cowboys telling him that the team had drafted him in the first round, he assumed it was Bruce Weinstein playing a practical joke. It wasn't. Hill was the first Ivy Leaguer ever to be selected in the first round of the NFL draft. Over the course of his twelve-year NFL career, Hill was named Rookie of Year, set the team's single-season rushing record, was named to the Pro Bowl four times, helped the Cowboys win a Super Bowl, ran for 6,083 yards, caught 271 passes, scored 65 touchdowns, and served as what one sportswriter called "a moral force" wherever he played. Not long before injuries forced him to retire, Hill told a reporter that the hardest-hitting game of his football career had been at Harvard, in 1968.

During his first two years in Dallas, Hill studied part-time at Southern Methodist University's Perkins School of Theology. He now plays something of a pastoral role as a special assistant to the Cowboys, counseling young players as they adjust to life in the NFL. He has been married for forty-eight years to Janet McDonald, the Wellesley student whom he met the night of the 1968 Harvard game and charmed despite the lisp occasioned by his infected tongue. He was in the audience when McDonald's roommate, student body president Hillary Rodham, delivered the commencement address at their graduation. Hill has tried to be as good a father to his son as his own father was to him. (Grant Hill would go on to become a seven-time NBA All-Star and a three-time winner of the league's Sportsmanship Award.) In 2016, Hill was awarded an honorary degree by Yale; his citation described him as "one of the most revered student-athletes in Yale history." Although his long jump record was broken in 1985, his triple-jump record still stands a half century after he set it—as do his football records of 22.2 yards per catch for a season (1968) and 18.8 yards per catch for a career. In 1999, a street in Turner Station was named for Hill. Hill and Dowling, whose names will be linked forever in the annals of Yale football, remain good friends.

Although several NFL teams expressed interest in signing him, Pat Conway went to Harvard Business School. He has run his own financial services company for forty years. Conway isn't proud of the circumstances that led him to the Marines, but he is proud of being a marine, and believes that his experience in the Corps was the making of him. "You're a Conway," he reminds his grandchildren. "You do not take shortcuts."

In 2008, on the fortieth anniversary of the siege of Khe Sanh, Conway attended a weekend reunion for his regiment at Quantico. He had a wonderful time. Not long after returning home, he was driving on a back road when, inexplicably, he began to weep. This happened again, and then again. He started to have recurring nightmares in which he was back in Vietnam. His wife insisted he see a counselor. Conway was resistant—he pointed out that many veterans had gone through far worse than he had—but eventually went to the VA hospital, where he was diagnosed with post-traumatic stress disorder. The doctors wanted him to go into therapy, but exploring his feelings only made things worse. "People said it's good to talk about it, but it wasn't good for me. If you let those demons out, they can take you over." For two years after the reunion, Conway was, he says, "a wreck." His marriage ended. Eventually, he righted himself. "It took time to put those demons back in the box," he says. "I don't want to let them out again. If I let them out, I'll get mushy again, and I don't want to get mushy."

Epilogue

* * *

"These will be the greatest memories of my life," said Frank Champi in the locker room after the 1968 Harvard-Yale game. "But I really take things in stride. Moments of glory are all right, but they die so soon." At first, the hero of the Yale game seemed to enjoy his moments of glory. He was interviewed, wined, and dined; he was inundated with letters from grateful alumni. He and Brian Dowling were flown to Los Angeles to appear on *The Dating Game*. (Neither won the date.) Four months after the game, however, he told a reporter, "I just wish everyone would quit talking about it." He wanted to be known for who he was as a person, he said, not for what he'd done in the last forty-two seconds of a football game.

The following season, with twenty returning lettermen and Champi picking up where he left off, Harvard was favored to win the Ivy League championship. But as two-a-days approached, Champi, finally getting his chance to start, realized he didn't really want to play. All the frustration that had built up over the years had dissolved on November 23, 1968: he had proved he could play quarterback at Harvard. At the same time, he worried that he could never live up to his performance that day. "When you're an instant hero, people expect you to come back and be a hero every game," he says. "I thought, 'What if I come back and I'm a flop?'"

Two games into the season, so anxious and distracted he could hardly play, Champi quit the team. The story was picked up across the country. "It wasn't me out there," Champi told the *New York Times*. "I was just going through the motions." His teammates were furious, feeling he'd left them high and dry. Without Champi, Harvard went through four more quarterbacks and finished 3-6, its first losing season since 1958. Yale, predicted to finish in the bottom half of the league, finished 7-2, and won a share of the Ivy League title for the third year in a row. In the final game of the season, Yale shut out Harvard, 7–0. Champi listened to snatches of it on the radio while working on two English papers in his Win-

342

throp House room. He would write his senior thesis on another conflicted soul, Hamlet.

Champi's moments of glory against Yale were a subject with which he would wrestle for many years. Although he didn't want that one game to define him, he struggled to find out what else might. He spent the summer after senior year hitchhiking across the country before getting his master's at the Harvard School of Education. He coached football and taught high school English for several years, but his introversion made classroom work emotionally exhausting. He has spent much of the rest of his career in service, sales, and administration for the tech industry. He isn't passionate about the work. "I envy people who are successful at something they love to do," he says. "The trick is to find what you're good at, and hone that skill. Looking back, I see that what I was good at, the thing I loved best, was throwing a football. And it sort of punctuated my life with that Harvard-Yale game."

For many years Champi resisted talking about the one thing everyone wanted him to talk about. He seldom gave interviews and dreaded mid-November, when reporters called, asking him to relive the game. "It's as if, when you were a kid, you rode a bike," he says. "You were seven years old and you rode it one day in May for the first time and you shouted *hallelujah* and your parents loved you for it and the world was a great and wonderful place. But twenty years down the road a friend of yours comes up to you and says, 'Hey, remember the day you learned to ride a bike? How did it feel? It must have been fantastic!' And all they want to talk about was that day when you were seven years old." There have been times when Champi has wished he had never played in that game.

Champi and his wife, a librarian, live in a modest house on Boston's North Shore. He still loves reading, mostly history; he occasionally writes poetry. The boy who liked to watch his grandfather in his forge now spends a great deal of time tinkering in his basement workshop. He has invented and patented an ingenious back-saving snow shovel he calls the LeverLift.

Epilogue

Though he has sold dozens of prototypes to friends, he hasn't yet found an investor.

As long as his grandmother was alive, Champi felt it would be disloyal to the woman who raised him to try to find the mother he'd last seen when he was three. But after Theresa Champi's death at the age of ninety-three, Champi tracked down his mother to a town in New Hampshire, only to be told by a neighbor that she had died several years earlier. Champi found out that he had a half sister in the area. From her, he learned more about his mother and came to understand better why she—a young mother in a troubled family in an unfamiliar country—had left. It was then that he found out that she had tried to stay in touch with him and his sister. He realized that the time he'd picked up the telephone and heard a woman say she was his mother, she really *was* his mother.

For decades, Champi avoided going back to Harvard, knowing everyone would want to talk about the game. But as he grew older, he mellowed—"I learned to roll with things better," he says—and he began showing up at an occasional football game or team gathering. He has come to accept that long-ago afternoon in Harvard Stadium as a small but important part of his life. "I had my one moment of greatness, and I'll take it for what it's worth."

Champi, who continues to dabble in astrology, occasionally ponders what might have been. "Physicists talk about alternate realities and how different versions of ourselves may work their way out in other dimensions. Sometimes I speculate about the alternative paths my life might have taken. What would have happened if I hadn't played in that game—if, instead, I had come back and played the following year? Or if I had been the starter all that year and George came off the bench and was the hero against Yale? Or if I hadn't played in the sixties, with the Vietnam War going on—if I had played in the seventies instead? How would my life have changed?" But sometimes he thinks that maybe everything worked out the way it was meant to. Maybe it was all in the stars.

Frank Champi still loves to throw. He threw the javelin in

master's meets till he was forty; seeing him practice on the local fields, nervous townspeople occasionally called the police to report that there was a man in the park throwing a spear. He keeps a shopping bag filled with four or five footballs in his closet, and from time to time, when the weather is nice, he lugs it down to a nearby playground. For several years, there was a neighborhood teenager who'd catch his passes, but now Champi throws alone, sending long, arching spirals, one by one, to the far end of the field. Then he walks the length of the field—he no longer runs—and throws them back.

Appendix

1968 SEASON RECORDS

YALE (8–0–1)				
Sept 28	Connecticut	W	31	14
Oct 5	Colgate	W	49	14
Oct 12	Brown	W	35	13
Oct 19	Columbia	W	29	7
Oct 26	at Cornell	W	25	13
Nov 2	Dartmouth	W	47	27
Nov 9	at Pennsylvania	W	30	13
Nov 16	Princeton	W	42	17
Nov 23	at Harvard	T	29	29

HARVARD (8–0–1)				
Sept 28	Holy Cross	W	27	20
Oct 5	Bucknell	W	59	0
Oct 12	at Columbia	W	21	14
Oct 19	Cornell	W	10	0
Oct 26	Dartmouth	W	22	7
Nov 2	Pennsylvania	W	28	6
Nov 9	at Princeton	W	9	7
Nov 16	Brown	W	31	7
Nov 23	Yale	T	29	29

Appendix

YALE VS. HARVARD, NOVEMBER 23, 1968

Yale	7	15	0	7	29
Harvard	0	6	7	16	29

Yale: Dowling, 3, run (Bayless, kick)
Yale: Hill, 3, pass from Dowling (Bayless, kick)
Yale: Marting, 5, pass from Dowling (Marting, pass from Dowling)
Harvard: Freeman, 15, pass from Champi (kick failed)
Harvard: Crim, 1, run (Szaro, kick)
Yale: Dowling, 5, run (Bayless, kick)
Harvard: Freeman, 15, pass from Champi (Crim, run)
Harvard: Gatto, 8, pass from Champi (Varney, pass from Champi)

Attendance: 40,280

	YALE	HARVARD
First Downs	19	17
Yards Rushing	251	118
Yards Passing	116	104
Return Yards	60	30
Passes	13–23	8–22
Interceptions by	0	1
Fumbles Lost	6	1
Punts	3–36	8–36
Yards Penalized	66	30

Appendix

YALE VS. HARVARD, NOVEMBER 23, 1968
INDIVIDUAL LEADERS

Rushing

Yale: Hill 23–92, Davidson 7–63, Dowling 10–55, Levin 13–41
Harvard: Ballantyne 13–65, Crim 8–45, Reed 1–26, Gatto 8–15,
Hornblower 6–8

Passing

Yale: Dowling 13–21–116, Hill 0–2–0
Harvard: Champi 6–15–82, Lalich 2–6–22, Gatto 0–1–0

Receiving

Yale: Marting 4–35, Hill 4–28, Weinstein 3–29, Levin 2–24
Harvard: Freeman 4–51, Gatto 2–20, Varney 1–23, Hornblower 1–10

YALE FINAL 1968 STATISTICS

TEAM		
	Y	Opp
Points	317	147
First Downs	211	138
Yards Rushing	2,101	1,042
Yards Passing	2,006	1,236
Total Offense	4,107	2,278
Interceptions by	10	14
Fumbles (Lost)	31 (20)	31 (14)
Punts (Avg.)	39 (35.3)	71 (35.4)

Appendix

RUSHING				
Player	**Att**	**Yds**	**Avg**	**TD**
Calvin Hill	138	680	4.9	8
Bob Levin	102	356	3.5	4
Brian Dowling	82	313	3.8	6
Nick Davidson	56	265	4.7	0
Bob Kropke	47	147	3.1	0
Buzzy Potts	22	132	6.0	0

PASSING						
Player	**Att**	**Comp**	**Pct**	**Yds**	**TD**	**Int**
Brian Dowling	160	92	57.5	1,554	19	10
Bob Bayless	31	17	54.8	182	2	1
Joe Massey	18	11	61.1	170	1	2
Calvin Hill	12	7	58.3	80	4	1

RECEIVING				
Player	**Rec**	**Yds**	**Avg**	**TD**
Del Marting	28	428	15.3	6
Calvin Hill	24	532	22.2	6
Bruce Weinstein	23	299	13.0	4
Lew Roney	14	202	14.4	2
Nick Davidson	10	159	15.9	4
Bob Levin	3	45	15.0	0
Brian Dowling	2	38	19.0	1

Appendix

HARVARD FINAL 1968 STATISTICS

TEAM		
	H	Opp
Points	236	90
First Downs	159	135
Yards Rushing	2,025	1,249
Yards Passing	818	1,064
Total Offense	2,843	2,313
Interceptions by	17	7
Fumbles (Lost)	19 (9)	27 (19)
Punts (Avg.)	58 (37.2)	63 (35.9)

RUSHING				
Player	Att	Yds	Avg	TD
Vic Gatto	149	678	4.6	5
Ray Hornblower	126	649	5.2	5
John Ballantyne	39	269	6.9	2
Gus Crim	47	213	4.5	4
Ken O'Connell	15	91	6.1	2
Jim Reynolds	15	69	4.6	0
Tom Miller	12	73	6.1	0

PASSING						
Player	Att	Comp	Pct	Yds	TD	Int
George Lalich	110	55	50.0	628	3	4
Frank Champi	27	11	40.7	128	4	0
Vic Gatto	10	3	30.0	56	0	1
Ray Hornblower	9	2	22.2	21	0	1

Appendix

RECEIVING				
Player	Rec	Yds	Avg	TD
Pete Varney	20	306	15.3	3
Vic Gatto	18	179	9.9	1
Bruce Freeman	11	144	13.1	2
Gus Crim	8	39	4.9	0
John Kiernan	6	53	8.8	0
Ray Hornblower	5	66	13.2	0
John Ballantyne	2	18	9.0	0
Tony Smith	2	13	6.5	1

1968 COACHES' ALL-IVY FIRST TEAM

Offense: Bruce Weinstein (E, Yale); Del Marting (E, Yale); Kyle Gee (T, Yale); Tom Hamlin (T, Penn); Tom Jones (G, Harvard); Mike Guerin (G, Princeton); Gerry Murphy (C, Brown); Brian Dowling (B, Yale); Calvin Hill (B, Yale); Marty Domres (B, Columbia); Vic Gatto (B, Harvard); Eliot Berry (K, Penn)

Defense: Pete Lawrence (E, Dartmouth); Pete Hall (E, Harvard); Mike Chwastyk (T, Penn); John Sponheimer (T, Cornell); Dick Williams (G, Yale); Mike Bouscaren (LB, Yale); John Emery (LB, Harvard); Pat Conway (B, Harvard); George Burrell (B, Penn); Keith Mauney (B, Princeton); Ed Franklin (B, Yale); Bill Arthur (P, Cornell); Gary Singleterry (P, Harvard)

Notes on Sources

Although this book is based primarily on my interviews with the players, it also draws on a wide variety of written sources. I'd like to cite those on which I relied most.

I was fortunate that both Harvard and Yale are served by student newspapers of uncommon excellence, and that back issues of the *Harvard Crimson* and the *Yale Daily News* are available online. I was also fortunate that the *Yale Alumni Magazine* and *Harvard Magazine* (known as the *Harvard Alumni Bulletin* until 1973) chronicled their institutions' mid-sixties growing pains with admirable thoroughness and candor. Harvard and Yale yearbooks of the era also provided valuable contemporary accounts of campus life. My descriptions of individual games during the 1968 season were aided by *News and Views of Harvard Sports*, a weekly newsletter published by the Harvard Varsity Club, and by *Football Y News*, a weekly publication for Yale boosters assembled largely by Charley Loftus, Yale's director of sports publicity.

I: Two-a-Days

My portrait of John Yovicsin owes much to "John Yovicsin Celebrates His Tenth," a profile of the coach by John T. Bethell (*Harvard Alumni Bulletin*, November 12, 1966).

II: Hell No, We Won't Go!

My description of 1960s Harvard borrows from two highly readable histories, *The Harvard Century* by Richard Norton Smith and *Making*

Notes on Sources

Harvard Modern by Morton Keller and Phyllis Keller. *Veritas*, a comparatively jaunty tour of the same territory by Andrew Schlesinger, was also helpful. I found a trove of good stories in *Harvard: Through Change and Through Storm* by E. J. Kahn Jr., a *New Yorker* writer and Harvard alumnus, who did much of the research for his book in 1968. *The Prince of Tennessee*, a biography of Al Gore by David Maraniss and Ellen Nakashima, includes a lively account of Gore's undergraduate years at Harvard. I drew from several anthologies, especially *The Harvard Book*, a sampler of three centuries of writing about the university edited by William Bentinck-Smith; *My Harvard, My Yale*, a collection of essays by notable twentieth-century alumni and alumnae, edited by Diana Dubois; and *Our Harvard*, another collection of essays by well-known graduates, edited by Jeffrey L. Lant. *Mapping Norwood*, a memoir by Charles Fanning, gave me a sense of what life at Harvard was like for a public schooler in the early sixties. *Harvard Observed*, an illustrated history of the university in the twentieth century by John T. Bethell, and *Harvard A to Z*, a compendium of Harvardiana by John T. Bethell, Richard M. Hunt, and Robert Shenton, were fonts of institutional knowledge from which I frequently and gratefully drank. The story about the national magazine seeking to publish a piece on "pot parties at Harvard" can be found in Faye Levine's essay "When the Bright Colors Faded," in *My Harvard, My Yale*. The story about the master of Adams House and the parietals-breaking couple is taken from Anne Fadiman's essay "Where Is the Grace of Yesteryear?" in *The Harvard Book*. For jogging my memories of Cambridge in the sixties, I could have had no more evocative guide than *Harvard Square: An Illustrated History Since 1950* by Mo Lotman.

My discussion of Nathan Pusey was helped by *The Harvard Century*. My description of Social Relations 148 draws from *Making Harvard Modern*. I benefited from reading *Push Comes to Shove*, a blow-by-blow, protest-by-protest account of the internecine struggles of the radical left at Harvard. Its author, Steven Kelman, belonged to the Young People's Socialist League as an undergraduate in the sixties. I was inspired by "O Harberg, My Harberg," a bittersweet account of sixties student idealism by former SDS member Jesse Kornbluth, which can be found in *My Harvard, My Yale*, and by James Fallows's untitled essay in *Our Harvard*. My discussion of ROTC owes a debt to *My Detachment*, a memoir by Tracy Kidder, who was an ROTC cadet during his years at Harvard.

My brief description of the 1968 Columbia uprising was informed by *The Strawberry Statement: Notes of a College Revolutionary* by James

Notes on Sources

Simon Kunen; *The Battle for Morningside Heights: Why Students Rebel* by Roger Kahn; and *Underground: My Life with SDS and the Weathermen* by Mark Rudd.

III: God Plays Quarterback for Yale

My understanding of Yale football's long and glorious history was enriched by *The Yale Football Story*, an anecdotal tour of the program's first eighty years by Tim Cohane. (This is the book Carmen Cozza sent to Brian Dowling and other incoming freshman recruits; guard Jack Perkowski read it twice—not only because he wanted to soak up as much of the Yale ethos as possible but because he worried there might be a quiz on it.) Even more helpful was *Gridiron Glory: Yale Football 1952–72*, an elegant account by Thomas G. Bergin that picks up where Cohane's book left off. Also of use were *Yale Football* (from the *Images of Sports* series) by Sam Rubin and *The Blue Football Book*, which chronicles selected seasons of Yale football through 1969 and includes a chapter on the 1968 team. I am especially indebted to "Portrait of a way of life," an intimate and revealing essay on the 1968 team written by the future Pulitzer Prize–winning arts critic William A. Henry III when he was a Yale sophomore. I also dipped frequently into *A Bowl Full of Memories*, a cornucopia of oral histories assembled by Rich Marazzi for the hundredth anniversary of the Yale Bowl.

Details of Dowling's storied high school career can be found in "Brian Dowling: A Living Legend," a chapter in *Pass the Nuts* by Dan Coughlin, as well as in *The Charity Game: The Story of Cleveland's Thanksgiving Day High School Football Classic* by Timothy L. Hudak. Dowling's exploits at Yale were extensively documented in the pages of the *Yale Daily News*, among other publications. Frank Deford's marvelous profile, "The Man Called B.D.," originally published in *Sports Illustrated* on September 5, 1988, can be found in *The Best of Frank Deford*.

My description of *bull tales* and its creator was helped by *Doonesbury and the Art of G. B. Trudeau* by Brian Walker and by *40: A Doonesbury Retrospective* by GB Trudeau, as well as by "Doonesbury's War," a profile of Trudeau by Gene Weingarten in the *Washington Post* (October 22, 2006). The strips that gave birth to *Doonesbury* were published in paperback form as *bull tales* by the *Yale Daily News* in 1969, with a foreword by Brian Dowling. Among the many pleasures of researching *The Game* was the chance to relive the sixties through the work of one of our most witty and insightful social commentators.

Notes on Sources

Some of the material on Carmen Cozza was gleaned from *True Blue: The Carm Cozza Story* by Carm Cozza with Rick Odermatt.

IV: The Melting Pot

My discussion of Harvard's changing student body was aided by "Poor but Hopefull Scholars," an essay by Stephan Thernstrom in *Glimpses of the Harvard Past*. Some of the details on the link between football and war derive from *A Team for America*, a book about Army's 1944 national champions by Randy Roberts, and *When Saturday Mattered Most*, a book about the undefeated 1958 Army team by Mark Beech.

V: Opening Up the Club

Several memoirs offered insight into life at Yale in the years leading up to the mid-sixties: *Remembering Denny* by Calvin Trillin, *On the Cusp* by Daniel Horowitz, and *Class Divide* by Howard Gillette Jr. "A Keening of Weenies," an essay by Christopher Buckley in *My Harvard, My Yale*, was also helpful. Of the many articles and essays that chart the mid-sixties transformation of Yale, I am especially grateful to "In the Days of DKE and S.D.S.," by Carter Wiseman, in the *Yale Alumni Magazine* (February 2001).

The Chosen by Jerome Karabel, a masterful, insightful, and frequently appalling look at admissions practices at Harvard, Yale, and Princeton over the course of the twentieth century, is essential to understanding the shifting demographics of Harvard and Yale. I also benefited from *The Big Test* by Nicholas Lemann, *The Half-Opened Door* by Marcia Graham Synnott, *The Power of Privilege* by Joseph A. Soares, and "The Birth of a New Institution" by Geoffrey Kabaservice (*Yale Alumni Magazine*, December 1999).

For background on William Sloane Coffin, I relied on his memoir, *Once to Every Man*, and Warren Goldstein's biography, *William Sloane Coffin Jr.: A Holy Impatience*. For background on Kingman Brewster, I am indebted to Geoffrey Kabaservice's fascinating group biography, *The Guardians: Kingman Brewster, His Circle, and the Rise of the Liberal Establishment*. The story of R. Inslee (Inky) Clark's appearance before the Yale Corporation is told in *The Guardians*. The meeting at which a Corporation member pointed out that there were no Jews and no public school graduates in the room is said to have taken place in the spring of 1966; in fact, William Horowitz, a prominent New Haven banker (and

Notes on Sources

father of *On the Cusp* author Daniel Horowitz) had been elected to the Corporation as a petition candidate the previous year. "Trustee of Yale Breaks Tradition: Horowitz, Jewish Executive, Is First Non-Protestant on University's Board," was the *New York Times* headline of June 21, 1965. (By way of comparison, not until 1985 would a Jew be elected to the Harvard Corporation.) Horowitz was, furthermore, one of two public high school graduates on the sixteen-member board. It should also be noted that Inky Clark, who left Yale in 1970 to become headmaster at the Horace Mann School, would, many years after his death in 1999, be implicated in an extensive pedophilia scandal at the secondary school, as detailed in *Great Is the Truth* by Amos Kamil with Sean Elder.

My description of Yale's journey toward co-education was assisted by *"Keep the Damned Women Out"* by Nancy Weiss Malkiel. My knowledge of Yale's attitudes toward Jews was enriched by *Joining the Club: A History of Jews and Yale* by Dan A. Oren. For information on Yale's senior societies, I am indebted to *Skulls and Keys*, an eight-hundred-page history by David Alan Richards; I also made use of the considerably briefer *Secrets of the Tomb* by Alexandra Robbins and *"Go to Your Room,"* a slim 1960 volume about the society system by Loomis Havemeyer.

VI: Playing Football for the Man

My account of John Tyson's years at Harvard owes much to *The Prince of Tennessee*, with its description of Gore's Dunster House roommate group, and to *Inventing Al Gore*, a biography by Bill Turque. The story of Tyson and Gore's bunk bed conversations, as well as their reactions to Martin Luther King's assassination, are taken from "On Campus Torn by 60's, Agonizing Over the Path" by Melinda Henneberger (*New York Times*, June 21, 2000). My brief discussion of the 1967 Newark uprising was informed by *How Newark Became Newark*, a history of the city by Brad R. Tuttle. "The Killing of Billy Furr" ran in the July 28, 1967, issue of *Life*.

Blacks at Harvard, a compilation of essays and historical documents edited by Werner Sollors, Caldwell Titcomb, and Thomas A. Underwood, was an invaluable resource. The book includes W. E. B. Du Bois's essay "A Negro Student at Harvard at the End of the Nineteenth Century" as well as "The Crisis of 1969" by Lawrence E. Eichel, a detailed history of events leading to the founding of Harvard's Afro-American Studies department. The freshman dormitory crisis of the early twenties is told in painful detail in *Blacks at Harvard*, as well as in "Jim Crow at Harvard: 1923," an essay by

Notes on Sources

Nell Painter in *The New England Quarterly* (vol. 44, no. 4, December 1971). *Black Harvard/Black Yale*, reminiscences by graduates of the two schools edited by Jesse Rhines, was also useful. Herbert Nickens's essay "Travels with Charlie: In Search of Afro-America" can be found in *333*, the yearbook of Harvard and Radcliffe's class of 1969. *The Black Revolution on Campus*, a pioneering work by Martha Biondi, placed the rise of black activism at Harvard in a larger context, as did "Black Power Hits the Campus," an article by Ernest Dunbar in *Look* (October 3, 1967). My discussion of Social Sciences 5: The Afro-American Experience draws from "Soc. Sci. 5: 'A Place for the Black Man at Harvard?,'" a summary of the controversial course published in the November 14, 1968, issue of the *Crimson*.

For more than a century, Richard Greener (Harvard 1870) was believed to be the first African-American to graduate from an Ivy League college. (In 1847, Beverly Williams was admitted to Harvard, but he died of tuberculosis before his freshman year began.) In 2014, an archivist at a Manhattan auction gallery came across evidence that Greener had been preceded, at Yale, by Richard Henry Green, the son of a New Haven bootmaker, who graduated in 1857.

VII: The Most Dangerous Back in the History of the Ivy League

My portrait of Calvin Hill owes an immense debt to a wide-ranging interview with the former Yale star conducted by David Zang for the *Journal of Sport History* (vol. 15, no. 3, Winter 1988). Many of the details about Hill's upbringing, including his quotes about his father's influence, can be found there. Details about Hill's experience at the Riverdale Country School are drawn from a speech he gave at the school on November 14, 2014 (available on the school's website). I also made use of a speech Hill gave at the Ivy Football Association's 2013 dinner. Hill recalled the 1963 March on Washington for an episode of *Personal with Bill Rhoden*, a cable television series in which the *New York Times* sportswriter interviewed Hill and his son, Grant. The story of Hill's father's flight from South Carolina is told in *Breakthrough 'Boys* by Jaime Aron. *Game of My Life: Dallas Cowboys* by Jean-Jacques Taylor, in which Cowboy players discuss memorable games from their NFL careers, includes biographical information about Hill. *Change the Game: One Athlete's Thoughts on Sports, Dreams, and Growing Up* by Grant Hill includes an affectionate portrait of the author's father. *Turner Station* by Jerome Watson (from the *Images of America* series) provided a helpful photographic glimpse of Hill's former hometown.

Notes on Sources

The long and difficult journey traveled by African-American quarterbacks is outlined in *Third and a Mile*, a collection of interviews with pioneering black players by William C. Rhoden. *Breaking the Line* by Samuel G. Freedman, which tells the story of a seminal 1967 game between two historically black colleges, Grambling and Florida A&M, also touches on the subject. (Grambling's James Harris would go on to become the first African-American quarterback to start an NFL opening-day game, in 1969.)

Information on the history of African-Americans at Yale was derived from *The Chosen* by Jerome Karabel and from *The Guardians* by Geoffrey Kabaservice. I also found much of use in *Black Harvard/Black Yale*, in particular the untitled essay by Ronald Matchett. I benefited from reading "Parable of the Talents," an essay by Henry Louis Gates Jr. on his experiences as a student at Yale in the late sixties and early seventies, in *The Future of the Race* by Gates and Cornel West. The story of Pierson College's "slave quarters" is recounted in Sarah Maslin's article "In Pierson's Lower Court, a tainted history," published in the *Yale Daily News* on September 23, 2013.

VIII: Coming Home

My understanding of the Vietnam War was immeasurably enriched by reading two of the best books written about that war or any war: Michael Herr's *Dispatches*, which contains two chapters on Khe Sanh, and *A Rumor of War*, whose author, Philip Caputo, was part of the first combat unit sent to Vietnam, in March 1965. I also made use of *Last Stand at Khe Sanh* by Gregg Jones, a gripping account of the siege. (Pat Conway has given copies of *Last Stand* to family members to help them understand what Khe Sanh was like, while making it clear that his experiences were less harrowing than those of the marines whose stories are told in the book.) *Patriots: The Vietnam War Remembered from All Sides*, a fascinating and moving collection of oral histories assembled and edited by Christian G. Appy, was also helpful.

IX: Most Determined Guy Out There

David Halberstam's *The Amateurs* provided background on the role of sports in Mike Bouscaren's family. It also provided a model of fine sportswriting.

Notes on Sources

The story of George W. Bush's truncated career on the Yale varsity football team is based on the accounts of several players. Bush went on to play for his Davenport College intramural football team as well as for the Yale rugby squad, and he remained a passionate supporter of Yale football throughout his undergraduate years. He roomed for two years with tackle Ted Livingston (who played in the 1968 Harvard game), and their postgame parties were the stuff of legend.

XI: Ballyhoo

The creation story of The Game is engagingly told in Mark F. Bernstein's *Football: The Ivy League Origins of an American Obsession*, from which I have drawn extensively. *Ivy League Football Since 1872*, a thoroughly researched and gracefully written history by John McCallum, also provided helpful details. *The Only Game That Matters*, by Bernard M. Corbett and Paul Simpson, tells the tale of the 2002 Harvard-Yale game but includes much background lore. *The Game: The Harvard-Yale Football Rivalry, 1875–1983*, an illustrated history by Thomas G. Bergin (the Thucydides of Yale football), was another invaluable source. *Ivy League Autumns* by Richard Goldstein also contained useful material.

My grasp of Harvard's gridiron heritage was strengthened by several books, including *The H Book of Harvard Athletics*, a three-volume compendium commissioned by the Harvard Varsity Club, which describes in granular detail the evolution of every sport played at Harvard; *Harvard Football* by Bernard M. Corbett (from the *Images of Sports* series); and *Crimson in Triumph: A Pictorial History of Harvard Athletics, 1852–1985* by Joe Bertagna (himself a former Crimson hockey goalie), which contains an excellent chapter on the football team. For a hilarious reimagining of Houghton's bulldog-strangling, see George Plimpton's *Paper Lion*.

The story of Frederic Remington is well told by Judith Ann Schiff in "Artist in the Backfield" (*Yale Alumni Magazine*, October 1998). Remington was hardly the only man to play for Harvard or Yale and go on to success in another field. Indeed, a pretty fair team could be assembled from such players. Remington could be joined in the backfield by three-time Pulitzer Prize–winning poet Archibald MacLeish, who lettered for Yale at halfback in 1913. ("Conventional wisdom notwithstanding, there is no reason either in football or in poetry why the two should not meet in a man's life if he has the weight and cares about the words," reasoned

MacLeish.) The interior line could be anchored by Massachusetts governor Endicott "Chub" Peabody, an All-American guard at Harvard in 1941, and United States senator William Proxmire, who, as a member of the Yale junior varsity in the late thirties served, in his own words, as "a blocking and tackling dummy" for Heisman trophy winners Larry Kelley and Clint Frank. Proxmire's position coach, Gerald Ford, who was a starting center at the University of Michigan before he took a job with the Bulldog JVs to help pay his way through Yale Law School, might be pressed into service.

A second Pulitzer Prize–winning author, John Hersey, who was a second-string receiver for Yale in 1934 and 1935, could play end. The other end could be manned by a Kennedy. Neither Joe (Harvard '38) nor Jack ('40), the stars of Hyannisport touch football games, progressed beyond the Harvard JVs, but Bobby ('48) played—sparingly but tenaciously—for the varsity; after the five-foot-ten, 155-pound receiver fractured his leg early in his senior season, the coach put him in the Yale game, cast and all, long enough for him to win his letter. Ted ('56), dominated (and humiliated) by his older brothers in backyard touch, turned out to be the best football player in the family. In 1955, with his father and brothers watching from the stands, the six-foot-two, 200-pound end made a spectacular reception in the snow to score Harvard's only touchdown in a 21–7 loss to Yale. A photo of the catch hung on the wall of his Senate office.

Cole Porter (Yale '13) could be the team composer; as an undergraduate, he wrote many of Yale's most memorable fight songs, including its unofficial gridiron anthem, "Bulldog." Journalist John Reed (Harvard '10) could be head cheerleader, just as he was during his senior year. "As song-leader of the cheering section, I had the supreme blissful sensation of swaying two thousand voices in great crashing choruses during the big football games," he wrote. After graduating, he would teach some of those songs to striking factory workers in Paterson, New Jersey, before traveling to Petrograd and becoming an unofficial cheerleader for the Russian Revolution. Crooner Rudy Vallee (Yale '27) could lead the band; he sang and played saxophone for the Yale Band as an undergraduate and learned what would become his first big hit, "The Whiffenpoof Song."

The history of the Harvard-Yale gridiron rivalry is long and storied, and the facts are occasionally a matter of disagreement. Tad Jones's immortal words to his team about the importance of the Harvard game, for example, are, depending on the source, said to have been uttered in either 1916, 1923, or 1925. (I settled on 1916, in large measure because Chester LaRoche, the quarterback of the 1916 team, says so in his foreword to *Ivy League Football Since 1872*.) As for the origin of the phrase "The Game," most writers date it to 1959, when Charley Loftus, on the phone with Red Smith, is said to have referred to the upcoming Harvard-Yale clash as "the game," and Smith, hearing the implied capitals, rendered it that way in his *New York Herald Tribune* column. But as Rich Marazzi points out in *A Bowl Full of Memories*, the phrase was used at least as far back as 1952, when *New York Times* sportswriter Joseph M. Sheehan deployed it in his coverage of that year's Harvard-Yale game. It was in regular use in the *Times* thereafter. ("Yale-Harvard Skirmishes Precede THE Game" was the *Times* headline on the eve of the 1958 contest.) It was Loftus, however, who institutionalized the phrase.

XII: With Almost Contemptuous Ease

My account of the 1968 game itself is based largely on repeated viewings of the WHDH-TV broadcast. It also owes much to Kevin Rafferty's *Harvard Beats Yale 29–29*, the companion book to Rafferty's gripping, heartwarming documentary film of the same name. I also drew on contemporary accounts in the *Harvard Crimson*, the *Yale Daily News*, the *Boston Globe*, the *Boston Herald*, the *New Haven Register*, the *New Haven Journal-Courier*, the *New York Times*, *Sports Illustrated*, the *Yale Alumni Magazine*, and the *Harvard Alumni Bulletin*. (The *Bulletin* is the source of the anecdote about the sociologist and the statistician.) I am further indebted to *The Only Game That Matters*, whose opening chapter is devoted to The Game's 1968 iteration. Roger Angell's moving account of the 1968 game, "Harvard Wins, 29–29!," originally published in *Harvard Football News* on November 18, 1978, was reprinted in *The Harvard Book*. The game has been immortalized in numerous sports anthologies, including *College Football's Most Memorable Games, 1913 Through 1990* by Fred Eisenhammer and Eric B. Sondheimer; *Ten Moments that Shook the Sports World* by Stan Isaacs; and *It's Not Over 'Til It's Over: The Stories Behind the Most Magnificent, Heart-Stopping Sports Miracles of Our Time* by Al Silverman, which ranks it alongside Bobby Thomson's ninth-inning, pennant-clinching 1951 homer and the U.S. hockey team's upset of the U.S.S.R. in the 1980 Olympics.

Notes on Sources

XIV: Forty-Two Seconds

Tom Peacock's quote about "a weird force" descending on the stadium can be found in *Harvard Beats Yale 29–29*, Kevin Rafferty's 2008 documentary film.

XV: Pandemonium

Details about imprisoned former Yale footballer John Downey, whose remarkable story is worthy of its own book, are from "Ex-C.I.A. Agent John Downey Talks About His 20 Years in a Chinese Prison—and His Readjustment" (*People*, December 18, 1978); from "'Your Future Is Very Dark'" by Andrew Burt (*Slate*, September 24, 2014); and from Downey's own words in *A Bowl Full of Memories*.

XVI: Strike

Much has been written about the events at Harvard of April 9 and 10, 1969. Where accounts disagree, I relied on the *Harvard Alumni Bulletin*, whose issues of April 28, 1969, and May 19, 1969, are exemplars of journalism. I am also indebted to the detailed narrative laid out in *The Harvard Strike* by Lawrence E. Eichel, Kenneth W. Jost, Robert D. Luskin, and Richard M. Neustadt—all reporters for WHRB, the Harvard student radio station, which broadcast from inside University Hall throughout the occupation. The *Harvard Crimson* and the *Boston Globe* both had reporters inside the building, and my account has profited from their fine work. *Coming Apart: A Memoir of the Harvard Wars of 1969* by Roger Rosenblatt provides a thoughtful and unsparing look at the crisis. *Random Curves*, a memoir by mathematician Neal Koblitz, who joined SDS two months before he entered University Hall on April 9, contains an illuminating chapter on the occupation and bust. Other valuable sources include "Confrontation in Harvard Yard," *Life*'s cover story of April 25, 1969; E. J. Kahn's *Harvard: Through Change and Through Storm*; Steven Kelman's *Push Comes to Shove*; and William Martin's untitled essay in *Our Harvard*. Martin, a freshman in the spring of 1969, was housed in Thayer Hall, which was next door to University Hall and gave him a ringside seat.

Although it fell beyond the scope of this book, I would be remiss not to point out that in May 1970, a year after the Harvard occupation, Yale would have its own sixties day of reckoning when Bobby Seale, co-founder of the Black Panther Party, went on trial in New Haven, charged with orchestrating the murder of a local Panther suspected of being an informant. For America's radicals, it seemed an ideal opportunity to "take down" Yale, one of the few college campuses that had been spared widespread disruption. They called for a massive protest on the New Haven Green over the May Day weekend. "Not only will we burn buildings," promised Panther Chief of Staff David Hilliard, "we will take lives." It was said that 50,000 antiwar radicals, Panthers, Yippies, and hippies would descend on the city. The governor called out the National Guard. Four thousand marines and paratroopers were placed on standby. Administrators and alumni urged Kingman Brewster to send the students home, shut down the university, and lock its gates. Instead, after sub rosa meetings with prominent radicals and BSAY leaders (including football player Kurt Schmoke), Brewster declared that Yale would remain open and unlocked; indeed, it would offer to house and feed its May Day visitors in the courtyards of its hallowed Gothic colleges. He would treat the invaders like guests.

In the event, the rumored 50,000 radicals numbered about 15,000. And though downtown New Haven resembled an armed camp—store windows boarded up; trash cans, in which fires could be started, hauled away; flagpoles greased to discourage would-be desecrators of the American flag; bayonet-wielding National Guardsmen on every corner—much of the weekend had a festival air: speeches, music, dancing, poetry. ("O holy Yale Panther Peaceful Conscious populace awake alert sensitive tender," chanted Allen Ginsberg.) On Friday night, however, a tense standoff took place on Church Street when a thousand protestors were confronted by hundreds of New Haven policemen and National Guardsmen. William Sloane Coffin hustled back and forth between the two groups trying to defuse the tension. Senior football player Bart Whiteman, one of 200 designated student "marshals," was among those attempting to keep the peace. But when a few radicals ("from Cambridge," Coffin claimed) began throwing bottles, the Guardsmen responded with tear gas; Whiteman was among hundreds of teargassed students caught in the crossfire. Sporadic clashes between rock-throwing anarchists and policemen continued for hours. Carmen Cozza spent the night with a loaded rifle in his office in Ray Tompkins, prepared to fire a warning shot if radicals stormed the building. National Guardsman and former Yale defensive end Pat Madden spent the night in the Goffe Street Armory, relegated to clerical work because he hadn't yet had firearms training. He was glad he hadn't, as he listened to jittery fellow Guardsmen return from street patrols, terrified they might have to shoot someone. Former fullback Bob Levin had come to New Haven for the weekend to check out the scene. His senior society, Elihu, located just across the street from the New Haven Green, served as the communications center for teams of medics who tended to injured and teargassed demonstrators on the Persian carpet of the Elihu library.

By the end of the weekend, after the tear gas had cleared and the radicals had moved on, only thirty-seven people had been arrested, no one had been badly injured, and Yale was still standing. Brewster's decision to keep the campus open had been a risky but deft strategy, like a jiujitsu move in which, by giving way, a potential victim puts his attacker off balance. Yale was still breathing a collective sigh of relief the next day, when Ohio National Guardsmen opened fire on students at an antiwar rally at Kent State University.

Epilogue

George Pataki's quote is from his foreword to *The Only Game That Matters*. Kyle Gee's quote about his 29–29 "lesion," Mike Bouscaren's quote about the meaning of the 1968 game, and Frank Champi's quote about bike riding are taken from *Harvard Beats Yale 29–29*, the documentary film by Kevin Rafferty.

Acknowledgments

Five years ago, my wife and I watched *Harvard Beats Yale 29–29*, a documentary film about the 1968 Harvard-Yale football game by Kevin Rafferty. Like me, Anne had attended Harvard in the early seventies. Unlike me, she hadn't been at the 1968 game, and had no interest in football. But she was transfixed by the film no less than I was. After it was over, we talked into the night about the game, the players, the Vietnam War, the sixties, our younger selves, and the differences between Harvard and Yale. I woke up the next morning knowing that I wanted to write about the game and the era in which it was played.

I owe a great debt to Kevin Rafferty, who not only gave his blessing to this book but also provided contact information for the players, granted me permission to quote from his marvelous film (available at www.kinolorber.com), offered support at key moments, and was, in all things and at all times, the soul of generosity.

It has been suggested that if you can remember the sixties, you probably weren't there. The players on the 1968 Harvard and Yale football teams *were* there, and they remembered a great deal. For entrusting me with their memories, I will forever be grateful to Mike Ananis, John Ballantyne, George Bass, Rick Berne, Frank Champi, Andy Coe, Pat Conway, John Cramer, Gus Crim, Bob Dowd, Brian Dowling, John Emery, Gary Farneti, Ed Franklin,

Acknowledgments

Bruce Freeman, Rick Frisbie, Vic Gatto, J. P. Goldsmith, Pete Hall, Ray Hornblower, Jim Hudak, Neil Hurley, John Ignacio, Bob Jannino, John Kiernan, Mick Kleber, George Lalich, Brad Lee, Bob Levin, Ted Livingston, Alex MacLean, Pat Madden, Jerry Marino, Del Marting, Fred Martucci, Rich Mattas, Joe McGrath, Joe McKinney, Fred Morris, Dale Neal, Jack Perkowski, Bill Primps, Milt Puryear, Jim Reynolds, Scott Robinson, Lew Roney, Gary Singleterry, Ted Skowronski, Tony Smith, Bob Sokolowski, Ken Thomas, John Waldman, Bruce Weinstein, Dick Williams, and Coach Seb LaSpina. Thank you for responding so graciously, patiently, and honestly to my questions—and to my follow-up questions, and to my follow-up-to-my-follow-up questions. Extra credit to Mike Ananis, Rick Berne, Bob Dowd, Seb LaSpina, Bill Primps, Bob Sokolowski, John Waldman, and Dick Williams for lending me scrapbooks, yearbooks, game programs, and other memorabilia. And thanks to the wives, girlfriends, and mothers who compiled those scrapbooks and saved that memorabilia.

For helping me get to know John Tyson, whom I never met, I am grateful to George Tyson, Lorena Tyson, Lee Daniels, Robert Hall, Mike Kapetan, Glenn Price, Wesley Profit, Roger Rosenblatt, Bob Somerby, Tom Williamson, and, especially, Ron Burton.

A number of other people with connections to the game or to the players generously shared their thoughts and memories. Thanks to Cris Coffin, Kathy Hurley, Elizabeth Kilbreth, Jamie Kilbreth, Delia O'Connor, Jack Reardon, Jane Reed, Susan Schraft, and Jeff Wheelwright. Thanks to Jon Stein (who, as a 125-pound rookie reporter for the *New Haven Journal-Courier*, suited up for Yale football practice one afternoon and lived to tell the tale) for describing what it was like to cover the 1968 Yale team.

Thanks to Tim Driscoll, Ed Copenhagen, Robin Carlaw, and the staff at Harvard University Archives for making my visits to Pusey Library both fruitful and enjoyable. Thanks to Michael Lotstein, Michael Frost, and the Manuscripts and Archives staff

Acknowledgments

at Yale University Library for expertly and patiently attending to my needs and for pointing out archival treasures I didn't know existed. Thanks to Steve Conn, Yale's Director of Sports Publicity, for allowing me to root around to my heart's content in the athletic department archives at Ray Tompkins House. Thanks to Tim Williamson, Harvard Associate Director of Athletics, for providing access to Harvard's collection of game programs and press books. Thanks to John Rosenberg and Robert Bonotto of *Harvard Magazine* for letting me comb through back issues and test the stamina of their photocopying machine, and to my old friend Jean Martin for rummaging through the magazine's collection of vintage photographs. Thanks to Kathrin Day Lasilla and Mark Alden Branch at the *Yale Alumni Magazine* for allowing me to camp out in their conference room for three days, poring over *YAM* back issues and old yearbooks. Thanks to Deborah Smullyan and the Harvard Alumni Association for guiding me to their collection of alumni reunion "Red Books." Thanks to Jacqueline Lipton for helping me navigate the world of photo permissions. Thanks to Isaac Amend, Ana Barros, Jalen DaVon, and Daniel Stern for running to ground a miscellany of arcane factoids. Thanks to the members of Journalism 428 ("Sports in Film, Journalism, and Literature") at the University of Massachusetts, Amherst, for their suggestions. Thanks to their professor, Maddy Blais, for her warm support—and for giving the title of this book a final tweak. Thanks to John Bethell (a.k.a. "Cleat"), former editor of *Harvard Magazine*, for his exemplary coverage of Harvard in the sixties, for helping me track down savory morsels of Harvard arcana, and for his mentorship over the years.

For advice and encouragement—or for just continuing to nod supportively as I nattered on about a football game that took place a half century ago—I am grateful to Beth Colt, Sarah Colt, Lawrence Douglas, Rob Farnsworth, David Modest, Billy Shebar, P. K. Simonds, Forbes Singer, Henry Singer, and Rod Skinner.

I am grateful to the many Old Blues who advised me to talk to

Acknowledgments

Bob Barton (Yale '57), former sportswriter and editor at the *New Haven Register* and "resident historian of Yale University football," as one editor described him. Bob generously shared his encyclopedic knowledge of all things Bulldog (as well as his breathtaking memory for names, dates, and statistics), and tracked down what little he didn't already know with Sherlockian doggedness.

Thanks to Mark Feeney for his sage advice at critical junctures, and for casting his gimlet editorial eye over an early draft of this book, an act of generosity that saved me from dozens of embarrassing mistakes, grammatical, geographical, and institutional. Those that remain are entirely the fault of the author.

I am especially grateful to Dick Todd, who on November 23, 1968, was listening to The Game on the radio with his wife and infant daughter in their third-floor Cambridge apartment (the baby clapped in delight each time the crowd roared), and to whatever forces led us to wind up in neighboring towns in western Massachusetts nearly five decades later so that I could benefit from his wise and forbearing editorial counsel. At a point when the manuscript was swelling to a size that threatened to suffocate its creator, Dick helped trim it down to more manageable dimensions. Our monthly editing sessions were among the most pleasant, productive, and regenerative hours I spent during the writing of this book.

As I worked in my study in rural Massachusetts, it comforted me to remind myself that *The Game* had its supporters in midtown Manhattan. Having Amanda Urban as my agent has always made me feel as empowered as a boxer with Angelo Dundee in his corner. Thank you, dear Binky, for your unerring advice and unflagging enthusiasm. Having Scribner as my literary home away from home makes me among the most fortunate of writers. Thank you, Nan Graham, for inviting me into that home twenty years ago, and for backing this book with your trademark gusto and keen editorial attention. Thank you, Susan Moldow, for your support. Thank you, Jason Chappell, Kyle Kabel, Jaya Miceli, Amanda Pelletier, and Ed Klaris for helping *The Game* become its best self. Thank you, Daniel

Acknowledgments

Loedel, for your patient guidance and astute suggestions—and for proving that a football-indifferent Brown graduate could be the ideal editor for a book about a football game between Harvard and Yale that took place long before he was born.

I owe everything to my family. To Cathy Robinson and Carlyle Singer, for sanctioning my one-man, one-dog writer's colony on Goat's Neck. To Typo, for keeping me company there and everywhere else. To Mark Colt and Liz Collins, for getting married. To Harry and Sandy Colt, for commenting on chapter drafts and for periodically transforming their Maine home into a literary B&B. To Susannah Colt, for nourishing conversations about the book and about the challenges of the writing life. To Henry Colt, for his enthusiasm on hearing me read aloud the first draft of the first completed chapter of this book (which sustained me for many months), and on hearing each subsequent chapter. A college student-athlete himself, Henry also taught me something about the sacrifices that role requires and the rewards it can bring. To my mother, Lisa Colt, for always asking about the book (and for always being interested in the answer), for her insightful comments on each chapter, and for being supportive of my writing ever since I penciled my first essay, calling for peace in Vietnam, in sixth grade.

Above all, I am grateful to my wife, Anne Fadiman. When I began work on this book, Anne was barely able to distinguish between an end sweep and a chimney sweep. Despite her shocking ignorance of all things gridiron, and despite the demands of a full-time teaching job and a book of her own to finish, she supported *The Game* no less thoroughly and enthusiastically than she did its predecessors: sharing my excitement after particularly fruitful interviews; tracking down old Yale yearbooks and vintage *Street & Smith's* football guides on eBay; using her dual perspective as an alumna of Harvard (and a former member of its Board of Overseers) and as the Francis Writer-in-Residence at Yale to help me ponder the vicissitudes of the two institutions; and applying her matchless editorial skills to each chapter at least twice. In countless ways, Anne (who is now perfectly capable of drawing up an end sweep) has given this book—as she has, for thirty-four years, given its author—her unwavering support, loyalty, and love.

*   *   *

Fifty years ago, a month after attending the 1968 Harvard-Yale game, my fourteen-year-old self found, under the Christmas tree, two presents that spoke to my diverging interests. One was from my mother: the Beatles' *White Album*, which had gone on sale two days before the game. The other was from my father: *29–29 "The Game" 1968*, a record album of Ken Coleman's WHDH radio play-by-play of the game's final minutes. I cherished both presents, as I will always cherish the givers.

This book is dedicated to my father, Harry Colt, who took me to my first Harvard football game when I was seven. Dad, a gifted and graceful athlete, was the best kind of sports father: always willing to throw another baseball or play another down, and always showing up for our games, matches, and races without ever making us feel judged. This book is also dedicated to my brother Ned. Though less sports-obsessed than I, Ned shivered alongside me in Harvard Stadium, was a fine oarsman and sailor, and, in middle age, became my favorite doubles partner on the tennis court—not least because he kept the opposition (and me) laughing uncontrollably between, and often during, points. Both Dad and Ned died during the years I worked on this book, but their spirit informs every word of it.

Index

Index

Index

Index

Index

Index

Index

Index

Index

About the Author

George Howe Colt is the author of *The Big House: A Century in the Life of an American Summer Home*, which was a *New York Times* Notable Book and a finalist for the 2003 National Book Award. He also wrote *Brothers*, winner of the 2013 Massachusetts Book Award for nonfiction, and *November of the Soul*, a critically acclaimed study of suicide. His work has appeared in the *New York Times*, *Civilization*, and *Mother Jones*, among other publications. He has taught at Smith College and was for many years a staff writer at *Life* magazine. He lives in western Massachusetts with his wife, Anne Fadiman.